THE
WATER GARDENER

THE
WATER GARDENER

A complete guide to designing, constructing and planting water features

ANTHONY ARCHER-WILLS

Foreword by John Brookes

FRANCES LINCOLN

The highest good is like water.
Water gives life to the ten thousand things and does not strive.
It flows in places men reject and so is like the Tao.

Lao Tsu
Tao Te Ching, 6th century, new translation by Gia-su Seng and Jane English, © 1972, Wildwood House, London

Frances Lincoln Limited
4 Torriano Mews, Torriano Avenue
London NW5 2RZ

The Water Gardener
Copyright © Frances Lincoln Limited 1993
Text copyright © Anthony Archer-Wills 1993
Illustrations copyright © Frances Lincoln Limited 1993
The copyright in the photographs is the property of the
photographers unless otherwise stated.
All rights reserved.

British Library Cataloguing in Publication Data
A catalogue record for this book is available from the
British Library
ISBN 0-7112-0775-5

Set in Guardi Linotype
by Frances Lincoln Limited

Printed by Graphicom in Italy
First Frances Lincoln Edition September 1993
2 4 6 8 9 7 5 3

HALF-TITLE PAGE *Nymphoides cordata*, the floating heart

FRONTISPIECE A corner of a small water feature at Brook Farm Cottage in Surrey

OPPOSITE Formal centrepiece with a lead fountain at Lower Hall, Worfield in Shropshire

Contents

Foreword

Water is the source of life and one of the Four Elements: it must be that which makes its use so irresistible in the garden! For I certainly find it so. When it comes to how we use it, of course, modern garden designers can draw on a huge number of watery precedents - both old and new - for inspiration, but this very bounty of ideas can prove a mixed blessing. For even one good idea to be successfully transposed, it is essential to understand the context from which it emanates: the time, place and climate and, above all, the way it was used. The temptation to amalgamate 'a piece of this and a piece of that', however, is great - and, almost always, doomed to failure. As a designer I am all too aware that this approach can rarely work either in visual or practical terms. It is here that the amateur often welcomes professional guidance, and for that he or she can do no better than delve into the pages that follow.

All the elements of a garden, whether large or small, should read as a balanced whole. What often happens is that the garden is surrounded by planting - pushed back against the edges like the chairs in a parish hall - and the best way to fill the void in the middle seems to be to dig a hole and fill it with water! This *can* work , if it creates a balanced reading across the garden - of fence, planting, grass, water, grass, planting and fence again. But if the planting is too thin, or there is too much grass and too little pool, the section will be disproportionate and the water will look lost. Scale is important. How right Anthony Archer-Wills is to recommend a bold approach. If you want to get away from a strict geometry, avoid small wriggles at the edge of a pool - look at the shape of rivers, see what natural curves are like, formed by the pressure of wind and current, and make a strong statement.

Water draws the light and provides a baseline to which all neighbouring elements relate. Its very horizontality makes it an ideal foil to the vertical lines of willow, rush or reed. Plant associations with water can, and should, be strong and architectural - and for this quality alone a pool merits inclusion in a garden layout.

There are so many ways in which water can enhance a scene and Anthony Archer-Wills knows how to exploit its myriad moods in an imaginative as well as a practical way. In this book he moves beyond the boundaries established by the existing literature, which has for too long failed to grasp the nettle of earth moving and machinery or to deal adequately with the minutiae of water usage in the garden. He shows how to avoid the pitfalls and attain the pinnacles, on whatever the scale.

The Water Gardener raises the art of design with water and the craft of its usage to new levels of excellence. After reading it you will realize that art and craft are equally important: your priorities will be clear - and the results, I am sure, spectacular!

John Brookes   Denmans   March 1993

For my pool at Denmans, Anthony Archer-Wills constructed a wide shingle beach to make a visual link with the dry gravel stream that runs through the garden. On the side where the lawn meets the water's edge, the sides are well defined. A narrow ledge accommodates marginal plantings of flag iris.

The bulk of the excavated material was mounded up on the far side of the pond to make a backdrop of sheltering trees, including existing hollies, cotoneaster and viburnums, with bamboo at the higher level.

The pool is lined with butyl that is securely wedged behind concrete blocks (on the water side) and capped in places by bricks. Exactly how this was done is shown on p.56.

Introduction

Water – in all its moods – is compelling. We are beguiled by its still beauty, awed by its ferocity and power: its presence can never be ignored.

At an early age, when I had demonstrated my ability to swim, my parents would allow me to take a punt out on to the lake near our farmhouse. This sun-blistered muddy-green craft became my passport to a bright new world. From the dark shadows of the yews overhanging the landing stage I could propel myself into a dazzling new domain where sunlight sparkled and water lily pads slapped gently against the bow.

Most of us have similar childhood memories of the joys of playing on, with or around water – and of trying to control it. Who has not placed a stone in a small rivulet and observed the water check, circle like a trapped creature, then swell and expand to form a pool before discovering a fresh way out of its temporary prison? Who can resist moving a blockage of twigs in a ditch to start the water once again into swift motion? It was through just such experiments – diverting and damming small streams in the woods – that as a youth I gained my first practical experience of controlling water, and through them my fascination and passion for it grew.

Today my greatest pleasure is seeing the joy with which a new water feature is received by my clients. For I know well the satisfaction and pleasure this fresh new element in the garden will bring, involving as it does the sense of sight in its light and movement, touch in its liquid sensations of warmth or chill, sound in the gentle soothing ring or chuckle of its music, smell in the fragrance of its planting.

It is hardly surprising that water has been revered throughout history and that in many cultures rivers, springs and streams have possessed their own deities. The name of France's most famous river, the Seine, is derived from that of the Celtic goddess Sequana. From earliest times, too, people, in the same way as the masterful beaver, have contrived ways of controlling and altering the flow of water for practical purposes. In places where an abundant supply could always be relied upon they learned to lay stones and branches across a stream to create an upstream pool, or to change the course of the flow for irrigation. But it was in the hotter parts of Asia and North Africa that, through necessity, people found the most ingenious means of controlling, diverting and storing water.

Water channels dating as far back as the sixth century BC have been excavated in the Middle East. Known as *ganats* in Persia, modern-day Iran, these channels conducted water away from wells sunk where it was plentiful to irrigate distant fields and sustain settlements. Hand in hand with the introduction of permanent water supplies came the introduction of water gardens.

The beauty and refreshing pleasure of water in the garden was particularly prized in lands subjected to the relentless heat of the desert sun, and Paradise in the *Koran* is likened to a garden symbolically divided by four rivers. The typical Islamic garden was also divided by four water channels, to produce a quartered garden known as *chahar bagh*. Fountains cooled the air and brought life and movement to courtyards and gardens; there were brimming pools for bathing. For me, the beauty of a well-constructed brimming pool is unsurpassable, and much of my own creative thinking about formal pools is inspired by the Islamic garden, notable examples of which were created in other parts of the world with the spread of that religion. Among the most outstanding are those at the Alhambra Palace and the neighbouring Generalife in Granada, Spain.

Inspiration for formal gardens comes, too, from the great European tradition, though few people today can emulate the spectacular and fabulously costly creations of the Italian Renaissance. Waterfalls, fountains, ornamental lakes and grottoes were splendidly laid out in the formal manner, though a note of frivolity was often introduced in the form of water 'tricks', installed to surprise, and drench, the unsuspecting. Effects with water reached their most flamboyant in France, in the gardens of Versailles, where King Louis XIV himself occasionally delighted in controlling the water jets. Britain's finest formal water gardens, with immensely impressive cascades, were created in the seventeenth century at Chatsworth in Derbyshire.

It was in China, where nature offered plentiful supplies of water and beautiful mountain landscapes that the informal or natural style of water gardens first developed. Water and rocks have always been the two principal elements of these gardens, and the Chinese word for landscape, *sanshui*, literally means 'mountains and water'. The two elements were used together to express balance and harmony, with rocks representing the male *yang* and water the female *yin*. A particularly auspicious use of water was held to be the rock island, and in the Han Dynasty, 206 BC to AD 220, ponds were created with islands linked by bridges and paths to waterside pavilions. The Taoists, from the first century AD, created miniature landscapes with special stones representing mountains or large rocks. These, they believed, embodied a concentrated source of energy.

A keen plantswoman commissioned me to build this small informal pool to transform a corner of her garden. I used large pieces of Sussex sandstone to form a 'natural' rock outcrop to retain the existing bank. The rocks rise up out of the water from a ledge formed as part of the excavation, and there are pockets between them for planting. The pond is lined with butyl, protected with a layer of concrete beneath the rocks. Within six months the planting was established. Mosses were encouraged to form on the rocks and, cascading over and between them, plants such as the pretty daisy-like osteospermum, hebe and Juniperus squamata 'Blue Carpet' complete the informal appearance.

To provide safe access to the water and a firm mowing edge, the rim beneath the lawn is constructed of engineering bricks laid on a narrow ledge within the pond.

Great effort and resources have been put into creating vast and lavish water gardens throughout Chinese history and as recently as the eighteenth century the Ch'ien-lung Emperor created a colossal complex of lakes, ponds, pavilions and grottoes, known as Yuan Ming Yuan or the Garden of Perfect Brightness. Many of these gardens still survive and are open to visitors today.

In Japan, too, water has long played an important role in the garden. Early gardens contained large ponds, with pavilions round their shores, interconnected by covered walkways and bridges. With the influence of Zen Buddhism, the water in some monastery gardens came to be depicted by a smooth sweep of sand or pebbles representing a dry stream bed between rocks. Contemplating such gardens left the mind free to meditate in tranquillity. When it became the custom to take tea, imported from China, to provide refreshment and stamina before a long session of meditation, the teahouse evolved, set in a secluded part of the garden and reached by a winding pathway. Along this pathway a stone basin or *tsukubai*, fed by pure running water, was provided for the ritual cleansing of the hands before the ceremony.

Planting was for the most part simple, using carefully pruned and clipped shrubs and trees. Where flowering plants were used, mass plantings were employed. A stream bed filled with, say, *Iris ensata* would twist and turn, always inviting one round the next bend to see what lay beyond, exploiting one's natural curiosity in what was known as a 'strolling garden'. Japanese gardens are still built like miniature landscape jewels, with their meticulously placed rocks and ponds, the water often alive with brilliantly coloured carp.

So gardeners may turn to Europe and the Middle East for outstanding examples of the formal use of water, and to the Far East for inspiration in the creation of informal water features. I have incorporated elements of both traditions, as appropriate, in my own work which has focused since the mid-1960s on designing and building water features and growing aquatic plants. My prime goal has always been to ensure that people get the maximum enjoyment possible from a water feature. To achieve this, the feature must be right for its setting, it must be reliable, cost effective, durable, easy to maintain and, of course, beautiful. My aim in this book is to provide information, based on my own practical experience, that will enable you to create a water feature tailored to your own situation and preferences, that fulfils these requirements. It may be that certain aspects of a particular design or complex electrical installations demand more specific professional advice. In general, though, I have set out to deal comprehensively with all the problems and possibilities you are likely to encounter: above all my intention is to inspire and equip *you* to create a successful water garden that will bring into your life the same magic that has for so long filled mine.

Designing a water feature

The legacy of more than three thousand years of gardening with water in different cultures presents us with a dazzling array of possibilities when planning our water gardens. But it is crucial to examine all the aesthetic and practical aspects of your own situation before making any irrevocable decisions. Then, with a little imagination and by following some simple guidelines, you should arrive at an appropriate design. Be clear first and foremost about what you are trying to achieve.

Ponds and other water features tend to fall into two general categories, formal and informal, though some contain elements of both. Formal, obviously designed, features are usually incorporated into the existing architecture of the site, perhaps as an extension of the geometry of the house. They may stand alone, making their own powerful statement, or they may complement a piece of sculpture or statuary. Informal water works, by contrast, attempt to emulate natural features whether streams, waterfalls, rock pools, ponds or placid tranquil lakes.

In deciding on a style you need to take into account the surrounding natural features and buildings. If, for example, the angularity of the house is extended into the garden, with rectangular enclosures and planted areas, a formal, symmetrical pond would probably be most suitable. A more naturalistic design might be the obvious choice if the pond is to be located some distance from the house in an informally landscaped garden. If, however, the pond is to be sited near the house in an informal garden with soft, rounded lines in lawn and planting, a fusion of the two may be called for; thus the edges of the pond nearest the house could have straight lines and angles while those farther away from it could curve and merge with the planted areas. A word of caution, here, though: the point where a straight edge meets a curved one can look awkward, and it is best to soften this area with some strategic planting. Another way of achieving a harmonious fusion between the two basic styles is to extend terrace paving or timber decking up to the nearer edges of an informal pond; this creates the pleasing impression that the house and surrounding structures have been built out to meet an existing natural water feature.

An approach that works especially well with modern architecture is the asymmetrical formal pond. Here the intrinsic formality of straight lines is offset by the relative informality of the asymmetrical shape. Natural flagstones or timber decking could be used for the surrounding area, perhaps forming inlets or promontories around the pond, making for an exciting interplay of land and water.

Formal ponds

I can think of no garden feature that more beautifully sets off a handsome building than a well designed and executed formal pond. A simple rectangle of brimming water, rimmed in stone or brick, forms a continually fascinating living element, offering an endless interplay between light and shadow, stillness and movement, solid and ephemeral reflected form. Walls and hedges, doorways, windows and arches, sharply reproduced at one moment, quiver and vanish in a breath of wind at the next. Mirroring the house, or complementing open areas, ponds of formal or geometric design – whether square, octagonal, circular or oval – can be easily constructed with the materials now so readily available.

The main characteristics of a formal pond – its geometrical shape, clearly defined edges and restrained planting – impose certain requirements on its construction and positioning. First of all, the pond must be carefully oriented in relation to adjacent structures: there are few things so disappointing as the discovery on completion that a pond is not quite parallel with the terrace or does not quite align with the view from the bedroom window. Then, the sides of the pond must be sufficiently firm to remain vertical (or near-vertical, if so designed) for many years, as any subsidence will destroy the regularity and angularity that characterize the formal pond. For this reason a hard construction material such as concrete – whether poured, sprayed or in the form of blocks – or premoulded GRP (glass-reinforced polyester resin) is appropriate, but a flexible liner used in conjunction with hard materials gives the greatest scope for varied and durable designs.

Exuberant planting banishes any hint of severity in an essentially formal design. Symmetry is retained in the carefully trimmed box and the standard bays, but the closeness of the plant groupings has eliminated hard outlines. Beyond the semi-raised pool, the distance is beautifully planted to recede, using the blues of Rosa glauca, Picea pungens, eucalyptus *and purple plum.*

Timber edging, in this case old railway sleepers, lends itself well to use with a formal pond such as this where a more natural mood is required. It can be used to clad concrete or GRP structures, but is particularly effective used in conjunction with a flexible liner.

Another consideration is that keeping the pond clean is more important for a formal pond than for an informal one, in which a modicum of natural disarray may be acceptable. Partly for this reason, you may wish to consider a semi-raised pond, which is more accessible for cleaning and collects fewer leaves.

Informal ponds

In contrast to formal water features, which are often sculptural or geometric in concept and in which the hand of the designer is always obvious, informal features are far more relaxed, often attempting to emulate nature by perfectly fusing with their natural setting. Ponds, pools and placid lakes – naturally abundant in certain localities – can all be created artificially and, once established, are virtually indistinguishable from the real thing.

While some people already enjoy natural water sources in their gardens, most have to start from scratch. Though initially more expensive, this may in the long run be more satisfactory since you do not have to contend with an unpredictable or erratic natural water supply. Even if you have inherited a highly formalized garden, there is no reason to be deterred if the idea of an informal feature appeals: it is usually a relatively simple matter to soften the severity of lines by planting to create a more sympathetic setting. The flexibility of approach that is possible with natural-looking water features means that it is easy to adjust the size to suit the pocket.

A completely natural-looking pond, or a wildlife pond, surrounded by wild-looking planting, is easy enough to achieve. The pond is dug with gently sloping sides all around, lined to make it waterproof, and the base and sides are overlaid with good topsoil. This may then be planted with native plants, which are allowed to flourish and rampage at will – reeds, rushes and sedges, with the occasional marsh marigold (*Caltha palustris*) in temperate zones; sedges, reedmace or cattails (*Typha latifolia*), swamp lilies (*Crinum americanum*) and pickerel weed (*Pontederia cordata*) in hotter climates. Or, if you wish, you may be more selective, choosing plants for maximum interest and beauty and keeping them moderately controlled. Shrubs and small trees could come in close to the water in one or two places and provide cover for amphibians and waterfowl, receding in others to create open spaces.

It is more likely, however, that you will want to integrate the pond more closely into the garden design, opting for a 'naturalistic' rather than a 'natural' look. The main differences between the totally natural and the naturalistic pond lie in the planting of the shallows, and the treatment of the edging at the rim of the pond. While the deepest parts of the pond are similar in both cases, the shallower parts of the more artificial pond are planted with cultivated, rather than wild and naturally occurring, plants. And while the natural pond merges imperceptibly into the surrounding land, the naturalistic pond has a defined edge, even if it is sometimes combined with contrived areas of bog or marsh.

You can also bring grass right up to the edge of at least part of the pond, which eliminates the fringe of planting at that point, enables the water to be seen from some distance away and makes it possible to walk to the brink of the pond, as long as it has a firm edge.

The shape of the pond

Most informal ponds are freeform and curvilinear. There are good practical, as well as aesthetic, reasons for avoiding complicated shapes. Simple shapes are both easier to excavate and easier to line. Sharp promontories are not advisable in a pond with a flexible liner. They are especially problematical if they are to be lined – it is almost impossible to fit the lining without welding or complicated pleating – and the promontories use up nearly as much liner as bays of the same size, while merely reducing the water surface. If you wish to add interest by creating promontories in a lined pond, make a pond of simple shape and line it first. Gentle, unlined promontories can then easily be built out on top of the liner when adding the soil for planting around the margins of the pond: soil raked back close to the rim forms a 'bay'. This kind of contouring must be considered at the planning stage, however, because shallower areas will be needed to form a base on which to build out.

In an unlined pond, which will never be 100 per cent watertight, it is at the sides that most leakage occurs. Intricate bays, inlets and promontories greatly increase the pond's margins in relation to the volume of the water, and hence the amount of possible leakage.

AN APPROPRIATE SIZE

The size of water feature is often best determined by the constraints of the site, whether it is a small yard or garden or a well-defined area of a large one. On patios, balconies or terraces, where space is severely limited, a single water lily floating in a half barrel or small wall fountain can make an impressive display. Wall fountains that are designed to fit entirely on a wall take up no ground space, are quick to install, and are comparatively inexpensive. Generally, however, a useful maxim to keep in mind when thinking about the size of a pond or pool is 'Big is Beautiful'. There are several reasons for this, some aesthetic, some practical. A large water surface offers greater possibilities for beautiful reflections as well as increasing planting opportunities. In addition, a large body of water reacts more slowly to temperature fluctuations and stabilizes more readily, coping better with decaying leaves, and accommodating more varieties of plant and minute forms of animal life, making for clear water and minimum maintenance. An important safety consideration is that over a larger area a greater depth is achievable while maintaining shallow or gently sloping sides.

A formal pond designed primarily to reflect beautiful architecture should be as large as possible. The question of cost obviously comes into the equation, but to a lesser extent than you might expect, for by doubling the area of the pond you do not double the cost since much of the expense lies in actually setting up the job. Equally, by doubling the surface area of, say, a square pool, you do not double the perimeter (where much of

15

the cost is involved) but merely increase it by 50 per cent. Increasing the width of a rectangle could be even more cost effective.

There are other ways of maximizing the area of a pond at comparatively little cost. Take, for example, the case of a small square walled garden, where a large, centrally placed square or rectangular pond is desired. On consideration, it may be realized that the corners of such a pond would encroach uncomfortably on the walking space. While it would be simple to make a smaller pond, a more imaginative solution would be to remove the corners, thus forming an octagon that retains the full length and width of the original design. Triangular beds of plants in the four corners of the courtyard could complement its shape.

The octagonal pond, being close to circular, contains a large surface area within a comparatively small perimeter, which makes it economical to construct. It is also easy to get around, and is thus a useful shape for a front garden where a driveway leads up to the house, or for public places where pedestrians, and people in wheelchairs or with shopping trolleys, can negotiate it with ease.

With informal, natural-looking water features, the setting, whatever the scale, is usually less constraining and the size of the pool is equally likely to be determined by your budget. There are many approaches. In a wild corner of a country garden, for example, in which trees extend to the boundary and natural rock is prominent it would be quite feasible to create a rock pool of about 2x1.2m/6½x4ft, with water trickling down through mossy rocks in a series of waterfalls perhaps 3m/10ft in total length. The pond could contain a small water lily or, if it were too shady, the water hawthorn, *Aponogeton distachyos*, similar in habit and with its forked white flowers smelling sweetly of hawthorn or vanilla. Some submerged aquatics would be good, and even a few fish. Many kinds of moisture-, shade-, and woodland-associated plants could flourish here: *Matteuccia struthiopteris*, the shuttlecock fern, and *Smilacina racemosa*, with its deliciously scented creamy plumes, spring to mind.

Even the tiniest pond can be made to appear large by judicious planting. The softening effect of well chosen plants breaks the hard outline, deceiving the eye into imagining that the stretch of water may continue farther than it actually does. Whatever the size of the pond, it should be well integrated into its setting, with other elements chosen and positioned to enhance its effect. Focal points such as fine specimen plants, sculpture, or a well placed urn or seat can help to create a sense of theatre, as in the Japanese 'strolling garden', which draws you onwards by a series of invitations to see what lies around the next bend.

Room for growth

When planning a small informal pond, consider the life it will support, and allow room for growth. Plants and animals are an essential characteristic of a natural pond, even when it is artificially created. Planted areas around its fringes, water lilies floating on its surface, with goldfish swimming among them or basking beneath their pads, all contribute to its beauty and natural effect. It must be said that a pond smaller than about 2x1.2m/6½x4ft will present problems in this respect and more work will be entailed in keeping the water clear and various species in balance. Water plants will need occasional pampering and fish will require even more care in order to last the year round in a small pond that is quickly affected by changes in temperature.

Bear in mind that as marginal plants flourish, they strain to the very limits to colonize fresh ground, encroaching 2m/6½ft or more across the water surface. Shallow water can easily become congested with plant growth. Small ponds need steeper sides than large ones in order to quickly reach a sufficient depth to discourage such proliferation.

It is impossible to specify an optimum depth for a given size of pond, because so many different factors are involved. For example, in order to prevent rampant plant growth, a pond receiving a great deal of sunlight may need to be deeper than another of the same size in the shade, or a small pond might need to be relatively deep in order to accommodate certain breeds of fish. However, the following approximate guidelines may be helpful: for a pond with a surface area of 4 sq m/43 sq ft or less, at the very least 45cm/18in, and preferably 60cm/24in; of 10 sq m/108 sq ft, a depth of 90cm/3ft; of 50 sq m/540 sq ft, a depth of 1.2m/4ft; for a pond of over 1,000 sq m/1,200 sq yd it would be desirable to include an area 2.5-3m/8-10ft deep, in order to restrict the growth of algae and rampant plants, thus keeping part of the surface clear and preserving the pond's reflective quality, especially in midsummer when excessive plant growth can make this a problem.

Size and context

Rules about relative size sometimes can or must be broken. For example, the space available may be so large that even the most ambitious-sized pond will be dwarfed. I recall having to design a small lake in a 20 hectare/ 50 acre open field – a context in which even a 0.5 hectare/1 acre pond would look like a puddle. The answer was to adjust the landscape to suit the pond, and the introduction of gentle moulding and groups of trees soon made the pond look more comfortable. The Oriental gardener's technique of hiding parts of the pond was used to make it look larger.

It is generally thought that if a pond is too big in relation to the house it will look 'out of proportion'. I, too, subscribed to this theory until, some years ago, I was forced to disprove it when I was asked to build a pond as large as possible next to a bungalow in a small country garden. With some reluctance, because the site was so small, I agreed, and the pond was duly completed and filled with water. On returning some weeks later I could hardly believe my eyes! The property was transformed. Instead of an enormous pond filling the garden and dwarfing the bungalow, there appeared before me the most delightful lakeside residence. It was as though the lake had always been there and some enlightened person had built the bungalow beside it. Lawn swept down to the water's edge, and there, on a small landing stage, stood my client, feeding the ducks.

The simple fact is that water can look more permanent than buildings and trees, and play the dominant role.

SITING THE WATER FEATURE

Water is the most magical element: it brings the sky down to earth and forms a focal point of reflected light in the garden. Its therapeutic effects are well known, and if the pond is situated next to the house these can be enjoyed indoors as much as outside. Strong light reflected from the water's surface can brighten an otherwise dark and gloomy room; a pond situated just beneath the windows on the sunny side of a house can send lovely rippling patterns across the ceiling. These are most restful, and they are of special benefit to people who, for health reasons, are confined to the house. If there is moving water, its soothing sounds can be enjoyed through the windows.

When siting a water feature, there are a number of practical as well as aesthetic considerations to take into account. For instance, you must find out what type of soil you will be working with by digging sample holes. Different terrains are discussed on pp.28-33.

Once used for swimming, the elevated rectangular pool beyond the water-lily speckled canal has been converted to grow water plants. It is visually linked by stepped ponds to the immaculately sharp-edged canal with its brimming water. A symmetrical design such as this lovely Belgian example might be oriented from an important viewpoint in the house, a doorway or an upstairs window, for instance. Alternatively, it could be a surprise feature in a secluded compartment of the garden.

Swimming pools are often conceived of as part of a grander design, relating with adjacent pools, cascades or fountains, though the water does not actually interconnect.

LEFT *Sunlight glints and glistens on a descending curtain of water in an imaginative curved cascade. A focal point of sound, movement and refreshing coolness, this delightful wall feature in the South of France, designed by Jean Mus, makes the stone terrace irresistible in the noonday sun.*

The mechanics are simple. With a surface or submersible pump, water can be drawn from an underground chamber and piped to a channel let into the top of the wall. It spills out over the sill into a collecting trough and back into its underground chamber, whence it is recirculated.

In hot climates, splashing and evaporation can lead to considerable water losses, so such systems need a large reserve of water or an efficient built-in top-up system to prevent their running dry.

OPPOSITE *It is sometimes tempting to break the rules! In fact, although caveats about siting ponds under trees are true for very small ponds - and it would certainly be unwise to allow a complete overhang of any pool - most ponds will tolerate a few sparser-leaved trees. The occasional grooming is well worth the wonder of shafts of sunshine piercing foliage and the sparkle of water beneath a dappled canopy.*

An inviting timber walkway allows one to brush through this lush foliage to take a close look at the pond and its creatures. Here, in the foreground, the waxy, heart-shaped leaves of Pontederia cordata *contrast with the crimped blades of* Acorus calamus, *the aromatic sweet flag.*

A place in the sun

The position from which the pond is most likely to be viewed, whether from the house, a patio or deck, or from a particular place in the garden, is important. Try to locate it so that the reflective qualities of the water can be best enjoyed. You will want the pond to mirror surrounding features, and the direction of sunlight in relation to your usual or best viewpoint has an important bearing on the reflective quality of the water. The best effects are achieved when the sun shines from behind the observer, lighting up the farther side of the pond. If the sun shines towards you, the water reflects a strong glare, rather than clear images of waterside buildings, plants or trees.

The effect of evening light, which imparts a rich brilliance to the coloured bark and stems of waterside plantings of dogwoods and willows, is also particularly lovely when the light is falling from behind the viewer. As buildings that are enhanced when struck by sunlight from across the pond will thereby give enhanced reflections of themselves, it could also be that the pond should be sited to reflect the house when viewed from the garden, with a garden sitting area forming an important part of the design. Study the direction and quality of the light at different times of day and in different seasons in order to choose a site that heightens the beauty not only of the pond but also of surrounding features.

To support a thriving plant and animal community, a pond must have sun. Admittedly, streams and rock pools that are in full shade still grow moss and ferns and allow a few cold-water-loving fish, such as golden orfe, to survive. Provided few dead leaves fall into it, this dark or brackish water will remain reasonably trouble free. However, to reach its full potential, a pond should be located where the sun can shine upon it for at least half the day and preferably all day in cold and temperate climates. In very hot countries slightly less is required; indeed, some shade is beneficial in preventing algae. Water lilies especially need lots of sunshine – at least six hours a day – and they prefer warm, still water.

Although nearby walls can cause a pond to be in shade, they are less likely to be a problem than are large trees. Formal ponds, especially, are often sited within walled areas, which may shade the pond for 25-50 per cent of the day without detriment.

It is best to site the pond out of the wind, and in some cases walls can provide the necessary shelter. Sometimes a wind break in the form of a belt of trees, hedges or suitable fencing is needed to give shelter from strong winds, which can blow the taller and more delicate emergent plants over and cause water lily leaves to capsize. In addition, in hot countries winds increase evaporation, while in colder climates they can chill the pond.

Frost pockets, where the pond is more likely to freeze over, should also be avoided if possible.

Ponds near trees

As a general rule ponds should not be positioned under trees. However, this rule is not iron-clad – it depends on the size of the pond and the size and type of tree. The first consideration is how much sun the tree will take from the water. If this is more than half the daily quota then it is too much, and the pond should be sited elsewhere (or the tree suitably pruned or removed).

Another question, possibly more important, is how much leaf fall will occur over the pond. Small, sparse-leaved trees that do not overhang more than a small portion of the surface, such as the pollarded willows grown for their bark, the small weeping willows, *Salix purpurea* 'Pendula' and *S. caprea* 'Kilmarnock', or Japanese maple (*Acer palmatum* var. *dissectum*) can make ideal pondside trees. But ponds overshadowed by large deciduous trees can receive such a downpour of leaves in the autumn that, unless these are cleared away or caught by netting, the water becomes black and will grow practically nothing – nothing, that is, except curled pondweed (*Potamogeton crispus*). This plant's seaweed-like bronze and green fronds appear remarkably delicate and translucent in the unpromising dark water, growing up through deep drifts of partially decayed leaves, and their finely curled and crimped appearance is a welcome sign of spring (the weed disappears towards the end of the summer). Another plant that often colonizes deeply shaded ponds overburdened with decaying matter is the far less desirable common duckweed (*Lemna minor*). This light green, disc-like floating plant spreads with alacrity on the surface, fed by the rich nutrients. It can cover the entire surface, and is only temporarily checked during the winter months.

Ponds should also be kept well away from trees that are toxic, such as laburnum, laurel, holly and yew, even though they may not necessarily shade the water.

In natural or clay-lined ponds, tree roots are also a considerable nuisance, since they make straight for the banks of the pond, where they form a fibrous mat that allows water to seep out of the pond. Tree roots are not a problem to lined ponds, however, as they are unable to detect the presence of water through the liner, unless there is a hole in it, in which case they will grow through it. (Bamboo, however, should be kept well back from liner ponds – see p.150.)

Electricity supplies

Although proximity to an electricity supply is helpful where any sort of fountain or waterfall features, pumps or lighting are envisaged, this is not essential. Cable can be run without any difficulty for up to 100m/110yd, and it is quite feasible to site a pond up to 300m/325yd away from the electricity supply, although in this case much heavier cable is needed, thus increasing the cost. The cable will normally have to run below ground (see p.75). In all cases it is necessary to have a clear idea in advance of the work and cost involved.

THE WATER SUPPLY

Contrary to expectations, the pond does not necessarily have to be situated very close to a water supply. As long as it is well made, it will be watertight, and any water lost through evaporation will normally be replaced through rainfall. Only in very hot weather, when there is excessive evaporation, or in times of drought, will topping up be necessary. In temperate climates this will be rare, although in hot climates water will have to be added more frequently. It is convenient if the pond is within 100m/110yd of a tap, unless it has a natural water supply, but this is certainly not a prerequisite.

Until comparatively recent times every pond, fountain, cascade, bathing pool, and irrigation channel depended on harnessing a natural water supply – often using the principle of gravity. Provided that levels and falls are well calculated, it is possible to conduct water over great distances by gravity, taking it, if necessary, through channels hewn in mountain rock and, as in Roman aqueducts, across ravines. Traditionally, water has also been obtained by mechanical means. Windmills and waterwheels, as well as other mechanical devices, such as the Egyptian *shaduf*, are still in common use in certain countries.

Wells

Before mains water was available, many households had their own wells. They are generally not far from the house, and sometimes even under the house itself, usually in the kitchen area. Any likely-looking stone slab, millstone, circular flower bed or hollow-sounding patch in a path should be investigated. To help locate one, it may be possible to engage the services of a water dowser.

If you find a well, first test its yield: some provide only a few litres or gallons a day, and would be useless for filling a pond or maintaining a water garden. The procedure for testing a well is extremely simple. First, pump out the water; wait a few hours for the residual water in the immediate vicinity of the well to drain into the well, then pump it out a second time. Wait again, pump for a third time – the water will come back more slowly each time – and after the third pumping, measure how much water comes up in an hour. Measure the diameter of the well, divide this in half to get the radius, multiply the radius squared by pi (3.142), multiply the result by the rise in water just measured, and finally multiply by 1000 for metric measures or 6.25 for imperial, which gives the number of litres/gallons per hour yielded by the well. My own well yields 6,800 litres/1,500 gallons per hour continuously, which is excellent, but even 340 litres/75 gallons per hour is useful, and a 1.2m/4ft diameter well needs only to come up 30cm/1ft in the first hour to produce that.

If you do not have an existing well on your property, it is possible to sink one but for amenity ponds the costs can easily become prohibitive. The deeper you have to go, the more expensive it becomes, and the deeper you have to pump from, the greater the running costs. In very porous ground, pumping will be needed more frequently to maintain a high water level, and this is an ongoing expense. It is always more efficient to push water than to suck it, so the pump should be of the submersible type (see p.74), and situated in the bottom of the well. Although wind pumps work very well indeed in breezy areas, they would detract from the beauty of an ornamental pond or lake. It is possible to construct a rather beautiful windmill, like a piece of mobile sculpture, although it would be more costly to build, and possibly less efficient. It should be mentioned here that in most countries wells and the abstraction of water are governed by water rights, and are not necessarily owned by the owner of the land. It is advisable to make enquiries before installing a pumping system. Sometimes a pump may not be needed: I have managed over the years to keep several ponds full by tapping the resources of wells located on higher ground. The best way of doing this is to dig a deep trench from the pond to the well, below the water level (as long as it is not too far down), and run a pipe through the side of the well down the trench to the pond.

Reservoirs and dew-ponds

Catching rain in suitable receptacles is one of the simplest methods of using water. In their earliest form, reservoirs consisted of animal skins stretched out to catch the rain, and from these humble beginnings have evolved the vast reservoirs we know today.

Most reservoirs work by being positioned in the centre of a large catchment or run-off area, so that when it does rain, the water falling on a wide area forms rivulets and runnels and is fed into the reservoir. This will not yield a lot of water all the time, but it will yield either a lot of water for a short period or a little water constantly, the water being stored so as to be available when needed. Many marvellous water features have been supplied by reservoirs formed high up in the hills behind gardens, providing sufficient head water to operate fountains and water steps, cascades and waterfalls. In some cases, of course, fountains supplied by reservoirs can operate for only a few hours during the day, especially in dry weather.

Dew-ponds are curious clay ponds dug at the tops of hills in various places in Britain, and apparently fed only by dew and rainfall. They are thus a form of reservoir, and were used in the past to water cattle grazing on the hilltops. Although the term 'dew-pond' dates only from the nineteenth century, the ponds themselves are thought to be of extremely ancient origin. According to one hypothesis, the word 'dew' in this context is a corruption of the French word *dieu*, meaning god.

Exploiting a high water table

The most usual way of exploiting natural water supplies for garden water features is to dig into a high water table. In many parts of Florida, for example, where there is a very high water table, you merely have to dig a hole and it fills with water. However, a high water table may still be 60–90cm/2–3ft below the surface and excavating may entail careful shaping and grading of the surrounding soil to achieve a brimming pool.

In countries with wet winters, the water table is lower in autumn and early winter, taking a long time to come up after rainfall. Fluctuations in

1 Tapping springs

Natural water supplies can be tapped and piped to your pond or water feature by collecting any available issue, even trickles, into a sump. This box or chamber can be a ready-made tank or formed from concrete. It should be approximately 1m/3ft square and 60cm/2ft deep, and placed so that its rim is slightly above the gravel or silt layer, and a rigid plastic pipe should be set into it, near the top. The water will flow over the rim and into the chamber, and from there be conducted via the pipe to the water feature. The box will also serve as a silt trap and can periodically be dug out, should gravel and silt be washed in.

More diversely spread wet areas can be channelled into the sump by means of land drains.

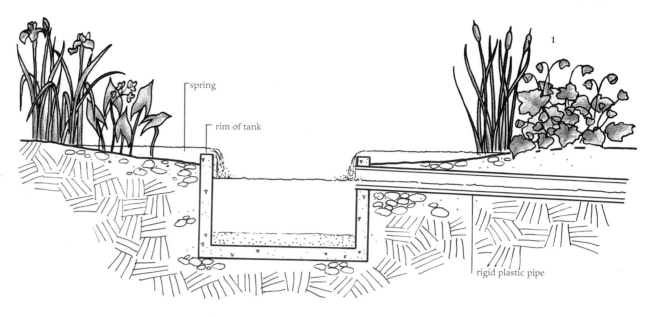

level are less noticeable in clay soils and most apparent in shingle and gravel layers. Close proximity to a river, or the bournes that flow through chalk, can cause dramatic fluctuations in the level, which rises and falls with the river. Natural unlined ponds, or clay- or bentonite-lined ponds are generally unsatisfactory in such conditions, the water going up and down like a yo-yo. Furthermore, when the water does come, it comes up from underneath, causing the bottom of the pond to erupt; when the water table falls again, the pond water finds its way out through these fissures.

Before deciding to rely on a high water table to fill a pond, establish exactly where its level is by digging down until you reach water; do this in a dry period and make sure that the water is not running from another source. When excavating, you should first clear the soil down to within about 15cm/6in of the water table, and then excavate for the pond itself; in this way a more natural-looking brimming pond can be achieved.

Tapping springs

A high water table is often – though not always – associated with springs. A relatively vigorous spring that yields a strong flow of water can be utilized with very little work. A few judiciously placed stones or boulders can funnel the water into an open ditch, or, better still, a pipe leading down to the point where the water is needed. A slight gradient, say 1:200, is necessary. Cover the end of the pipe with a large strainer or basket to prevent leaves and debris from entering. If the spring issues up out of gravel, a slightly more sophisticated approach is called for. Because of the loose, shifting nature of the gravel, an open pipe leading straight from the spring would immediately become blocked, so a catchment box must be constructed and pushed down into the gravel,

near the point where the spring emerges (diagram 1).

In peaty or marshy ground, springs are usually indistinct and are indicated by an area of rushes and soggy ground, until eventually small rivulets of water can be seen running from the area. In cases like this, water needs to be collected from more than one point. If the ground is flat, select a position roughly in the centre of the wet area and dig a sump, or construct a catchment box 1-1.2m/3-4ft square by about 60cm/2ft deep. The box could be a preformed galvanized iron or GRP tank, or may be made from concrete blocks (but a ready-made box is better). Into this you can run land drains – lengths of purpose-made perforated pipe – from the wettest places in the immediate area. They should lie snugly on soil at the bottom of the trench, to prevent the water from running under them, and be topped with gravel to prevent the small holes from being blocked. The water will be conducted away, down the main pipe, and to your required position. Long lengths of rigid plastic soil pipe are best for this purpose, as open, unlined ditches tend to lose water *en route*.

If the spring area is on gently sloping ground then the sump or catchment box should be placed in the lower side of the slope, approximately centrally within the collecting area. The pipes can be run into this from the upper side in herringbone fashion, two or three pipes entering the box at different angles, and further pipes radiating out from the main ones like the branches of a tree. The radiating pipes can be led to the most obviously moist places and covered with shingle in the usual way.

Important developments are now taking place in land drainage materials, and the increasing use of non-woven geotextile membranes bonded to plastic pipes now provides for nearly every land drainage requirement. When planning operations of this kind on a large scale, you should seek expert advice from an appropriate land drainage supplier.

A natural brook flowing down through this beautiful valley garden has been dammed in puddled clay to open out into a deep, still pool. The water is halted only temporarily in its tracks, spilling over beneath the picturesque rough-cut stone that provides a path across the bank.

On either side of the stream, cushions of waterside plants revel in the movement of water through their roots. In the foreground, the few remaining white flowers of Caltha palustris var. alba remain on their mound of tight glossy leaves. They contrast wonderfully with the blades of iris and the fronds of fern.

Beyond the bright golden mint the double flowers of Caltha palustris 'Plena' peep out above a carpet of multicoloured Houttuynia cordata 'Chameleon', which spreads out into the water and is mirrored on the opposite bank. Here the fresh cream blades of Iris pseudacorus 'Variegata' cleave their way up among the bluebells.

Streams

A stream that runs all year round can be an ideal water source for a garden, as well as being potentially a water feature in its own right (see pp.83-91).

Some streams can be subject to sudden and violent influxes of water, making them rise a metre or more/several feet above the normal level. If this is likely to occur, build weirs across the stream to slow the force of the water and keep fluctuations in level to a minimum so that waterside plants can be grown successfully.

When using a stream to feed a pond or lake, it is tempting merely to widen the stream or construct a dam to form a pool behind it. This requires very little excavation work, only a small outlay of money, and in a 'V'-shaped valley may be all that you can do. However, it is better, if possible, to build the pond or lake next to the stream, rather than allowing it to flow in one end and out the other. This makes it possible to impose a measure of control over the quantity and quality of water entering the pond. A small feed pipe or ditch can be set at such a level that even if there is only a small trickle coming down the stream, it will keep the pond or lake topped up; but should there be a violent spate, the water, carrying all its debris, leaves, silt and branches, will be carried harmlessly past. If a flow is required, both an inlet and an outlet can be made, which can be controlled either by the size of the pipes used or by a valve or controlling sluice gate.

If you are stocking the pond with trout, a good flow of water is required, so a large proportion of the stream water might be allowed through the pond. For carp and water lilies, the flow should be kept to a minimum.

If you have no alternative but to make your pond by widening a stream, one or two silt traps, in the form of small, deep ponds with easy access, should be made higher upstream. Most silt and debris will settle here and can be dug out comparatively easily and cheaply every few years. This may not be necessary in rocky terrain where some streams pick up little debris and carry hardly any silt. A pond within such a stream could be ideal for trout fishing.

DESIGNING FOR SAFETY

It is possible to drown in 2 or 3cm/1in of water, and where there is water of any kind there is some degree of danger. However, one must keep things in perspective or one would never dare to have a pond at all. Several practical steps can be taken to make ponds safer.

A pond can be provided with a steel or wooden frame fitted with a mesh strong enough to take the weight of an adult. This can be laid on when children are playing unsupervised. However, such a frame is impractical if there are plants growing abundantly around the pool edges. If it is left on for long, water lilies and other pond plants may grow up through the mesh, which distorts their growth, looks unsightly, and makes it difficult to remove the frame.

A better way, and one recommended for a large pond, is to fence off the pond area completely. This is frequently done in the United States – as required by law in most areas – where deep ponds and swimming pools must be surrounded by a fence at least 1.2m/4ft high (the precise depth of the pond and height of the fence vary according to local legislation). Fencing need not be unattractive: it can be completely hidden by plants and the entrance to the pond area can be a (lockable) gate between shrubs or trees. Smaller ponds can have a walled and gated enclosure, which is particularly appropriate for formal ponds.

The slope of the sides is a crucial aspect of safety. There is nothing so dangerous as a 45-degree slope: it makes it difficult to reach the edge and no amount of struggling will give you a foothold from which to climb out. If you are out of your depth, this can be a truly frightening sensation, even for a good swimmer. A sheer side is much easier to reach and hold on to and is the safest design for a formal pond. A pond that is only 60cm-1m/2-3ft deep, and with a level base, is reasonably safe, and so is a pond with ledges all the way around, provided that these are not occupied by precariously balanced baskets of plants. As an additional precaution a formal pond could incorporate an extra-wide ledge at an intermediate level, say at a depth of 45cm/18in on the habitual viewing side.

In an informal pond that is more than 1m/3ft deep, sides with a shallow slope are by far the safest. Where a clearly defined edge is required, with the water restrained by brick, stone or timber, then the profile of the pool can be such that the straight sides extend only 30cm/1ft down below the surface, then give way to a very gradual slope, which could be overlaid with shingle or gravel.

For some informal ponds a beach is appropriate and safe for both animals and people who can easily get in and out of water that gradually deepens. The rest of the pond might be fenced off with posts and rails, and the beach area left open. The fencing could run through reed beds and be quite inconspicuous.

Establishing a wide planting strip – of bog or emergent plants – around the edge of the pool is another good safety measure appropriate for informal ponds, since this makes the approach to deep water very difficult. Alternatively, you could form an effective barrier with thickly planted dry-ground shrubs growing right up to the water's edge. A combination of these possibilities could result in a comparatively safe pond or lake without the need for fencing or permanent barriers. None the less, especially where children are concerned, a fence with a secure gate is the wisest choice.

Many formal ponds have a firm rim with a broad capping that forms part of a hard surface surrounding the pond. People can walk and sit around the edge, and children will be tempted to run along the capping; this is particularly inviting on a semi-raised pond. If the capping is loose, not only may someone fall into the pond, there is the added danger of their being struck on the head by a falling slab of stone. It is therefore essential that all capping is very firmly fixed. Both surfaces to be joined should be moistened, and a 3:1 mortar mix generously applied so that the capping squeezes out the surplus, ensuring a complete bond. On a dry-stone wall the capping stones must be sufficiently large and heavy to provide complete stability.

Thriving in the marshy margins of this informal pond, the lush foliage of Iris laevigata *spreads and produces its lovely purple-blue blossoms. Equally at home here in wet mud, and in beautiful contrast with the iris leaves, the bright flowers of* Mimulus *'Wisley Red' are borne in profusion. This plant slowly carpets moist or wet ground. Emerging from the water rise the blotched purple and green leaves of*

Nymphaea *'Marliacea Chromatella' with their speckled undersides.*

A shallow planting bed like this not only hides the pond edge but provides scope for a range of plants with differing moisture requirements. In a more natural setting a few weeds can be tolerated, though all pernicious perennial weeds must be eliminated before planting begins.

DESIGNING FOR PLANTING

The planting of a pond is an essential part of its character, and must be considered before the digging and shaping begin. I have seen beautifully constructed pools finished, full of water, ready to be planted, and the task made extremely difficult, if not impossible, because no provision for planting enclosures had been made in the shaping of the pool: the sides sloped steeply to the bottom without ledges, and the bottom was too deep for water lilies.

It is wise to plan from the outset to incorporate a ledge around most of an informal pond even if you are not sure what sort of planting you will want. In a small pond the ledge can be fairly narrow since cultivation is usually managed from the bank, and the inner edges of very wide ledges can be difficult to reach (diagram 2). Beyond the ledge, the pond should slope fairly steeply down to the bottom. A larger pond can have very wide ledges, or the sides may slope down very gradually to the full depth (diagram 3). In a larger pond, you should also leave level areas at intermediate depths, so that water lilies can be established. It is much easier to leave an area only 50cm-1m/20in-3ft deep at the digging stage than to have to build up water lily containers from a depth of 2m/6½ft. However, even the task of building up from a flat bottom is easier than trying to lodge containers or build up enclosures on a 45-degree slope.

Where emergent or marginal plants are required for a formal pond, ledges should be provided for them. Some premoulded ponds have ledges built in. These are usually narrow and lend themselves only to the standard planting crate obtainable from most aquatic and nursery suppliers. These baskets come in several sizes and are shaped to conform to the slope of the pond side, therefore fitting quite snugly. An entire straight ledge can be packed with them, and when the plants have become established, the baskets are fairly well concealed beneath apparently continuous planting. (For the planting of baskets, see diagram 1, p.124.)

These planting crates can also be used in other types of pond construction. However, they are rather restricting and tend to impart an artificial feeling to the finished work; they are also prone to being knocked or blown over. A properly constructed soil retainer allows for more root growth, longer periods between maintenance, and a bolder, more natural effect. If the pond already has a ledge, a low retaining wall can be constructed on the front of this and the resulting trough filled with a suitable planting loam. If there is no ledge, you can construct one by building up a retaining wall from the pool bottom to within 20-23cm/8-9in of the top and filling this with loam.

A simpler method, which requires less material, is to build piers of brick or concrete blocks from the bottom and bridge these with concrete slabs. The front edge of these can then support a low retaining wall, behind which the planting medium is packed (see diagram 14, p.56). A great advantage of this method is that it provides 'caves' beneath the shelf where fish can escape attacks by birds. It also forms useful places in which to hide a pump or underwater lighting. A similar method can be used to

2 Designing small informal ponds for planting

Plan a small informal pond with planting ledges around the perimeter. These need to be wide enough to hold rocks or stones to retain the earth but not so wide as to be out of reach of the banks: 23-30cm/9-12in is comfortable. From ledges the sides must slope steeply to provide enough depth for a well-balanced pond.

3 Designing larger informal ponds for planting

Ledges tend to look contrived in larger ponds, whereas gently sloping sides allow plants to grow in a natural-looking way. Water lilies can be grown in enclosures (see p.124) or directly from the bottom of the pond. In ponds deeper than 1m/3ft, an area should be dug less deeply to allow for this.

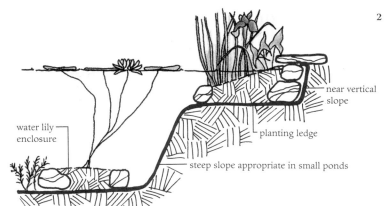

near vertical slope

water lily enclosure

planting ledge

steep slope appropriate in small ponds

gently sloping side in larger pond

4 Designing formal ponds for planting

Plan a formal pond with ledges on which to sit containers for emergent plants or, if raised just above the water level, for bog plants.

Plinths of brick or blockwork, bridged with concrete slabs, will support containers for water lilies and other aquatic plants. Build them to suit the water depth requirement of the particular plant.

In flexible liner pools, set the plinths on broad slabs that protect the liner and spread the load. In concrete ponds, the bricks or blockwork can be built directly on the base.

provide island plantings in the middle of large formal ponds (diagram 4). These can be placed anywhere over the bottom to enhance a modern geometrical shape or to show off groups of specimen plants, where a fringe of planting around the periphery is not appropriate. Structures such as this built on the bottom of a pond can also act as support for water lily planters where the pond is too deep for these plants to grow on the bottom. I have seen this done effectively in parts of the United States with tropical water lilies, which do much better in shallow water.

Water lilies can be planted in premoulded crates or baskets on the pool bottom, or special enclosures can be built for them. Personally, I prefer the special enclosure or large concrete, brick or plastic container. It should be made of material to match that used for the ledge, if any. Submerged plants that serve to oxygenate the water need no specially constructed enclosures and can be planted in simple containers, such as seed trays, at the bottom of the pond.

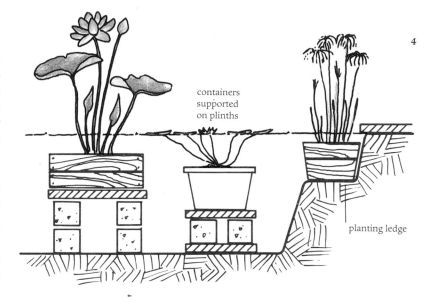

containers supported on plinths

planting ledge

OPPOSITE *By harnessing the water from natural springs occurring higher up this sloping site, and constructing a weir across a natural flow, I created a pool in which a wide variety of aquatic plants flourish.*

BELOW *Requiring minimal earth moving, a semi-raised pond is ideal for the town garden where there may not be access even for a wheelbarrow. It could be constructed cheaply from a plastic water tank, partially sunk below ground level, and disguised by a brick or stone wall.*

Now that you have drawn up a design for your pond and selected a site, it is time to get down to the groundwork. This includes not only the marking out and excavation of the pond, but also the shaping and forming of the area surrounding it. With a large water garden, these works could be extensive. Whatever the scale, it is vital that they are well carried out, because they can make or mar the finished result. Make every effort to ensure that the new works will look 'comfortable' in the existing landscape or in the new landscape you form with excavated materials.

Before excavations can begin, scrub, undergrowth and trees may have to be cleared. If there is any danger of confusion between trees that are to stay and those that should go, mark trees that are to be removed. Small areas can be cleared by hand, which makes for a neat job and causes little disruption to the surroundings. Small trees and shrubs can be hauled out by hand winch. On larger sites, where a digger is to be used for the excavation, it may be cost effective to use this for the site clearance as well. Remove all organic matter from the working area, since it is not satisfactory to have grass, weeds and roots mixed in with the topsoil that you are planning to reuse.

Whether you are digging a small garden pond or a large lake, the same rules apply. Having cleared the site, first strip off all the topsoil from the pond area, including a margin for edging and/or planting, and save it. Also strip off topsoil from areas where you are proposing to dump the subsoil (spoil) excavated from the pond – topsoil should never be wasted or buried, and you can never have too much of it. Remember that topsoil should not be moved during heavy rain. If it gets mixed into a slurry its structure is broken down and it takes an age for the natural free-draining and open characteristics to return. Place the topsoil strategically so that it can readily be graded back over the subsoil when the excavation work is complete. Wherever possible, plan to incorporate excavated subsoil into the landscaping of the water feature – filling hollows, extending banks or making new ones, creating contours – and arrange to dump it in such a way that as little earth moving as possible is required.

MOVING EARTH

Moving earth adds enormously to the work (and the cost, when paid labour and machines are being used) and carting spoil away from the site in trucks can double the cost of the job.

Little more than a spade and wheelbarrow are needed for small excavations. Use the wheelbarrow running on a track of planks to cart away the soil when excavating a small pond. Small machines can also be hired for home use, and the size of pond you have in mind may make this worthwhile.

A dump truck can be used for larger ponds, when possible in conjunction with a 360-degree excavator. Some of the smaller dump trucks run on tracks – a godsend in very wet conditions. They are unfortunately rather hard to obtain and slow, but no doubt in future improvements will be made to this type of machinery.

For very large earth-moving jobs, six-wheel, all-wheel-drive dumpers, capable of carrying over 10 tonnes/10 tons at up to 55km/35 miles per hour are the usual method of transportation. Two or more will be required, so that one can be loading while the other is carting the spoil away. It is essential to hire these machines with their operators. I have always maintained, incidentally, that the operator is more important than the machine. Before hiring operators, talk with them to assess their competence. Someone who is calm, amenable, familiar with the work and willing to listen patiently to your requirements is ideal. Show them the site and your plans to make sure they are confident of their machine's ability to tackle the work.

Digging machines

Digging machines come in a wide range of sizes and capacities, but there are two basic types: wheeled and tracked. In general tracked machines are preferable, particularly for large jobs and difficult ground conditions. They usually exert less pressure on the ground than the human foot, and they can track across a lawn in straight lines, hardly leaving a mark; they can also traverse hollows and ditches. It is in changing direction that they chew up the ground and sheets of timber can be laid down for them to turn on when necessary. Wheeled machines make deep ruts in soft ground and are more likely to get stuck. For smaller jobs they are well worth considering, although the arm is only able to move through 180 degrees, since they can be driven to the site (instead of having to be transported), which saves both time and money.

Wheeled machines normally have a back hoe attachment, while tracked machines have either a front blade or a huge digging arm that can swing around 360 degrees, thus enabling them to dig a large area while remaining stationary. Machines with digging arms are efficient for deep ponds, but for shallow excavations or for moving material across a wide area, a bulldozer, which digs down by pushing the soil out in front with its blade, is useful. The motor or box scraper, either self-propelled or towed by a bulldozer (the well-known D8 and scraper), has a box into which the planed earth is shovelled. It scrapes and deposits the earth in the chosen place in one continuous operation. This machine is economical and efficient since it does not have to stop.

Site access

Difficult site access can greatly limit the use of machinery. The smallest tracked vehicles will squeeze through an opening just over 1m/3ft wide; but although a machine even of this size (about 1 tonne/1 ton) can be a boon when digging out a large pond, consider the pros and cons carefully. It may be that the obstacles to overcome in gaining access to the site and the damage that will inevitably be caused by the machine, especially if the ground is soft, outweigh its advantages. If the only access to the site is via the house, heavy machinery is ruled out – apart from a type of mini-tractor with a back-hoe attachment, which can be dismantled and manhandled through the house.

Digging techniques

When bulldozing or using a motor scraper the technique is to plane off the whole of the pond surface, layer by layer, working your way down; when using a mechanical excavator or digging with a spade, the technique is different. With a spade it is easiest to dig the depth of the spade (a spit) each time, working backwards from the open hole. Similarly, with mechanical excavators, it is easier to dig backwards to the full depth of the pond, keeping the machine up on the level ground. These machines can dig almost all round themselves, and should start at the edge and work towards the middle, where they stand, always leaving a promontory on which to travel back - this also serves as an exit route for the dump trucks, so that they do not have to climb up out of the hole each time. The correct profile – that is, cross section of the pond – can be cut in each area as the work is in progress. (Whatever the size of the pond, dewatering may be necessary - see p.31.)

Any tight curves in the pond's outline that cannot be cut neatly with a large machine may have to be finished off at the end with a smaller one or by hand. Ledges, too, may sometimes have to be cut separately at the end of the operation.

DIFFERENT TERRAINS

It is essential to know what kinds of subsoil you are likely to encounter during excavation. This can vary considerably from one spot to another, and unless you are already familiar with the subsoil in the pond area it is advisable to dig one or two test holes – or several on a large pond site. I recall a case where five holes dug in an area 30x90m/100x300ft yielded three soil samples of pure clay with a seam of chalk, one of solid chalk and one of sand!

Clay soils

Generally speaking, clay soils are easy to dig. A spade will slice through them as if through putty. If it is raining hard the surface can become puddled and sloppy, but the rain does not usually penetrate far, and the

This ancient clay-lined pond on the Sussex Weald was once used for watering horses. Clay is easy to excavate and makes a natural-looking pond. It is not, however, an economic option if the clay has to be imported.

Today the horse pond at Great Dixter, home of eminent plantsman Christopher Lloyd, plays host to many desirable water subjects. These include the water lily Nymphaea *'Rose Magnolia' in the foreground, the stellate pink N. 'Rose Arey', the huge bright red N. 'Escarboucle' and the velvety cup-shaped flowers of N. 'James Brydon'. Beneath the water, green clouds of water violet (*Hottonia palustris) *mushroom up to bear their pretty mauve flowers above the surface in early summer before the water lilies bloom.*

top can be sliced off, revealing good, firm ground underneath. However, in hot, sunny weather, clay forms a rock-hard crust through which it is almost impossible to cut. The crust may be quite thick, and can only be prised off or chopped away with a pickaxe. It presents no problem for machines, but it does cause the finished cut to be much rougher than would normally be the case. Once the offending layer has been sliced off, the clay will dig well. The problem comes when you wish to remove only about 5cm/2in, perhaps to form an accurate, level edge; then the best thing is to moisten the ground and cover it overnight with wet sacking.

Solid rock

Striking solid rock could ring the death knell for a small garden pond (or at least prescribe a raised one); but before giving up it is advisable to investigate a little further. The 'rock' could be chalk, which can be cut away reasonably easily with a pick, or it may be only a boulder, which can be prised out of the way. More extensive rock may call for a rethink. Can you be a little flexible in your design and move the pond to a different site? Or could the rock work to your advantage? The top of most rock deposits is not flat but contains hollows, depressions and fissures, and by remov-

ing the overlying soil to expose it you may find revealed a series of natural 'pools', almost ready made; or perhaps by moving a little to one side you may locate a hollow deep enough for the pond.

For a large pond, where machinery is to be employed, chalk should present no problems – machines can cut it away fairly easily, and it makes a beautifully smooth surface. Embedded flints, often found in chalk deposits, can be a problem, though, and if you are using a flexible liner you must dispose of them. If the pool is not too large you can simply pick them out and fill the resulting holes with clay or sand. Small, loose flints can easily be drawn off using the back of a garden rake. For a larger pond, this method would require an army of helpers; here the excavating machine can be used, not to remove the flints but to squash them down. There is little point in trying to dig flints away with the front edge of the machine bucket, for as you scrape away those that protrude, other sharp, splintered pieces appear underneath and it is impossible to make the surface free of them. A far more practical and effective method is to track over the entire pond with the machine itself, using its caterpillar tracks to push the flints down to prepare an amenable surface over which sand or suitable underlays can be placed before lining.

Soft, wet ground

Ground may be wet during excavation – either permanently because of a high water table or a constant ingress of water, or sporadically because of rainy periods – and this causes problems when excavating. While it can be a sheer delight to dig in dry peat or sand, either by hand or machine, when they are wet these types of earth become difficult to move by any method. Wet running sand is particularly problematic. Many of us have spent happy hours by the sea scooping sand away to make a pool, and what happens? As fast as we deepen the pool, the water draws sand from the edges and maintains the level of the bottom. No matter how hard we try to make it deeper, it just becomes wider and wider. In the construction of a real pond, running sand, which may be just loose or may be caused by a high water table or by springs, can create similar problems. I was once digging a pond that was intended to be 2m/6½ft deep in the middle (luckily it was fed by a small stream so it did not require lining), but because of the soil's wet, runny consistency it stabilized at a depth of 1m/3ft, and no amount of trying would make it deeper. So, where the ground is composed of running sand, you must usually be content with a shallow pond.

Digging in soft, wet soil is made easier if you make a stable working platform – a few planks will suffice – and use the edge of the platform as a fulcrum for the spade. Dig backwards in strips, digging one spit (spade's depth) at a time and move the planks back about 10-15cm/4-6in after completing each row. Long scaffolding boards can provide a good wheelbarrow run away from the soft area. If there is a lot of carting, and you are not very good at steering a straight course, you can make a sturdier run with two planks battened together at 1m/3ft intervals.

As you dig down, layer by layer, first dig a deeper area at each level to act as a sump in which the water can collect. If the flow is only slight, the water can be emptied out of the sump periodically with a bucket; for a stronger flow a pump with a suction pipe and strainer (to prevent clogging) will be needed. Submersible pumps, which come ready-fitted with strainers, are excellent for this, and some have their own built-in float-switch that automatically switches off the pump when it has emptied the sump. They are readily hired.

If machinery is being used, wet sand, as long as it is not wet running sand, generally causes few problems. The machine will sink in a little, but not usually enough to prevent its operation. Wet peat can be a different matter: I have seen a 15 tonne/15 ton excavator disappear out of sight, save the top of its boom, in peat! And there are other soil types often encountered in wetlands that are similarly dangerous: thick deposits of slowly rotting and decaying vegetation; peat that has not properly formed; marsh, silts, and mud deposits that you find in low, swampy areas, or where there was once a pond that has gradually become choked with vegetation. Such places should be entered with great caution in a machine. It may be necessary to operate on 'mats' – long balks of timber wired or chained together to form a mattress or raft on which the machine can stand. At least three are needed so that the machine has one or two to stand on while it picks up the mat over which it has just travelled and lifts it round to the front, ready to track on to. In this way, it is possible to traverse even the most swampy terrain.

In the case of large pools, where machinery is being used, a deep sump can be dug to begin with, into which all the water will drain during operations. So quickly and efficiently do modern machines dig that a new sump can easily be dug wherever necessary. It would, of course, be inadvisable to dig it close to the intended rim of the pond. A temporary sump is best located in what is to be one of the deeper parts of the pond, but if a permanent sump for dewatering (to prevent water from accumulating under the liner, for example) or for draining is part of the scheme, a suitable location should be chosen a little distance away from the main excavation. The water draining into the sump can be handled by a submersible pump. When large volumes are involved – say 22,800 litres/ 5,000 gallons an hour or more – a petrol- or diesel-driven surface pump standing close by will be needed.

It is important to bail or pump the water to a place where it cannot find its way back into your excavation, such as the other side of a mound into a ditch, storm drain or gully. (Do not utilize the foul water drains, which are not designed to cope with large influxes of water.)

Sometimes it is more practical to dig ponds 'wet' – without dewatering at all. This happens, for example, in the case of existing ponds that are being enlarged or redug after becoming silted. The method is usually to dig from the banks using a dragline machine, which runs on tracks and has a long latticework jib from which a scoop is slung far out into the pond by means of steel ropes and pulleys. Dragline machines range from a mere 10 tonnes/10 tons to truly colossal specimens; the cost of transporting and reassembling them can be prohibitively expensive.

Draglines cannot be operated near power lines or overhanging trees because of the height of the jib. In these situations the traditional method, still operated by one or two companies, is called for. A scoop is drawn backwards and forwards across the bottom of the pond by powerful machines, each with a large winch. The old steam ploughing engines were best for this, and some are still in use today. The advantage of this method is that no matter how soft the bottom, no machinery is put at risk by having to operate inside the pond; also, the excavated material can be unloaded some distance away by just one pulling operation of the winch. It is best to drain the pond before dredging by this method.

Revelling in the leafy ooze, the naturalized Primula florindae *hybrids lighten this shady hollow with their bell-shaped yellow-orange flowers. Although peaty from the leaf fall, the dark waters of this woodland pool reflect the giant leaves of* Petasites japonicus var. giganteus *and birch trees with their feathery leaves and russet peeling bark.*

Heavily canopied sites such as this, in

Frank Cabot's garden at La Malbaie, north of Quebec, are ideal for moisture- and shade-loving plants but unsuitable for most fish.

Take care when excavating or dredging pools in which centuries of leaf matter may have built up. Though the ground may appear solid and firm enough, it could prove to be soft and unstable, and the pool could be deeper than you had realized.

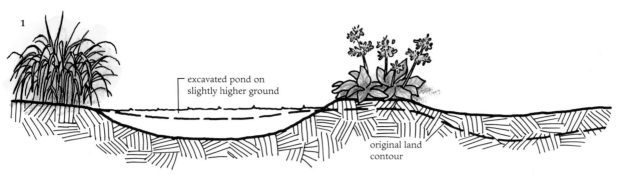

1 Excavating wet hollows
To avoid accumulations of water which could cause 'hippoing' under a flexible liner, excavate the pond at a higher point so that its bottom is slightly above the lowest level of the land. Use the excavated material to raise the ground slightly on the lower side of the pond by filling the original hollow. This side of the pond will form a natural bog garden.

2 Draining surplus water
Dig a trench in the bottom of the pond in which to run a perforated land drain, surrounded with gravel, to a sump (fitted with a pump if necessary). From the sump, water can be drained to the nearest ditch.

3 Excavating on a slope by the cut-and-fill method
Cut in at the top of the slope and place the excavated soil on the lower side to make the lower and upper edges the same level. Plant shrubs to stabilize the lower slope.

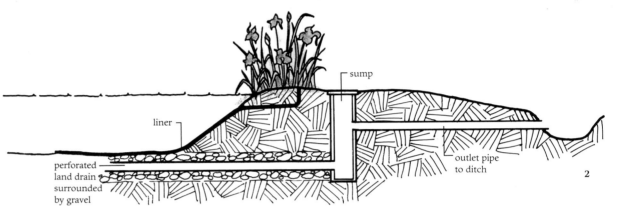

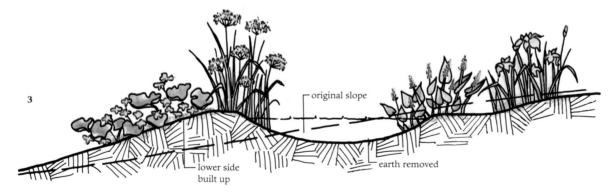

OPPOSITE *Gently graded, carefully worked surrounds ensure that this pond fits naturally into its sloping site. Always avoid steep banks running into the water: they are not only dangerous but unpleasing to the eye, since the pond appears to be half empty.*

The high water level and interruptions in the fringe of planting around this pond allow it to be viewed from distant vantage points.

If this is impractical or unnecessary because of the pond's location, or if you only wish to remove the top half metre/ foot or two of a deep layer of silt, then a suction dredger can be employed. This consists of a large pump capable of lifting mud and silt that is usually operated from a raft or, for smaller ponds, by means of long suction hoses, from the bank.

Of course, it is also perfectly possible to perform these operations by hand if enough people are available and there is plenty of time. Many wetland sites have been restored for conservation purposes by the admirable work of volunteer teams.

Wet hollows
It is obviously tempting to situate a pond in a wet hollow, and this is undeniably the place to choose for a large stretch of water with an unlined bottom. You will, however, encounter the usual difficulties in excavating wet ground, and problems may arise through storm water that tends to collect in this spot, possibly carrying undesirable silts and nutrients into the pond.

If you wish to line the pond, this position is far from ideal. It is better, if possible, to dig the pond just above the lowest spot in the hollow, using earth from the excavation to raise the hollow slightly (diagram 1).

If you have to excavate in a wet hollow, and the pond is to be lined, special precautions must be taken during the excavation. Excess water or gases from decomposing organic matter may collect under the liner, causing it to rise up from the bottom to form a sinister black hippopotamus-like lump, known in the trade as 'hippoing'. If there is even the slightest suspicion that this problem could arise, provision must be made before the excavation is complete to drain surplus water or funnel off gases from beneath the liner.

Dig a trench from the bottom of the pond to a suitable low-lying ditch or drain and lay in it a 10cm/4in perforated land drain, backfilling it with round gravel, which increases the catchment area off the perforated pipe and reduces the risk of its becoming clogged. (The same trench can be used if a bottom drain is to be fitted in the pond.) If gases are likely to be a problem, install several perforated air vent pipes, in addition to the land drain, running under the pond and extending to the surface.

If a lower-lying ditch or drain is not available, the pipe can be conducted to a sump situated nearby. Lined with brick or with concrete tubing, which is cheaper and quicker to install, the sump can be covered with a paving slab, or a metal inspection cover if appropriate. Piping can then be run from this at any level lower than the rim of the pond (diagram 2). Provided the level of the water in the pond is higher, sufficient downward pressure should be exerted on the liner to force the water down this exit pipe. In the unlikely event that no lower position of any kind is available, then the sump can serve as a pumping position from which the water can be drawn from beneath the liner should a 'hippo' occur, or better still, to prevent it in the first place.

Dry hollows, incidentally, do not normally present problems, though in areas prone to temporary flooding after storms the pond surrounds should be contoured so that storm water is diverted around the side of the pond rather than into it.

Sloping ground

Positioning pools and streams in relation to ground contours requires careful consideration. On sloping ground, earth adjustments will be necessary, as water will not conform to a slope! On hillsides and in valleys water should be made to fit in as naturally as possible, running along the contours of the land rather than across them. It is possible for the pond to be dug in at the top of a slope and made level with the ground at the bottom; it can be set level with the ground at the top and built up at the bottom; or a compromise – known as 'cut and fill' – can be made.

The first method requires a lot of work, involving digging down a long way before even reaching the proposed water level, and then disposing of all the excess soil. It also results in a steep or long bank on the upper side, which can prove a difficult, even dangerous, approach to the pond.

The second method is very economical with earth moving, as the material from the pond is merely scooped out and placed a little lower down the slope. However, the result looks most unnatural and contrived, with the pond apparently perched up in the air. It also often happens that the excavation does not provide enough earth to build up the lower side of the pond.

The third method is the one that is usually adopted. The material dug out to make the pond is normally sufficient to contour the lower side

convincingly, and the pond fits snugly into the sloping land (diagram 3).

Problems arise when the slope is steep or the pond big. There comes a point where the enlargement of the pond makes the necessary excavation at the top and the building up at the bottom out of all proportion to the extra area of water obtained and it becomes problematical and costly to construct too high a bank. Such ponds can look unnatural and are usually constructed only for reservoir purposes.

Water does not normally collect on hilltops, and they are not an obvious location for a pond. However, a very small pond could nestle in comfortably and its surroundings be suitably planted to disguise its unusual location. In the case of a large pond, the material gained from the excavation could be banked up around the pond to create the effect of a natural hollow on the hilltop.

Drainage presents no problems in situations such as these, and if the pool is artificially lined to prevent seepage any excess water that collects under the liner can easily be conducted away by means of a land drain leading from beneath the liner to a point lower down the hillside. In ponds that are even slightly elevated, both top drainage, for normal overflow situations, and bottom drainage, for water collecting under the lining, can easily be installed.

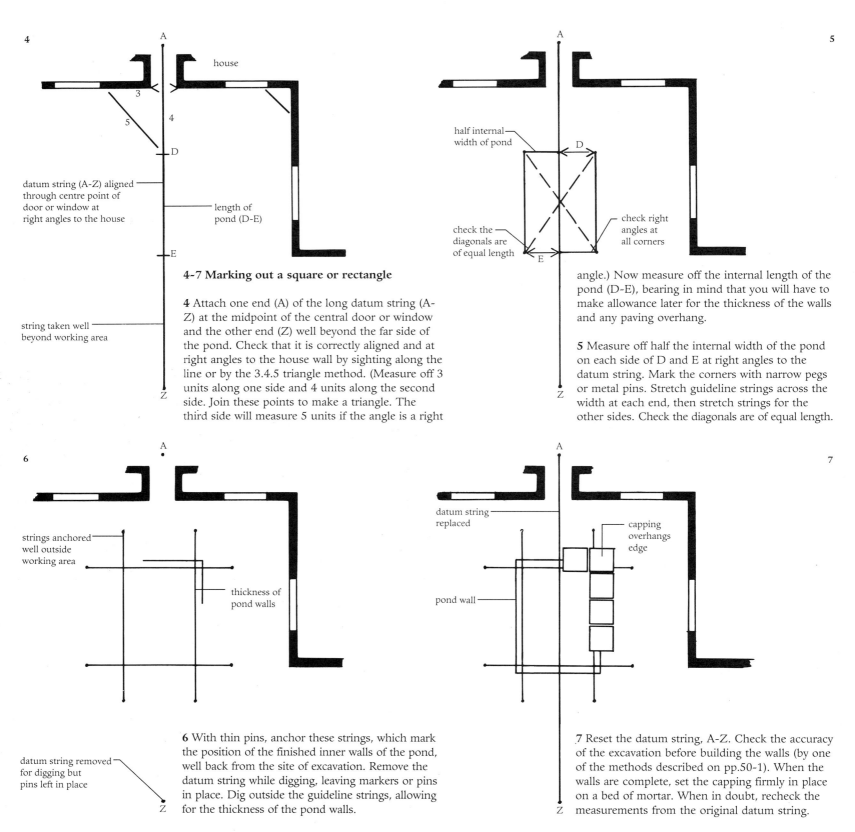

4 A

house

3

5

4

D

datum string (A-Z) aligned
through centre point of
door or window at
right angles to the house

length of
pond (D-E)

E

4-7 Marking out a square or rectangle

string taken well
beyond working area

Z

4 Attach one end (A) of the long datum string (A-Z) at the midpoint of the central door or window and the other end (Z) well beyond the far side of the pond. Check that it is correctly aligned and at right angles to the house wall by sighting along the line or by the 3.4.5 triangle method. (Measure off 3 units along one side and 4 units along the second side. Join these points to make a triangle. The third side will measure 5 units if the angle is a right

5 A

half internal
width of pond

D

check the
diagonals are
of equal length

check right
angles at
all corners

E

Z

angle.) Now measure off the internal length of the pond (D-E), bearing in mind that you will have to make allowance later for the thickness of the walls and any paving overhang.

5 Measure off half the internal width of the pond on each side of D and E at right angles to the datum string. Mark the corners with narrow pegs or metal pins. Stretch guideline strings across the width at each end, then stretch strings for the other sides. Check the diagonals are of equal length.

6 A

strings anchored
well outside
working area

thickness of
pond walls

datum string removed
for digging but
pins left in place

Z

6 With thin pins, anchor these strings, which mark the position of the finished inner walls of the pond, well back from the site of excavation. Remove the datum string while digging, leaving markers or pins in place. Dig outside the guideline strings, allowing for the thickness of the pond walls.

7 A

datum string
replaced

capping
overhangs
edge

pond wall

Z

7 Reset the datum string, A-Z. Check the accuracy of the excavation before building the walls (by one of the methods described on pp.50-1). When the walls are complete, set the capping firmly in place on a bed of mortar. When in doubt, recheck the measurements from the original datum string.

MEASURING AND MARKING OUT

First try out the proposed shape of the pond from your rough design, using temporary markers such as sticks or battens (or ropes for curves) to plot the outline in its correct position. At this stage bear in mind the effect that sloping ground will have on your impressions: ground sloping towards you will make the water surface appear larger, ground sloping away will cause the surface to seem smaller.

When you are happy with the shape and location of the pond, make your accurate working drawings, noting all the details necessary for the digging. These include the depth and position of proposed planting ledges, and the thickness of the walls – including any cavity in double-walled ponds. Once the final plans have been made you are not likely to want to depart from them for a formal pond, whose site and shape are precisely related to its built surroundings.

Geometric ponds

Accuracy is essential when marking out a formal pond for excavation. Only when you are entirely satisfied with the position and shape and have recorded all the information necessary for the digging should marking commence. It must be done very carefully, and therefore takes a little time. You will mark out the exact shape and dimensions of the pond on the ground, and dig the excavation out from this. When working off your own plan it is often best to write down the key measurements rather than relying on scaling off the drawing each time.

First, level the site so that the geometrical shape of the pond is not distorted by uneven ground. Next, set up strings to ensure that the sides of the pond run exactly parallel with the existing path or wall and the axis runs truly in line with the planned view. The strings can be checked with a spirit level at several points during marking out. Diagrams 4-7 explain

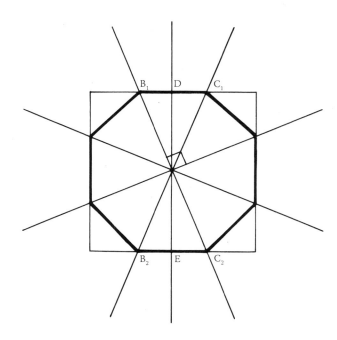

8

8 Marking out an octagon
Mark out a square the length and width of the pond, as described in diagrams 4 and 5. Set a peg in the centre of the square. Multiply the width of the pond, D-E by .4142 to determine the length of the straight sides, B-C, positioned centrally on and at right angles to D-E. Mark out the axis lines, B_1-C_2 and B_2-C_1, and use a right angle at the centre to mark the remaining corners of the octagon.

RIGHT *Cleverly designed by Nathaniel Lloyd to fit into the sunken garden at Great Dixter in Sussex, the elongated octagonal pond aligns with the short flight of steps. The advantage of an octagon over a square is that no sharp corners stick out to impinge on the walking area. This makes it easier to negotiate with prams or wheelchairs; at the same time, when space is at a premium, the area of the surround is increased, though the dimensions of the pond itself do not appear any less generous.*

the principles of aligning rectangular or square ponds. Diagram 8 shows how to mark out an octagonal pond.

Often a relatively complex shape, incorporating curves or points, is desired for a fountain pond. For a large pond, the string method works well. For a small pond, the easiest way is to construct a template in timber battens and mark around this for the excavation. If you are making a circular pond, mark out the ground with an improvised compass. Tie one end of a piece of string to a pin inserted firmly at the centre point of the projected pond (first making sure that this is correctly aligned). Measure off the radius of the circle and tie the other end of the string to a sharp pointed implement, a paintbrush or a washing-up liquid bottle filled with diluted white emulsion paint, which will pour out a fine white line. Hold the string taut, and use the point, the bottle, or the brush dipped in paint, to mark the outline of the pond on the ground.

While a circular pond looks the same from all angles, oval or elliptical ponds offer opportunities for interesting changes of perspective. According to the angle from which they are viewed, they may appear perfectly circular or narrow and lenticular. A simple, roughly oval shape can be formed by linking two circles. Diagram 9 shows how to mark out an elliptical shape.

Freeform ponds

For most informal ponds, the marking out is best done by eye. Simply form the temporary outline with a length of thick rope or hose, then stand back and view it from different angles. Remember that things never appear on the ground as they do in plan: perspective distorts the shape from whatever the viewing angle, so make adjustments at this stage, if from one angle the effect is not pleasing.

There may be circumstances in which more precise marking out is required and several measurements may be needed to get the pond correctly oriented. Diagram 10 shows how to scale up a freeform shape in relation to two fixed points.

When you are satisfied with the shape, mark the outline with lime or white emulsion paint.

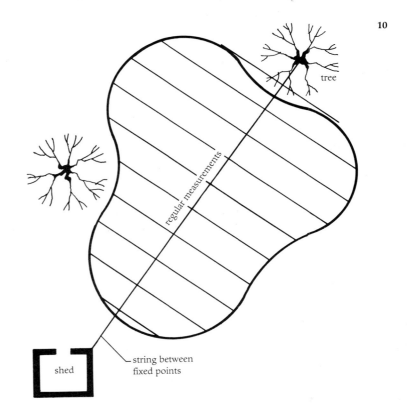

10

tree

regular measurements

shed

string between fixed points

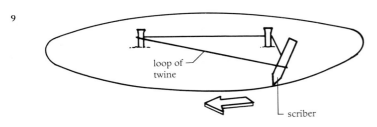

9

loop of twine

scriber

OPPOSITE *Circular ponds always look elliptical, unless they are viewed from directly above. This unchanging characteristic evokes a feeling of calm and reassurance - unlike asymmetrical ponds which look dissimilar from every angle and thus stimulate frequent glances.*

A round pond may form a central focus from which paths radiate out or it may be placed, as in this garden in South Africa, to emphasize and enhance the curvature of a bay in the lawn. Its circularity is emphasized by the surround and ground cover planting.

9 Marking out an ellipse
You can do this with two stout poles and loop of strong twine. Set the poles firmly in the ground. The distance between them, and the length of the loop, will determine the finished shape. The closer the poles are together, the squatter the ellipse will be. Place the loop of twine over the poles and pull it taut with a scriber. Drag the scriber, keeping the twine taut, around the poles to mark out the elliptical shape on the ground. The scriber can be a washing-up liquid bottle filled with diluted emulsion paint or a strong sharp object that scores the ground.

10 Scaling up a freeform shape
Even though it has a freeform shape, an informal pond can be easily scaled up from a plan and marked out on the ground. This is done by stretching out a central line (using string or measuring tape) on the ground taken from two fixed points such as a tree and the corner of a garden shed. To translate the shape on to the ground, mark off regular measurements along this line at 30cm/1ft or 1m/3ft intervals, depending on the size of the pond. From these equal points mark off in each direction at right angles from the line the distances to the outside edge of the pond. Then use a loop of rope or hosepipe to form the final shape of the pond.

DIGGING THE POND

The first spit of 20-23cm/8-9in is likely to take you down to planting ledge level, whatever the size of the pond (except for concrete ponds, where extra depth should be allowed for the thickness of the concrete). If the pond is to have a hard edge, it is essential that the ledge, from which it will be built up, be quite level.

Informal ponds

As a general rule, the smaller the pond, the steeper its sides. For the smallest garden pond a batter (or slope) of about 15 degrees from the vertical is normally appropriate. With larger ponds or lakes, the angle can be considerably more gradual – perhaps 1:3 or even 1:4. A vertical cut should be used only where a hard edging is to be applied above a planting ledge, or if a wall or landing stage for a boat is to abut the pond. For the remainder of the pond, the contours can be kept gentle and the sides not too steep.

Formal ponds

As well as allowing room in the excavation for the walls of the pond, it will also be important to make sure that the digging is done to exactly the right depth, with allowance for any concrete base, footings for the pond walls, and any slabs or wall footings within the pond according to the design and construction method. Make sure that you also take into account the thickness of any paving or other edging to be laid above the rim of the pond, and the mortar in which it will be set.

If you plan to install a bottom drain, you will need to dig a ditch for the pipe. Otherwise, dig a shallow sump (in the form of a hollow about 10cm/4in deep) into which the dregs of the pond water can be swept when the pond is cleaned by pumping or siphoning.

To gauge the correct depth of the digging, take a straightedge and spirit level out across the pond from the datum peg (see diagrams 11-13). Then measure down at right angles into the excavation from several points along the straightedge, to calculate for the full depth of the pond including all allowances.

When the main excavation is finished, the datum string can be replaced and accurate measurements again taken to determine the position of the internal walls of the pond (including any walls or pillars within the pond) and surrounding paths. This must be done with absolute precision, as no adjustment can be made to finished walls.

Dig as carefully as possible, so as not to disturb the ground forming the sides of the pool, but do not be too dismayed if part of the side does collapse: this can be cleared away and the gap stopped up with earth or even filled with concrete, if smooth sides are needed for a liner-only pond. Most formal ponds have masonry walls built within the excavation, and here such gaps can be backfilled with earth, rubble or a 'lean' concrete mix during construction. Smooth sides are not vitally important in the case of preformed ponds, as gaps will be left around the pond to be filled in with earth or sand.

PERFECT LEVELS

Water is always level – you cannot have a sloping pond! It follows that the rim of the pond must be perfectly level also. Nothing looks worse than a lopsided birdbath effect, with the water slopping over one side and an ugly edge showing on the other. Precision is especially vital to achieve the classic effect of brimming water characteristic of Islamic ponds; any discrepancies are offensive to the eye. Where walls near the water's edge are to form part of the water feature, great care must also be taken to keep their top parallel with the water level.

Using a spirit level

For most ponds, an accurate builder's or carpenter's spirit level, used with a straightedge, is convenient, inexpensive and gives good results. The straightedge can be either a long straight piece of planed timber approximately 15x3cm/6x1in, or, ideally, a piece of extruded aluminium section, of the type used in conservatory roofs, for example. The important thing is for it to reach as far as possible without bending: the longer the straightedge, the fewer times it will need to be transferred from peg to peg. Not only will fewer pegs then be needed, but, more important, there is less opportunity for slight inaccuracies to build up.

To ensure that the pond is level, a datum point has to be established, from which readings are taken during excavation and construction. This is marked with a wooden peg after the topsoil has been removed, when the shape of the pond is pegged out more precisely. It is usually best to make the datum point correspond with the level of the rim of the pond. For brimming ponds this also represents the water level, which will be at the very rim of the pond. The position and level of the surface of the pond will already have been decided according to the contours of the land.

The peg marking the datum point (known as the datum peg) is tapped into the ground just outside the perimeter of the pond, its top marking the datum level. Once the datum peg has been inserted, the whole contour of the pond is mapped out by pegs, which are inserted, like the datum peg, about half to one metre/yard outside the perimeter of the pond, leaving enough room for the edges to be dug without the pegs impeding the work. Plenty of pegs will be needed, as, for the simplest method of measuring, they must be within straightedge reach of each other.

The top of each peg must be exactly level with the top of the datum peg, and this is established by taking a spirit level reading from the datum peg to its neighbour, and so on, round the pond (diagram 11). When going round a large pond in this way, slight inaccuracies can occur, and you should go round in both directions, ironing out any discrepancies.

Using a water level

To obtain the level for a large pond, one of the oldest building techniques, using water itself, can be used. In its crudest form, a modern water level consists of a length of transparent hosepipe. Simply fill the hose with water, making sure that no air is trapped in it, then fasten one end,

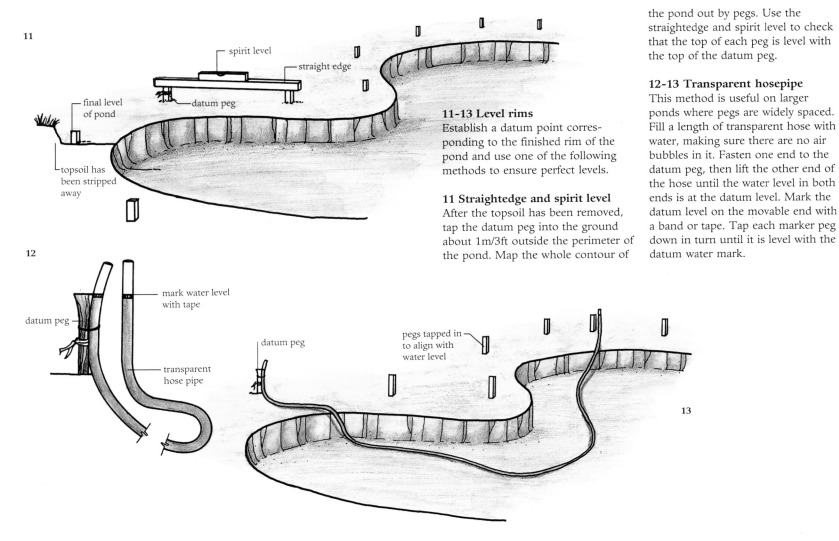

11

spirit level

straight edge

final level
of pond

datum peg

topsoil has
been stripped
away

12

datum peg

mark water level
with tape

transparent
hose pipe

datum peg

pegs tapped in
to align with
water level

13

the pond out by pegs. Use the straightedge and spirit level to check that the top of each peg is level with the top of the datum peg.

11-13 Level rims
Establish a datum point corresponding to the finished rim of the pond and use one of the following methods to ensure perfect levels.

11 Straightedge and spirit level
After the topsoil has been removed, tap the datum peg into the ground about 1m/3ft outside the perimeter of the pond. Map the whole contour of

12-13 Transparent hosepipe
This method is useful on larger ponds where pegs are widely spaced. Fill a length of transparent hose with water, making sure there are no air bubbles in it. Fasten one end to the datum peg, then lift the other end of the hose until the water level in both ends is at the datum level. Mark the datum level on the movable end with a band or tape. Tap each marker peg down in turn until it is level with the datum water mark.

pointing upright, to the datum peg. Lift the other end of the hose until the water level in both ends is at the datum level (diagram 12), and mark the movable end of the hose with tape or an elastic band.

Now take the free end of the hose from one peg to another, holding it so that the water level remains at the position marked, and tap each peg down until it is level with the datum water mark (diagram 13). If you should lose any water from the hose during the operation, you will have to refill and start again.

Professional levels
On large sites, more sophisticated methods of taking levels are required. Apart from the greater distances involved, it may be necessary to check that a bank beside a pond slopes to the required angle or to ensure that different parts of the work bear the desired relation in height to one another. Used mainly by professionals, these methods may involve expensive equipment.

The self-levelling Cowley level is easy and quick to use, and gives a high degree of accuracy within a radius of about 30m/100ft. Telescopic levels, or theodolites, are used for long-distance work around a large pond or lake, or for determining the height of rockworks or waterfalls. Very expensive, and worthwhile only to professionals, are laser levels; their great advantage is that they can be operated over long distances by only one person.

Sometimes on a large site, when excavations are likely to take a long time, it is left to the machine operator to gauge the accuracy of the work without constant recourse to expensive equipment. In this case conspicuous profiles, accurately set by instruments in the first place, are positioned across the working area. These pieces of batten, horizontal for gauging levels or angled for gauging slopes, are arranged wide apart, in such a way that they can be 'eyed through' using a 'traveller', with a matching cross piece. When the 'traveller' matches up with the profiles, the ground is at the same level.

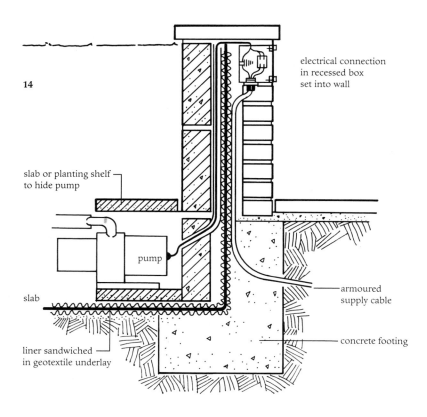

14

electrical connection
in recessed box
set into wall

slab or planting shelf
to hide pump

pump

slab

armoured
supply cable

liner sandwiched
in geotextile underlay

concrete footing

14 Concealing services in semi-raised ponds with double walls
Semi-raised ponds with double walls provide a simple means of conducting electrical cable to the pond, as the armoured cable, junction box and supply to the pump can be housed invisibly between the walls. Bring the supply cable from the house between the liner and the outer wall and up to a junction box concealed within the wall. Direct the supply to the pond across the top of the liner and down between the liner and the inner wall as shown in the cut-away section. Set the capping above the supply, so that it can be removed for maintenance, but use heavy material so that it will not be dislodged.

A slab can be built off the wall inside the pond on brick or blockwork supports so that the pump can be hidden.

CONDUCTING SERVICES TO THE POND

There are several simple ways of conducting services - electricity, drainage and water supplies - to and from the pond and these should be considered at the planning stage.

Formal ponds lend themselves to fountain and lighting features, so that in practically all cases an electricity supply will be needed. If possible, plan to conceal junction boxes in nearby flower beds. Alternatively, the armoured cable can terminate in a hollow planter or inside the hollow stand of a garden ornament. From there run the waterproof cable to a pump or lights through a conduit beneath the capping to emerge, ideally, at a point where it is readily disguised. It may be necessary, when the capping is in place, to chip away the underside (taking care not to spoil the front edge) to make room for the conduit. The cable can be fed through the soil of a planting ledge or, more elaborately, down a specially built plinth surmounted by a statue.

By taking services in over the edge, leaving the pond structure or liner intact, you avoid the risk of making the pond less waterproof. Where it is essential for services to enter below the water line, the number of entry points should be kept to a minimum. If pipes to fountains and electrical cables are required, they may all pass together through one simple duct that can be carefully flanged and sealed (see p.75).

Normally, when electricity cable is needed, the best construction method for the pond is to build walls within a liner. This enables cables to be taken behind the wall – or between inner and outer walls in a semi-raised pond (diagram 14) – to conceal them and protect them both from ultraviolet light and from possible damage. For access, you can include a removable slab on the capping or (better still), if the pond is raised, a removable stone in the outside wall just beneath the capping. Into this cavity connections can be made from the waterproof cable that comes ready-supplied with the pump and lights to the armoured cable feeding the pond from the house.

Top-up supplies and overflows

Top-up supplies and overflow pipe work can also be brought in via the cavity wall of a semi-raised pond or behind the wall of a sunken pond. If you do not want a brimming pond (and remember to make allowance for occasional brimming after heavy rain) then you can incorporate some sort of overflow system that will prevent the water level from reaching the brim. Make sure that the water level will not be lowered too much as a result of the position of any overflow pipe. Also, make sure that a mains water delivery pipe does not finish beneath the water level, as this will make the flow so inaudible that it will be easy to forget that the water has been left running. Moreover, in most countries it is against the law to have pipes feeding in where they could possibly siphon back into the water system and thereby pollute the drinking water. It is, therefore, necessary to fit a non-return or anti-siphon valve to any permanent top-up system, even if pipes terminate above the normal water level. Alternatively, use a remote pressure-fed tank (in a garden shed, for example), to feed the top-up valve by gravity.

In ponds that are formed in hollows or valleys by the building of a bank or dam, a simple and cheap method of emptying and controlling the level of pond water can be devised using large-diameter interlocking plastic pipes connected to a pipe laid almost horizontally through the bottom of the bank (diagram 15). In normal use, the upright pipe acts as an overflow and to lower the level of the water or drain the pond right down to the bend, you merely have to pull out one or more vertical sections.

For large ponds a more sophisticated system of water control, known as a 'monk', will be needed at the pond end of the horizontal pipe. It can be bought as a preformed structure. It incorporates boards that can be

This water chute forms part of a more extensive system at Docton Mill in Devon, dating back beyond the eleventh century. Water flowing along the mill race (just visible at the top of the photograph) can be diverted before it reaches the mill wheel by opening a sluice and allowing the flow to enter a by-pass channel. Here it can be seen plunging down into a deep rock-cut chamber formed in the lower channel, itself an overflow from the mill pond. Bulbs and moisture-loving subjects give year-round interest and colour to this imaginative and animated water feature.

15

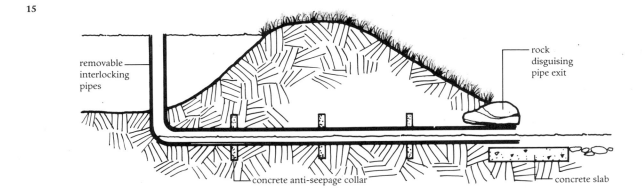

removable interlocking pipes

rock disguising pipe exit

concrete anti-seepage collar

concrete slab

15 A simple overflow system
Through the bottom of the bank, lay a pipe of sufficient diameter to take the anticipated wet-weather flow. Fit anti-seepage collars to prevent water tracking along the outside of the pipe. On the pond side, just beyond the foot of the bank, fit a 90-degree bend and connect it to vertical sections of pipe to reach the desired water level. Position a concrete slab and a few stones at the pipe exit to act as a wearing course, and conceal the exit itself with rock.

raised, lowered or parted in the middle to allow water to be drawn off.

In an alternative method that is more appropriate where the silting of the pond is unlikely to cause a blockage, a pipe is laid horizontally from the bottom of the pond to an inspection chamber within the bank or dam (similar to the principle shown in diagram 2). At the end of the pipe a 90-degree bend is fitted with lengths of vertical pipe to the height of the water level. The overflow from the pond will spill out of this and fall into the chamber, continuing down the pipe which is taken to lower-lying ground or a suitable drain. Again the pond can easily be emptied .

A wide ditch should always be dug through the ground to one side of the bank. It can be used as the normal overflow to the pond instead of pipework or as an adjunct to a piped spillway or sluice to take occasional excess storm water. This channel must be wide enough to take the most severe anticipated flows so that floodwater does not rise above the earth dam or bank. Once the water rises over it, a bank will quickly be eroded. The spillway channel must be dug to a gentle fall to prevent excessive water speeds being reached. The steeper the slope, the faster the flow, and the more protection required to prevent scouring of the channel bottom. In extreme cases this may need to be encased in concrete. Usually, however, a covering of stone scalpings will suffice. Stones should always be laid below the outfall of a sluice pipe or bypass channel to prevent scouring and undercutting by swift water currents.

OPPOSITE *The hard structural elements of this unusual water feature are an integral part of its stylish design. Although incorporating some planting, its bold architectural lines, best appreciated from above, are in keeping with the urban setting. In relation to the water surface area, such a feature would be expensive to construct.*

BELOW *Easier, and cheaper, to construct - whether using a flexible liner or poured concrete - an open expanse of water fits naturally in a rural surrounding, with its edges disguised by planting.*

At its simplest, to make a pond you need something that holds water reliably over a long period of time. A lining of some kind is required for most water features, the only exception being an informal pond or lake that has a natural, fairly constant flow of water or a solid, pure clay subsoil that will retard water loss. A lined pond offers a constantly high water level: only occasional topping up is needed to replace losses through plant consumption and evaporation. All manner of materials have been employed in the past: lead sheeting lined with ashlar stone, as used by the Romans at Bath; wooden casks sawn in half; clay; concrete; brick; and, more recently, reinforced concrete, huge sheets of plastic or other manmade fabrics.

Cost, durability and size, as well as finished appearance, are the governing factors in selecting a construction method. Having examined the practical aspects of your own situation and decided on the style of water feature – formal or informal, sunken or semi-raised – you need to consider the materials available.

If your ground is suitable, you may consider constructing a clay-lined pond (p.44) but remember that this can be time-consuming and require more maintenance. A preformed pond (pp.45-6) is the obvious choice if you want something small, inexpensive and quick to install.

Poured or sprayed concrete is often used for crisp geometric shapes and for naturalistic ponds with gently sloping sides; for durability, concrete should be reinforced (see pp.47-8). Over large areas the danger of cracking increases due to ground movement and this method becomes less practical and more costly.

Although concrete blocks are appropriate for angular pools, they do not conform well to tight curves. They constitute a simple method of constructing vertical sides and are an excellent way of containing poured reinforced concrete.

In terms of time and money, there are many arguments in favour of using flexible liners; the advantages of this method increase with the size of the pond. 'Flexible' really is the operative word since liners can be used in many different circumstances. The smallest garden pond or water feature can

quickly be installed without special skills; equally, a good sized lake can be made. The liners can be used for both formal and informal ponds and can also be used to repair and waterproof old ponds that have sprung leaks. Better quality liners are especially suitable for the curvilinear shapes of an informal pond. They can be protected to withstand all kinds of applications – domestic, recreational and industrial. In combination with brick, stone or concrete, liners can be used to construct highly durable water features and are the best choice for most ponds.

The materials for edging and surrounds need to be considered, too, according to their suitability for formal and informal designs.

CLAY-LINED PONDS

It is immensely satisfying to construct a pond without any artificial materials, and this is the allure of the clay-lined pond. But it is only worth attempting to build a pond by this time-consuming method today if your ground is of pure clay (see pp.28-9). It is certainly not an economic option if clay is not available on site and has to be imported.

Clay also has certain drawbacks. Although it will retard water loss, it is not 100 per cent watertight, so a clay-lined pond needs to be large and deep, at least 6m/20ft across: a slight drop in water level may go unnoticed in a lake but it is readily manifest in a small pond. Water lilies love clay and their roots can penetrate a clay lining. This is fine as long as they are growing vigorously, but when they die and shrivel, they leave holes. Tree roots, irresistibly drawn towards the water can form a fibrous mat through the clay, causing considerable water loss. (If you are importing clay, a layer of polythene placed under it will help reduce this effect.) Moles and other tunnelling animals can make passages through the clay. Be prepared for all these eventualities if you propose to embark on such a project, whether it is formal or informal in concept.

In its most basic form the clay pond can simply be scooped out of the clay, maintaining a shallow batter, or slope, all the way around the pond's sides. The clay must be good right through to the bottom of the pond, of course, and will need careful inspection beforehand. It is found in various qualities and colours, ranging from brown, red, and yellow to blue: a change in colour from brown to blue can indicate the proximity of liquid running sand or water (see pp.31-3) and you should be wary of this colour change as the digging progresses. Pure, freshly dug clay needs little treatment to be made to hold water, but it must not be allowed to dry out. Arrange to fill the pond very quickly on completion, or as the work proceeds.

If the clay is wet, or soft and putty like, you can work it by wedging or puddling to enhance its water-retentive properties. This can be done by hand with wooden rammers, with your feet or with mechanical compactors. On very large areas, however, the best method is to use a lamb's foot roller, a heavy vibrating roller with knobs sticking out all over it. It is best to start at the bottom of the pond, letting in water as you work up the sides, so that the clay will not dry out.

Beware of intermittent springs in the pond bottom, as they may force their way through the clay, causing it to 'blow'. This will create fissures through which the water will leak out of the pond when the spring pressure diminishes. When using the 'wet' method it is very important that deep cracks are not allowed to form. To prevent this, take care to fill the pond as quickly as possible: start filling even before the sides are completed, so that you can work up just ahead of the water.

If the clay proves to be completely dry on excavation – and I have seen this in a particularly dry summer – it must be treated differently. In this state it will come out in a mixture of hard lumps and powder as you dig, and the nature of the clay can be exploited to make the pond retain water. Do not wet the clay. First break up the lumps until a deep (10-12cm/4-5in) layer of fine particles covers the entire pond. On large sites agricultural-type harrows or rotivators drawn behind a tractor can be used to break up the clay. When the water is allowed in, the particles of clay powder expand to form a mush that settles to provide an extremely impervious seal over the entire surface.

Clay ponds can be overlaid with soil or gravel to protect the clay and prevent it from drying out. The soil provides a good bed for plants to grow in, greatly preferable to the clay lining itself, which would be damaged if subsequent dredging or weed clearance were needed.

Waterproofing with bentonite

If you are fortunate enough to have a large, naturally occurring pond, or a reliable natural water supply to feed one that you have excavated, and you simply want to enhance its water-retentive properties without any visible artificial means, bentonite is the ideal waterproofing material. This form of clay derived from fossilized volcanic ash is named for Fort Benton, Montana, where it was first discovered; it is sold in powdered form under various trade names. Its ability to waterproof comes from its remarkable qualities for expansion when moistened. It is easier to handle in its prepared form, sandwiched in a textile quilt; the powder is better suited for use on informal ponds, with gently sloping sides, than on formal ones with vertical sides to which it will not adhere. Bentonite, which is suitable for use only on certain soils, is adversely affected by high or fluctuating water tables, chalk or gravel, encroaching tree roots and heavy vegetation growing down into the water. It can also be damaged during weeding and dredging and by large numbers of ducks or geese.

In order to form an effective seal the bentonite particles must swell, when wet, to 12 to 15 times their original volume under the weight of the earth lining. Before choosing bentonite to line a pond, you must test the subsoil. On soil containing calcium – in the form of chalk or limestone – the calcium ions replace the sodium ions in the bentonite and inhibit the swelling process, so that the material may be able to swell to only twice its volume. If the soil is suitable, it must be carefully prepared before the bentonite is applied. The excavation depth should include an allowance of about 30cm/1ft for the layer of soil that will cover the bentonite, and the base and sides of the excavation should be clean and smooth, free of all organic material, and reasonably dry.

Spread the bentonite evenly over the entire pond surface at a density of 10kg per sq m/20lb per sq yd. Using a rotivator (if necessary), work it finely into the subsoil to a depth of 10cm/4in. Go over the surface with a vibrating roller to compact the material. Finally, cover the surface with a layer of subsoil or topsoil to a depth of 30cm/1ft, to protect and add pressure to the treated area. When the pond is filled with water, the moisture will penetrate to the bentonite, causing it to swell and form an impermeable layer under the soil.

PREFORMED PONDS

If you are not practised in the use of building materials and want something simple and inexpensive to install, a preformed water feature is the obvious choice, provided you can find a suitable size and shape for your requirements. Ready-made ponds, usually made of glass reinforced plastic or fibreglass (GRP) are available from most garden centres and nurseries. They come in a variety of styles and shapes, the maximum ready-made size being about 3.5m/12ft across. GRP ponds can be made to order, but at considerably greater cost. Formal preformed ponds are preferable to informal or naturalistic ones, in my opinion, since they can be entirely surrounded by paving and thus moderately well disguised. Incidentally, black is always the best colour choice.

GRP, which consists of glass matting, resin and hardener, can also be applied as a coating on to a concrete shell, a method sometimes used for swimming pool construction. This process is extremely expensive, however, and is best carried out by a professional team. Liquid resin is sprayed or brushed on to successive layers of fibreglass matting, building up a very durable waterproof structure. The best use for this product is in repairing concrete ponds (see p.181), when a complete new GRP shell is built inside.

Installing a preformed pond

Symmetrically shaped ponds can be inverted and scribed around to get the precise shape to dig. The hole itself should be several centimetres/inches larger and deeper than the shell, so that when the shell is lowered into position it does not pinch any hard projections sticking out from the ground, and no uneven stresses are imposed on it.

The base of the excavation must be very solidly compacted and then dressed with an even layer of about 5cm/2in of sand or sifted soil. Check with a spirit level to make sure that it is perfectly level. Next, place the shell in and test it for height. If adjustments are necessary, lift it out while they are made, then position the pond carefully, making sure the shell is sitting snugly on the base, so that its weight is not taken by its edges. This is

The effect is pleasing, the outlay modest. A small premoulded pool is surrounded by paving, embedded in mortar round the rim for stability. Other stones are scattered at random, and the gaps between them infilled with gravel. Simplicity is the keynote in the planting, too: the yellow of Alchemilla mollis, *which thrives in stony situations, combines with the green pond foliage, the white petunias and the beige planters in a restrained but attractive scheme.*

1

1 Installing a preformed pond
It is vital for a pond to be level. Excavate the hole deeper and wider than the pond and provide a base of well-compacted sand or sifted soil. Check the base with a spirit level before inserting the pond.
Continue to check the levels while simultaneously filling the pond with water and infilling the sides with well-compacted sand or sifted soil to provide a firm support to the rim. With a straightedge and spirit level, double check that the rim is level all round before fitting the capping in a bed of mortar.

mortar

good support needed
beneath rim and capping

spirit level   straightedge

water level increased
as sides are infilled

premoulded
pond

well-compacted sand
or sifted soil

particularly important if a fountain or other heavy object is to be placed in the centre of the pond. Check that the rim is level, using a straightedge and spirit level (diagram 1). When you are satisfied, start to fill the pond with water, at the same time pouring sand or sifted soil around the edges to support the sides, and tamping it down firmly, but not too heavily, as you go. If these operations are not done simultaneously, the pressure of sand on the outside of the shell can cause it to rise up like a pip between the fingers. When the pond is about a quarter full, check the level once more. If the gap between the shell and the ground is narrow, you can wash the sand down around the sides with a hosepipe. This ensures that every void has been properly filled and that the whole structure is evenly and well supported. Finally, whatever capping or edging you have chosen – stone, brick or timber – can be placed around the perimeter. Again it is vital that the edges of the moulding, over which the firm edging is laid, are well supported – with concrete if necessary. Nothing must pierce the moulding, and any fixings, such as posts for timber decking or edging, must be set around and beyond the pond. Stone or brick can be set on a sand and cement bed.

The procedure for installing a freestyle premoulded pond is virtually identical to that for a symmetrical one, except that you cannot simply invert it and scribe around it, for this will give a mirror image. Instead, place the pond right-side up in the chosen position, and use a plumb-line (a piece of string with a weight tied on the end will do) to make an accurate outline. Hold the string against the outside rim, and let the weight just brush the ground. Mark the outline with a pointed instrument such as a nail as you move the weight around the edge. (This is more easily done by two people.) The hole can then be excavated and the shell put in place as described. Judge the shape by measuring and by eye, leaving ample room to ensure that the pond will not be squashed against the side. When you have dug part way down, push the pond into the loosened ground to mark the shape of the bottom itself for the remainder of the excavation. Finish the edges with plants, paving or rocks. (If you are placing heavy rocks on the rim, first provide a good concrete bed under the rim to spread the load.)

USING CONCRETE

This ancient and versatile material was extensively used by the Romans, some of whose structures survive today. However, its quality and durability can vary considerably; for instance, on very acid soils, concrete will eventually break down, unless an acid-resistant cement is used. For long-term durability, a pond with steep sides measuring more than 12m/40ft across is safer built on a butyl or similar membrane, even if the concrete is reinforced (see pp.47-8). Large ponds certainly need reinforcing rods, or reinforcing mesh and/or some expansion joints. Mixing and curing the concrete are all important. For smooth inner walls, a coat of rendering may be applied. Before plants and fish can be introduced to the pond, the concrete has to be neutralized. Do not lay concrete or cement in freezing conditions; if in doubt, use a frostproofer in the mix.

Mixing concrete

For reliable results, the mix is important. This generally consists of 1 part fresh cement dust and an aggregate of 2 parts clean, sharp sand and 3 parts washed gravel in the form of 2cm/¾in stones. Alternatively, stones graded from 20ml/¾in or 10ml/¼in down to dust can be used as an aggregate, mixed with cement at 5 parts aggregate to 1 part of cement. As a rough guide to quantities when mixing concrete, for a depth of 10cm/4in you will need 1cu m/1cu yd of concrete to cover an area approximately 10sq m/12sq yds.

Mix the constituents thoroughly together, adding water to form a thick, 'fatty' consistency that can be worked without being too runny; too much water makes the concrete weaker. Mixing may be done by hand – usually on a board – for smaller ponds; use a mechanical mixer if large amounts are required. Concrete can also be bought ready-mixed, when it is usually supplied at a mix of 5:1, which is strong enough for most pond work. However, unless you are well prepared, this can be difficult to handle, as it is cost effective only if bought in full truck loads and tends to go off very quickly; ask for a retarder to be added to be on the safe side. You may also ask for the addition of a waterproofer in the mix, which is available in certain countries.

Reinforcing concrete

For any pond bigger than about 2.5x3m/8x10ft reinforced concrete is advisable, and it should be considered for any concrete pond, except the very smallest, where severe frosts are likely. It is also necessary in concrete ponds built in clay ground that is likely to shrink in times of drought. Here a separation layer of gravel between the clay and the concrete will also help to prevent cracking.

In the case of intricately shaped ponds, reinforcing may be difficult to apply. However, it is now possible to buy ready-mixed concrete with strands of glass incorporated in the mix. This greatly reduces time and cost, and is an excellent choice for a freestyle pond. But, although this

When a high degree of precision is called for, as in this pond at Wave Hill in New York, which relies for its effect on the flawless execution of vertical sides and convex curves, shuttered and poured concrete is a good choice for the construction. Bricks, too, can be readily persuaded into curves, and an equally effective construction method would be a combination of concrete blockwork (for straight runs) and brickwork (for tight curves) used as a permanent shutter with poured concrete behind.

Here the concrete wall provides a solid support for the large well-tailored capping stones. Impressive clumps of ornamental grasses provide interest year round and contrast in their soft cascades with the rigid hardness of the stone. In summer, the water flickers like fire with the reflections of the flame-red cannas.

reinforcing prevents the cracking caused by shrinkage, it does not measure up to the strength of steel reinforcing. For deep, vertical-sided structures, such as swimming pools, reinforcing steel bars are always recommended to ensure a good strong structure (see diagrams 6 and 7).

To reinforce poured or sprayed concrete, bars are applied to form a continuous mesh; ready-made sheets of mesh may also be used. The reinforcing runs through the middle of the concrete and must not protrude through the surface anywhere, as this quickly leads to oxidation, causing the concrete to 'blow' and subsequently to leak.

The continuous mesh over the base must be firmly connected to a similar mesh in the sides, either with wire ties, for ready-made mesh, or with the appropriate connections, where rods are used. This is particularly important where the sides meet the base, which is the weakest part in a formal concrete pond. To give strength to this area, pre-bent rods are usually used round the edges of the base, extending up the sides by 30cm/1ft or more, and the rods for the sides are wired firmly to these.

Curing concrete

It was the Romans who discovered that the hardness of concrete is not dependent on air drying but is the result of chemical curing, which allows it to set under water. Premature curing or drying can occur when working in strong sunlight, and this can be prevented by keeping the surface covered with polythene or wet sacking as the work proceeds. When finished, the pond should be allowed to cure as slowly as possible, and this is best done under water. If circumstances permit, fill the pond slowly with water as soon as the initial set is completed (this takes from 8-24 hours) and leave it for the curing to take place. Only in cool, damp conditions will a satisfactory finish be obtained through air curing. After a first, rapid stage, curing is very slow – the concrete continues to harden for years; however, after even two or three days it is strong enough to stand on while continuing with the construction. After about 28 days the concrete can be considered strong enough for most building purposes.

Neutralizing concrete

At this stage the concrete is toxic to both plants and fish because of the free lime released from the cement, and steps must be taken to neutralize this. Perhaps the best method of all is to fill the finished pond with water and leave it over winter. The lime will gradually come to the surface and settle out as a precipitate of chalk at the bottom of the pond, which you can then empty and thoroughly scrub out in spring before refilling and planting. A quicker method is to use potassium permanganate crystals. Add them to the water until it is the colour of blackcurrant juice and allow it to stand for at least a week, by which time the water will have turned brown and the pool can be emptied, scrubbed out and refilled ready for use. Even quicker, though less effective, is to swill and scrub the pond out repeatedly for a day with a strong solution of potassium permanganate. Never allow a strong solution to drain off into a stream or wildlife pond.

Instead of potassium permanganate, vinegar may be used as a neutralizer at the rate of approximately 1 litre or gallon of vinegar to every 250 litres or gallons of water. Again the solution has to be left to stand for about a week, after which the pond is emptied, thoroughly rinsed, and refilled. To save time, a strong solution of about 4 parts vinegar to 1 of water can be scrubbed and swilled around the pond repeatedly for a day, followed by a thorough rinsing and refilling. Again, this method is less effective than the slower one.

Adding acid is another common method for removing free lime. This can be done with a 10 per cent solution of hydrochloric acid and water. Wearing protective clothing, gloves and goggles, brush on the acid solution. Hose it off and fill the pool, leaving it to stand for a week. Drain the pool and repeat the process. Drain and refill a week later. (The same technique can be employed for etching the concrete prior to painting with a rubber-based paint; it ensures long-lasting adhesion.) Rinse protective clothing in fresh water after use.

There are various proprietary products that effectively cure, neutralize and seal the surface at the same time. Some specially formulated waterproof paints, including liquid neoprene rubber, form a seal and make neutralizing unnecessary. A substitute is waterglass (sodium silicate), which is transparent and absolutely non-toxic. It has the advantage of being mixed with water so that it is easy to apply and much more likely to seal every crevice. Products that are painted on are particularly useful in areas in which water is in short supply, but they are of no use unless the entire shell is treated. If rocks, fountain structures or islands prevent the entire coverage of the pool, harmful lime will continue to leach out from inaccessible places.

However carefully concrete is neutralized or sealed, lime can still be a problem in a pool, whether because of the surrounding soil or because of a high lime content in the water supply itself. To check the lime content of the water in the pool, use a pH test kit: a value of below 8.5 should be achieved. One or more mesh bags filled with fine peat can be suspended in a small pond to help lower the pH value if it is a little too high.

Rendering concrete

In concrete ponds made in any of the ways on the following pages, a smooth rendering coat of 3 parts clean sand to 1 part Portland cement can be applied to the surface within the next day or two, or as soon as the concrete has hardened. This is advisable for swimming pools, where smooth inner walls are required. A proprietary waterproofing powder or liquid can be added to the mix to help with plasticity, bonding and general waterproofing. However concrete, if well applied, is waterproof in its own right, and no amount of rendering will make up for concrete that has been badly laid. The essence of successful concrete is a good mix, well tamped. Do not render, or use concrete, in frosty weather, as this causes it to disintegrate before curing, and in hot weather, apply polythene or wet sacking to assist curing. If you do apply rendering, you can paint it black, or use black pigment in the mix, to make it unobtrusive.

2

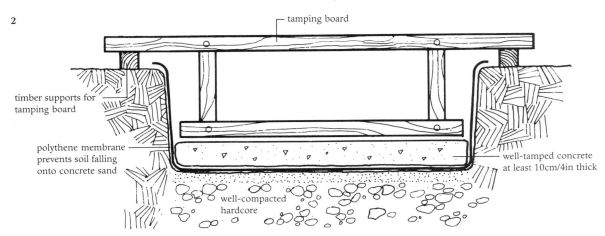

tamping board

timber supports for
tamping board

polythene membrane
prevents soil falling
onto concrete sand

well-tamped concrete
at least 10cm/4in thick

well-compacted
hardcore

3 Poured concrete walls

Make the concrete base as in diagram
2. Even when not reinforcing the
whole pond, a few rods at the
corners will ensure a strong link with
the base and sides. Put 2cm/¾in
greased shuttering plywood spaced
out from the walls according to the
chosen thickness of the concrete and
hold it firmly in position with cross
pieces well braced back to the
opposite wall or to the bottom to
take the thrust. Pour concrete into
the cavity, tamping it down well as
you proceed.

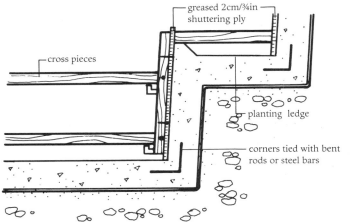

3

greased 2cm/¾in
shuttering ply

cross pieces

planting ledge

corners tied with bent
rods or steel bars

2 Constructing a concrete base

Lay a bed of well-rammed hardcore
overlaid with sand. Line it with a
polythene membrane brought well
up the sides of the excavation.
Particularly where the sides are steep,
this will prevent dirt from dropping
onto the concrete. Pour in the
concrete and tamp it down using a
purpose-made tamping board - two
vertical battens fixed between two
wooden beams, one long enough to
stretch across the hole, and the other
fitting the base. Rest the top board
on beams placed along the sides of
the 'pond'. The lower board sits on
the surface of the concrete. Two
people can tamp down the surface
completely flat from above. Climb
down onto the lower board and
trowel a shallow dip or sump in the
base (see diagram 4), into which
water and mud can be swept when
cleaning the pond.

CONSTRUCTING WITH CONCRETE

Concrete can be poured or sprayed to form any shape. It is frequently
used in swimming pools and for formal water features, but it can be
equally well employed for naturalistic shapes. In fact it works well in
ponds with gently sloping sides and the slope eliminates the need to take
any special measures to make the concrete adhere.

Concrete pond base

A poured concrete base can be used with almost any construction
method. For ponds with concrete sides, both base and sides should be
poured as one on the same day. Walls constructed from concrete blocks
may be built the day after the base has been poured, provided it is
protected by planks.

In all cases, the pond should be dug deep enough to allow for a base,
normally 15cm/6in deep. In severe climates considerably thicker bases
(up to about 38cm/15in) may be required, with correspondingly thicker
walls. In soft ground, also allow for a layer of hardcore (broken stones and
bricks) well rammed into the bottom. On clay ground, which shrinks and
cracks when dry, a layer of well compacted shingle or stone chippings
should also be applied.

Fit any necessary pipes for drainage, filtration or electrical wiring (see
p.75), then position a polythene membrane in the bottom of the pond.
Pour in the concrete and tamp it down well as you work backwards. If the
pond is not too large, a tamping board can be made to fit it (diagram 2).

To reinforce the base, pour one complete layer of concrete first, to a
thickness of about 5-15cm/2-6in, then position the mesh or rods (see
p.48) and apply a second coat. Wherever possible apply both layers of
concrete in one day, so that they fuse together, for any joints will be points
of weakness. If this cannot be arranged, roughen the concrete up as you
lay it and wet it well before recommencing the following day. The second
coat will bring the shell to its final thickness, which will vary from some
10-15cm/4-6in in temperate climates to as much as 38cm/15in in the
northern United States, Canada and Scandinavia.

If you are using sprayed concrete, both the base and sides can be
completed in one stage so that the result is a solid, seamless shell. Position
the reinforcing over the base and bring it up the sides of the pond, leaving

a similar gap all round. Tie the reinforcing carefully in the usual way. Keep it about 8cm/3in off the bottom of the pond by propping it up on one or two clean stones or on short lengths of strong galvanized wire that can be removed as the concrete flows under and around the mesh to form a solid coating.

Poured concrete walls

Shuttering is required when pouring walls for formal ponds with vertical or near vertical sides. It is not usually needed for informal ponds, with their gently sloping sides, although it may be applied to the upper edges of a concrete-lined informal pond to hold the wet concrete in place above a ledge, or on a large pond where a quayside or architectural feature is to be added.

While the base is still wet, roughen the edges with a builder's trowel or stiff brush to provide a key for the walls, which can lean back at a slight angle, say 10-15 degrees, from the vertical. If the base and walls are to be reinforced (see p.47), leave the base bars upturned at the edges to link into the walls. Position the shuttering timber so that the same size cavity is maintained right round the pond and hold it in place with cross pieces (diagram 3). If the top of the shuttering is kept precisely level, at the correct height, no further adjustments will be necessary. Make sure that the ends of the shuttering boards do not cut into the corners of the pond, as this will cause weakness, and try to prevent earth and stones from being dislodged from the bank and falling on to the edge of the concrete base. One way of doing this is to extend the polythene membrane covering the base up the side walls of the pond as well. Remove any debris that does fall with the hose of an industrial-strength vacuum cleaner. If there is to be a joint between the walls and the base, this area must be kept scrupulously clean; use a hose to wash it off if necessary.

Pour concrete into the cavity between the earth wall and the shuttering timber. (It must be emphasized that better results are obtained by pouring the sides immediately after the base.) As you fill the cavity, tamp the concrete down well with a wooden rammer or vibrating poker. Trowel off the top precisely level on the inside, with a slight slope back towards the bank. This allows for better adhesion of any stone edging that may be laid, or any planting that is to come to the edge.

If the excavated sides are uneven, a considerable amount of concrete may be required to fill the gaps in some places. In this case, close off the gaps with a second line of shuttering, later filling the gap behind it with stones, rubble or a 'lean' (8:1) concrete mix.

Concrete blockwork walls

Concrete blocks can be used for any formal, angular pool. They may be solid or hollow. Solid blocks come in various thicknesses (10cm/4in is commonly used for pond work) and measure about 46x23cm/18x9in; hollow ones are usually 23cm/9in thick and measure approximately 46x23cm/18x9in. These thicker hollow blocks will form a wall more quickly than the solid ones, but the hollows have to be filled with a strong

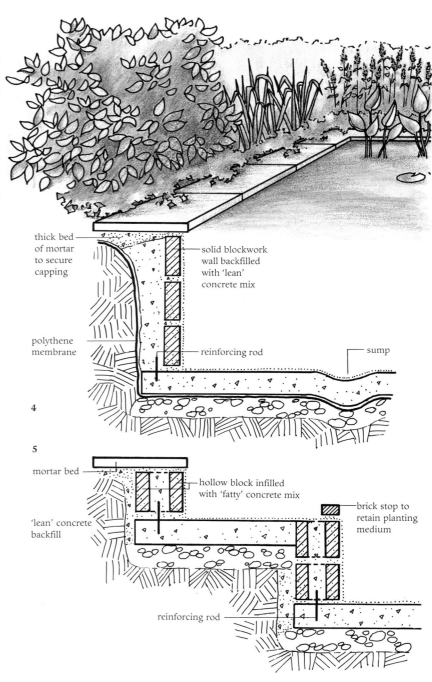

thick bed of mortar to secure capping

solid blockwork wall backfilled with 'lean' concrete mix

polythene membrane

reinforcing rod

sump

4

5

mortar bed

hollow block infilled with 'fatty' concrete mix

'lean' concrete backfill

brick stop to retain planting medium

reinforcing rod

'fatty' mix of concrete as you build up the sides (diagram 5). The 10cm/ 4in blocks can be used singly to form a solid wall, backfilled with concrete (diagram 4) or side by side to form a cavity wall of any required thickness with the cavity being filled with concrete. In this method, the cavity becomes an uninterrupted wall of poured concrete, which provides greater strength than infilling hollow blocks.

Blockwork walls can be built the day after the base has been poured. For extra strength, reinforce the concrete where base and sides join or reinforce the whole structure (diagrams 6 and 7). Once the walls have been built to the desired specification, any extra voids between these and the earth sides can be filled with a 'lean' (8:1) concrete mix.

If planting ledges are to be accommodated, take the blockwork up to about 15cm/6in higher than the level dug for the ledge, to allow for the thickness of the concrete on the ledge (with the blockwork forming the front of the ledge). If another row of concrete blocks would make the wall too high, one or two courses of engineering bricks can be used to bring it to an appropriate level. Use metal ties to reinforce the concrete at the joints between ledge and wall.

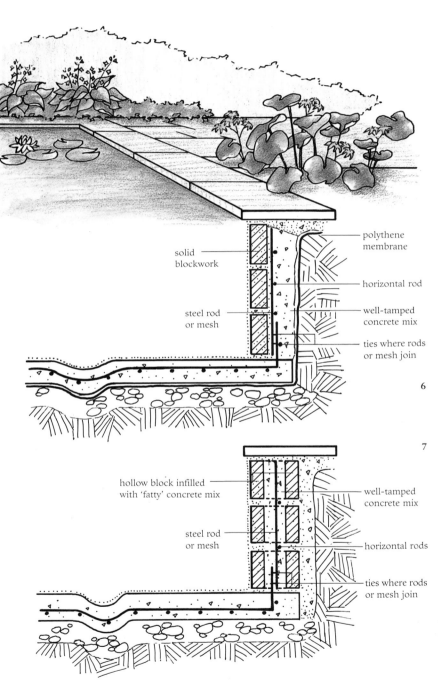

solid blockwork

polythene membrane

horizontal rod

steel rod or mesh

well-tamped concrete mix

ties where rods or mesh join

6

7

hollow block infilled with 'fatty' concrete mix

well-tamped concrete mix

steel rod or mesh

horizontal rods

ties where rods or mesh join

4–7 Constructing concrete blockwork walls

With all methods the base is made of poured concrete, and has a central hollow or sump for pumping and cleaning. The gap between the walls and the earth or polythene membrane is filled with a strong 'lean' concrete mix (about 8:1 graded aggregate to cement), raked back at the top to allow plenty of room for a thick bed of mortar beneath the capping stones. The blockwork walls can be rendered in sand and cement to give a smooth finish.

4 Solid blocks backfilled with concrete

Leave a substantial cavity behind walls built in solid concrete blocks, and fill this with poured concrete, reinforced where it joins the base.

5 Hollow blocks infilled with concrete

Fill hollow concrete blocks with a 'fatty' (about 3:2:1) mix of poured concrete as you build up the wall; reinforce the joins between walls and base/ledges.

6 Reinforced solid blocks

For extra strength, use reinforcing rods or mesh behind a solid blockwork wall. They must be carefully tied in to the upturned edges of the base mesh or rods. The reinforcement is embedded in the poured concrete, well tamped down behind the blockwork wall.

7 Reinforced hollow blocks

Insert reinforcing rods or mesh within a hollow block wall. They should be firmly tied in, both at the base and wherever they join. They should run both vertically and horizontally between the courses. Infill with concrete, well tamped down around the rods or mesh. Use rods to reinforce planting ledges made of poured concrete.

Exactly the same method applies to building twin walls of blockwork with reinforced concrete in between.

FLEXIBLE LINERS

A wide range of different liners, with different characteristics and qualities, is available. By far the cheapest, but generally also the least durable, is polythene, which normally has a life expectancy of only three to five years. However, its extreme cheapness makes it tempting to use in certain circumstances. For example, a polythene membrane can be used to give added water retention to a clay-lined pond; overlaid with 15-30cm/6-12in of clay or fine earth it is well protected from ultraviolet light, which is its chief enemy, and from being accidentally pierced. The material is, however, delicate, while also unwieldy, and extreme care must be taken during installation. Polythene would be most unsuitable for anything but dish-shaped reservoirs or informal ponds, which are fairly easy to fit because of their smooth, sloping sides. I would certainly not recommend it for formal or geometric ponds of any kind.

Of somewhat higher quality, and also more expensive, is PVC in a variety of weights and thickness, together with a wide range of PVC-based materials, including laminated and reinforced types. Most expensive is nylon- or polyester-reinforced PVC, which has great strength. PVC is more durable than polythene, and pieces can be joined together easily to form sheets suitable for large ponds and lakes. The life expectancy of these materials can vary enormously from one brand and type to another, but something in the order of twelve to fifteen years' wear could be expected. Durability, flexibility and elasticity are all of great importance in lining materials: flexibility not only makes installation easier, but also affects the appearance and finish of the end product. PVC is marginally more flexible than polythene and more resistant to puncturing, although heavy gauges and some reinforced types are not particularly flexible.

Vinyl is also available in heavy gauges and is quite durable, but rather more expensive than PVC materials. Vinyl handles similarly to PVC and both are comparatively quick and straightforward to weld, but the heavy gauges can be difficult to position, owing to their rigidity. Vinyl and PVC products are widely used for custom-made swimming pool linings, and this, I think, is the best use for them. If used for ponds they are best suited to large, gently sloping informal ponds.

Probably the best material available to date, and certainly the most amenable to handling, owing to its 300 per cent elasticity – it can stretch to three times its size – is butyl. Butyl has a very stable molecular structure, and does not 'creep'. It can therefore remain stretched over a sharp object indefinitely without parting or puncturing. Butyl is so congenial that it just flops into place, and it is now widely used both in Great Britain and in Europe; a comparable product in the United States is specially formulated EPDM (ethylene propylene diene monomer) sheeting. Both butyl and EPDM have excellent resistance to ultraviolet rays and a life expectancy of approximately 50 years. They cost about the same as the heaviest gauges of PVC and vinyl. Although sheets of butyl are somewhat time-consuming to weld, they are available in very large sizes, which may make welding unnecessary.

Flexible waterproof linings can be formed *in situ* by overspraying a geotextile membrane with a two-part solution that cures to form a rubber sheet. This technique is useful for awkwardly shaped ponds.

With flexible linings there is a choice of stone, blue or black in colour. My own feeling is that both blue and stone lend artificiality, and that only black is acceptable – except for swimming pools, where blue can be a good choice. Even in the most natural ponds, where the bottom and sides are covered with soil, the lining tends to be exposed by fish, which keep the areas where they gather to be fed well-manicured with the movement of their fins: here stone or blue would strike a jarring note.

Underlays and overlays

Underlays and overlays are used in conjunction with flexible pond liners to cushion and protect them, and many excellent products are now available. Originally developed for civil engineering uses, in road making, as a separation material and for drainage, these non-woven geotextiles are extremely resistant to tearing, and the thicker gauges are almost impenetrable by the sharpest stone. They come in rolls 2m/6½ft wide and over, and are therefore ideal for quickly covering a pond base. Their relatively low cost makes their use particularly sensible, considering the high degree of protection they offer. It is advisable always to use an underlay with flexible liners, and when planning for a bog area or a shingle beach it is best to put a layer of the same material on top to give the liner extra protection.

Calculating quantities

To calculate the required length and width of the liner for a rectangular or square pond, take the maximum length of the pond and add twice the maximum depth; similarly, take the maximum width and add twice the maximum depth. With a vertical-sided pond an extra 30cm/1ft can be added to both length and width to allow for folding over at the top or slight errors in calculation. It is always a nuisance to find that the liner is just 5cm/2in too small! However, should this occur, you can gain a few extra centimetres/inches by adding some sand to the bottom corners of the excavation so that they are slightly rounded. Without reducing the pond's dimensions, this will reduce the area the liner has to cover – you can literally 'cut corners'.

For a freeform pond, you can first dig and roughly shape it so that the amount of liner needed can be calculated or use the same method as for formal ponds: measure the maximum length and add twice the maximum depth to get one measurement, and measure the maximum width plus twice the maximum depth for the other. However, the more gently sloping sides of an informal pond will result in a greater surplus of liner after it has been fitted. While this can be used to create a wider bog ledge on one or two sides, and may involve relatively little waste on a small pond, it could be significantly wasteful on a large pond. In this case, or whenever a precise measurement is required, drape the tape measure down into the pond and up the other side to take more accurate length and width measurements. On large ponds (15m/50ft or more long), the size will always work out at least 1m/3ft less than when calculated by the first method as a result of their extremely gentle slope.

An alternative method is to buy the liner and then dig the hole to suit it. In this case, a perfect fit can be achieved.

CONSTRUCTING WITH LINERS

There are so many ways of constructing ponds with liners that just a few of the more tried and tested methods are described here. The most straightforward method, requiring the least time and expenditure on materials, and one that can easily be tackled by an amateur, is to use a lining placed directly within the excavation. Alternatively, a liner can readily be used in conjunction with hard materials, such as concrete, to create a pond which has both firm sides and a completely waterproof lining.

Fitting a liner in an informal pond

Carefully pick out any large or sharp stones from the excavation and cut back below the surface any projecting tree roots. Cover any sections that are particularly rough with a 5cm/2in layer of sand. Then put protective underlay on to this smoothed surface, with extra protection in areas that are likely to be subject to heavy wear. Open the liner out and if possible lay it in the sun for a while to flatten the creases, but do not lay it on the lawn in hot sunshine for too long or it will kill the grass. Now position the liner, leaving any surplus around the bog areas if these are planned.

Contrary to popular belief, it is bad practice to stretch the liner over the hole and allow the water to drag it into position, particularly with the more sophisticated, highly flexible liners such as butyl. Stretching the liner reduces its elasticity to some extent so that it is less able to conform to any sharp objects it encounters. Leave it relaxed but smoothly fitted, and gather it neatly where necessary into definite folds rather than leaving a multitude of creases (diagram 8). The pond can be filled with water at the end of construction and the water allowed to settle, as described on p.110, before planting and stocking.

Check that the rim is still level and flat, and then lay the edging around the pond, allowing an overhang of about 5cm/2in to hide the edge of the liner and protect it from sunlight. This may be in the form of paving, or brick, rock or soil according to the design. The important point is that the edges are level, and the liner is invisible and protected from sunlight.

Liner used alone in a formal pond

Although suitable for the gardener who wishes to install a steep-sided pond quickly and easily, the liner-only method (diagram 12) of installation cannot be considered durable in the long term. It is also impossible to rely on the soil coming away cleanly and precisely when it is dug and the pond sides may gradually crumble beneath the liner, causing the surrounding stone slabs to sag down towards the water and become dangerous, while the sides bulge out into the pond. When excavating, work as accurately as possible, trying not to disturb the ground on the sides of the pond. It is best to dig the sides at least 10 degrees off the vertical. Carefully smooth them over, removing any sharp stones or roots from the sides and base. Line the base with a 5cm/2in layer of sand. Carefully place polythene bags or pieces of old carpet on the sides for protection. Ideally a proprietary non-woven geotextile underlay should be applied to the whole pond at this stage.

8

8 Fitting flexible liners in freeform shapes
Lay the liner into the prepared excavation, making sure it is positioned with sufficient material to come up all round the sides. Do not stretch it into the hole: under tension it is more likely to puncture. Good modern liners are around 300 per cent elastic and this allows them to conform around a sharp object. Smooth the liner over the base and gather up any pleats or wrinkles in the sides into a few neat folds. Where possible, position the folds on the ledges where they will be hidden by planting or rockwork. Finishing touches can be easily made as the water rises.

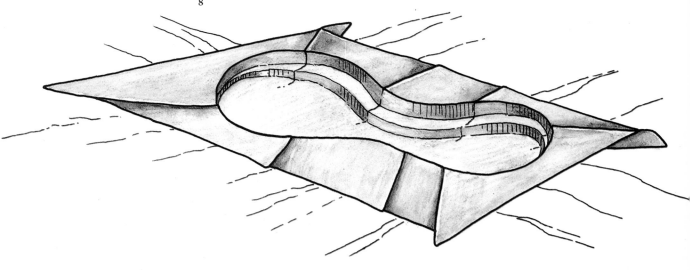

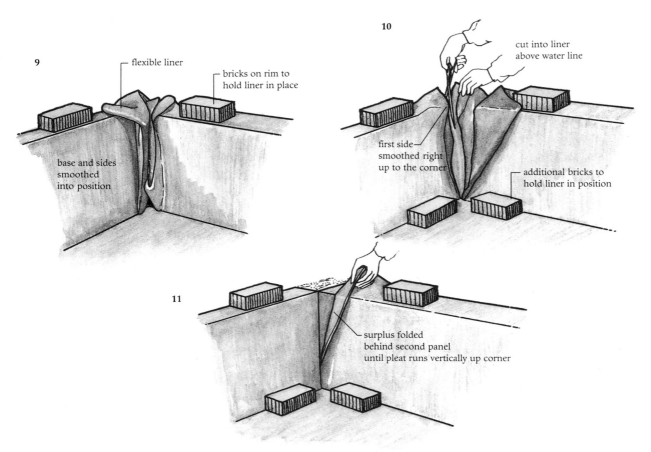

9 — flexible liner
— bricks on rim to hold liner in place
base and sides smoothed into position

10
cut into liner above water line
first side smoothed right up to the corner
additional bricks to hold liner in position

11
surplus folded behind second panel until pleat runs vertically up corner

9-11 Fitting flexible liners in geometric shapes

This method can be used for all geometric shapes with internal angles - squares, rectangles, hexagons and octagons.

9 Position the liner centrally, making sure there is sufficient material to overlap the edges on all sides. Smooth the base flat; then smooth the sides into the corners/angles, bringing the liner up evenly all round. Place bricks round the rim to hold the liner in place.

10 Place additional bricks on the base. Smooth one side panel along until it is pressed hard into the first corner, letting the top flap over the edge of the pond. Cut into the flap to 5cm/2in above the top corner of the pond. (Do not cut too far: the slit must not extend to below the waterline.) Adjust the brick to hold the flap on the smooth side.

11 Smooth and position the second side, leaving the surplus flapping as you approach the corner. Take the flap in one large pleat, and tuck it back on itself. Adjust the pleat until the fold runs vertically up the corner. Fold the top flat at ground level.

Fitting the liner will produce a mass of vertical folds that need to be smoothed into the corners so that no folds or wrinkles are visible (diagrams 9, 10 and 11).

Fitting a liner around projections, as found in 'L'-shaped or even more complicated ponds, can be difficult. One solution is to have it custom made. Another is to dig a simple large rectangle, fit this with a liner, and then build in the desired shape in masonry, concrete or other suitable material. Circular and elliptical ponds also present problems. To avoid having numerous little pleats around the sides, you can have a liner fabricated to fit the pond, or you can buy one ready made and adjust the size of your pond, if necessary, to fit the nearest available size.

Liner inside the walls

You are not reliant on the ground remaining firm and supportive for the vertical sides of a formal pond if you construct a simple retaining wall over which to apply a lining. Having dug an excavation large enough to allow for a single wall all round, construct the walls within the excavation and then apply a liner over the base, bringing it up the sides on the inside of the walls (diagram 13). In appearance the result is the same as for the liner-only method described above, but the sides are firm.

The simplest way of doing this is to excavate the shape required and dig a shallow footing some 15cm/6in deep by 23cm/9in wide around the perimeter. Fill this with a carefully levelled concrete foundation, and on it, using 10cm/4in concrete blocks, construct an inexpensive wall, up to the level of the pond rim, jointing the blocks with a 3:1 sand and cement mortar mix. When the mortar has hardened, backfill any space between the wall and the earth with a 'lean' concrete mix (of some 8:1 aggregate to cement). For ponds deeper than about 75cm/30in, make a larger footing to support a 23cm/9in concrete wall, or a carefully built 10cm/4in wall with a 15-23cm/6-9in layer of concrete infilling behind it.

Having constructed the walls, cover the base of the pond with soft sand and the walls themselves with some protective cushioning material (as for liner-only ponds), fit the liner and finish off with an edging (see pp.61-8). A good 'cushion' is always needed when lining against a hard wall; if planting ledges have been built in with blockwork, special care must be taken to protect the liner from the sharp front edge of the blockwork.

Large paving slabs overhang the water surface, concealing the pond's inner rim and lining materials. It is particularly important to use large slabs when following the simplest method of edging (diagram 12) since they take much of the weight away from the rim. If a lot of foot traffic is anticipated, blockwork walls should be built to support the sides and provide a solid edge on which to lay the slabs (diagram 13).

Ledges or shelves for emergent plants can form part of the original excavation or be built up afterwards where required.

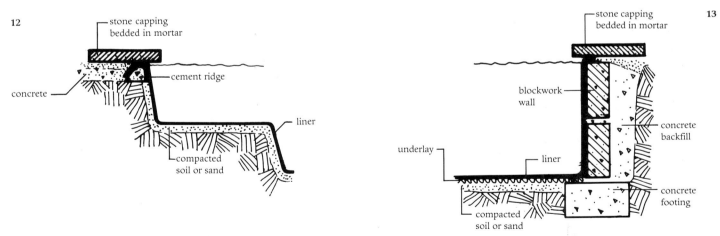

12 Liner used alone

This simple method works best in ponds where there are to be no heavy objects or complicated planting structures in the pond. Dig the pond, and make the base and sides of firmly compacted soil or sand. The ground must be smooth. If necessary, pad the walls with old carpet or underlay to protect the liner. Form a 'nose' or ridge of cement around the rim. Place the liner inside the pond, smooth over the bottom and up the sides and bring it up over the back of the 'nose'. Bed a capping in mortar, to form a surround. An additional concrete bedding can be provided to make sure the capping will not tilt back and to keep the lining in place.

13 Liner inside the walls

Excavate, allowing for a single blockwork wall, and dig a footing round the perimeter of the pond. Lay a concrete footing and build the retaining wall over it, backfilled with concrete. Place a layer of underlay and lining inside the pond on a base of compacted soil or sand, and bring both up smoothly over the tops of the walls. Bed capping stone securely in mortar.

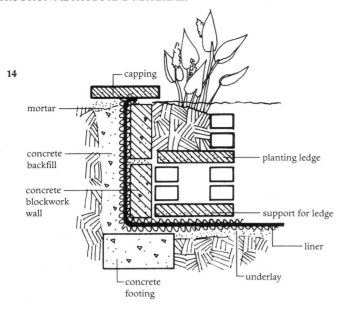

14

- capping
- mortar
- concrete backfill
- concrete blockwork wall
- planting ledge
- support for ledge
- liner
- underlay
- concrete footing

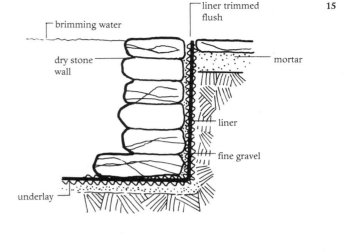

15

- brimming water
- liner trimmed flush
- dry stone wall
- mortar
- liner
- fine gravel
- underlay

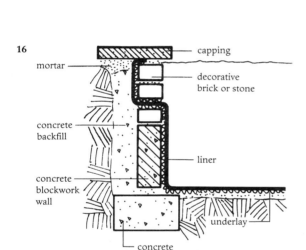

16

- capping
- mortar
- decorative brick or stone
- concrete backfill
- liner
- concrete blockwork wall
- underlay
- concrete footing

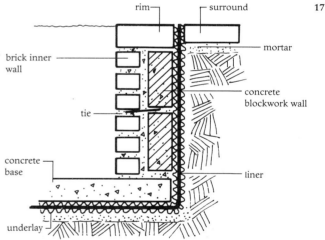

17

- rim
- surround
- mortar
- brick inner wall
- concrete blockwork wall
- tie
- concrete base
- liner
- underlay

14 Liner behind the walls

This method enables planting ledges supported by piers resting on solid slabs to be built off the pond walls and base. Excavate the pond and make a footing as in diagram 13. Bring the lining, sandwiched between layers of underlay, up the sides of the excavation and temporarily hold it in place. Build the wall (here in concrete blockwork) within it over the footing. Bring the lining up over the top of the wall, backfill with concrete and finish it off with capping bedded in mortar.

15 Liner behind dry stone walls

Dig the pond and lay a base of compacted soil or sand. Place the liner sandwiched between underlay inside the pond, bring all layers up smoothly over the top of the excavation. Use bricks to hold them in position while you build a wall, with broad stones at the base for stability. Backfill with fine gravel. If you want a brimming pond, set a stone surround on a bed of mortar right up against the top of the wall, wedging the lining in between. Trim the liner flush with the top stones.

16 A combination lining method

With this method the upper part of the wall is built of decorative brick or stone within the liner. Make a footing, as in diagram 13. Build the lower part of the wall (here using a combination of blockwork and a course of bricks to bring it to the desired height) and backfill it with concrete. Place the lining and underlay in position and take it back over the course of bricks. Then build the upper part of the wall within the liner, over a protective layer of underlay. Tuck the lining in and cap off the wall.

17 Vandal-proof liners

This method makes very strong walls and no extra foundations are needed for heavy structures such as fountain plinths and statues. Construct a concrete base and a double wall inside the liner. Tie the decorative inner walls in to the concrete blockwork outer walls and finish off the double wall with a deep stone block to form the rim. Use matching stone to form a surround that sandwiches the liner tightly into place as in diagram 15, and the pond can be filled to the brim.

Liner behind the walls

If you intend to build a formal pond embellished with walls of brick or stone you can set the liner in place over an underlay and then build the pond walls in front of it. The walls may be built mostly of concrete blocks, with just the top 20cm/8in or so nearest to the rim finished off in the brick or stone of your choice or, for the most attractive effect, the entire wall can be of brick or stone to suit the house and garden (diagrams 18-20). When the walls are built mainly of concrete, this can be painted in a suitable, non-toxic black paint or rendered in black-pigmented mortar to make them unobtrusive (see p.48). When building over the liner it is import-ant to lay it centrally, with enough material left for all sides, as it will not be possible to adjust it once the walls have been built. There are several variations in method, some of which are illustrated in diagrams 14-17, but the first step is, of course, to dig out the pond, allowing as usual for the thickness of the walls.

As you build up the walls within the lining, make sure there are no sharp projections at the back that might damage the liner. Any mortar that has squeezed out of the joints at the back can be smoothed out over the surface. Make sure at all times that no flaps of lining material are allowed to slip down below the intended water line. When the walls are finished, pull the liner gently up around all the edges and carefully back-fill the void between the underlay and the bank with a 'lean' mortar mix of about 6 or 8:1 sand and cement or 'lean' concrete using a rounded aggregate. In all cases, the walls should be set well to the back of the footings, to ensure stability.

It is not necessary to form a concrete base over the liner with these methods, but covering the liner completely, as shown in diagram 17, is the best method to adopt for a pond in a public place, where an exposed liner is more likely to be damaged, accidentally or through vandalism.

With this type of construction, particularly where the whole base is concreted over, it is simple to build planting ledges within the pond, using columns of brick with stone slabs on top built straight off the base (diagram 14). These provide excellent hides for fish and can also be used to conceal a fountain pump. The concrete slabs can be adapted for basket planting or soil planting.

SEMI-RAISED PONDS

Ponds with supporting walls that raise them above ground level offer several advantages. They entail far less excavation – a matter of some consequence when planning a pond for a garden that is accessible only through the house itself, where the less material that has to be carted away the better. A semi-raised pond is easier to keep clean than a fully sunken pond, which is always the final resting place of leaves blown along the ground. It is also easier to empty.

The safety advantages of the semi-raised pond are clear. A baby at the crawling stage cannot fall in, and even the liveliest toddler will take a minute or two to scale the wall – by which time an adult can have come to the rescue. For disabled people, the raised pond is ideal. People in wheelchairs can come close to the pond and enjoy the sensations of the water in safety. In fact, most people will enjoy observing the pond and its life from this closer, more comfortable vantage point. The pond becomes a social focal point – the walls are a convenient place for family and guests to sit and talk, or place a glass of wine.

Raised ponds have slight disadvantages that must be kept in mind. Water above ground level is more subject to temperature fluctuations: it gets warmer during the daytime and freezes more thickly during the winter than a pond that lies snugly below ground level. In colder climates the pond may need to be designed and constructed with extra depth to prevent the water from freezing solid.

The shaping and digging for a semi-raised pond are virtually the same as for a sunken pond. However, the fact that the pond rises some 40-50cm/16-20in above the ground means that the excavation is that much shallower. It is not advisable simply to build a wall around the top of the excavation, for the soil will almost certainly collapse beneath it. Whether the pool is lined with concrete, a flexible liner or a premoulded shape, always build up the inner walls from the base of the pond to the finished level for strength.

However the pond is constructed, it is important that the water level be as high as possible. To ensure this, bring the liner or concrete right up to the capping level, and make the mortar joint between the wall and its capping as thin as possible.

The outer, visible wall above ground level can be of concrete block-work – rendered over or plastered – or of brick or stone. It should be at least 23cm/9in thick to take the pressure of the water, and the additional pressure of ice occurring in colder climates. In zones experiencing severe frost, walls thicker than this, or well-reinforced ones, will be required.

Semi-raised ponds with flexible liners

For ponds with flexible liners, there are several methods of construction. As with fully sunken ponds, they can be divided into those in which the liner is applied to the inside, and thus exposed, and those in which the liner is set behind the inner walls – and is therefore encased within inner and outer walls above ground level. For both kinds it is important to make sure that the liner is large enough to go up the full height of the wall, with a generous margin for fitting at the top.

The simplest method is to form the sides of the pond from a single wall, before fitting the lining. Dig out the excavation for the part of the pond that will be below the ground, allowing for the thickness of a blockwork wall all round. Around the edges of the base, dig a footing approximately 40cm/16in wide and 23cm/9in deep, and construct on this a single wall of 23cm/9in concrete blocks, which can be solid or hollow. The upper part of the wall can be rendered on the outside with sand and cement, or plastered, to give it a pleasing stucco finish.

Alternatively, the inner wall can be built up in blockwork from the base and an additional outer wall, in a more attractive material, can be constructed at ground level. The outer wall can be built on its own footing

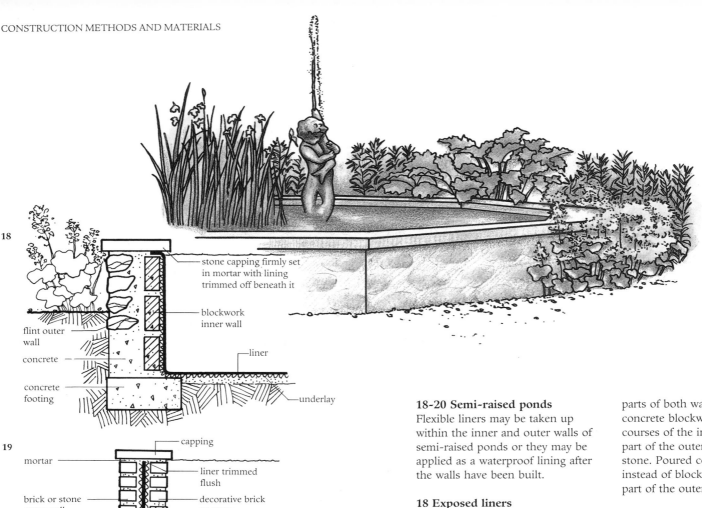

18

stone capping firmly set in mortar with lining trimmed off beneath it

flint outer wall

blockwork inner wall

concrete

liner

concrete footing

underlay

19

capping

mortar

liner trimmed flush

brick or stone outer wall

decorative brick or stone

concrete blockwork wall

liner

concrete footing

underlay

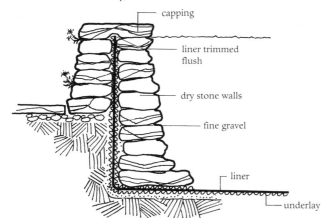

20

capping

liner trimmed flush

dry stone walls

fine gravel

liner

underlay

18-20 Semi-raised ponds

Flexible liners may be taken up within the inner and outer walls of semi-raised ponds or they may be applied as a waterproof lining after the walls have been built.

18 Exposed liners

Excavate the site, allowing for a double wall, and make a concrete footing wide enough to accommodate it. Build a single wall on the inner edge of the footing, up to ground level, and backfill with concrete before constructing the outer wall. Here, the inner wall is in concrete blockwork and the outer wall in flint bedded in concrete (see photograph opposite). The outer wall can be of rendered concrete block or of brick or stone. Place the liner in the pond and pull it up over the top of the inner wall and cap off, setting the capping firmly in mortar. Slabs can be laid on the base, over underlay, to form a planting ledge, which hides the lining. In soft soil, set the slabs on a concrete base.

19 Concealed liners

Here the liner is simply a waterproof tanking within two walls. The lower parts of both walls are made of concrete blockwork and the top few courses of the inner wall and visible part of the outer wall are in brick or stone. Poured concrete can be used instead of blockwork for the lower part of the outer wall.

20 Concealed liners with dry stone walls

This method is very popular in areas where there is hard frost in winter. The inner and outer walls are both made with dry stones and the lining (which makes the structure waterproof) is taken up between the walls. Fold the liner over the sides of the excavation while you build up the inner wall to ground level, filling the gaps between and behind the stones with fine gravel.

Continue building the inner wall to the desired height and fold back the liner over it while building up the outer wall. When both walls are of equal height, fill the gaps with gravel. Trim the liner and cap the top of the walls with heavy stones, without mortar.

Plant between the stones to achieve a 'natural' look.

John Brookes and I collaborated on this semi-raised octagonal pool built in the Sussex garden of Sue and Peter Holland. The skilfully crafted outer walls are built of the local flint, with corners in cut stone (diagram 18). Sawn York stone is used for the capping.

The pond is lined in butyl, and the central plinth is set on a large stone slab to spread the load and protect the liner. The water for the lead fountain is recirculated by means of a submersible pump, concealed beneath the planting ledge, with its electrical connections housed in a box set into the side of the outer wall.

just below ground level or on a 'wall' of poured concrete (diagram 18). The dimensions of the walls can be increased to suit the pressures imposed by extra height or adverse climatic conditions.

To line the pond, cover the base with a layer of sand or protective underlay and apply a protective underlay to the sides. A special insulating foam or a layer of polystyrene will help to prevent freezing in winter. Fit the lining over the cushioning, bring it up the sides of the pond, take it over the top of the inner wall, and apply capping to finish off.

The other approach is to treat the flexible liner as merely a waterproof tanking within two walls. The principle is shown in diagram 19. Begin by digging a footing below the level of the pond base. Pour a wide footing flush with the base and construct the outer wall on it. Place the liner, sandwiched between two layers of underlay, on the base and bring these three layers up and over the wall, temporarily holding them in place at the top with loose bricks. Then construct the inner wall on top of the liner, on the front of the same footing. If preferred, for total protection, the pond base can be concreted over – approximately 10cm/4in thick – and the inner wall built on the edge of this. Finish the liner and capping as for the basic method.

Liners may be concealed in many ways, not only within dry stone walls (diagram 20) but also by adjusting the methods illustrated on p.56.

Semi-raised ponds with premoulded liners

A semi-raised pond can also be made with a symmetrical premoulded shape (see pp.45-6). As for a sunken preformed pond, you should first invert the shell in the chosen position and mark around it. Guided by this outline (and allowing for the overlap round the edge of the pond), dig out and pour the concrete footing that will support the wall.

The proportions of the wall that surrounds and supports the pond can be adjusted to suit its size. The footing should be about 15-23cm/6-9in deep and 30cm/12in wide – there should be about 10cm/4in free on the inner side, so that the wall can be set well back on its footing. Care must be taken to ensure that it will not catch the side of the pond as it is lowered in. Premoulded ponds are usually constructed with sufficient slope to their sides to clear 10cm/4in of footing, but it is as well to check by measuring the width and length of the pond at the relevant level. If when the pond is inserted it scrapes against the footing, all is not lost – chip the offending part away with a hammer and cold chisel.

The excavation can then be made for the submerged part of the pond, allowing an extra depth of about 5cm/2in for cushioning the base, and working out from the centre to the sides. Where the wall is to be, for example, 45cm/18in high and the pond is 90cm/3ft overall, you will need to make an excavation that is some 50cm/20in deep.

Level off the base and line it with builders' sand up to the required depth; the pond can now be lowered into place and the wall built up around it. If you prefer, the wall can be built first and the pond inserted afterwards. In either case, the gap between the pond and the wall must be firmly packed with sand to keep the pond stable, and the top of the pond must be absolutely level. Remember to partially fill the pond with water, to prevent the sand from lifting it, and continue to fill and add sand until you reach the top.

When the pond is installed and the wall complete, cover the top of the wall and the pond edge with a suitable capping of stone or brick.

EDGES AND SURROUNDS

The edging that secures the lining of the pond should ideally lie within its rim, and the pond lining – whether a flexible liner, concrete or blockwork, or a combination method – should be concealed behind it. In the case of formal ponds, this narrow band of edging may be topped with a capping set flush with the rim which is extended to form a wider solid surround to the pond. For informal ponds, a hard surround may not be necessary – instead the rim is concealed by planting to the water's edge or by stones or a shingle beach.

Fitting an edging can be the most time-consuming part of constructing a pond. Consider, first, the effect you want to create and then choose a method from those that follow to suit your pocket as well as the style of your water feature.

Edging formal ponds
A well-designed, well-executed rim and surround, in a material that is in keeping with the surrounding architecture and planting, imparts the qualities of harmony and stability that are so necessary in formal situations. From the water itself, which is always first to claim attention, the eye is immediately drawn to its framework, the point at which the water meets the land.

Brimming ponds look best, and the edging to the rim helps to disguise a practical way of preventing seepage, in which a flexible liner is taken up between two courses of brick or stone, or other aesthetically pleasing hard edging materials. The liner is trimmed off flush with the surface (see diagrams 15 and 17).

Capping must be absolutely level, and must follow precisely the shape of a formal pond. It can, however, be slightly adjusted to align correctly if, when completed, the walls prove to be a little out of true. The capping itself will normally be bedded on mortar, which should be thin at the rim (where it will be visible); the bedding must be thick and strong at the back to give stability.

The capping of the walls of semi-raised ponds can be severely formal, made of sawn stone, slate or marble (diagrams 18 and 19), or more informal, made of rough riven (split) stone, brick or even timber. If you want the pond to look old and well established, you can use rough stone for the wall capping, then carefully chip out parts of the edges to form pockets and fill these with soil and plant them with suitable cushioning or trailing plants. For a truly ancient appearance, place soil and mosses in the joints, and apply earth and moss to the outer vertical walls to complete the effect (diagram 20).

Form – materials and their use – must always follow function. The rim edging and the pond surround must be of materials that are appropriate for the use to which the area around the pond is to be put. In a courtyard, small garden or confined area where there is to be a lot of foot traffic, for example, a hard edge that is comfortable and safe to walk on is clearly called for; if a strong visual statement is required, a luxurious material such as marble or a striking one such as stainless steel could be used to edge the pond itself.

Stone slabs, granite setts, cobblestones, large pebbles, bricks, marble, and slate are all possible choices for rims and complementary surrounds to formal ponds. They may echo the materials used in the surrounding architecture, or they may contrast with them in both colour and texture. In practice, it is far preferable to use a contrasting material than to select a poor match: instead of a slightly different shade of brick or stone, for example, consider edging the pond with another type of stone, a contrasting material, or cobblestones. In a white-painted courtyard, the grey of slate or engineering bricks would provide an attractive foil to the white. Different paving materials can also be combined to give interesting and unusual effects – cobblestones and stone slabs in alternating squares, for example – and there are many different bonds for giving texture and pattern to brickwork. Timber also makes a good edging and ponds that are incorporated into decking areas or have timber staging running adjacent to the water look delightful near some houses.

The choice of edging is also important for small formal features. A shallow basin, perhaps surrounding a fountain, bubbler or small geyser on a large modern patio, could be filled with a layer of large pebbles, sloping slightly upward from the centre, and contained by a hard edging material, in granite, paving or brick. Pebbles look particularly beautiful when wet, for the water brings out their colours. Beware of juxtaposing pebbles and grass, however, for the grass will take root among the pebbles, spoiling their effect.

In a large garden, with a lawn that is subject to only medium or low foot traffic, a hard surround to the pond may not be necessary. Grass can grow

A precisely constructed rim in dark engineering brick picks up the colours of the brick pavement and adds a smart finishing touch to this well-executed cruciform pond, which was also a collaborative effort, with John Brookes, for the Hollands in Sussex (see p.59).

A specially tailored butyl liner taken up behind the 23cm/9in internal brick wall is backfilled with concrete. The liner is wedged between the brick pavement and

the rim and is trimmed off flush with the path to maintain the brimming water level.

Simple water jets, each with its own control valve, spout from the corners to join in a flourish at the centre of the pond. They are all worked by the same submersible pump which is concealed beneath the planting shelf on which the white Zantedeschia flourish and is connected to the copper fountain manifold by a flexible 2.5cm/1in hosepipe.

virtually up to the water's edge if the pond is constructed with this in mind. If the inside wall of the pond is concrete, the very top can be chamfered back into the ground, to allow grass to root right up to the water and avoiding an unsightly expanse of concrete between lawn and water. Turves or sods can also be laid to the edge of premoulded ponds, on top of timber and engineering bricks (see p.66).

Edging informal ponds
The simplest and cheapest option is to have marsh (bog) and marginal planting or grass around the edge of a liner pond, with no hard edge. For this very natural-looking wildlife pond, or in cases where the budget does not allow for a more sophisticated treatment, you can cover the wide, shallow, ledge around the pond with heavy loam, above the liner, to hide the liner completely and protect it well below the water line. This can then be overlaid with meadow turf or planted with suitable indigenous plants. Without a hard edge, the surround will always be rather marshy, making routine maintenance of the grass difficult. However, with a wildlife pond this is unlikely to be touched except for an annual cutting and removal of dead vegetation. Because the earth within the pond is continuous with that outside it, some leakage will occur through capillary action. (This effect is particularly apparent in sandy or fibrous soils, and least noticeable in clay soils.) This will extend any marsh area and absorb overflow

water, but it also means that the pond may need frequent topping up.

In ponds other than wildlife ponds the liner needs to be protected by a hard rim around the perimeter to prevent it from being pressed down by foot traffic, which lowers the water level. Even with natural-looking ponds up to 10m/33ft across, a hard edge is usually needed to provide access, and in larger ponds and lakes, wind and wave action, or the presence of waterfowl, may call for robust edging to prevent erosion.

A firm rim in brick, timber, stone or concrete can sever completely the connection between the pond planting and the surrounding ground. The methods for invisible edges can be adapted to retain the perimeter of the pond as well as to support a hard surround. A hard edge, taken right up to the surface in sandy soils prevents the otherwise inevitable excessive water loss. If the hard edge finishes below the surface, a line of gravel sandwiched between soil on top of the brickwork will reduce capillary action. This barrier will quickly be hidden by growing plants.

Planted edges and bog areas
Between the zone of emergent plants and dry land lies a potentially fascinating area where damp or marshy conditions prevail. This area can have a variable degree of moisture content, to suit a wide range of plants. The only prerequisite is that the damp soil should not become stagnant. The bog plants need to have water moving through their roots, so provide them with wide shallow shelves covered in wet soil (diagram 21), rather than containers in which they might become waterlogged. If a small area of the bog is hollowed out so that just a hint of water appears, this will attract frogs, newts and dragonflies, while less desirable creatures, such as midges and mosquitoes, can be kept in check with plants like *Utricularia vulgaris*, the bladderwort, which lends interest to the dark waters of bog pools.

This same dark water will also vividly reflect the cool greens and lemons of the surrounding marsh plants. Beautiful contrasts in foliage can be achieved by juxtaposing, say, *Iris sibirica*, with its thin, upright blades, and *Lysichiton americanus* or *L. camtschatcensis* (skunk cabbages), whose huge green leaves follow the lemon or white spathes that rise out of the marsh in early spring. *Matteuccia struthiopteris*, the shuttlecock fern, contrasts its spring-green fronds with the dark, serrated, palmate leaves and black stems of *Ligularia przewalskii*.

Planting edges can extend beyond the pool to create a bog area that is not dependent on water in the pond for keeping it moist (diagram 22). A separate, self-contained bog garden can also be established as a water feature in its own right (diagram 23).

Evocative of primeval swamps, bog gardens are exotic and mysterious, even dangerous. Yet numerous plants of outstanding beauty are at home in these seemingly hostile places. When exploring a bog garden it is sensible to keep to the path for who knows if the ground underfoot will be firm or if treacherous pockets of deep mud are disguised by the lush leaves of fern, iris or skunk cabbage? With little more than a plastic sheet with a few holes punched in it, and a convenient water supply, a bog garden like this can be constructed in virtually any space.

21 Shallow planting ledges

Bring the pond lining over the ledge and up behind a hard edge to keep it in place (see pp.65-8). At the front of the ledge, place more bricks or stones to retain the soil. Water will overflow into the soil on the outer side of the liner, making a damp area for moisture-loving plants.

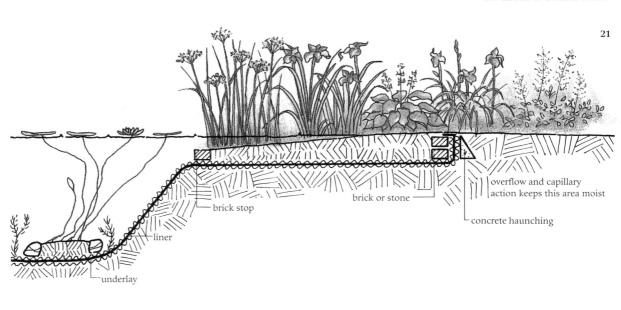

overflow and capillary action keeps this area moist

brick or stone

concrete haunching

brick stop

liner

underlay

22 Planted edges adjacent to the pond

Add surplus liner to your calculations or use an offcut from one corner of the pond to form a broad bog garden in a hollow next to the pond. As before, bring the liner up behind the hard edging. Lay the surplus liner in the hollow and up the sides of the hollow to the same level as the rim of the pond. Make holes in the liner to allow some water to seep away and prevent the water becoming stagnant. Put a layer of pebbles and gravel (for drainage) on top of the liner and set a perforated pipe attached to the water supply into the fibrous loam or growing medium. In impervious soils an overflow pipe can be laid from the edge of the bog garden to a storm drain to prevent the hollow becoming over full.

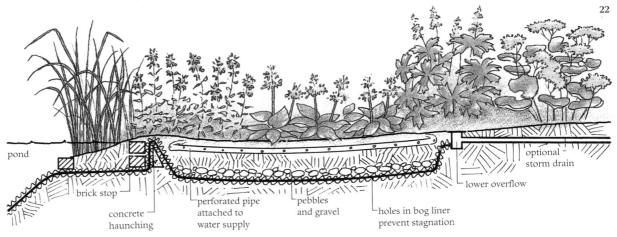

pond

optional storm drain

brick stop

concrete haunching

perforated pipe attached to water supply

pebbles and gravel

holes in bog liner prevent stagnation

lower overflow

23 Bog features

A bog independent of the pond is simple and cheap to create. Make a hollow and line it with low-grade liner. Punch holes in the liner (one hole in the liner per sq m/sq yd). Bring the water supply through the liner and into a perforated pipe set in pebbles and gravel over the liner. Put a further layer of gravel on top of the pipe followed by a sheet of geotextile separation medium, then fibrous loam or other suitable growing medium. Keep the bog area moist by turning on the water supply when needed. Alternatively, control the flow of water by fitting a float valve into a supply cistern to automatically release water when the level is low.

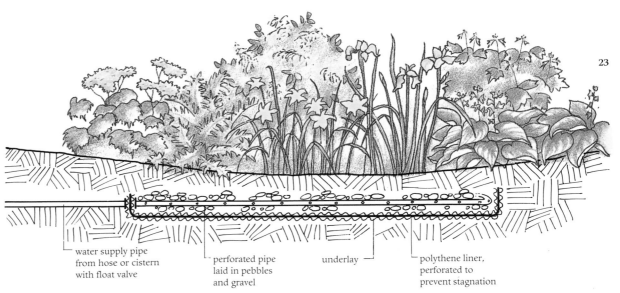

water supply pipe from hose or cistern with float valve

perforated pipe laid in pebbles and gravel

underlay

polythene liner, perforated to prevent stagnation

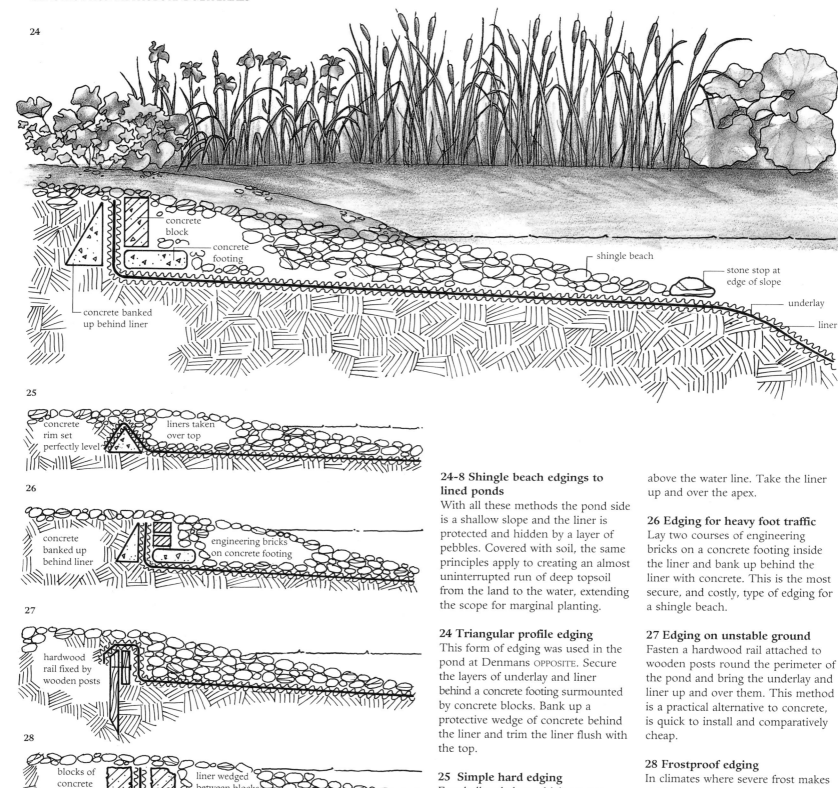

24

concrete
block

concrete
footing

concrete banked
up behind liner

shingle beach

stone stop at
edge of slope

underlay

liner

25

concrete
rim set
perfectly level

liners taken
over top

26

concrete
banked up
behind liner

engineering bricks
on concrete footing

27

hardwood
rail fixed by
wooden posts

28

blocks of
concrete
or stone

liner wedged
between blocks

24-8 Shingle beach edgings to lined ponds

With all these methods the pond side is a shallow slope and the liner is protected and hidden by a layer of pebbles. Covered with soil, the same principles apply to creating an almost uninterrupted run of deep topsoil from the land to the water, extending the scope for marginal planting.

24 Triangular profile edging

This form of edging was used in the pond at Denmans OPPOSITE. Secure the layers of underlay and liner behind a concrete footing surmounted by concrete blocks. Bank up a protective wedge of concrete behind the liner and trim the liner flush with the top.

25 Simple hard edging

For shallow ledges which are not subject to much foot traffic, trowel up a level wedge of concrete to just above the water line. Take the liner up and over the apex.

26 Edging for heavy foot traffic

Lay two courses of engineering bricks on a concrete footing inside the liner and bank up behind the liner with concrete. This is the most secure, and costly, type of edging for a shingle beach.

27 Edging on unstable ground

Fasten a hardwood rail attached to wooden posts round the perimeter of the pond and bring the underlay and liner up and over them. This method is a practical alternative to concrete, is quick to install and comparatively cheap.

28 Frostproof edging

In climates where severe frost makes rigid cement work unsuitable, secure the liners between heavy blocks of stone or concrete laid dry.

Three distinct types of edging details are called for in this butyl-lined pool at Denmans (see also pp.6-7). Around the perimeter, the layers of underlay and liner are secured between a concrete footing surmounted by concrete blocks on the pond side and a protective wedge of concrete banked up behind (diagram 24). The triangular profile of this kind of edging gives an almost uninterrupted run of deep topsoil from the land to the water, extending the scope for planting through the margins.

The pond is approached on one side by a shingle beach which is built up on a very wide, shallow shelving ledge. On the far side of the pool, a narrower ledge is completely covered with soil for emergent plants and forms a continuation of the shrub planting on the bank. The viewing side of the pool is for the most part lawn and here a firm brick edge enables people to walk right to the brink of the water. Large clumps of water lilies are grown in stone-built enclosures filled with heavy clay loam.

Bog areas can be created in impervious soil merely by omitting the liner. If the bog area forms part of a clay-lined pond it will receive all the moisture it needs from the main pond, but if it is self-contained, it will need to be artificially supplied with water.

Alternatively, a completely automatic watering system can be made by excavating and installing a liner that comes only part way up the sides of the hole. Instead of puncturing it, cover the liner with a layer of gravel. On this place a layer of perforated pipe, overlaid with more gravel to a depth of about 3cm/1in. Cover this with a protective underlay (see p.52), which serves as a separation membrane through which water, but not soil particles, can pass. Fill the remaining area with any rich, fibrous organic material, including clay loam mixed with well-rotted cow manure, and plant out.

The pipe can be led back to a small tank nearby, where the water level is controlled by a ballcock float valve or an electric sensor and valve. As the ground dries out, more water will be provided from the cistern, and capillary action will draw it through the matting to the roots of the plants. Any surplus water resulting from heavy rains will run over the top of the liner and disappear into the surrounding earth. (If the area is bordered by impervious ground, a separate drain can be taken from just above the float valve level in the cistern and led to a suitable storm drain, permitting surplus water to be drained from the bog.) In wet periods the ball valve will not come into operation, as enough water will be trapped under the membrane to keep the bog healthy.

Gravel, pebble and shingle edges

This type of edging gives a lovely textured contrast with the water and provides a firm area to walk on. Offering a gradual transition from dry ground to water, it is safe for small children who, once alerted to the presence of water, have plenty of time to stop and turn around before getting out of their depth, and it is ideal for ducks or other creatures that need to get in and out of the water easily. The shallow slope required for what is really a beach takes up a lot of space, which may not be available in small gardens. On larger sites, however, a beach area can be ideal: it does not suffer from erosion due to wave action, it can accommodate flocks of wading birds without the usual problems of muddy banks, stripped of their vegetation, and – although I prefer a landing stage – it is also good for boats.

A shingle beach is an ideal way of hiding and protecting the edge of a flexible pond liner. It also enables large animals such as horses and cattle to walk into the pond without damaging the lining. The methods shown in diagrams 24 to 28 are relatively easy to execute, and inexpensive.

grass laid to the brink

engineering bricks

concrete haunching

concrete footing

liner

underlay

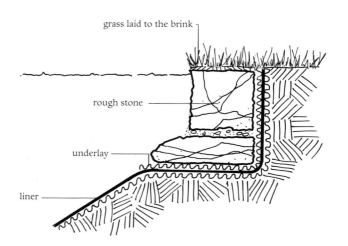

grass laid to the brink

rough stone

underlay

liner

Stone edges

Stone is widely used to edge natural-looking ponds. It is a good way of securing a lake edge, and can be treated in the same way as brick, with lawn coming right to the edge of the pond, or with pieces of stone slabbing laid as a broad capping to create a path or standing area beside the pond. Again, the effect created will be of a natural pond enhanced by a designed feature which facilitates its use.

The use of stone is most appropriate in regions where it is widely used for walls and buildings, and you should, in general, try to use the local stone. Choose building stone that has not been neatly sawn to shape, but cut into more or less square pieces so that the natural look is retained (the pieces need to have tops and bottoms that are roughly flat and level). Fairly large pieces can be used, and the edging can be built up without mortar, on the same principle as a dry stone wall (diagram 29). If stones in the order of 70-140kg/150-300lb are used for the capping, they should be sufficiently stable to be used dry.

Brick edges

A brick edging around the rim gives stability, precision and support to the pond edge. It can be entirely hidden by grass (diagram 30), but it could also take a more visible form, used both round the rim and as a capping crisply outlining the pond and clearly defining the grass edge. In the latter case brick might also be used for a firm path leading up to the water's edge.

Engineering bricks, or the shallow pavers designed for outdoor use, are best for this purpose, as they are hard and impervious to frost. As to colour, bright red is best avoided; black or brown are ideal, and some of the russets and ochres are very effective; or the colour can be matched with that of the house or garden buildings. A black brick edging capped with green lawn looks superb, and the black hardly shows at all beneath the water while clearly defining the rim. If you wish to grow grass right up to the edge, engineering bricks with holes in them allow the grass to take root over them and hide them completely.

29-30 Grass to the water's edge

A beautifully brimming pond can be achieved with these forms of edging, with grass growing right to the brink. To bring grass to the edges of a lined pond, you need to build an inner wall of brick or stone.

29 Brick-edged ponds

On a concrete footing, build the wall up to the intended water level. Lift liners right up to the top of the brickwork, haunch up behind with concrete for protection and trim to keep the liners in place. Then lay turves on top of the hard edges, over the top of the liner and onto the surround, thus creating a crisp edge where grass and water meet.

30 Stone-edged ponds

Use large, flat pieces of stone for the footings on which to build up the inner wall of rough stones. Wedge the liners, trim them and lay the turves as for brick-edged ponds.

Timber edges

Timber edging can be applied to almost any type of pond. It combines happily with grass and suits natural-looking ponds (diagrams 31 to 34). It may consist of horizontal planks, in hardwood or treated softwood, or round logs, vertically set. Grass can be taken right to the top of the logs or planks, all around the pond or in chosen areas. The timber theme can also be developed further to make a platform along part of the edge (see p.100) – a use of timber that makes a natural-looking extension for a seating area or terrace adjacent to the house.

Rock edges

Unlike stone slabs which have obviously been deliberately placed, rocks should never be positioned evenly around the entire edge of a pond, for they will look unpleasantly artificial. For best effect, the rocks must always appear as if they were there first. They may resemble natural outcrops or may stand alone as specimen boulders in traditional Oriental water garden style. To achieve this, they should be placed on a ledge within the pond, and partly submerged in the water.

In a well-built concrete pond the rocks can be merely lowered into position on a suitably constructed ledge (diagram 35), although smaller rocks, or those with uneven bases, may need to be bedded in a fresh

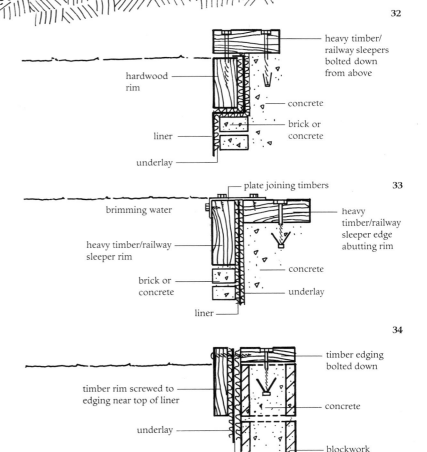

31-34 Timber edgings

A timber edging is less durable than stone, brick or masonry but provides an attractive finish to formal and informal ponds and can be useful in hiding concrete walls. Laid longitudinally, however, it will not readily accommodate a tight curve.

31 Brimming ponds

Drive hardwood posts into the ground at 1-2m/3-6ft intervals around the pond according to the length and weight of the timber. These should have tops cut back at an angle so there is more soil for the grass growing here. Position hardwood rails on either side of the liner. Bolt the back rail to the posts, making sure that the fixings do not puncture the liner. Use bent galvanized steel bars or staples to clamp over the front and back rails, sandwiching the liner in between. Screw the staples onto the front rail. Lay turves onto the pond surround, covering the clamps and timber edges.

32 Lower water level

In this method the timber rests on a brick or concrete wall inside the pond. Bring the pond liner over the brick and up behind the hardwood beam that forms the rim. Place railway sleepers or other stout pieces of timber on top and firmly bolt them into the rim. To secure them, bolt the railway sleepers into concrete behind the liner.

33 Timber rims

This is an adaptation of the method shown in diagram 32, with the liner behind the bricks and the hardwood rim. It is an alternative way of making a brimming pond. Set the edging timber at right angles to the rim, sandwiching the liner in between, and bolt it into the concrete. Join the timbers with securely bolted stainless steel or galvanized plates.

34 To disguise concrete sides

Lay the timber edging round the pond and bolt it into the concrete blocks that form the pond sides. Bring the liner up on the inside and place the hardwood rim so the liner is sandwiched in between. Support it with bricks while you secure it in position from the pond side through the lining and into the edging timber. The screws will puncture the liner and determine the water level.

For timber edging (diagrams 31-4) use hardwoods (from a renewable source) or softwoods treated with a compound that you know is safe to use with fish, birds and plants. Even treated wood can curl when exposed to the heat of the sun, so choose heavy, sturdy timbers that are better able to withstand the effects of both sun and rain.

For timber edging (diagrams 31-4) use hardwoods (from a renewable source) or softwoods treated with a compound that you know is safe to use with fish, birds and plants. Even treated wood can curl when exposed to the heat of the sun, so choose heavy, sturdy timbers that are better able to withstand the effects of both sun and rain.

Although the rigid constraints of timber dictate straight lines for a pool edge, the fact that it is a natural product, and weathers to look grey, imparts a rustic feeling to this design. This characteristic is taken further by the random planting that has been allowed to soften the pool and its surrounds.

concrete mix. On a small liner pond, using comparatively light rocks, it is possible merely to place the rocks on the ledges over an extra layer or two of protective underlay. Obviously, however, such rocks cannot be walked on, and are dangerous to children. It is safer to set them into a thick bed of mortar. With large rocks, more protection is required for the liner, and it is best to cover the extra layer of underlay with a concrete raft approximately 10cm/4in thick, which will allow you to move the rocks without the risk of damaging the liner. The rocks can be set on the concrete in mortar to ensure that no movement will take place during subsequent maintenance. The liner itself is taken up behind the rockwork, held in position and further protected with a haunching of concrete as illustrated in diagram 36.

The space between the rocks and the rim of the pond can be filled with loose stones or gravel, and a few further rocks can link this marginal area to its surrounding, to create the illusion that the stone runs back into the ground.

Planting containers and pipework or cables can be installed as described on p.75 or concealed in surrounding rocks or planted areas.

ROCKWORK

Rock should be chosen to look right for the area in which you are going to use it. Some imported stone can look out of place, especially if the immediate surroundings already include stone. Check that the type of stone you like is available in the size you need and that you have the means to handle or manoeuvre it (see pp.70-1).

Choosing rock

Historically, the Chinese and Japanese were masters of the use of rocks. The Chinese prized rocks that were deeply faceted, full of holes, and contorted by wind and water into grotesquely beautiful shapes, while the Japanese preferred – and still prefer – smoother, more rounded forms.

There are many different types of rock, ranging from soft tufa to marble and granite, suitable for water gardens. Leaving aside rock that has been cut into dressed stone, rocks fall roughly into three categories: stratified rock, grainless or fissured rocks, and boulders and field stones.

Stratified rock has an obvious grain to it, with streaks, flecks, lines or hair cracks running through in one direction. Individual pieces usually

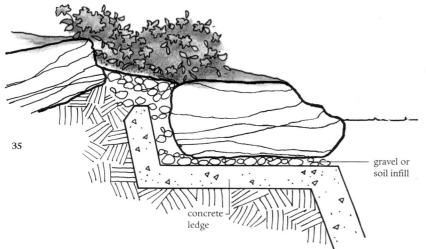

gravel or
soil infill

concrete
ledge

35 Rocks on concrete ledges
To achieve a natural look, place the rocks on concrete ledges within the pond so they appear to rise out of the water. Keep heavy flat-bottomed rocks steady by putting a thin layer of gravel or soil underneath them. Smaller, rounder rocks should be set in a soft mortar bedding to give stability. Pack the space behind the rocks with gravel or soil.

36 Rocks on lined ledges
On a layer of protective underlay, lay a concrete 'raft' over the planting ledge, to spread the weight of the rocks. Set the rocks in gravel or soil, or mortar them in place, depending on their size, weight and shape, and on the degree of stability required. Haunch up in concrete behind the rocks to keep the liner in place. Finally, place a few rocks in groups around the pond to break the line of rocks at water level. They should appear to be 'growing' out of the earth in natural-looking outcrops.

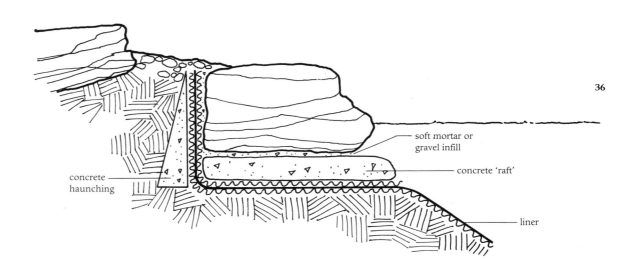

soft mortar or
gravel infill

concrete 'raft'

concrete
haunching

liner

have flat tops and bottoms and are suitable for building large rock structures and waterfalls or to form outcrops fanning out into the water of a large pond.

Grainless or fissured rocks are oddly shaped lumps which may have no apparent grain or may have a mass of swirling colours and rhythms within them. Some are cuboid, others totally random in shape, deeply scored and fissured by the action of ice and water. Where the random fissures are deep, the rocks can be fitted together so cunningly that it becomes impossible to tell where the joints are.

Boulders or fieldstones are smooth and rounded, worn and pummelled by the action of ice and water. Ranging in size from pea-sized grains to huge boulders shaped like balls, pears or cottage loaves, they are effective on beaches, by large ponds or in streams, under running water or fountains. A few placed beneath a waterfall will create a natural effect.

Positioning rocks: basic principles
The golden rule of rockwork is that a few large pieces of stone are more convincing than lots of smaller ones. Rocks should look as you would find them in nature. If, having excavated soil for a pond, you are left with a mound of earth, do not feel that you must sprinkle the whole surface with rocks, for the result will not be pleasing. They should appear in patches, groups and outcrops, with spaces in between for scree and plants. Rocks should be placed so that the grain follows on from one rock to the other. First decide which way the grain should run – horizontally is probably the easiest, but a tilt running through the entire rock landscape can be very effective. It is also legitimate for the grain to bend gently, as in nature, where an upheaval has occurred. This can work well – for example, through a stream bed punctuated by a series of waterfalls.

A rock will always look bigger and more convincing if it is not fully visible, giving the impression that it is merely the tip of a much larger piece or part of the solid underlying bedrock. It is therefore important, particularly with the stratified types of rock, that they be well bedded in the ground. Round boulders and fieldstones are obviously handled differently, for in nature they would have been washed down and left scattered on the surface. Much more of the surface of these rocks can be left exposed to look correct.

The stork sculpture, stone lantern, rocks, moss, water, convoluted banks and maple trees are all suggestive of an Oriental water garden: this one is at Tatton Park in Cheshire.

The effect is disarmingly uncontrived, yet great thought went into the positioning of every element. New rocks can be made to look as though they are the ancient backbone of the setting: partly submerged to look natural and larger than they in fact are, they can also be encouraged to grow verdant coatings of moss and lichen, another convincing indicator of longevity. This can be done by spraying them with rice water, milk or diluted manure.

Manoeuvring rock

The handling of rock is governed by the facilities available, and these in turn are governed to a large extent by the amount you have to spend. Access to the site is a primary consideration: will the stones physically pass through the doorways? Can they be manoeuvred up steps? Is the ground over which they are likely to pass marshy? If you are planning a rooftop garden, will the roof be sufficiently strong to take the weight? Most access problems can be overcome with sufficient funds. With the

equipment available nowadays practically anything can be achieved; it all boils down to the amount you can spend. For example, in city gardens, where the only access is through the front door and straight through the house, the solution would be to hire a crane and swing the stone over the roof and into the backyard. Handling materials by crane is the usual practice in big towns and cities.

The maximum weight that can be handled without mechanical means is about 150kg/3cwt. For weights in excess of this you must resort to using some mechanical advantage, such as levers or block and tackle. When handling rocks weighing more than approximately 500kg/half a ton, it usually becomes more cost effective to use a machine – a hydraulic digger or excavator for weights up to perhaps 5,000kg/5tons and a crane for anything heavier.

By hand

When moving any heavy weight by hand, do not strain yourself and keep the back and neck straight. Wear protective gloves and strong boots or shoes with steel toe caps. Even a light rock rolling back on the feet can severely damage toes. It is easier to roll rock than to lift it. Firmly position yourself close to the rock and use its weight to your advantage. It will usually roll more easily one way than another, and can be twisted to suit the direction you wish it to travel.

If you are handling a rock that is approximately cuboid in shape (as would be used in the construction of a waterfall), each time you roll it over, roll it on to a small stone, so that the flat base of the rock is approximately centred over the stone. The rock will then already be partly off balance, ready for the next roll, rather like a seesaw. Rocks are always easier to manoeuvre on hard than on soft ground. Never allow a rock to get bogged down in soft ground; it is almost impossible to get it out again. Planks and sheets of plywood facilitate rock-moving operations. Once levered on to small rollers (short sections of scaffolding tube or pipe will do), a rock can easily be pushed along planks.

Wheelbarrow and ropes

It is possible to roll a surprisingly heavy stone into a wheelbarrow by laying the barrow on its side; it can then be hauled back level with the stone in it. A rope attached near the front of the wheel and pulled by a second person makes transportation easier. When rolling a rock into the final position you may find you have to plan several moves ahead, rather as in a game of chess. Remember to keep the rock on hard ground until the very last moment when you roll it into its prepared bed.

An extremely useful appliance is a purpose-made sack barrow with pneumatic tyres, and handles over which tubes can be slipped to give extra leverage in lifting the rock off the ground. Once balanced over the wheels, the rock can be pulled and pushed on the barrow. The job is easier with two people, one holding the handle bars and the other pushing – or pulling with a short length of rope.

Crowbar and fulcrum

For rocks that are too heavy to roll by hand you will need a crowbar and fulcrum – any hard object on which to rest the crowbar. Blocks of hardwood are good, as they tend not to slip as bricks do. Place the fulcrum on a larger block, itself placed on planks or plywood. It is unlikely that you will be able to turn a rock with just one levering of the bar: have lumps of stone or bricks or wood ready to push under the gap as the bar lifts the rock. A second purchase can then be made, and perhaps a third

or fourth will be required before the rock is sufficiently out of balance to roll over into the desired position.

Hand winch

The Tirfor is a form of hand winch with a long steel wire that can be attached to the rock by a chain or strop; by working a hand lever the wire is drawn through the winch. With this powerful and versatile tool rocks can be winched a considerable distance. Firm anchorage points for the winch are essential: you could use a tree or another large rock in the vicinity. Make sure that a tree is well protected with sacking and that the winch is attached low down on the trunk.

Block and tackle with sheerlegs

A block and tackle, or endless chain hoist, is a centuries-old means of lifting things. It is normally used in conjunction with a sheerlegs, a tripod formed of three poles fixed securely together at the top rather like a wigwam. The tripod needs to be securely fixed in three places to anchorage points some distance away. Modern safety regulations in some countries are phasing out the use of wooden poles in civil engineering, and metal tripods are now considered to be safer. However, they tend to be shorter than the old wooden ones, so that you have little opportunity to move the rock much beyond the centre of the lifting point – there being little lateral movement.

Hydraulic machine

It is often cheaper, weight for weight, to put in large rocks by a machine (preferably running on tracks) than smaller ones by hand. The rock can simply be lifted by chains, carried over by machine and carefully lowered into place. The only problems arise when the machine is operating to the full extent of its reach, particularly on uneven ground. The weight tends to cause the hydraulics to sink, and the operator will constantly be having to counteract this. If the machine is not standing level, the weight will also make the load swing to one side or the other. This makes the final placing much more difficult than it would be otherwise. The machine should be equipped with special valves, so that in the event of a burst hydraulic hose, the rock will not suddenly drop.

Crane

Whenever possible a crane should be used for moving heavy rocks, as it is quicker and easier than the methods just described. Rocks can be carefully and accurately slung using chains so that they hang exactly level at the correct angle for final placing. The crane has infinite control and can let them hover effortlessly a few centimetres/inches above where they are to go, while you swivel them round and round deciding on the best position. Make sure that you have a sufficiently large crane for the job. The farther the load is out from the crane, the less it can be lifted. If you find, with a particularly heavy rock, that you are outside the radius, you will have to move the crane closer.

71

Fountains, streams and waterfalls

The sight and sound of moving water never fails to refresh, charm and delight. In nature it can be soothing, like the gentle murmur of a brook, or exhilarating, like the crash of surf on rocks. There are all sorts of water features that can bring the pleasures of moving water to the garden, and it is of no consequence if the room available is limited - there is a suitable feature for even the most modest space.

A fountain can be installed in any kind of pond or purpose-built basin. Traditionally built in stone, bronze and lead, more recently sculptors have exploited the potential of modern materials including cast iron, glass and stainless steel. The smallest garden can be enhanced with fountains and water mobiles available in a seemingly unending variety of shapes and designs to suit every taste and budget: jets that play into copper bowls and ring bells as they fill and empty; flow-control mechanisms that produce spurts and squirts, jets and pirouettes, sprays and displays. There are wall fountains and spouts as well as jets that rise straight from the ground to introduce the sound of trickling water while occupying minimal space.

A stylized water staircase can be constructed on raised ground in the larger garden, and for features emulating nature there are streams and waterfalls. The movement and chuckle of a stream, meandering round stones and boulders, or churning down falls and rapids, always invites exploration and, with today's pond-lining materials, the illusion of a natural water course can be created even on a perfectly level site, with pump-operated falls built with concrete, flexible liners, or using premoulded sections. Terminating in a pool or basin, the water is pumped back for recirculation.

Waterfalls or weirs can be constructed across natural waterways, perhaps to impound a pond or lake, or simply to slow down the flow of a stream so as to raise the water level and provide more scope for waterside planting.

Electric pumps are used for all artificial moving water features. Their installation and operation is simple, practical and inexpensive, making fountains, streams and waterfalls attainable for every gardener.

RECIRCULATING SYSTEMS

In the past, water features worked on the pressure created by gravity. Water can be supplied under pressure from the piped domestic supply, but to work fountains and waterfalls from the mains would be expensive and wasteful – and probably in breach of local regulations. Nowadays, the water which is contained within the feature is recirculated by means of an electric pump.

There are two main types: submersible pumps, which run under water and are always the centrifugal type, and surface pumps, which are centrifugal, positive (piston) or Archimedean screw. With centrifugal pumps – by far the most common – water is drawn into the pump by an impeller that revolves at high speed, and flung out by centrifugal force to be expelled through the outlet pipe (diagram 1). These pumps can be regulated to restrict the flow, which puts less strain on the motor. You should not, however, stop the flow completely while the pump is switched on. In the case of piston or positive pumps, the more the flow is reduced the greater the load on the motor.

The performance of a pump is given in litres or gallons per hour for a given head. A head is the height to which the water is being pumped above the surface of the source (usually a pond) from which it is being drawn. The depth or the position of the pump in the pond makes no difference. Waterfalls, unless they are very high, usually require a pump that gives a large volume and comparatively small head. This relationship, however, can alter if the distance is great and the pipe runs are consequently very long. The longer the pipe run, the greater will be the resistance, or pipe friction. This will in practice increase the head and reduce the amount of water you get from the end of the pipe. As a rule of thumb, the pipe should be increased to the next size up from that of the pump outlet: thus, a 4cm/1½in pump outlet would take a 5cm/2in pipe. For very long runs it is best to consult pipe friction tables, which are available from most pump stockists.

Surface pumps

These pumps have a long life expectancy and the larger sizes tend to be cheaper than their submersible counterparts. However, more time and money has to be spent housing a surface pump which requires shelter from rain and frost, adequate drainage and ventilation.

The pump can be installed some distance away from the water feature, preferably below the level from which it is drawing water. This causes what is known as 'flooded suction' – meaning that a constant water supply, drawn by gravity, enters the suction pipe and cannot drain back to leave the pump empty. The cellar of a house would be a good location. In any event, it should be sited so the hum of the pump does not detract from the beauty of the water feature.

Pumps can push water more strongly than they can suck. Surface pumps require a proper suction pipe to prevent collapse. This should usually be one size larger than the delivery pipe and of as short a run as possible. A long suction pipe will reduce the pump's efficiency far more

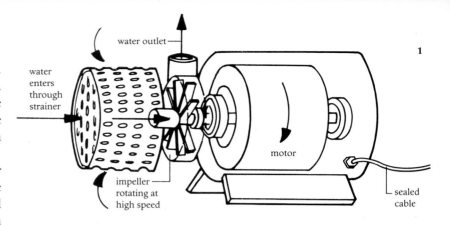

1 A centrifugal, submersible pump The impeller, rotating at high speed, draws in water through the strainer, then expels it by centrifugal force through the outlet pipe. A sealed cable leads either to the mains electricity supply or to a transformer which reduces the voltage.

drastically than the equivalent length on the delivery pipe. Always try to install the pump so that it has flooded suction. If this cannot be arranged, fit a foot valve on to the end of the suction pipe; this one-way valve prevents the water from flowing back after the pump has been switched off. However the slightest particle getting underneath the valve will prevent it from closing properly, and the water will then drain back. If the system is drained of water, the pump must be reprimed. Some surface pumps are self-priming and can be situated a metre or so/a few feet above the pond from which they are drawing – but they should, nevertheless, always be kept as low as is practical. A strainer must be put on the end of the suction pipe to prevent the ingress of large foreign bodies.

When installing the flow and return pipes for a surface pump, make sure that there are no loops or hummocks in which pockets of air could get trapped, for they can be very difficult to remove.

Submersible pumps

Submersible pumps have many advantages and are generally quick and easy to install. The pumps do not, of course, need priming; they are silent in operation and, provided they are situated deeply enough, frost protection is not necessary. Only an electricity cable and perhaps a delivery pipe are required. They come in all sizes, from the smallest unit delivering 450 litres/100 gallons an hour and suitable for a wall fountain, to pumps for enormous waterfalls capable of moving approximately 230,000 litres/50,000 gallons an hour.

When choosing the size of pump for a small water feature, you can experiment with the garden hose, trying different volumes until you arrive at the flow rate you need. Then place the hose in a bucket, time how long it takes to fill and divide the size of the bucket by the time to get the litres/gallons per minute. Remember that it is best to have some power in reserve, for although the flow can easily be reduced (by a gate valve set anywhere in the delivery pipe), it cannot be increased if the pump is already running at maximum capacity. As a general guide, a natural stone waterfall spillway 15cm/6in wide will require approximately 2,750 litres/

600 gallons per hour and a rock spillway 50cm/20in wide will require approximately 9,000 litres/2,000 gallons per hour to look effective.

Apart from volume, the pumps also vary in pressure but most domestic fountain or waterfall pumps are designed to move large volumes of water at low pressures. A deep well pump, on the other hand, will move a comparatively small volume, but at a very high pressure.

Installation and pipework

The pump should not be installed on the very bottom of a pond or stream, where it will pick up all the detritus, but set on a concrete block, stone or slab, where it will draw neither debris from the surface nor rotting material from the bottom. Where possible any delivery pipes and cables should be taken up over the edge of the pond structure so that holes do not have to be made in the pond fabric and resealed. In formal ponds, pipes and cables can be taken up inside the masonry structure. With butyl pond liners, since they are so elastic, it is simple to flange a water pipe through a hole of about half the diameter of the pipe. Make sure that the hole is exactly round. It will form a trumpet, around which adhesive tape can be applied, and the pressure of water will form a seal. Less flexible liners can be flanged through using a conventional screw assembly, sometimes called a tank connection, or using two flanges connected through with nuts and bolts. Proper gaskets must be used on these, and a clear silicon sealant is advisable.

Fit a malleable pipe union just beneath the water surface so that you can disconnect the pump without having to turn it underwater. Very small pumps are connected by means of a hose clip and flexible tube.

Submersible pumps come with a length of perhaps 3m/10ft of waterproof electrical cable already fitted. This must be carefully handled and well-protected, by a conduit or by stone or concrete, where it comes out of the pond. It should be terminated in a waterproof connector concealed a little distance from the pond. This could, for example, be fixed on a short stake above ground, hidden by a flower pot or evergreen shrub. Do not bury it in a subterranean chamber, which can become waterlogged or full of condensation and cause a short circuit.

Use armoured cable back to the main supply. This should be buried 60cm/2ft deep in the ground, with a strip of electricity warning tape in the trench above it. All outside electrical wiring installation should be protected by a sensitive trip which will cut the supply should any earth or ground fault occur, and prevent electrocution. If there is any doubt, have the installation carried out, or at least checked, by a qualified electrician.

If it is important that the pump is safely out of sight, it can be installed in a purpose-built watertight chamber (diagram 2).

Water-delivery pipes should run from the pump to the delivery points of the feature. Copper, plastic or polythene rather than lead are now generally used for pipework. However, while minute quantities of copper in the water – less than .02 parts per million – can be beneficial, inhibiting the growth of algae, too much will kill molluscs and fish. Short lengths of copper tubing in a relatively large pond, where plastic is used for the main pipe runs, will have little effect, but an elaborate system of copper pipes could make the water toxic.

2 External submersible pump chamber

The watertight chamber should measure about 60x60x60cm/ 24x24x24in to accommodate the pump and a valve top-up system or overflow. Connect it to the pond via a balancing pipe or duct (10-15cm/ 4-6in in diameter) through which a delivery pipe and any required electric cables can be passed. The water returns through the duct or balancing pipe to the pump. Seal or flange the duct at both ends.

To feed a fountain, run the delivery pipe to rigid tubing set in a circular concrete block and screw the jet on the end. To supply water to a stream, cascade or waterfall, set a gate valve in the delivery pipe. Where more than one waterfall is operating or if the water is to be increased halfway down the system, insert 'Y' or 'T' connections in the pipe with a gate valve to control each branch.

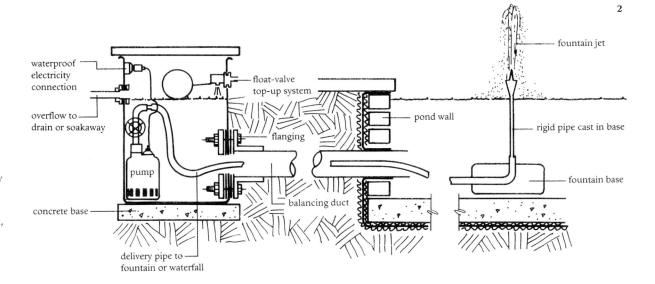

waterproof electricity connection

overflow to drain or soakaway

pump

concrete base

delivery pipe to fountain or waterfall

float-valve top-up system

flanging

balancing duct

pond wall

fountain jet

2

rigid pipe cast in base

fountain base

FOUNTAINS

A fountain can be installed in almost any kind of pond or purpose-built basin, the water spouting from a single jet or a series of jets from an ornament.

Many modern fountains rise straight from the ground, through gravel or from hidden orifices in stone or brick, with the water draining back into a concealed reservoir to be recirculated. Children can play among the jets in complete safety, so a walkway or courtyard can easily double as play area and fountain display. In public places it may be necessary to filter or treat the water to prevent the risk of infection via water droplets.

Fountains should complement the mood and character of the house and setting. Being man-made features, they are best suited to the more formal and architectural features and areas of hard landscaping. Their presence in a natural or apparently natural setting is discordant, though a single high plume or jet could be set in a natural-looking pond or lake, provided the setting and scale were suitably imposing.

Sight and sound

The way a fountain catches the sunlight is one of the key factors in its appeal. The water droplets are radiantly silver when the sun shines through them and this effect should be fully exploited by placing the fountain in a sunny position. It is particularly effective when seen from far off, through deep shade.

The other important reason for having a fountain is for the sound it makes. The design, like that of a musical instrument, radically affects the quality of the sound it produces. Water landing on a hard material, such as cobblestones or a stone fountain ornament, makes repetitive sharp slaps, the volume governed by the quantity falling. Water falling into water sounds different. A thin, vertical jet will not hold together for long and by the time it returns to its source it will be descending in beads that, on entering the water, produce some of the most musical sounds of all. I have known three jets in a row in a small rectangular pond to each produce a sound in a slightly different pitch, resulting in perfect harmony. Multitudes of fine drops tend to produce a high-pitched tinkling sound; larger drops, or a column of water returning to the surface virtually unbroken, produce deep tones. Fine high-pressure jets hitting the surface tend to hiss; drops showering down in more desultory fashion tend to plop. A quite different sound is produced by a geyser or welling water – more of a burble. A simple adjustment to the valves and nozzles controlling the flow can make a lot of difference to the sound.

Planting near fountains

Fountains are powerful features: the movement, light and sound they bring require little else in the way of embellishment. Textural contrasts are already provided by the brick or stone, lead or bronze of the fountain and its surrounds and the water itself. As with any garden feature, too many materials in close proximity create a cluttered effect, and far from embellishing, they detract from it. Brightly coloured plants and flowers

ABOVE *In hot countries every town or village square has its fountain and the enticing sound of water playing can be heard behind many garden walls.*

An Islamic-style fountain set in a chequered basin provides the focus of this walled courtyard in Morocco. Audible from the rooms and balconies above, its gentle splashing is a pleasant and soothing accompaniment to siestas.

A single vertical jet is a good choice in simple formal settings, since it never conflicts with its surroundings. Also important, in hot weather, evaporation is kept to a minimum.

OPPOSITE *Towering plumes have a dramatic and unexpected impact in this wild corner of a large garden. Fountains in natural settings must be sensitively sited so that their artificiality does not conflict with their surroundings. If nearby planting is well-spaced and restrained in colour, water and foliage can work together to create a symphony in silver and green. A fountain bursting into bright sunlight is particularly impressive when viewed from the shade of buildings, arbours or trees. The water droplets appear silver white in the counter light and rainbows form when light streams from behind the viewer.*

are not usually appropriate, restrained planting is preferable. Evergreen foliage, such as that of a simple clipped box, looks wonderful in full sun as the water droplets produce a brilliant picture in silver and green.

The shapes of plants should also be considered. Low arching jets are complemented by the rounded shapes of bushes and shrubs. Tall vertical jets can run parallel to the straight trunks of trees – if room allows, the majestic trunks of the royal palm and the arching leaves of the coconut palm almost resemble fountains themselves. Cypress and, for the smaller garden, *Juniperus communis* 'Hibernica' and *Juniperus scopulorum* 'Sky-rocket', are complementary pencil shapes. Clipped evergreen arches would make an excellent frame through which to view such a picture.

Water lilies cannot withstand being splashed by fountain jets and therefore should be planted well outside the range of falling water. Conversely, water falling continuously on stonework encourages some plant life and ancient fountains can become completely clothed in a dome of beautiful mosses, lichens and dripping ferns.

Fountain jets

A single thin vertical jet is the best choice for circular ponds and basins. For a long, narrow rectangular pond that would look awkward with just one jet, two or more placed down the middle will complement the elongated shape. Alternatively, jets could come in from the sides or from each corner, arching into the centre, the latter arrangement being particularly effective for square, octagonal or short rectangular ponds.

The rules of classical architecture provide formulae for determining the height of the jet in proportion to the diameter of the pond, but I prefer to be governed by the setting and by the crucial factor of the exposure to the wind. In a sheltered garden with high walls, a high jet could be equal in height to the diameter of its basin and serve as a focal point, perhaps where two paths cross. In windy spots its height could be reduced to as little as half the radius, or the desired height can be created by a fountain ornament, rather than by the jet itself. The water can be adjusted to hug the sculpture, with only short, free-fall plunges to catch the light.

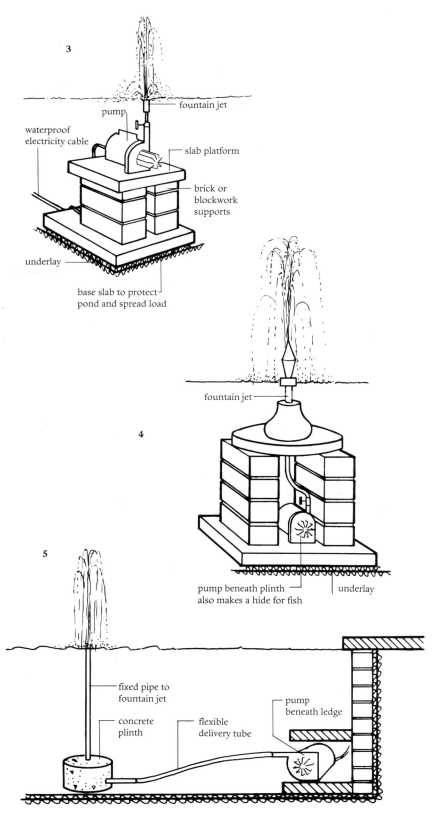

3

waterproof
electricity cable

pump

fountain jet

slab platform

brick or
blockwork
supports

underlay

base slab to protect
pond and spread load

4

fountain jet

pump beneath plinth
also makes a hide for fish

underlay

5

fixed pipe to
fountain jet

concrete
plinth

flexible
delivery tube

pump
beneath ledge

Installation

For the simplest fountain feature, a small jet attached to a submersible pump can be bought as a single unit. The pump is set up on bricks so that the jet is held just above the water surface (diagram 3). It will need frost protection and also has the disadvantage of leaving the pump visible, although it will be partly concealed while the fountain is operating. A more attractive alternative is to build the plinth large enough for the pump to fit underneath it (diagram 4) which will also serve as a 'hide' for fish. A simple, discreet arrangement is to hide the pump at the edge of the pond and set the jet in a round plinth made of poured concrete (diagram 5). The jet can be arranged so that it is pointing absolutely vertically and subsequent cleaning of the pump filter will not disturb its positioning.

For a larger pond, however, it is better for the pump to be near the edge, perhaps installed in a chamber covered with a concrete slab which can be removed for access to the pump (diagram 2). A flexible tube can lead out to a fountain plinth, built in brick with the protruding pipework or a purpose-made fountain ornament emerging from it. Water can enter the chamber through a fine mesh, or, better still, via perforated pipes buried in shingle or gravel in the pond base. This will largely solve the problem of jets becoming blocked.

If several jets are operated by the same pump, each must have its own control valve, so that you can balance the heights of the jets. Water always takes the line of least resistance, and will tend to flow strongest at the nearest jet, or down the pipe of the largest diameter with fewest bends.

3-5 Jet fountains with submersible pumps

Pumps installed within the pond may be exposed or concealed, and with both methods (outlined below) the plinth must be strong enough to take the weight of a plank for access to the pump to adjust it or clear the filter, otherwise you will have to get into the pond. With remote installation, which is also suitable for waterfalls, cascades and streams, the pump is easily cleared of debris from the pond side. Installation in a chamber outside the pond (diagram 2) provides the best means of access to pumps for larger water features.

3 Exposed pump installation

Attach a small jet to the pump and set it on a plinth or stand within the pond so the jet is held just above the water surface. On a large paving slab, build two columns of bricks or blockwork to the required height. A smaller slab on top of the plinth provides a platform for the pump. Run the waterproof electricity cable down the side of the plinth and across the bottom of the pond, with a waterproof connector to join it to the main supply.

4 Concealed pump installation

Conceal the pump by constructing a simple plinth for the fountain stand or ornament, under which the pump can sit. Set the plinth on a concrete block, stone or slab at least 10cm/4in high to prevent the pump picking up the detritus that falls to the bottom of the pond. Make a hole in the upper slab through which to run the rigid delivery tube to the jet.

5 Remote pump installation

Construct a ledge at the side of the pond to hide the pump and run a flexible delivery tube to a concrete plinth set on the base of the pond. Set a vertical rigid supply pipe firmly in the plinth.

6 Casting a raised free-standing basin

Make a plywood template shaped to the profile you have designed, to fit the radius of the bowl. Attach it with wire to a firm tube hammered vertically into the ground through a heap of sand. Revolve the template through the sand to form the curved underside of the basin. Pour in a strong mix of concrete using a fine aggregate, preferably reinforced with mesh. Raise the template to the desired thickness of the concrete and revolve it again to make the shape for the top of the basin.

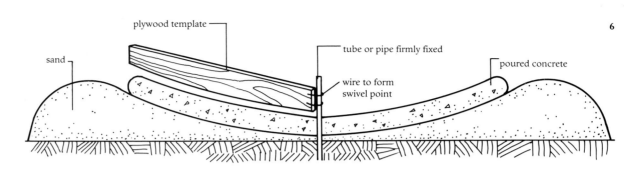

plywood template

sand

tube or pipe firmly fixed

wire to form swivel point

poured concrete

6

Taking separate pipes to each fountain from close to the pump is an ideal solution if they are all to be controlled from one place. However, in a long narrow pond with a line of jets this would be extravagant on pipework and unnecessarily expensive. In this case a single large-diameter pipe running the length of the pond could feed smaller diameter pipes linked to each jet. The large diameter of the manifold pipe relative to the others cuts pipe friction to a minimum and ensures that there is a fairly even pressure to each jet before final adjustments are made.

Fountain basins

Fountain basins are shallow in form, with the bowl at least as wide as the spread of the fountain. Water is pumped to the jet or jets through a central feed pipe in galvanized or stainless steel, copper or rigid plastic. The area on which the basin stands should be well-compacted.

For a small garden, a premoulded basin in concrete or GRP is the obvious choice. If the basin is large enough, an inner wall of squared stone or brick can be built inside the pool to hide the preformed structure. In a private garden where the wall is not likely to be disturbed, it is not even necessary to cement it: the stone can be laid dry and capped with wide pieces of heavy stone of the same type.

For large features and to support heavy ornaments in cast or moulded concrete or stone, concrete is the best material for the basin. Flexible liners in conjunction with stone or brickwork will allow for the construction of complex shapes.

Constructing a concrete basin

Simple, round fountain basins can be made from poured or sprayed concrete. When excavating the site, allow for a compacted base of hardcore and the required thickness of concrete. Mould the inner surface of the basin by means of a plywood template, the length of the radius shaped to the profile you have designed for the basin. Attach this to a firm central tube and then revolve it through the wet concrete to produce the

basin shape. The tube can be used to supply water to the jet or, if not required, may be pulled out and the hole blocked off with concrete. To make a raised, free-standing basin for which the underside needs to be carefully shaped, the template can first be drawn around a pile of sand to produce a temporary mould into which you pour the concrete, and the inner surface formed as above (diagram 6).

Once the technique has been mastered, you can form more intricate shapes, for example by shaping the end of the template to form a flat-edged rim.

Make the basin with a level rim, which can, if you wish, be capped with an attractive stone. An interesting rough texture can be produced for the basin by using round aggregate in the concrete mix and spraying the uncured concrete with water until the pebbles are exposed.

Basins with flexible liners

The method of constructing a fountain basin with a flexible liner is identical to that for an ordinary formal pond (see pp.54-7). Take care, though, to allow for the weight of the fountain ornament. The base beneath the liner should be well-compacted and protected with a suitable underlay, and the top of the liner similarly protected from the base of the fountain. For a small fountain, a flat slab can be laid on the base and the fountain ornament built on top of this. For large ornamental structures a concrete slab may be cast on the bottom to spread the load, or for neatness the whole base can be concreted over to a thickness of 10-15cm/4-6in, with reinforcing, if necessary. Take extra care when moving ornaments, for the risk of damage is increased by the anvil effect where the liner is caught between two unyielding surfaces.

The use of a flexible liner greatly facilitates the construction of complex geometrical shapes where stone or brickwork walls are desired. Any shape can be constructed on a level concrete base without the need to make the structure waterproof, the liner being simply brought up behind the wall and fixed in place with a poured concrete haunching.

Every corner of Anthony Noel's tiny walled garden in Fulham, London, is used to advantage.

Terracotta pots of clipped box are an integral part of the design of the elegant water feature. They stand on a loose flagstone that covers a small underground water tank. From here a submersible pump pushes the water up via a copper pipe chased into the wall, to emerge through the lion's mouth. An overflow pipe from the sink conducts the water back to the tank beneath. The pots planted with box disguise the bricks on which the stone sink has been raised to an appropriate height beneath the water spout.

Wall fountains

Some of the smallest, and most rewarding, water features are wall fountains, or spouts, through which water splashes into bowls, basins or sinks. Ideal for town gardens, patios, small enclosed courtyards and even for balconies, they occupy little space, while offering the refreshing sight and sound of moving water. Wall fountains should look appropriate in their setting, and must function well mechanically. The advent of small reliable submersible pumps has made this aim much easier to achieve.

Spouts, perhaps in the form of a wall mask, may be of stone, terracotta, lead or a more ambitious material such as bronze, glass or stainless steel. Basins may be small, and wall-mounted, or larger and sited on the ground beneath the spout. Old-fashioned porcelain sinks, solid handcut stone troughs, antique lead cisterns beautifully and elaborately cast, matured oak casks (with every trace of their original contents removed) – all make suitable receptacles. An attractive lined basin can be built against an existing masonry wall, with liner held in place by lead flashing set in a mortar joint on the wall, folded down over the liner and embossed with a pattern. The sides and front can be built up in materials to match the wall.

Because the volumes of water involved are so small, splashing must be reduced to a minimum, and this governs the height of the spout above the basin. As a basic guide, the height of the spout should be equal to the diameter of the basin. This rule of thumb may, however, be modified by the presence of strong air currents, which deflect the flow and reduce the quantity of water falling into the basin. Whether the water breaks up *en route* or falls in a continuous stream also determines water loss through splashing. If in doubt, keep the drop to a minimum; this can be easily done in the case of a free-standing basin by raising it off the ground. When installing a small water feature of this kind, always ensure that there is provision for flow adjustment.

The water may also fall into stones or gravel, flow into a 'stream' or be directed from the spout into a purpose-built formal pool or rill.

Installation

Whatever the design of the external features, the water circulation system must be carefully planned. You may be fortunate enough to have a conveniently situated permanent natural water supply, such as a spring or rivulet, that can be tapped by running a pipe downhill to the back of the spout. If this is the case, provide the basin or pool into which the water spills with an overflow system through which the water is redirected to continue on its course, or, better still, take further advantage of the natural water supply by routing it via a bog garden.

In most wall fountains, the water is circulated by a miniature submersible pump inside the pool or basin. Such systems are simple to install but make it difficult to disguise the delivery pipe and the electricity supply cable feeding the pump itself. Also, if the basin is small, there is very little water reserve to operate the system continuously; this is particularly crucial in hot climates where the water in a basin 30cm/1ft in diameter and, say, 20cm/8in deep would quickly be consumed through evaporation and splashing. In summer a small, wall-mounted basin may have to be topped up from the watering can on a daily basis.

It is preferable to install the pump in a separate, larger, underground reservoir sited close by (diagram 7). The pump, and its related pipework and cable, can be readily accommodated in this tank and the whole disguised with a removable cover, such as a large flagstone, at ground level. The water may need to be topped up if there is loss through evaporation or splashing. A float valve may be installed to ensure a permanent supply of water in the system, but will entail laying a feed pipe from the mains water.

For best effect, the pipe from the tank to the spout must be invisible. The simplest way of achieving this is to drill a small hole through the bottom of the wall on which the spout is to be mounted and to take the pipe from the reservoir through to the other side of the wall and up into the back of the spout. A short run of 15mm/½in pipe on the back of the wall can be disguised or hidden, perhaps by planting, if necessary. If the pipe must remain on the same side of the wall as the water feature, consider mounting the spout or wall mask on a small brick or stone pier built out from the wall, which contains a cavity that serves as a conduit for the pipe. This is preferable to cutting a channel for the pipe, which is likely to disfigure the wall, and as long as it is executed in the same material as the wall, it will look like part of the original structure.

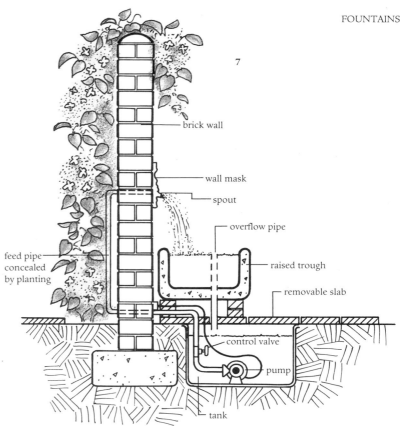

7

brick wall

wall mask

spout

overflow pipe

feed pipe concealed by planting

raised trough

removable slab

control valve

pump

tank

7 Installing a closed-system wall fountain
The water is pumped from the tank up a concealed pipe into a spout or jet, from which it spills into a container and returns to the tank via an overflow. A removable slab gives access to the pump and control valve. Conceal the feed pipe to the spout by running it behind the wall and planting around it or by boxing it in a channel of masonry on the feature side of the wall.

LEFT *Cleverly designed to capitalize on a steeply sloping site and well-constructed, this deep basin, though new, has a timeless air. The large body of water has ample reserves to operate the attractive stone waterspouts without the need for any extra tank or chamber. A natural water supply higher up the incline could also be exploited in a situation such as this.*

WATER STAIRCASES

A stylized water staircase in natural or polished stone, concrete or brick is essentially a formal feature that terminates in a pool or basin from which the water is pumped back to the top of the feature for recirculation. Although formal in concept it can harmonize well with a natural setting of trees and sloping ground. It may be more aptly sited in the farther regions of the garden although, provided there is suitable terracing or raised ground on which to construct it, there is no reason why it should not be as near to the house as a pond. In some of the great formal gardens of the past where no high ground was available, staircase cascades were constructed on an artificial mound.

The staircase should have a balanced look, with even weight in wall, balustrade and planting applied each side. If it is visually separated from other architectural features of the garden, its design can be as fanciful as you like; but the work must be well-executed and the materials should work well with those used in the surroundings

The surface over which the water flows may be constructed with bricks, sawn stone, field stones, cobblestones, timber – even railway sleepers; or any suitably hard, sculptural material such as slate or bronze. Splashing and evaporation losses are probably greater in cascades than in any other type of feature, so it is vital to construct an integral waterproof shell. The most satisfactory method is to construct a stepped concrete ramp (diagram 8) and face it with brick or stone blocks. These channel sections have great strength, and the stone or brickwork can be fitted into them in any configuration. Concrete alone, either block, poured or sprayed, may be used for the base. However, because there is always the risk, particularly for long cascades, that ground movement will cause the base to fracture, it is best also to provide a waterproof lining of butyl or EPDM to prevent water from being lost via leaks while the feature is in operation. The flexible liner can be laid in one piece, extending down and overlapping with the liner in the pond or catchment tank that provides the reserve of water for the feature. This will ensure that all the water returns. The upturned sides of the liner must be several centimetres/inches above the top of the spillway treads so that the water is funnelled into the centre.

8 Constructing a water staircase
On sloping ground, excavate a series of steps or a continuous ramp (which is easier to line) set well into the ground. Allow for the thickness of the facing material – brick or stone – and the concrete base. Excavate a pool or catchment tank in which to place a submersible pump. Bury the pipe that will take the water from the pump in the pond to the top of the staircase. Line the pond. Cover the ramp with one piece of liner, making generous allowance to come up the sides and to overlap the pond liner at the bottom. Over the liner, construct a base of poured concrete. Build the steps in decorative stone or brick, bringing the liner up behind the walls or between double walls.

Set a large slab across the top 'tread' of the staircase to conceal the incoming water supply.

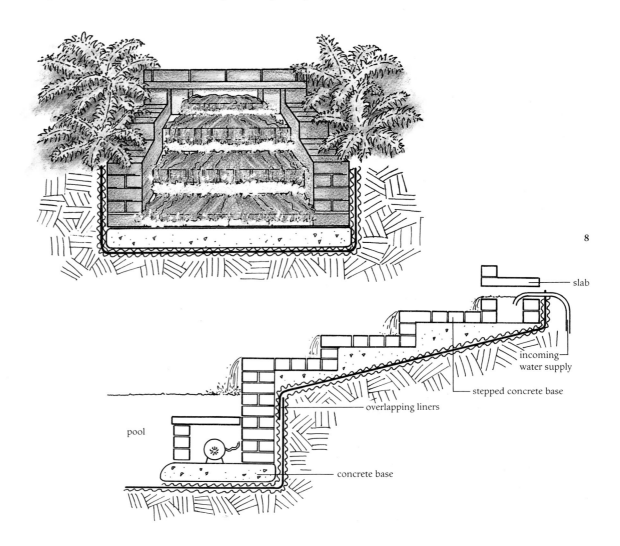

8

slab

incoming water supply

stepped concrete base

overlapping liners

concrete base

pool

STREAMS AND WATERFALLS

The character of a stream is determined by the setting through which it flows. A level ditch running through a meadow, for example, might have rough grass to the water's edge interspersed with the occasional clump of native iris or rush and would be easy to emulate. Where a change of level is required, a low waterfall can be created using a minimum of rock. This should appear as though the water, through its more rapid movement at this point, has exposed an underlying stone outcrop. Where ground slopes steeply, rocks of various sizes, including boulders and field stones, can be used to construct rapids.

By varying the shapes of rocks and the way the spillways are formed, it is possible to achieve a series of falls of great variety and ingenuity. Such details must be left to the artistic flair (and engineering skills) of the individual. Most important is that the waterfall should look uncontrived and function well mechanically.

Designing a stream

At its simplest, an artificial stream is a shallow ditch lined with concrete and/or flexible liner, covered in gravel or earth. Most rewarding for the gardener is the stream that meanders between banks on which hosts of water plants drift in gentle swathes. In places, the planting may give way to grass or an occasional run of flagstones, perhaps some herringbone brickwork, field stones or timber edging, or even a winding walk of forest bark or pine needles. The longer it is, the more scope there is for variety, but a general theme should be maintained to give continuity. Plan its course, if only roughly, on paper. Try to make sure there is always some fresh aspect to enjoy – perhaps one high waterfall, or a series of low ones resembling rapids, some a single chute of water, others broken and jagged. If big enough, the stream can be widened to incorporate an island at one point (see p.103). The water might run at a higher level on one side of the island and swoop and dive to rejoin the lower level at the confluence. The complexity can be increased according to your confidence and ability; technically, almost anything is possible.

Normally a stream is constructed on a slope as a series of level sections (or very narrow ponds), and the fall in ground level is taken up with waterfalls. The construction of a weir or waterfall will control the water levels, reducing sudden fluctuations in natural streams, and ensuring, in an artificial stream, that the level of water is maintained in each section after the recirculating system has been turned off – an important consideration for the creatures populating the waters of the stream.

It is possible to design and build a stream that meanders through a level garden, its movement being caused by the rate at which water enters at one end, either from a natural source – such as a spring – or with the aid of a recirculating pump. I have created the illusion of a natural water course by allowing it to emerge into view through an old brick culvert that also disguised the chamber and delivery pipe.

In totally flat situations you can create the impression that the stream is rising in higher ground by mounding the excavated material at the head of the stream and reducing the soil levels farther down. The reverse slope can be disguised with some judiciously planted evergreen shrubs.

Safety considerations
If young children frequent the area near a stream or waterfall, unless they can be closely supervised, it should be fenced off. The steep banks of some natural streams pose serious risks and can be extremely difficult to negotiate, making the maintenance of waterside plants more of a circus stunt than a simple crouching, weeding job. Where a natural stream runs through very steep banks, cutting a narrow path alongside can assist streamside planting.

Routing the stream
Natural streams tend to run in valleys, so look at the general contours of your garden and see if there is an obvious 'valley' through which it could be led. If there is not, consider some relandscaping, using materials excavated from the stream. It should appear snug and comfortable in its surroundings. Never take the easy option of piling up the excavated material on either side to form a kind of embankment; this makes the stream look more like a canal. The soil should be graded well back from the stream edge so that a gentle slope runs down towards the water.

The feeling that a stream is running through a natural valley can be enhanced by routing it so that it skirts around the canopies of trees. The trees give a feeling of height, substance and solidity, while the stream looks as though it is taking the easiest route – as it always will in nature. Trees or grouped shrubs can be added within the meander to enhance the natural appearance. An occasional outcrop of stone might be added on the inside of a bend to give the impression that the water has been forced around this obstacle.

The marking out is best done using a long rope, a hosepipe, a sand or lime trail, or a spray marker. Do not route the stream so that it runs at a constant width as this will lack interest. Where a change in levels occurs, it should waist in like a natural stream, for this is where a waterfall will be placed. It can then widen out into small pools in between the falls. Remember not to exceed the area of the bottom reservoir (see below).

Water circulation
If the stream is to be recirculated by pumping, a large reservoir of water is essential at the bottom end, preferably in the form of a pond. In order to prevent a significant drop in water level when the system is started, the surface area of this bottom pond should be at least as great as the entire surface of the stream and all its attendant pools combined. Some simple arithmetic will show the reason for this. In order to flow over a waterfall, the water in the pool/stream section behind it must rise by some 5cm/2in. (This applies to each section of the stream.) If, for example, the area of the stream and pools were four times as great as the surface area of the bottom pond, this would result in an unsightly drop of 20cm/8in in the bottom pond, assuming that all the sections of stream were brimming at the time of switching on the pump. If there has been loss of water through capillary action, leakage or evaporation, then more water will need to be pumped before it can return to the bottom pond. Leaves and twigs that clog the mouths of the waterfalls will also reduce the efficiency of the system. I have occasionally seen streams and waterfalls that require so much water to prime them that the bottom pond has been pumped dry before the water can return.

It is important to remember that if a bottom pond is topped up while the system is running, when the pump is switched off, the stream will continue to flow down until it has reached its static level and the bottom pond may overflow dramatically.

Where it is not possible or desirable to include a sufficiently large lower pond in the scheme, the problem can be overcome by building an underground compensating tank near the lower end of the stream. The water pumped from it to the top of the stream will flow down and simply disappear underground back into the tank. However, if you are in a position to choose, I would not recommend this as an alternative to building a larger pond for not only is it more expensive to construct, it affords none of the pleasures of a pond which is, after all, always there to be seen and enjoyed.

Bury the delivery pipe clear of the stream and rockwork , and at the top of the stream construct a small rock enclosure or miniature grotto to hide the influx of water.

Excavating the stream
Because a stream on sloping ground is treated essentially as a series of separate ponds – albeit long, narrow, shallow ones – the excavation and construction of streams is similar to that of informal ponds. The fundamental difference is the change of levels, and these need to be carefully worked out.

A stream excavated with a simple 'V'-shaped profile (diagram 9) requires the minimum of work and financial outlay.

Rocks are used only for the waterfalls where levels change. Attractive in themselves, particularly when covered with mossy growths, they perform an important function in maintaining the water level within sections, even when the flow is reduced to a mere trickle or stops altogether. At the same time, by slowing the flow of water and regulating its level, they ensure that the streamside plants have a constant degree of moisture.

Slowing down the flow also reduces erosion of the banks which would, anyway, be more natural and marshy in the case of a meadow stream where there is no defined border.

9 and 10 Stream profiles
The shape of the excavation will depend on the character of the stream. The depth should allow for a concrete base and the width for any walls.

9 A 'meadow' stream
Excavate a wide, shallow 'V'-shaped profile for a stream with grassy banks. A concrete base protects the flexible liner so that the occasional rock can be placed for a natural effect.

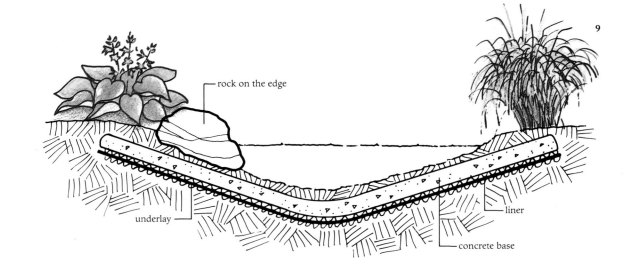

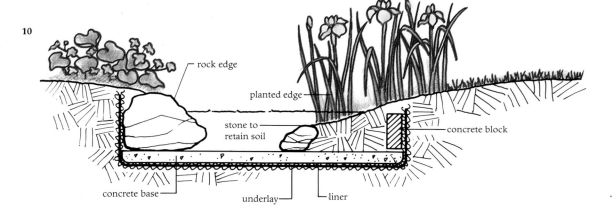

10 A rock stream
Streams with rock or planted edges are best built in a shallow 'U' shape, with a flat bottom to provide a base for rock edges or planting ledges. Bring the flexible liner up behind the rock edges or side walls. To retain soil for planting, place stones on the stream bottom and rake the soil up and over the banks.

As a general rule, the stream sections are dug as a series of 'flats' or level sections. The profile will vary according to the material used in the construction and the intended character of the stream. A meadow stream with grass running in on each side will be excavated as a shallow 'V', whereas a rock stream will be a straight-sided 'U' (diagrams 9 and 10). A planted stream more or less conforms to the planting ledges found in an informal pond, with a little extra depth in the centre, so this will also be dug as a shallow 'U'.

Always excavate sufficiently so that the lower end of each section is still below the surrounding ground level or a most unnatural appearance will result. The upstream end of each section must be below the top of the spillway rocks at the downstream end, and also deep enough so that the base of the upstream waterfall rocks will be well-hidden. This may necessitate digging the upper end of each section considerably below the ground level. The longer the reach, on steeply sloping ground, the deeper the top end must lie. Therefore it may be appropriate, in steeper places, to have shorter runs. Try, also, to avoid making each stream section exactly the same length.

Premoulded streams and waterfalls
Premoulded streams, which may also incorporate waterfall sections, are available in a variety of shapes and textures. Usually made of GRP, they are easy to install. To disguise the rim, you must plant them heavily with ground-covering and trailing plants.

Preformed waterfalls come in sections, which can be fitted together so that each slightly overlaps the next. Like GRP streams, some are moulded from natural features. Formerly available only in unnatural shades of blue and beige, they now come in more convincing colours.

They are made to look like rock so it is almost impossible to match them with natural rock – which will immediately betray their artificiality. It is therefore far better to confine them to a rock-free area. They can be softened and mellowed with creeping, carpeting plants.

Installation
Excavate a series of level steps, starting at the bottom and working up, and offering each stream section up against the next to test for height and angle. To create variety and interest, individual sections can be swivelled

round so that the falls do not enter in a straight line but at different angles. Dig to a sufficient depth to cover the base with 5cm/2in of well-tamped sand. It is essential that the ground on which the sections sit is well-compacted; use rubble or hardcore beneath the sand, to provide stability if the sections are being built into a bank. When all the levels have been dug and you have checked that there are no sharp projections that could damage the shell, position the sections. Use a spirit level and straightedge to make sure that the spillway really is the lowest point of each section; the lip over which the water flows should be 5-8cm/2-3in lower than the rest of the rim, so that the water does not spill over in another place. Be sure to make sufficient allowance for the rise of water once it is flowing. A section should not rest too heavily on the one below: once the shell is filled with water it is extremely heavy and this could cause the rim of the lower section to be pressed out of level. Once you are satisfied that all the sections are correctly positioned, partly fill each one with water while replacing the gaps around them with well-compacted sifted soil or sand.

Flexible liner streams and waterfalls

The better-quality flexible liners, such as butyl and EPDM, are ideally suited to stream construction. Their ability to move with the ground makes them suitable for long runs, and they can readily be obtained in lengths of over 30m/100ft. Edging and planting can easily be incorporated. Protection of the liner is advisable, because streams are shallow and therefore even more vulnerable than ponds. It is likely that you will overlay the stream sides and base with soil, rocks and gravel, to protect and hide all parts of the liner from view. For extra protection, first face the liner in concrete.

A series of waterfalls and pools can be lined with one continuous sheet of liner. Although there is little likelihood of water loss, if not done expertly the water will flow down between the rocks and up to the level of the fold in the liner, rather than over the rocks. Water would then need to flow into the upper pool for several minutes before rising sufficiently to surmount the rock.

This pool and stream could be made with a liner set in a shallow 'U'-shaped excavation, its upturned edges secured behind boulders or outcrops of earth where planting extends into the water. The stones, set on a concrete base, are placed at random for a convincingly naturalistic effect.

Such a pool could equally result from a pleasant afternoon splashing about in gumboots building a dam from larger stones and backfilling it with silt and gravel. This would result in a sufficiently impervious barrier to allow the water to rise up to create a shallow rock pool.

It is better to construct streams on sloping land as a series of long, shallow ponds linked by waterfalls and to line each section at a time, starting with the lowest (diagram 11).

Excavating

Excavate a 'V'- or 'U'-shaped stream bed according to the character of the stream. Where possible, cut into virgin ground for the waterfall ledge or ledges; if they must be built up, or if the ground is particularly marshy or soft, you need to make a special sub-base beneath the liner. Use hardcore, well-compacted and smoothed over with sand. It is essential that the ground should be firm and free of sharp projections. Carefully smooth out the bed of the excavation and remove all sharp stones.

Lining the lowest section

Begin with the bottom pond or lowest stream section. Cover the section with sand and protective underlay. Then position the section of liner, leaving the sides till last. Construct each waterfall before positioning the liner in the section behind it. It is important to get the liner sections securely joined at the waterfalls.

Constructing the falls

Place a further layer of underlay on the prepared ledge. Rocks up to, say, 50kg/110lb in small ponds can be bedded straight into a concrete mix. For heavier ones you will first need to lay a footing or raft of concrete on the lined ledge, approximately 10cm/4in thick, or thicker for heavier rocks. For very heavy rocks the concrete should be reinforced. The concrete spreads the load and protects the liner. Set the rocks in position as described below but do not grout them until the liner has been fixed.

Positioning the rocks

Consider the flexible liner as a waterproof bag into which to fit the rockwork. It imposes few constraints if handled correctly and if a rock is restricted you can simply dig out a little behind the liner to make room for its correct positioning.

Following the basic principles of rockwork, outlined on p.69, first position the spillway rock at the back of the ledge. This forms the sill over which the water will fall and it must be set correctly: if it is set too low, the bottom of the rocks upstream will be visible when the water is not running. The narrower the spillway, the higher the water will rise. Splitting up the fall by placing a small stone on the spillway will increase the thrust of the water, throwing it clear of the rock. This will make a modest flow look more effective. Unless the water is able to pick up some speed before it leaves the edge, it will cling to the surface of the fall in a desultory fashion: a slight run down to the brink of the waterfall is needed so that the water is thrown clear of the face.

Work out the desired finished level of the rock in advance so that you get the position right the first time. If you are dealing with rocks that weigh several tonnes/tons repositioning is extremely difficult.

I designed and constructed this series of small waterfalls (which continue out of sight at the top of the photograph) to flow down a bank into a pool near the house.

The entire system is lined in butyl sections, with the rockwork set into concrete ledges within the liner. The water is recirculated by means of a submersible pump hidden beneath a rock island in the lower pool. The delivery pipe runs up the side of the water feature to emerge at the top through a fissure in the rock.

The stream and falls are set in a 'valley' as they would be in nature with the rocks placed with the grain running in the same direction. The feature was designed for minimum maintenance so the surrounds are of gravel mulching, which conserves moisture and reduces weeds.

Iris laevigata 'Dorothy Robinson', which likes to be planted in a depth of 5-10cm/2-4in, thrives in the lower pool.

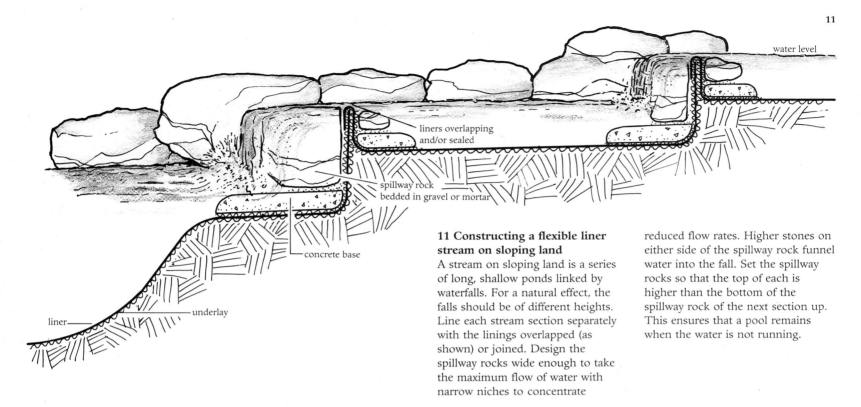

water level

liners overlapping
and/or sealed

spillway rock
bedded in gravel or mortar

concrete base

liner

underlay

11 Constructing a flexible liner stream on sloping land

A stream on sloping land is a series of long, shallow ponds linked by waterfalls. For a natural effect, the falls should be of different heights. Line each stream section separately with the linings overlapped (as shown) or joined. Design the spillway rocks wide enough to take the maximum flow of water with narrow niches to concentrate reduced flow rates. Higher stones on either side of the spillway rock funnel water into the fall. Set the spillway rocks so that the top of each is higher than the bottom of the spillway rock of the next section up. This ensures that a pool remains when the water is not running.

When the rocks are in position at the back of the ledge, smooth over the back of them with a concrete or sand and cement mix before bringing the liner up behind them.

Make sure that the liner comes at least 8cm/3in up above spillway level all round each section – to allow for the rise in water level. Also make sure that no sharp pieces of the concrete footing are sticking out at the bottom. There should be sufficient protective underlay on the ledge so that you can pull this, too, up behind the rocks at this stage. It is essential that the liner comes right up behind the waterfall spillway rock.

Now position the rocks to either side of the spillway. These should be a few centimetres/inches higher to funnel the water into the middle. Alternatively, they can be of the same height as the spillway rock, with cheek pieces set on top of each side. Set smaller rocks in the pond above, as shown in diagram 12.

Grouting the rocks

When you are satisfied with their position, carefully grout all the waterfall rocks with a strong waterproof mix of concrete, sand and cement, or self-expanding polyurethane. This ensures that the water flows over the rock rather than underneath it. The grouting can either be covered with small pieces of stone or dusted over with powdered rock. Keep the cracks between the rocks as small as possible to minimize the grouting and never grout or point flush with the rock, since it is difficult to disguise.

Deep clefts that have been grouted can be covered with gravel, grit, sediment, or clay pushed in and mosses planted.

Lining subsequent sections

Now line the next pond or stream above in the same way, and set more rocks into the back of the newly constructed waterfall. These will usually be smaller than the rocks used for the face of the waterfall, as the bottom of the pool above will be at a higher level.

At this point the two adjacent liners must be arranged behind the waterfall. If the lining material is sufficiently flexible, the liner in the upper pond or section can be folded over the top of the liner in the lower pond, as shown in diagram 11. This is quite tricky, but the rocks brought up behind the liner will hold it all in place. With less flexible lining, a satisfactory join can be made by bringing the two liners together vertically up close behind the spillway rock, cutting them off level and sealing them with mastic.

Finishing the bed and sides

Now finish the bed and sides in keeping with the design of the stream. The simplest way is with soil, gravel or rocks, but you can also use concrete. If it is 'V' shaped apply a layer of concrete 8-10cm/3-4in thick to the whole stream. If the stream profile is 'U' shaped and designed to take rock and resemble a series of rock pools, then lay a bed of concrete

The stream at Shute House in Dorset, designed by Sir Geoffrey Jellicoe, has a different mood, character and sound wherever it is encountered along its course, each fall being a different pitch on the musical scale. On a concrete base covered with pebbles, it leaps playfully downhill for a time beside lush plantings LEFT. Here the stream is crossed and recrossed by paths of large flagstones above the falls where ridge tiles set in a concrete base encourage the water into fresh frivolities. Always flowing straight, it then becomes more sedate ABOVE, changing in width and opening out into formal basins flanked by lawns, where the sides are held in trim with timber edging.

on the bottom of the stream and place the rock so as to link the waterfalls together. Break the line of rock here and there to incorporate some planting. To create enclosures for planting, place stones towards the centre of the stream, dipping down to below the water level. Backfill with soil to form a shallow flooded area, ideal for such plants as the marsh marigold (*Caltha palustris*). The stones will stop the soil from being washed away – although earth shows surprisingly little tendency to be washed away in an artificial stream, because of the constant flow and the lack of sudden spates. At the top of the stream construct a small rock enclosure or miniature grotto to hide the delivery hose and influx of water.

Concrete streams and waterfalls

For a stream with a short run, concrete block construction sides on a poured concrete bed can be used. The 23cm/9in blocks are an ideal height for this purpose, and a single course can make a good stream section. Each section, like a pond, must be an integral shell. However, a lot of work is necessary where the levels change and stone forms the waterfall. For longer stream sections concrete is not ideal because long runs are almost certain to fracture when the ground moves. The stream could be built in sections and fitted with expansion joints but this is far from satisfactory.

To form the stream sides from concrete blocks, excavate a 'U' shape and allow for the extra depth of concrete on the base. Also carefully consider the width. Even a very narrow stream will need to be dug at least 1m/3ft wide to accommodate planting on both sides.

Hand-mixed or sprayed concrete should be laid in one complete operation for each section of stream whether 'U' or 'V' shaped, using the same method of construction as for a pond. At the end of each stream section, where the waterfall will occur, the concrete, whether blockwork or hand-mixed, should be some 8cm/3in below the rest of the rim to allow for the water to spill over.

The ledges must be strong enough (reinforced if necessary) to take the weight of the rocks and wide enough to allow room for manoeuvring the rocks. Also, they should be deep enough to allow for 12-15cm/5-6in of rock beneath the surface of the pond, which in turn allows for a drop in water level in dry periods or when the waterfall is recirculating. The level of the water in each section will be dictated by the height of the rock leading to the section below. The structure should be completely finished off, including rendering, waterproofing and curing before rockwork or pebbles are introduced. Place the rocks on a bed of soft concrete mix to ensure that their weight is evenly spread on the ledge: this also helps manoeuvrability, as the rock can be pressed down until it is sitting at exactly the level and angle required. Make sure that the rockwork at each spillway is well mortared in, so that the water runs over the top of the stones, rather than underneath, or the effect will be spoilt. Do not weaken the integral concrete structure by setting rocks directly into it.

WATERFALLS ACROSS NATURAL RUNNING WATER

Waterfalls built across natural running streams to impound ponds and lakes can be infinitely varied in design and in size. If you are planning anything large-scale, you should first check that you are not breaking any law. In most parts of the world there are legal restrictions governing works on waterways. The most obvious of these concern safety: a poorly constructed dam, for example, can have catastrophic consequences. If the work involves impounding more than 23,000 cu m/5.5 million gallons of water or obstructing a watercourse, full constructional drawings need to be submitted.

Another concern is the effect on and possible inconvenience caused to neighbours up- or downstream of the work. Raising the water level in a stream can prevent the free drainage of land farther upstream, possibly causing flooding. Downstream the effect could be a variable and intermittent water supply. The increased water loss through evaporation and leakage created by an upstream pool could completely stop the flow and would have vital consequences for life downstream. It is essential that no waterfall or barrage of any kind should cause the cessation of water flow, and that some water be allowed to flow during the filling process, for fish and plant life farther downstream might be dependent upon it.

Emulating nature

Even the wavelets in a modest-sized pond can expose a fringe of rock or stones, but it is flowing water that exposes rocks in their most beautiful and varied forms. A natural running stream will quickly work away at the soft material of its banks, exposing the larger boulders and outcrops, which will cause it to turn this way and that looking for the line of least resistance. It is this alternation of hard and soft materials that makes the walk along a stream so fascinating; one moment it rushes between close jaws of stone, the next it may swirl into a deep cauldron, then spread out gently amid rushes and water plants, only to be checked farther on and forced into renewed contortions by more outcrops and hollows and drifts of stone. The most spectacular effects result when a bed of hard rock gives out; then waterfalls are formed – some modest, some extravagant.

It is worthwhile, before attempting any significant rockwork yourself, to go out and study nature. Observe how some rocks run in definite strata or layers, whereas other formations have a more random, boulder-strewn appearance. Try to get a feel for these different rock formations, so that you can decide what might be suitable for your own project.

Damming a stream

It is possible to construct a small pool and waterfall of the most rudimentary design from a barrier of rocks and stones in a constantly running stream (diagram 12). Some slight seepage will always occur, but provided there is a reasonable flow of water this will be of no significance. Waterfalls of this kind can be considered only as temporary. The water will eventually circumnavigate the rock barrage and pour straight around the sides or underneath.

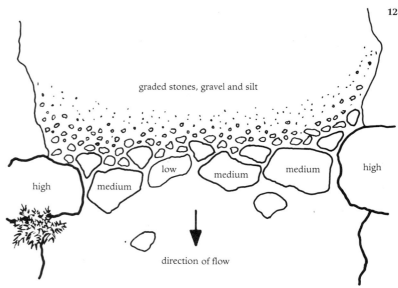

graded stones, gravel and silt

high

medium

low

medium

medium

high

direction of flow

ABOVE *Discreet but imaginative intervention diverts the flow of the small natural cascade over a sensuous lip of carved stone. Thus a corner of the garden that might otherwise have been overlooked is turned into a place of mystery and romance. A green coating of helxine (Soleirolia soleirolii) covers the wet rock around this fall which plunges into a fern-clad 'grotto'. Here is a place to pause, to enjoy the atmosphere and the sight and sound of the water.*

12 Damming a natural stream

To make a barrier, set higher rocks at the sides well keyed into the banks to prevent the water working its way round the edges. Place a low rock towards the centre of the stream, over which the water will flow, and complete the barrier with medium height rocks to take wet-weather flow. Behind the barrier, wedge successively smaller rocks into the gaps, followed by stones, gravel and finally silt, all sloped back on the upstream side of the barrier.

Constructing a durable waterfall

This is an effective way of making a watertight fall across running water. The same method of construction can be used for large and small ponds alike. With a deep valley and a high waterfall, the rockwork can be built in terraces, with each course of rock set slightly back from the fall of the one below. When backfilled with concrete, the terracing will add enormously to the strength of the dam. First, it may be necessary to divert the stream into a pipe – say, 10cm/4in in diameter – extending from well upstream of the dam to just past the point where the fall will be constructed. Water can then flow through this during the building process. Insert a bung into the downstream end when the work is completed. This will also enable you to drain down the water and release any sediment that may have accumulated above the fall.

Excavate a trench across the stream, just above the position for the waterfall, working well down into firm ground beneath the stream bed, and extend it into the banks about 1m/3ft or more.

A concrete wall and base

Now construct a wall of poured concrete, from the trench up to the chosen height of the waterfall. Simple timber shuttering must be built to provide a support for the concrete (see p.50). The wall can be continued in blockwork if preferred. If the wall is more than 1m/3ft high or 2m/6½ft long, add some reinforcing bars or steel mesh. Concrete or brickwork should be brought up several centimetres/a few inches higher at the sides to funnel the water through the centre.

13 and 14 Constructing a durable waterfall in a natural stream

A concrete wall built across the stream and well-keyed into the banks and the stream bed, makes a watertight fall in running water.

13 Constructing the wall and base

Divert the water into a pipe before excavating the trench across the stream and constructing the concrete wall and base. Extend the base about 1m/3ft in front of the wall to form a splash plate several centimetres/inches below the proposed water level.

Set the rocks in position as shown in diagram 14, with the low rock that forms the spillway at the same height as the concrete wall. Pour concrete between the rocks and the wall. Set flat pieces of rock on the concrete wall and push gravel and shingle behind them.

14 Arranging the rocks

First position the central, low rock that forms the spillway or sill over which the water will fall. Then set rocks on either side of it a few centimetres/inches higher so that they funnel the water into the middle of the fall and over the spillway. The high rocks adjacent to the stream bank keep the water on its course.

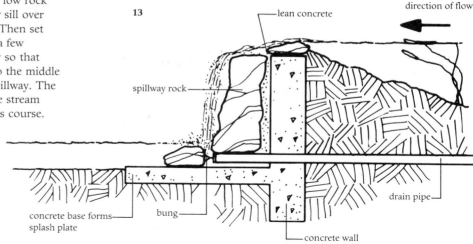

The spillways should be as wide as possible to allow for increased flow after heavy rain. A wide spillway will cope with a far greater volume of water with little significant rise in water levels. If you let the rocks form a spillway of two levels, the lower one can be quite narrow, so that even a small flow of water will be apparent and make a pleasing sound. A much wider one set 3-5cm/1-2in above this will act like a safety valve and accommodate the large volumes of water likely in times of spate.

At the same time that you construct the wall, pour a horizontal base of concrete, extending about 1m/3ft or so in front of it. This provides a base for the rock facing and a splash plate, to break the force of the water (diagram 13). Water falling from even a modest height on to an unprotected stream bed would scoop out a deep basin, and this could eventually undermine the structure. Place the splash plate several centimetres/inches below the proposed water level to ensure that the falling water actually lands in the water. River stones can hide the concrete.

Arranging the rocks

Place the rocks in position as described in diagram 14, following the basic principles of rockwork (p.69). Pour liquid concrete down between the rocks and the wall and grout all other rockwork with sand and cement. Cover deep clefts with gravel, grit, sediment or a layer of clay in which moss can be planted. Flat pieces of similar rock can be set on the concrete wall with gravel and shingle pushed in behind them.

Encourage mosses and lichens on fresh rockwork by spraying with the water left after boiling rice, with milk or yoghurt, or diluted farmyard manure.

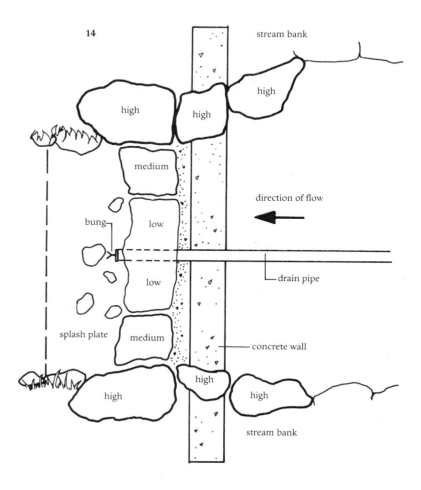

OPPOSITE *Immortalized in Monet's paintings, the Japanese bridge overhung with wisteria spans the water lily garden at Giverny. The French Impressionist's well-loved water lilies have inspired many gardeners and contributed much to the popularity of water gardening in this century.*

BELOW *Decorative as well as functional, natural rocks embedded directly in the base form stepping stones across an informal pool. Brightly coloured koi congregate where they know that people pass and there is a chance of titbits.*

Special features and leisure pools

The attraction of a water garden and the pleasure of having water on your property can be greatly enhanced by the addition of one or more special features. Anticipate the ways in which you wish to enjoy the water, providing access to it or across it. A row of stepping stones is a simple and practical embellishment, so appealing that it can be added simply for the fun of it. I once constructed a random row leading across a lake to an island using millstones arranged so that two people could leap across hand in hand, either side by side or one in front of the other. The stones were raised on circular brick columns, so that they appeared to rest upon the water like giant water lily pads.

Bridges may be beautiful as well as functional. The Chinese 'full moon' bridge, found also in Japan, is constructed in a perfect semicircle, so that its reflection completes the circle. Other Chinese and Japanese bridges were built in zigzag form, in the belief that demons could only move in a straight line: once an island or garden had been rid of its demons (by exploding firecrackers), the bridge would prevent their return. This fascinating style of bridge is often now used in Western countries to enable people to walk among water iris beds.

Decking or staging makes a valuable extension to the seating area in the garden and a platform from which to enjoy the pond. If carefully contrived, it can create the impression of a larger pond. Indeed, the presence of a landing stage implies a substantial body of water, and walking along solid planks, perhaps bordered on either side by banks of reed or water iris, gives a feeling of being transported from the terrestrial to the aquatic world. If your pond is large enough to justify one, an island will provide a sanctuary for wildfowl.

A swimming pool makes an ornamental, as well as an enjoyable, addition to the garden if its site and design are carefully considered. On the other hand, people who no longer use pools for swimming can convert them into fish ponds or water gardens.

The most obvious feature for enhancing a water garden is lighting, not only to provide safety around a pond or pool but also to endow it with a luminous quality after dark.

LIGHTING

Water is a strong attraction and powerful lure by day; after dark, if well lit, it can be quite magical. Lighting can sharpen and enhance many aspects of the pond or swimming pool and strikingly different effects can be achieved according to whether it is above or below the surface.

Surface lighting

Plants and objects illuminated above and around a pond by well-placed lights will be reflected with startling clarity in the dark water. Each water iris, each rhododendron or cascade of clematis or bougainvillea will be vividly duplicated. The image is so strong that a reflected wall or stonework appears to be a solid structure.

The light source should never be visible – nor, of course, should any of the cables or equipment related to it. Lamps should be well hidden behind rocks, shrubs or special enclosures – or, alternatively, well up in the tops of trees and buildings – remembering that people's gaze is normally directed horizontally or downwards. Light should play upon the plant or object you wish to illuminate; it should not shine directly on

the water because this creates an unsubtle effect.

Fountains and sculptures need to be picked out by a spotlight. This can be achieved with laser lighting. The light itself can be installed in a weatherproof chamber and a copper template cut and fitted over the lamp so that the beam falls only on the object. This enables people to walk all around a pond containing a central, illuminated sculpture without being dazzled by shafts of light coming from the other side of the pond. However, tall, narrow fountain jets are shown to their best advantage when lit from close beneath the nozzles.

Underwater lighting

Like surface lighting, underwater lighting should be well concealed, so that only the light and not its source is seen. Lights tucked under rocks and ledges around the sides, and shining towards the middle, are most effective. For a fountain, a light placed just beneath the surface, shining upwards so that it follows right up through the path of the water, is ideal; clusters of three or more lights can be arranged around the jet of a large fountain.

Underwater lights illuminate every underwater detail, every rock, aquatic plant and fish – as well as decaying leaves and clumps of algae. They quickly become dimmed by descending mud particles and coatings of algae, and need cleaning at fairly frequent intervals. Another drawback is that because mains voltage lights must be of very high quality for safety reasons, underwater lighting tends to be more expensive than the equivalent surface lighting. Here low voltage could be a good option.

Fibre optic lighting is becoming popular for underwater and surface lighting. The light is transmitted from a bright projector lamp inside a box (placed outside the water feature) along a flexible fibre-optic rod – either a single large one or a bunch of smaller ones. All sorts of effects can be achieved, and the light, being cool, can be used under water safely with less build-up of algae and scale.

Lighting installation

The switches for all garden lighting (and any pumps, too) should, for convenience, be located inside the house. The main electricity supplies out into the garden should be in armoured cable buried at a depth to conform to local regulations, normally some 60cm/2ft under the ground. It can be terminated in an approved weatherproof box fastened to a short stake above the ground. Metal boxes must be properly earthed or grounded. Before tightening cable glands or earth tag screws, ensure that any paint that might prevent a good connection has been scraped away down to bare metal. Some underwater lights come with waterproof cable attached, and this can be taken up out of the pond via a suitable route and connected up through the bottom of the box to the terminal block.

Many submersible lights, particularly those intended for swimming pools, are low voltage; these operate through a transformer, which can be housed inside the weatherproof box beside the pond or installed in a garden shed or garage with the low-voltage cables laid straight outside to the pond. The mains supply for this transformer can be switched wherever it is convenient – if possible, within the house. There is one problem, however, in that long runs of more than 30m/100ft will require heavy cables, otherwise a considerable voltage drop will occur. Therefore, the transformer should be installed as close to the lights as is practical. Transformers for low-voltage lights come in many different ratings, from those able to run just two or three lights to those capable of operating many lamps simultaneously.

If numerous outside lights of normal voltage are required, the armoured feed cable can be trenched around the garden and looped up from light to light. Some lights will permit the entry and exit of such a cable; others require a short length of cable leading from them to a small junction box let into the main armoured cable. Some may come with special mountings for direct fixing to a junction box. These lights will all switch on and off together if wired in parallel with two-core cable, but by using multiple-core cable you can arrange separate switching.

When fountain or waterfall pumps are to be run together with lighting, these will need to be separately switched and fused inside the house or other building. At least a four-core armoured cable will be needed.

All outside wiring should be protected by a safety trip or circuit breaker. Unless you are skilled in wiring, or if you have any doubts whatsoever, consult an electrician.

OPPOSITE AND RIGHT *I designed this tea or barbecue platform to be enjoyed by day as well as by night. Access is by a simple bridge, constructed from sawn oak, which draws the eye to the deck area and to invite exploration of the woods beyond.*

The glow of artificial light lends a magical intimacy to this area once night has fallen. Lights set unobtrusively in the trees high above create sharp reflections. Submerged lamps pick out aquatic plants and fish. A standard lamp provides a high level of illumination by the barbecue and millstone table.

When the green light mounted beneath the bridge is used alone, intensifying the green of nearby ferns, the setting takes on an ethereal quality.

Do not illuminate too brightly or you will lose the mysterious and seductive quality of the water garden by night.

STEPPING STONES

Stepping stones should be designed in harmony with the water feature and provided for at the planning stage. (You would not, of course, position them where steep sloping sides run down into deep water.) For example, a waterfall can form an almost ready-made crossing point and the addition of one or two well-selected boulders behind the lip will make it look less contrived and regular while increasing mobility around the garden.

Although especially suitable for informal ponds, stepping stones can also be incorporated into formal ponds, where squares of the stone or bricks used for the surrounds can be continued across the water. They need not follow a straight course nor, indeed, be the same size. The idea can be exploited to a point at which the area of stepping stones is almost equal to that of the surface of the water, and by imaginatively adjusting the pond edges one can achieve a fascinating interplay between water and solid ground.

For obvious reasons the stones should always be set securely. On natural and clay pond bases, large, heavy stones – provided they are of the right height – can be placed straight on the bottom if it is sound. If the ground is spongy or unstable, they must be set either in concrete or on a stable bed of stone chippings or gravel. In deep water, stone or brick columns can be built up from concrete footings, and the stepping stones embedded into these at the correct level.

In a liner pond stepping stones can be set on stone or brick piers (diagram 1). If the ground is extremely marshy, stabilize it by tipping in some rubble or stone chippings; smooth over the surface with fine grit or sand, followed by a layer of protective underlay, then install the pond liner. Place a further layer of underlay on top of the liner and then build up the column on a 'raft' or platform of concrete.

Where stepping stones have to be built up from a steep slope, a 15cm/6in layer of concrete can be laid down the slope and out across the bottom of the pond to form a good stable 'toe'. Horizontal ridges can be trowelled into this before it sets, to provide support for brick or stonework for the vertical columns.

BRIDGES, LANDING STAGES AND CAUSEWAYS

The function of a bridge should never be ignored and it should always be placed where it would have a practical justification. A neck at the far end of a pond, a narrow section of a stream or two promontories in natural rock would all make suitable bridging points. In a formal pond a bridge could be placed anywhere to become part of the geometry or design.

Bridges constructed in a single clear span can be used for any pond or stream; provided they have adequate footings and support outside the rim of the pond, the construction method used for the pond itself is of little significance. The bridge may be made of timber, steel, or cast iron, and I have seem small suspension bridges of various sorts, including one version spanning a river in the Ardennes that consisted of a single long plank cradled by loops of steel that were suspended from steel cables, securely moored between two stout trees. The regular users of this bridge were a flock of rather apprehensive-looking sheep.

Concrete and flexible liner ponds can easily receive timber, stone or steel bridges. Where upright supports are to be placed within the pond itself, they are anchored in a concrete base, or 'raft' (diagrams 2 and 3). If the bridge is high, a strong wind blowing down a pond can cause

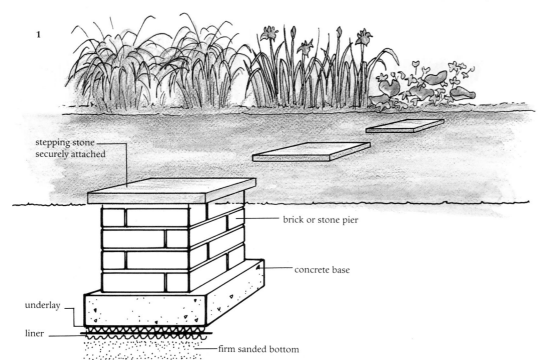

stepping stone securely attached

brick or stone pier

concrete base

underlay

liner

firm sanded bottom

1 Supports for stepping stones
Except in shallow water, set stepping stones on raised supports to adjust them to the water level. Make sure the base of the pond is firm and well compacted and, in ponds with flexible liners, protect the liner with underlay. Build the stone or brick supports on a series of concrete 'rafts' or on a continuous pad of concrete to spread the load and provide stability. Bed the stepping stones in concrete on the supports. Bridge piers within a pond and posts for landing stages and causeways can be constructed in the same way.

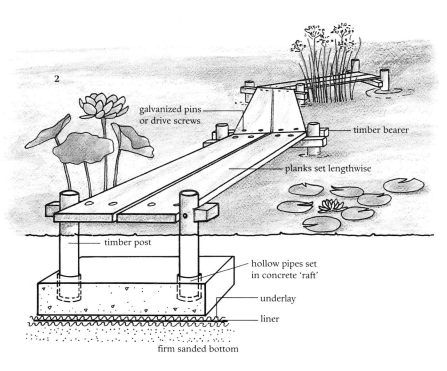

2

galvanized pins
or drive screws

timber bearer

planks set lengthwise

timber post

hollow pipes set
in concrete 'raft'

underlay

liner

firm sanded bottom

2 and 3 Timber bridges, landing stages and causeways

Timber constructions can be designed in many different ways but the essential difference is in how the timber is laid: lengthwise to lead you on or crosswise to encourage you to linger. In all cases, use hardwood or treated softwood at least 5-7.5cm/ 2-3in thick. Make sure the base of the pond is firm and well compacted beneath concrete 'rafts', 15-20cm/6-8in thick.

2 Chinese zigzag style

Set lengths of hollow pipe into the concrete 'raft' to take the posts. The pipes not only simplify the construction of the bridge but also make it easier to replace timber posts that have rotted under water. Cut notches into the posts and securely bolt timber bearers in position to support the planks and attach these with galvanized pins or drive screws.

3 Decking style

Set or mount the posts in a collar of concrete or on concrete blocks, secured with galvanized angle irons. Use string lines and a spirit level to ensure that the posts are aligned and vertical. Support the decking on timber bearers that run at right angles to it, like joists under floorboards. Run the bearers through mortices or bolt them to notches cut into the posts. Attach the decking boards to the bearers from the top, using galvanized pins or drive screws, with a 1cm/⅜in space between each so that rain water runs off the bridge to assist in the drying process. Make one of the end posts a suitable height for holding onto or for mooring a boat.

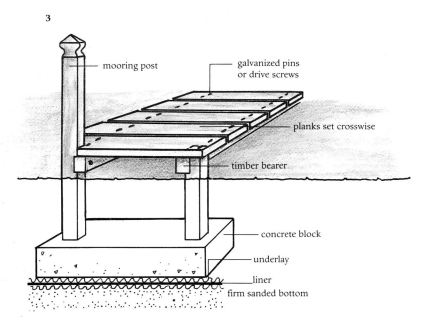

3

mooring post

galvanized pins
or drive screws

planks set crosswise

timber bearer

concrete block

underlay

liner

firm sanded bottom

RIGHT *The simplicity of this plank bridge is charming yet it is practical and robust enough to take a small garden tractor, as well as wheelbarrows, across the pond in safety.*

Planks are best in hardwood (from a renewable source) at least 5-7.5cm/2-3in *thick or in a thicker, treated softwood. Railway sleepers, either whole or sawn down, would be suitable. In all cases, the ends must be well supported and, in soft ground, the bridge should be placed on wooden supports laid parallel to the banks on each side of the water.*

considerable lateral pressure upon it, calling for increased width in the concrete 'raft' and increased mass of the concrete slab into which the uprights are set. Always construct securely, and provide strong handrails for curved bridges, or where there is any danger of slipping. Provide a lower handrail or rope if small children are to use the bridge.

Landing stages and causeways are, in essence, open-ended bridges that provide access from dry land through the shallows to clear water, where, if only in your imagination, a boat can come alongside. They make attractive features in their own right and can help create the illusion of size. Of course the pond must be reasonably large to begin with; anything less than 15x12m/50x40ft would not accommodate one comfortably. Their construction is the same as a wooden bridge spanning the pond: rot-proof wooden posts (either of hardwood or of treated softwood) set in pairs at intervals and bridged by timber bearers that support the cross planks. The distance separating the posts depends on the length of the bearers, but it should never be such a span that they will sag in the middle under the weight of the decking planks: about 2.5-3m/8-10ft is a reasonable length. The cross planks should have a gap of about 1cm/⅜in between them to prevent water from collecting. The height of the landing stage should be such that the bearers are always above the water. The width can vary according to the use to which it will be subjected, and to some extent it will be in proportion to the length. A width much less than 1m/3ft is impractical. The main cross members can be jointed and bolted through, using coach bolts or studding, preferably galvanized. It is a good practice, and also attractive, to leave one post at the end taller than the rest by about 60-90cm/2-3ft, cutting away the end plank as required, and to serve as a mooring post (diagram 3). The deck planks can be fixed with galvanized pins or drive screws.

DECKING

Lying on sun-warmed wooden planks with water lapping just beneath you is an exceedingly soothing sensation, for from this dry vantage point you can observe the play of light on the surface as well as the life within the pond.

Decking is constructed in much the same way as a landing stage, though it is usually more extensive and tends to run parallel to the edge of the pond. There is plenty of scope for imaginative arrangements, for instance with decking in an octagonal shape, or set at an obtuse angle partly overlapping the pond. Essentially most of the construction of decking can be done on dry land. The bearers project over the hard edge without the need for further support in the pond itself (diagram 4).

If you wish to make the water appear to run well back beneath the decking, it is important not to position the structure too high. The effect is spoiled if the edge of the pond is visible and the limited extent of the

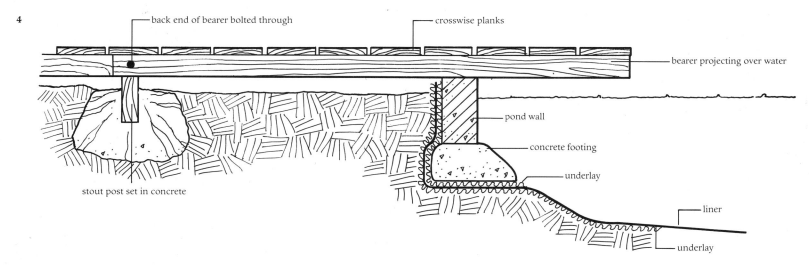

4   back end of bearer bolted through   crosswise planks   bearer projecting over water   pond wall   concrete footing   underlay   liner   underlay   stout post set in concrete

4 Decking or landing stages projecting over the pond
Decking need not extend far over the water but it is important to set it low so that the water surface disappears and the pond edge is hidden.

If the pond does not have a solid edge, build brick or blockwork supports on concrete bases. Set stout posts in concrete to hold the back end of the bearers at the same height as the edge of the pond. Bolt the bearers to the posts and attach the decking boards, at right angles, and approximately 1cm/⅜in apart, using galvanized pins or drive screws.

For decking or landing stages that project further over the water, build additional supports within the pond (diagrams 1, 2 and 3).

OPPOSITE *A sturdy timber terrace links the house with the 'L'-shaped informal pool in a Dutch garden. While decking often continues some distance out over the water, this well-constructed platform is firmly based on dry land, and the clump of Alchemilla mollis emphasizes this connection.*

In areas where children are likely to play, it is important to remember the hazards of water. Here a shallow ledge runs beneath the decking. Doubling as a planting ledge, this ingenious safety feature means that anyone stepping off the deck will find themselves just ankle deep in flowering rushes (Butomus umbellatus) and pickerel weed (Pontederia cordata).

overhang apparent. Furthermore, with a deep gap, the reflection of the structure itself in the water can become too dominant. If the decking is low, the back edge of the pond – which is not seen – can be constructed quite cheaply, say from concrete blocks.

Hardwoods (from a renewable source) or softwoods can be used – the hardwood left untreated to weather to its own beautiful natural silver or grey colour. Softwood must be treated, but since some treatments are highly toxic, it is safest to do it yourself, using a product that is known to be compatible with plants and livestock. Rough-hewn oak or other hardwood looks most appropriate with old properties or in rustic locations. Some planing or sanding may be needed to remove splinters – particularly where people are likely to go barefoot.

ISLANDS

People who are planning a larger pond or lake on their property often feel that it is *de rigueur* to have an island, whether they want one or not. Personally, I think that islands are best omitted unless they can be justified for some practical reason, or unless the pond is sufficiently large for the island to seem like a natural feature. Practical reasons for incorporating an island include the preservation of cherished trees or to create an enclosure or sanctuary for animals.

There are two basic ways to form an island. One is to dig out the pond, leaving the island behind. The other is to dig out the entire pond and then put the island back. For natural or clay-lined ponds, by far the simpler and cheaper method is to leave a piece of virgin ground behind. This will greatly reduce the volume that has to be excavated and carted away, and it will allow a sizeable tree to be grown within the pond. The island banks should be treated in the same way as the edges of the pond. If the fringes of the island are likely to suffer from erosion, they should be thickly planted or edged with solid timber (see p.66). With concrete or liner construction, unless trees are involved, it is better to build the pond and add the island afterwards. In a concrete pond, build the island in blockwork or set hardwood posts into hollow concrete blocks and pack gravel around them. Attach horizontal boards to the tops of the posts to give the appearance of a natural timber edge around the island. Infill with rubble or stony subsoil and finish with 45-50cm/18-20in of topsoil.

In a liner pond, the island is set on a concrete 'raft' at least 15cm/6in deep. Use rock or stone, if available, to build up the island or 23cm/9in blockwork infilled with rubble or stony subsoil and topped with timber, stone or topsoil. If the island is to be more than 60cm/2ft high, reinforce the blockwork with spokes of galvanized wire or stainless steel to resist the thrust of the rubble within the structure.

Thinking of Dr Dolittle, a floating island might be hard to take seriously. However, a small island raft is practical and inexpensive and with a little artistic flair a natural effect can be achieved (diagram 5). Moreover, if you get bored with it in one place, you can pull it over to a new position by attaching a length of nylon rope with a weight on the other end. A cord tied to the rope just above the weight and secured to

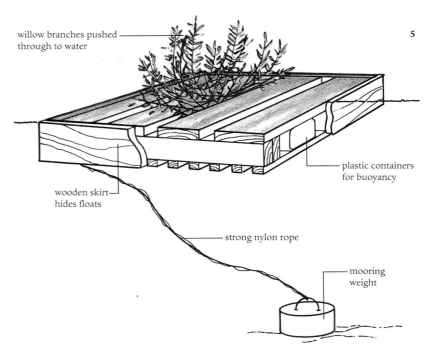

willow branches pushed through to water

5

plastic containers for buoyancy

wooden skirt hides floats

strong nylon rope

mooring weight

OPPOSITE *Apparently floating on the clear reflective water, a sweeping expanse of elegant decking is planed to a smooth and inviting finish.*

This coastal garden in Maryland, designed by Oehme and van Sweden, is an object lesson in the economic and harmonious use of three principal elements: water, timber and grass. The hard angularity of decking and furniture is offset by the soft, feathery sweeps of ornamental grasses whose beige tones echo that of the plain canvas parasol. The whole is reflected in the dark water of the pool. The effect is uncluttered, as suited to entertaining as to quiet contemplation.

5 An island raft
One or more wooden pallets anchored to a heavy weight make a simple but effective floating island. Slip plastic containers, polystyrene or cork between the top and bottom slats, to ensure buoyancy, and conceal them with a wooden skirting. With a little ingenuity you can get plants to flourish on the surface. Salix and cornus branches will sprout if they reach the water and grasses and rushes will also grow if their roots can get moisture. This structure would also take a small duck house.

the bank will enable you to move the island or pull it inshore. A lump of stone wrapped in liner or protective underlay, or a plastic container filled with sand, makes a safe weight that will not damage a pond liner.

To encourage ducks you can build a small house on the island. This can be built of timber and designed according to the type of duck. A brandy or sherry cask with an entrance cut into one end can be used on its side with a narrow plank laid out from the entrance to meet the water. Treads of batten nailed on to this will enable the ducks to ascend more easily. Contact your local ornithological or wildlife centre for advice on a suitable design.

SWIMMING POOLS

Until about the middle of this century people swam in rivers, lakes and millponds. It was great fun, even if sometimes cold and weedy. Pollution and greater awareness of hygiene have now deterred all but the most hardy from this rugged variety of swimming, and people prefer pools that are clean, clear and warm.

Any prospective swimming pool owner would be well advised to assess carefully the state of his or her finances in relation to the running costs before embarking on the project. A pool must be well maintained to remain sparklingly clear, warm and inviting. The clarity and purity of the water will depend on efficient plumbing, filtration and water treatment. Fortunately, running costs today are not as great as once they were – pool purification is becoming more cost effective every year. Most significant – at least in countries with cool summers – is the cost of heating the pool: the colder and windier the position, the more this will be. Another cost usually overlooked is that of the extra entertaining resulting when previously rarely seen friends emerge and require food and drink after an hour or two of vigorous activity. Apart from this proviso, a pool can be an excellent investment, providing fun and healthy exercise for all the family.

Siting the pool

Many people, if the truth be known, prefer to swim naked. To make this more comfortable and pleasurable, the pool and its approaches need seclusion. An attractive way of achieving this might be with trelliswork surrounds and perhaps a pergola walk, overhung with scented climbing plants. *Lonicera japonica* 'Halliana' makes a good evergreen screen with a sweet perfume from the yellow honeysuckle flowers. *Jasminum polyanthum* or *J. officinale* intertwined with a large-flowered clematis would also be suitable, or, in hot climates, *Passiflora, Hoya* and *Stephanotis*. Rampant climbing roses, with trailing, thorny shoots, should be very well tied in.

A sheltered position is important in a cool climate. Wind has a chilling

LEFT *Swimming in a natural setting is particularly pleasurable. In this unusual water garden, wooden walkways traverse a series of pools, each put to a different use but forming part of a visual whole. One pool, with its own filter system, is for swimming; others are treated as ornamental ponds where water lilies and emergent plants flourish.*

The proximity of planting that provides cover for animal life means that there is a risk of frogs, toads and newts finding their way into the swimming pool. They can be rescued if one or two small rafts are left floating on the pool surface. A plank laid from the edge into the water makes a safety ramp for them to climb out. Also, a strip of clear polythene fixed around the pool as a low wall, 30 cm/12 in high, will keep them out.

OPPOSITE *Ornamental as much as functional, this swimming pool is exceptionally well integrated into its formal setting. Reminiscent in its simple geometry of the classic Islamic pool, it becomes a decorative element in this enclosed garden largely because of its mirroring effect. This is due to the dark colour of its internal walls which allows reflections that would not be apparent in a light-coloured structure. Square paving and a well-designed wooden seat, carefully placed to preserve the symmetry of the composition, further enhance the classic design.*

effect, particularly on wet skin, and also drastically reduces the heat of an uncovered pool. Bear in mind, too, that high winds can carry poolside chairs and other objects into the pool, damaging a vinyl liner. Proximity to the house provides a greater inducement to use the pool.

Do not site the pool near trees that shed leaves every time there is a storm; leaves and twigs in the pool not only look unsightly, they can block the filtration equipment.

A normal domestic electricity supply is needed to operate the pump, lighting and heating, and if the pool is far from the mains heavy cables will be required to prevent voltage drop.

Designing the pool

Do not make the pool too big; the larger it is, the more water there is to treat chemically and also, if applicable, to heat. Unless you wish to provide for serious diving, 2m/6½ft is an adequate depth for the pool, and the width need not be more than about 4m/13ft, which will allow two people to swim side by side. In designing the pool, you should consider appropriate depths for people of different ages or swimming abilities.

Safety is of paramount importance, especially if children have access, and in parts of the United States an unclimbable fence at least 1.8m/6ft high is mandatory around the pool. If the pool is to be used by children, a large shallow area (about 1m/3ft deep) is also advisable.

Some of the design considerations that apply to formal ponds are equally relevant to swimming pool design. Early Arabic pools are an excellent model for the formal style. Sheltered and secluded, they were beautifully proportioned to fit within a walled courtyard – the surrounding area lush with scented flowers and fruit trees.

The basic rectangular pool has three main advantages: it offers the serious swimmer a straight swim up and down its length; it fits very comfortably into a walled enclosure and in a formal setting; and it can easily be fitted with a thermal or electrically operated cover. However, the pool need not be rectangular: shallow steps built into a semicircular 'Roman end' provide a safe entry point for young children, while the part that is out of their depth can be partitioned off with floats attached to a rope. Informally shaped pools can have a shallow 'beach' area with the water becoming deeper very gradually – a type of construction best suited to a concrete pool.

Unlike a pond, a swimming pool hardly ever looks completely natural because of the need for pure water and for a solid surround. Nevertheless, a great deal can be done to make the pool fit into its surroundings. Once I was called in to place rocks weighing 10 tonnes/10 tons around one side of a swimming pool and to form great outcrops with sheltered coves for sunbathing out of the wind. I planted these with cascading rock plants and large palms were placed all around. A waterfall, which one could walk behind, sent the heated, filtered water back into the pool and a rock tunnel led past this and into the pool machinery room.

It is a challenge to make swimming pools not only exciting but more

beautiful and imaginative schemes can be devised on even a modest scale, for instance with good planting. Ornamental grasses planted close to the pool are particularly effective and should be cut down once a year to encourage new growth. (Plants should never be in direct contact with the water.) The swimming pool can be combined with a garden pond or stream and waterfall feature, separated from it in an obvious way or invisibly by a sheet of thick glass beneath the surface. Lights can bring extra marvels to the pool after dark, and the poolside can become an area to be enjoyed by night as well as by day.

As for the interior of the pool, I find the shade of blue that verges on bright turquoise – though beautiful where it occurs naturally, in tropical waters – can strike a jarring note in a garden. There are plenty of alternatives. White and grey both take on pleasing tones of subtle blue, and deep green looks inviting. The colour of the house can be picked out in a band of matching tiles, which imparts a feeling of quality and permanence to the pool. I have seen pools painted black, which heats them up well, but which can seem sinister.

Choosing a construction method

The excavation, construction and plumbing of swimming pools should be carried out by professional installers. The choice of materials will depend on your budget. Liquid resin sprayed on to layers of fibreglass matting (GRP) over a concrete shell makes a long-lasting swimming pool but is very expensive. Another good method is to spray concrete on to a steel mesh or build reinforced concrete blockwork and then face it with tiles. Vinyl and PVC products within concrete blockwork or galvanized steel panels are the cheapest option, and prove very reliable.

Surrounds

Cost will be a major factor, too, in choosing a surround. Swimming pool surrounds must be well secured and constructed from non-slip materials: brick, slate, marble or other types of stone that are left 'riven', or rough, for safety. The ability to withstand constant wetting and possibly frost in winter is essential. Select brick or stone surrounds to complement adjacent structures. Grass – cool and comfortable to bare feet – can come close to the edge. Rocks, timber, pebbles and stone can all be used around the pool area.

Formally styled swimming pools usually have a bull-nosed coping around the edges, which helps return waves back into the pool. The coping can be in marble or even a terracotta finish; bricks with rounded edges are also available. Sometimes rocks are built on to the edges of pools; they may also, if safely smooth and of a non-flaking type, rise from the water itself, like rocks in an informal pond.

ABOVE *Sinuous lines, evocative of a tropical lagoon, ensure the successful fusion of this informal bathing pool into an imaginatively executed wild corner of an Australian garden.*

Well-laid stone paving unites it visually with the smaller splash pool, while an actual link is formed by the dry 'stream bed'. A small waterfall cascading over the rocks contributes movement and visual interest as well as its refreshing sound to this inviting setting.

Poolside planting is restricted to a few bold ferns springing from the impressive boulders. These are echoed in the smaller stones and ferns in the stream bed.

OPPOSITE *Water is sucked out at the bottom of the hot tub and pumped through a filter and heater before it returns again at the sides. Strong jets of water or bubble action are produced with hydro jets and air blowers. Hot tubs, available in kit form, are simple to install. Make sure the site you have in mind is strong enough to support the combined weight of water and bathers. A 10-15cm/4-6in concrete base should suffice.*

Here, stepped decking, a safe non-slip surface, conceals the walls of the tub and the associated mechanical parts.

Converting a swimming pool

If, for one reason or another, a pool is no longer needed for swimming, it can fairly readily be converted to an ornamental pool, graced by aquatic plants and supporting a natural ecology that helps keep the water clean.

Disguising a rigid outline and masking the rim are the most important first steps. This can be done by building up a retaining wall about 45cm-1m/18-39in out from the sides. Finish it approximately 15cm/6in below the water line and cap it with a material such as rough stone to create a pleasing finish beneath the water. Fill the space behind the wall with rubble topped with gravel, to cover the original pool rim, or top it with earth to form a planting shelf for emergent plants.

Retain the pumping equipment to operate a fountain or waterfall, or adapt it for filtration to keep the water fresh if fish are to be introduced.

Overwintering a swimming pool

In spite of the strength of a well-constructed pool, thick winter ice imposes great stress on the structure. A few precautions taken before the onset of frost will help to prevent damage.

To protect the skimmers from ice, lower the pool water to below their level and extract any residual water from them with a wet-and-dry vacuum cleaner. At the same time the pump, filter and boiler must be disconnected and thoroughly dried out; it is possible to do these jobs yourself but they are generally carried out by professionals.

It is not good practice to empty the pool completely – apart from being a waste of water, it exposes the structure to the enormous thrust of possibly saturated earth around it. Leave water in the pool at the reduced level, and place large objects such as 25 litre/5 gallon plastic containers or softwood logs in it to absorb some of the anticipated ice pressure. These must be partly underwater to be effective. Weight containers with sand or soil so that the bottom 20-30cm/8-12in is below the surface; logs will normally float low in the water without being weighted.

If you wish to keep the pool full during the cold months simply because it looks attractive – particularly relevant with more naturally styled pools and pools that are visible from the house – the plant can be left running throughout the winter, fitted with a frost-start device. This sets the pump in motion as the temperature approaches freezing so that relatively warm water from deep within the pool is circulated. This cannot be done in severe cold as the pump itself can freeze while still running.

Give the pool a double dose of chlorine or other chemical treatment to prepare it for winter. Cover it with strong nylon or polyester, attached round the edges with strong springs. This will prevent anyone from falling in and also keep out debris. Check the pool on a monthly basis while it is not in use to make sure that rainfall or melting snow has not raised the water level too high. Before the pool is put back into use, rainfall can be allowed to enter it to increase the water level for the next season.

SPAS AND HOT TUBS

A spa or hot tub can be installed in the smallest town garden. The barrel-shaped hot tubs, which are made of red cedar or other hardwood, can look most attractive, being easily integrated into the surrounding foliage. A hygienic surround, usually in timber or stone, is needed for bare feet. A spa – or Jacuzzi (a trade name) – is essentially the same as a hot tub, but may be tiled or premoulded in various shapes. The temperature is run at a therapeutic 32-38°C/90-100°F, and jets of water and air massage the body. Spas range in size from those big enough for two people to large family-sized units that will take twelve. They are compact and take up little space. Even the heating and pumping equipment comes as a neat package that is easily tucked away. Some have built-in under-tub heating, whereas others have separate remote heating and filtration units like a swimming pool.

A spa can be built into the sides of a swimming pool, although the main body of water is kept out, in order that the spa water can be made warmer than that of the pool. Usually they are separated by a low wall or flight of steps. The same boiler and equipment can be used to run both. Extra equipment will be required in the form of a strong water pump to produce the powerful massaging jets via a venturi tube or air pumps to produce the aerated water.

Bringing life to a pond

Life comes easily to water. Even a bucketful of clean tap water, placed outside, will quickly become colonized by algae. This is caused by the action of sunlight on the dissolved mineral salts in the water. In a pond there is a rich soup of minerals, salts, nitrates and other inorganic compounds in which this elementary form of plant life can thrive. Concentrations are particularly high following the winter months when plants have been dormant and heavy winter rains have washed in nutrients from outside. As the water warms up, bacteria get to work on breaking down the remains of last year's vegetation and the bodies of the small creatures that have not survived the winter. In sunlit water, huge quantities of phytoplankton – free-floating or self-propelled algae – develop and form the basis of the animal life that depends on plants for survival. In this broth grow tiny creatures called zooplankton. In turn clouds of daphnia (water fleas) will appear, feasting on the algae, and other small creatures, such as the nymphs of dragonflies, damselflies and mayflies, water boatmen and water shrimps rapidly grow and become active as the water warms.

Several creatures, which at some stage in their lives are dependent on water, are beneficial to the garden and it is largely thanks to people having ponds in urban, and indeed rural, gardens that many of them are again on the increase. The smaller aquatic dwellers – crustaceans, molluscs and invertebrates – bring life, movement and interest to the pond. Insects, such as water skaters and whirligig beetles, developed specially to spread their weight, hunt and gyrate upon the surface film. In the shallows among the vegetation the water teams with dragonfly larvae and with a variety of nymphs, snails, water spiders and fleas. There are also annual visits from amphibians such as newts and frogs. The presence of water and water plants may attract moths and butterflies to add to the life and movement of the garden. A well-planted, 'natural' pond, even if fairly small, may even attract wildfowl as well as various smaller birds. All are part of the ecology of the pond. Fish add movement, colour and interest and their languid swimming can be soothing after a stressful day. Given time, fish may become very tame, even eating out of the hand.

WATER QUALITY

To fill a pond without a natural supply, put the end of a hose in a watering can or jug on a sheet of newspaper. Turn the water on part way to begin with and increase the pressure once a few centimetres/inches of water cover the bottom of the pond. The water will gently spill over the rim of the watering can and trickle out across the paper without disturbing the soil. Remove the can and the paper when the pond is full. Wait for the water to clear; fine particles of earth may take many weeks to settle.

Green water may be unsightly, but do not be too eager to remove or poison algae in the spring, for it forms the first link in the food chain for creatures of the pond. The tufted forms that colonize the pool sides also provide a valuable sanctuary and breeding ground for small creatures on which fish can prey, and are particularly good for oxygenating and clearing the water. As the algae use up their supply of nutrients, they will gradually diminish, leaving the pond to other forms of plant life. Algae can occur in red, brown, blue-green and green forms, some free-floating, and others filamentous and attaching themselves to plants, objects and the sides of the pond. The action of sunlight on the chlorophyll (the green pigment) in the plant produces photosynthesis, making the algae absorb carbon dioxide and give off oxygen. This can cause the mat-like varieties to become buoyant enough to reach the surface in blobs or rafts. The form *Cladophora* – sometimes known as 'blanket weed' – is one of these and it feels rough and woolly to the touch. The brighter green slimy form, which grows in strands, is called *Spirogyra*.

Some fish will eat certain species of filamentous algae but, as most pond fish devour the small creatures that feed on algae, on the whole they aid its development. Too many fish – particularly when introduced too soon – will break the food chain by eating all these creatures, enabling the algae to grow unchecked.

Controlling algae

When algae do not die away of their own accord, this may be because they are being supplied with fresh nutrients. Tap water contains many dissolved minerals and salts and will provide nourishment for algae. Therefore, to control their growth, topping up of ponds should be kept to a minimum, simply to replace losses caused through evaporation. A pond that leaks and needs constantly topping up will develop an excess of algae. Equally, since decaying matter, both vegetable and animal, is broken down into nutrients by the action of bacteria, trees that drop leaves and small bits of twig all year round, are best avoided near to ponds. Excessive vegetation should be removed after it has died off and autumn leaves should be cleared away, although a large pond is able to cope with

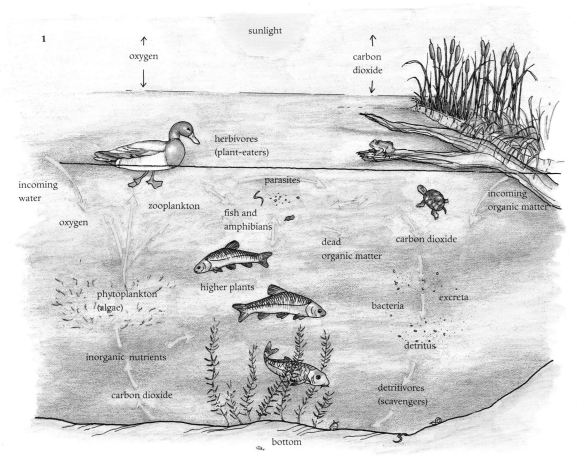

1 The life cycle in a well-balanced pond
An open surface allows sunlight to penetrate the water and prevents the build up of harmful gases, setting in motion the continuous process of breaking down and rebuilding. In a well-balanced pond, the plants and animals form a complex food web in which, for example, phytoplankton (algae) are eaten by zooplankton (small herbivores), which are eaten by fish and amphibians. All dead organic matter falls to form detritus at the bottom of the pond, where it is devoured by detritivores (snails, mussels and worms) and provides inorganic matter for plant growth. The plants are eaten by larger herbivores that fish and amphibians also eat.

a few leaves each year without excessive amounts of algae forming. Any dead fish or other decaying animals, such as bivalves (freshwater mussels), should also be removed immediately. Heavy rains can contribute to the growth of algae by washing in large quantities of nitrates from surrounding land. This can be combated by designing the pond in such a way that it does not receive run-off from paths, flowerbeds or cultivated fields. When this is unavoidable, take care not to fertilize near the pond.

Although sunlight is essential for both plant and animal life and ponds should always be placed in an open, sunny position, too much sunlight penetrating the water can result in excessive growth of algae. Water lilies, which relish the sun, can be planted to shade the water below their big leaf pads. Shallow ponds particularly need some shade, as the shallower the water, the greater will be the concentration of sunlight on its volume, and the greater the potential for algae growth. In regions experiencing long hours of bright sunshine small quantities of black vegetable dye, which is inert and harmless to fish and other pond creatures, are sometimes added to the water to counteract this. The dye also produces a pleasing, dark, mirror-like effect on the pond's surface.

Like algae, many of the submerged aquatic plants can draw most of their nutrients straight from the water, and this is particularly true of the elodeas, ceratophyllums, myriophyllums and other submerged plants known as 'weed' or 'oxygenators'. These higher plant forms are more robust than algae and can almost starve them out of existence. They should be planted in large drifts, say, one bunch per 0.2sq m/2sq ft of surface, and allowed to colonize about two-thirds of the pond. Floating plants, such as *Azolla* and *Eichhornia*, take all their nourishment from the water and these are not 'planted' but simply dropped in. Like the algae themselves, some will spread rapidly and should be used with discretion.

It has long been noticed by commercial fish farmers that giving annual doses of manure and straw to increase the numbers of zooplankton controls the growth of algae. Barley straw in particular contains a natural algicide, and also produces large numbers of water fleas (*Daphnia*) which feed directly on algae and are also an excellent food for fish. Research suggests that this is beneficial applied in loose bales each spring at the rate of approximately one bale per 23,000 litres/5,000 gallons of water.

FILTRATION

Not everyone likes crystal clear water in a pond. Some enjoy the mysterious depths, tinged green or brown, through which the fish appear as they near the surface to feed. Many fish feel vulnerable in gin-clear water, and carp actually stir up the bottom to make a 'smoke-screen' when aerial predators are about. I personally prefer a pond to be natural. I enjoy the challenge of assisting nature by planting, encouraging beneficial creatures and keeping fish to a minimum to achieve a comparatively clear and well-balanced pool (diagram 1). But for those who aim to have a collection of brightly coloured fish in full view at all times, and for koi ponds especially, some form of filtration will be needed.

To keep the water crystal clear mechanical filtration is of little help on

Symbols of love and strength in Japan, koi are gregarious, friendly fish that soon learn to eat out of the hand. Powerful and streamlined, they can grow to more than 60cm/2ft in length and thrive in warm water. Prized for the beauty of their markings – which should not merge or fleck – they are avidly collected and fine specimens change hands for large sums.

Koi co-exist happily with ducks and this one seems unperturbed by their activities just beneath the water surface.

Tiny young fish (fry) can also be seen swimming in this clear green water. Once they reach this size and are recognizable as fish, the koi are unlikely to eat them.

its own, as free-floating algae are so small they will pass through most filters and a filtration medium fine enough to filter out the tiny particles would quickly become blocked so that the system would need frequent cleaning out or back-washing. However, other, more successful methods of filtration are available. There are ultra-violet filters, in which the water is passed through a tube and bombarded by ultra-violet light, which partially sterilizes the water and kills algae, and ceramic filters, on which research still continues. For absolutely clear water, an ultra-violet filter coupled with a biological one is the solution. If you are considering the installation of a new filter system, check out the latest technology.

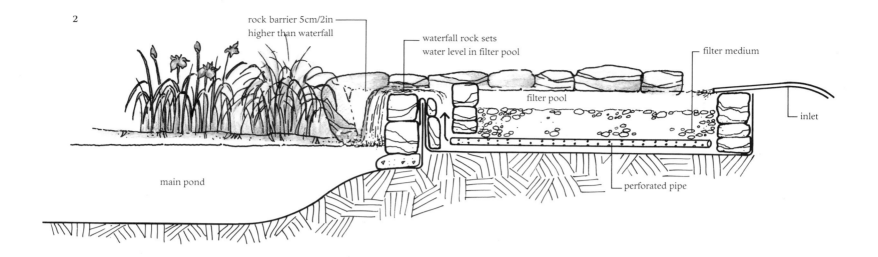

2

rock barrier 5cm/2in
higher than waterfall

waterfall rock sets
water level in filter pool

filter medium

filter pool

inlet

main pond

perforated pipe

Biological filters

It is possible to remove a large proportion of unicellular algae, and the nutrients on which they feed, by biological methods, using bacterial filters. If the pond water is passed slowly through a bed of gravel, clinker, crushed volcanic rock or other porous medium, bacteria together with oxygen will break down the ammonia and nitrogen and purify the water.

An internal filter is the simplest and quickest to construct: gravel beds are built into the bottom of the pond over a grid of perforated pipes and the water that filters through is pumped out from underneath. The filtered water can simply be recirculated within the pond. Preferably, however, it should be returned from a waterfall, spout or fountain as this oxygenates the water. The one snag is that, to keep the bacteria alive, the pump must run continuously, at least throughout the summer months. If it should stop, the bacteria will die off in a matter of 12 to 24 hours, their decay putting enormous oxygen demands on the pond, and possibly resulting in the death of the fish population.

An external filter, on the other hand, can stop without causing harm to the pond. This type of filter requires a flow and return pipe from the pond and a small pump to recirculate the water. The water is pumped out of the pond and into the filter and is returned by gravity through the return pipe. The system is ideal for returning water through a feature – which also beneficially oxygenates the water. A remote filter designed to resemble a rock pool can be incorporated in many informal designs (diagram 2).

The most natural biological filtration uses plants alone. Just as the floating plant, water hyacinth (*Eichhornia crassipes* var. *major*), can be beneficially employed to treat sewage and remove heavy metals from water treatment works, so can other plants be used for natural filtration. They remove nutrients from the water and convert them into plant growth which can in turn be composted and used as fertilizer. Other

2 Constructing a rock-pool filter system

The water is pumped from the main pond up to a filter pool, through a filter medium, into a perforated pipe, through a separate chamber, over a waterfall and back into the pond. At a higher level than the main pond, construct a flat-bottomed pool about a quarter of the surface area and 50cm/20in deep. To form the chamber which holds back the filter medium, build a rock barrier 5cm/2in higher than the outfall rock over which the water will flow. Cover the bottom of the pond with 10cm/4in perforated piping, evenly spaced about 60cm-1m/2-3ft apart. Overlay this with a filter medium to a depth of 30cm/12in.

This system will run for years without servicing but, if the filter pipes become clogged, backwash it by pumping water into the chamber and back up through the filter medium.

floating plants such as water soldier (*Stratiotes aloides*) also purify the water, and varieties of reed, *Phragmites*, planted in gravel, can make effective filtration and purification beds.

AN ENVIRONMENT FOR FISH

A pond will remain clear and in good health without them but, as well as adding interest, fish have practical benefits. In hotter countries no pond should be without its quota of gambusia or mosquito fish, and in cooler climates golden orfe are excellent, rising right out of the water to catch low-flying gnats or mosquitoes. Smaller, middle-feeding fish such as goldfish and the various fantails and long-tailed hybrids, with all their finny appendages, keep down the populations of water lily beetles and brown china mark moths that are so destructive to water lily leaves. For brilliant colour a collection of koi, the multi-coloured Japanese carp, will provide grace and movement, but these grow rapidly and may eat or dislodge many plants in a small pond. From the point of view of water clarity it is usually safe to have surface feeders, such as golden orfe, silver orfe, rudd, golden rudd, and, in hot countries, medeka and gambusia.

The right size pond

Fish need room to move freely and corners in which to hide, but even a very small garden pond can support one or two goldfish. It must not freeze solid in winter – a greater danger with small ponds – and it must supply sufficient cover. Fish feel vulnerable in shallow, clear water and will be constantly under stress unless they have some protection. Agitated fish are likely to dart about, stirring up mud and disturbing the plants. A ridge tile or terracotta pipe on the pool floor will provide a hide. In larger ponds the 'caves' underneath planting shelves or beneath a fountain plinth would also serve the purpose.

The number of fish a pond can comfortably hold will vary enormously. If the pond is being filtered and oxygenated mechanically, high concentrations are possible: the limiting factor is the potential for disease through overcrowding. In natural conditions, where you are relying on plants and the normal oxygenating content of the water to break down bacteria, a maximum of 25 centimetres of fish per square metre or 1 inch per square foot of surface area can be allowed.

The depth of the water

Deep water maintains a more equable temperature, while shallow water can heat up considerably during a hot summer day. When stocking large ponds and lakes, consider the requirements of various fish. Shallower, warm, muddy water is best suited to the carp family, and to tench, catfish and other bottom feeders. Carp will manage on 25 per cent dissolved oxygen in the water, while trout require cold, clear water with 75 per cent dissolved oxygen. Deep lakes with running or filtered water are most suitable for these fish, and gravel areas with shallow running water will encourage the spawning of brown trout. Where running water is not available, cool depths of at least 2.5-3m/8-10ft are needed.

Shallow, warm water can hold less dissolved oxygen than cold, so that a period of hot, sultry nights following scorching days can put a severe strain on fish. Although plants give off oxygen during the day, at night they release carbon dioxide. In waters thickly congested with plants and algae, this, coupled with the already reduced oxygen content due to the warmth of the water, may prove fatal for fish with high oxygen requirements, such as trout and golden orfe. Some areas of open water should always be maintained on the pond surface, to allow the vital exchange of oxygen. In periods of very hot weather, excessive weed or submerged aquatics should be pulled out and areas of leaf cover checked to ensure there are enough open spaces. A fountain playing at night will be an enormous help. In an emergency the garden hose can be played on the surface overnight, using a fine-spray jet.

Selecting and introducing fish

When purchasing fish, always look for the lively ones. A drooping dorsal fin (the one on top of the back) is the first sign of a sick fish. The eyes should be bright, the colours pure; there should be no lumps, ulcers, fungus or ragged fins.

The biggest cause of failure, of both fish and the ecology of the pond, is introducing too many fish, too soon. Fish should never be placed in a newly constructed pond which will always first go through a green period before slowly clearing, and in the height of the growing season this may take six weeks or more. The plants should always be given time to root and grow, and the small algae-eating creatures – a vital link in the food chain – allowed to build up their numbers, to keep the water clear. Although it is possible, thanks to modern water-maturing agents, to plant and introduce fish on the same day, it is preferable to give the pond time to become well established and a natural ecology to build up before the first fish are allowed in.

Before putting fish in a new pond check the pH level, which should be between 6.5 and 7.5. One or two small goldfish can then be introduced. If all is well after a few days, the other fish can follow. Those purchased from an aquatic centre are usually supplied in large polythene bags partly filled with water, and topped up with oxygen. Cover the bag to keep the fish in the dark to calm it and protect it from the sun. Then float the bag on the water surface for an hour. When the temperature in the bag feels the same as in the pond, the fish can be released. But do not simply tip it in: let a little water at a time into the bag and out again several times over a minute or two to allow the pH to adjust. Then lift the bottom of the bag and allow the fish to swim out into its new pond.

This is always a thrilling moment. The fish will either dive straight to the bottom and hide, or else lie pretty much where it was released, fanning the water quickly through its gills while it takes stock of its new surroundings. Should the fish rise straight up to the surface and start gasping there may be something drastically wrong with the water. Particularly after a long, hot journey, the fish may have become short of oxygen. Spraying a hose over the water surface to oxygenate it should solve the problem. If the gasping continues for more than a few minutes, remove the fish, as there is likely to be a serious pH problem, or some pollutant present, especially in the case of a new, untried pond. To revive the fish place it in fresh water, and lightly spray a hose on to the surface.

The less fish are handled the better. They have a protective mucus coating that feels slimy to the touch and this can be damaged by careless handling. Always wet hands before touching a fish, and if necessary, hold it in a soft, wet cloth. Rough nets can be more harmful than hands, and only the smoothest nets should be used. When moving a fish it is best not to lift it right out of the water with the net, which would cause it stress. If possible, coax it into a bowl by carefully wafting it with a net and carry it in its own water.

A healthy diet

A well-planted pond with plenty of green plants growing on the bottom and in the shallows should provide a good and varied food supply. Nevertheless, except in unusually large and well-planted ponds with few fish, supplementary feeding will be needed. The carp, including goldfish and nishiki-goi, will eat almost anything that human beings consume:

meat, peas, lettuce and sweetcorn, as well as brown bread. Greasy foods that would foul the water are not advisable. Many specially formulated foods are now on the market, but natural live food is best. Water fleas (*Daphnia*), freshwater shrimps (*Gammarus pulex*) and earthworms are excellent. Many aquarium keepers maintain a supply of red Tubifex worms in running water.

The young fish (fry) will eat phytoplankton and zooplankton and a culture of these tiny organisms, known as infusia, can be easily grown in a bucket, either by covering lettuce leaves in water or by softening a few handfuls of chopped hay or straw with boiling water and topping up with cold; fruit peelings or a little fresh milk can also be used. After a few days this culture will be teeming with minute creatures. It can be augmented with wheat germ (sold under various proprietary names) or finely ground fish food. On this brew the fry will grow quickly and after a few months they will have progressed to more adult foods.

During the cold months fish go into a semi-torpid state, moving little and hardly eating at all, living on fat reserves. In spring and summer, during the breeding season, when the fish are most active, and in the autumn, to build fat stores for the oncoming winter, their diet should be increased. As a general guide more harm can be done by overfeeding than by underfeeding. Aim for a maximum feeding time of 15 minutes per day, assuming that all the food is consumed in this period. Adjust the quantities you offer until this point is reached. When possible, three 2-minute feedings in the morning are better than one large evening meal, since the fish metabolize the food better. If they do not feed it is either because they are not hungry or because the food you are offering is not to their liking. Floating foods are preferable, as one can see what has been eaten. Prepared food that has not been eaten should be cleared away so that it does not rot in the pond.

In warmer winter spells, if the water warms up sufficiently to make the fish active for short periods, a little easily digestible food can be given to help them through the next cold period. Specially formulated winter feeds are available. Do not be tempted to feed fish on one warm day alone, as it may quickly become too cold for them to digest what they have eaten. After a long winter, fish may be emaciated and in this weakened state they are vulnerable to disease. As the water warms up, bacteria will increase rapidly before the natural purifying process of the pond can become established. Live food, such as earthworms, is particularly beneficial at this period.

Fish diseases
Provide the fish with the right environment – different depths and varied planting as would be found in nature – and avoid overcrowding to minimize the risk of diseases being transmitted from fish to fish. The pond should have no sharp projections or rough sides that could rub the fish raw and lead to infection.

Many different conditions may occasionally affect fish. Damage to the nervous system can cause bent spines, especially with young orfe.

Constipation, revealed by a trail of excrement, makes fish bloated and lethargic: provide a balanced diet with plenty of green food such as finely chopped lettuce. Parasites cause a wide variety of symptoms.

Check with a pharmacist, veterinary surgeon or fish specialist to find out about the most effective medication or treatment available. Always seek advice before using antibiotics as fish can build up resistance to them. Follow directions for all medications, never overdose and follow one course of treatment at a time. During treatment, provide plenty of oxygen with a pump and air-stone (also known as a diffuser-stone) and feed sparingly with a little live food.

An old-fashioned but still useful home treatment for fish is the salt bath. This involves placing the fish in a shallow basin or tank into which rock salt (pure sodium chloride) – *not* household salt – has been dissolved at the rate of 15g per 5 litres/½oz per gallon of water. The fish can bathe in this for half an hour but should be carefully watched and removed at the first signs of stress.

Fungus diseases
Although present in most water, fungus spores (*Saprolegnia*) attack only damaged tissues or weakened fish with low resistance. The fungus can attack the fins or body, appearing as fine white threads and, later, as tufts of cotton wool. If left untreated the fungus roots will work their way deeper into the tissues and eventually kill the fish. Treatment should be started as soon as possible. Use a soft net to carefully waft the fish into a clean washing up bowl and hold it in a soft wet cloth while applying one of the many available medications.

White spot disease ('ich')
Ichthyophthiriasis is a parasitic infestation that attacks tropical fish that have been chilled or stressed; cold-water fish are more susceptible in warm water. The fish look as though they have been sprinkled with salt. (This must not be confused with the white pimples that develop on the gill plates and sometimes other forward parts of the male fish during the mating season.) It is very contagious but can be cured by placing the affected fish in a bath of methylene blue diluted to 2.5 parts per million, measured out in drops from the dispenser bottle. This should be changed every three days and the treatment continued until the condition improves.

Flukes
These are microscopic flatworms that hook themselves into the fish. Fluke diseases are difficult to identify. Gill flukes cause the fish to bang themselves against the sides of the pond and rush along the surface gasping for air. The gill covers are wide open and the membranes inside are pale. Skin flukes cause similar symptoms and the fish lose colour, while their fins look ragged and drooping. Blood stains appear on the body, which produces excessive slime. The salt treatment can be tried but professional advice should be sought.

Swim bladder disorders

When fish have to struggle to stay down, or they swim upside down, something is wrong with the swim bladder that controls their level of buoyancy. This may be due to poor diet or constipation, chill or possibly a roundworm or other parasite, or even a bacterial attack. Live and green food can be tried as a first step. Moving the fish to shallow water can ease their distress and the salt bath may help. Veterinary advice should be sought because antibiotics might be needed.

Anchor worms

These are horrible parasites which hook their anchor-shaped heads in the skin. Luckily they can be seen as a 1cm/⅜in long thread protruding from an inflamed swelling in the skin. To treat this, hold the fish firmly in a soft, wet cloth and apply a fine paintbrush dipped in paraffin; this will allow the worm to be pulled out. Disinfect the wound with an antiseptic such as povidone iodide or mercurochrome and overseal with Orabase. Treat the pond at prescribed intervals with a specially formulated product to kill the larvae.

Fish lice

Fish may sometimes be seen to flicking and brushing themselves against plants and projections in the pond. This irritation is often caused by a fish louse (*Argulus*) or other parasite. Some can be seen and may be removed with the paraffin brush, followed by a dab of antiseptic; others may be invisible and a salt water, malachite green or proprietary bath will be needed.

Fin rot

The tail and fins may become ragged and bloodshot. This is caused by any of a variety of different bacteria and may be further complicated by a fungus attack. Antibiotics are usually the only cure; professional advice should be sought.

Dropsy

This disease causes the fish to become bloated and its scales to bristle out. It is not generally infectious but the afflicted fish should be isolated and given a saline bath; the diet should be changed to contain more green food. Antibiotics may help.

Dealing with predators

Fish may come under attack from herons, gulls, storks, kingfishers and cats as well as, in some countries, racoons, water snakes, turtles and large bullfrogs. If in your particular area there is only one type of predator to contend with, your task is made much easier. A fence or trip-wire, about 45cm/18in high around the perimeter and deep water – 60cm/2ft – near the edges, will be adequate both for animals and those birds, such as storks and herons, that prefer to walk down to the water rather than make hovering attacks. Special electric pet fences are used in the United States

to keep racoons away from the pond, and one of the most effective and least obtrusive methods of protection that I have found is the electric fence of the type used by farmers to confine livestock. Animals quickly learn after the first shock or two not to touch this, and interestingly, I have noticed that where one or two people in a locality have electric wires around the pond, the birds will not touch or approach any pond with a similar wire, whether electric or otherwise.

Netting needs to be strong enough to take the weight of the heaviest predator – bird or animal – and small enough to prevent diving birds such as kingfishers from darting through. It need not be immediately above the water surface. It is often a great inconvenience in this position as emerging plants and leaves get caught and distorted in the mesh so that it cannot be removed without causing considerable disruption. I do not advocate a net spread beneath the surface, however. Fish like to reach the surface, and a mesh large enough for them to rise through without restriction will also allow the passage of a sharp beak. With smaller mesh it is possible for some fish to be caught on the surface, unable to dive back down – fine mesh will, of course, also prevent fish from reaching the surface. A good solution is to arrange it high above the pond like a fruit cage. This allows an unobstructed view of the fish, although it is perhaps not the most attractive arrangement for a pretty garden. A popular method is to stretch the net tightly a few centimetres/inches above the open water with openings left for emergent plants.

A statue of a heron standing beside the pond is considered infallible by some people as a deterrent for these birds. Personally, I have found nothing to prove its efficacy. On the contrary, I have seen a photograph of a real heron standing next to a plastic one.

The kingfisher emerges after diving for a small fish.

POND CREATURES

The enjoyment of any pond is increased by the wide variety of creatures supported within its depths or attracted to its margins.

Fish for ponds

The fish described here are some of the most widely available. All, except for trout, belong to the Cyprinidae family.

CARASSIUS AURATUS Goldfish

The first mention of this fish appears to be in early seventeenth-century China, and it has become one of the most ubiquitous, best loved and easily kept fish. Capable of growing to 23-25cm/9-10in, but usually only about 15cm/6in, the common goldfish is ideal for the smaller garden pond. It is very hardy and breeds well, remaining active in water temperatures as high as 35°C/95°F and where the level of oxygen is below 25 per cent saturation. The predominant colour is red, which appears after six to twelve months (or longer) according to the temperature and amount of sunlight the fish receives. Occasionally the original black or grey remains all their lives. Sometimes they turn lemon or even white, the black remaining along the dorsal. As they get older, the white tends to creep up from the belly and the last patches of black disappear. These colours are very pretty in a pond.

In early summer fertilized eggs, the size of a pinhead and almost transparent, appear in great masses caught on the algae and stems of elodea. (Opaque eggs are infertile.) The young fish (fry)

A shoal of goldfish

appear a week or so later, according to the temperature, looking like tiny translucent grey-green sticks with two eyes. They are very vulnerable and are often swallowed by the parents, who relish eating their own eggs. They are also at risk from other pond dwellers. If a large hatching is required, move the eggs to another pond or fence off an area where the eggs and fry can develop.

Goldfish with unusually long fins are described as veiltails; they are generally more prone to damage and less hardy than the common goldfish. The comet's long dorsal, pectoral and tail fins are sometimes much longer than its body. Sarasa comets have clear bright red and white markings. Fantails have a doubled, fan-shaped tail that considerably reduces their speed in the water, making them vulnerable to predators. Black moors are rotund fantails, a pure sooty black in colour, with protruding telescopic eyes – a special characteristic generally only found in fantails. There are telescopic-eyed varieties of Japanese or red fantails (orange, red, white, black and combinations of these colours) as well as of calico fantails (blue with orange, black and gold spots).

A beautifully proportioned fantail, the oranda, also has bulbous eyes. Although often red with white tips to their fins, they come in many other colours – mauve, orange, lemon and grey-blue with black speckles. These lovely fish have a protuberance on the head that in some can be as large as that of the lionhead.

CARASSIUS AURATUS VARIEGATUS Shubunkin

With their transparent scales, these beautiful fish appear almost smooth skinned. They come in an extraordinary assortment of colours, with blotches and speckles. Their fins vary greatly in length and in the comet shubunkin the tails are over twice as long as the body. The Cambridge shubunkin is a soft blue with black speckles. The Bristol is the deep rich blue of Bristol glass. Again, black patches, streaks and flecks can adorn the fins and body, which is often further enhanced with blotches of bright crimson. These fish thrive in warm water and breed readily. The young, which colour up after a few weeks, appear as perfect miniatures (only 2.5cm/1in long) of their parents.

CYPRINUS CARPIO The Common Carp

This fish, like the wild goldfish (from which many of the more bizarre varieties of pet goldfish have been bred) and the mirror or German carp, is best suited to lakes. The carp's propensity to burrow, stirring up clouds of mud and uprooting water lilies, makes it unsuitable for ornamental ponds.

KOI Coloured carp or Nishiki-goi

The koi symbolizes strength and love in Japan, where the centre of koi breeding first grew, and where on 5 May paper and silk air socks in the shape of koi are flown.

First described in the eighteenth century by the naturalist Linnaeus, they probably go back a good deal earlier and possibly originated as colourful specimens of the common carp. One of the first to be standardized was the kohaku, which is a pure red and white. Some koi are evenly scaled all over, like the common carp, others, crossed with the mirror carp and called 'doitzu', have a row of distinctive plate-like scales along each side and another row on either side of the dorsal. Some of the most beautiful varieties are of this type, including the shusui, a blue-backed fish with a red underside. Others, such as the asagi, have very distinctive scales in a fishnet pattern. Taisho sanke is a striking white fish with red and black markings, while the showa sanke is red and white on black.

There should be a distinct boundary between colours, which should not merge or fleck. The depth and quality of colour and the position of the pattern make an enormous difference to the price of these fish. The colour can be enriched with special foods containing natural colour enhancers.

Koi are streamlined and powerful, with attractive smiling faces with two barbels. They are gregarious and easily become very tame, eating out of the hand and following one around the pond. They are long-lived, surviving for more than a hundred years in the right conditions. However, they are still carp, and like to rootle about among plants; they grow large – over 45cm/18in – and heavy and, in small ponds, few plants will survive them.

LEUCISCUS IDUS Orfe

These surface feeders devour midges and mosquitoes and make an excellent addition to the pond. The golden orfe are definitely the ones to have. They are the colour of carrots and look very similar when seen from above. With their compact bodies and powerful tail fins they move at great speed through the water and rise several inches in the air to catch mosquitoes. They seldom breed in a small garden pond, preferring larger expanses of water. The young fish colour up almost immediately after hatching (which can make the water look like carrot soup). They can double their length each year in the first few years, after which they continue to grow slowly to about 45cm/18in.

SCARDINIUS ERYTHROPHTHALMUS Rudd

These lively midwater and surface swimmers have distinctive dull red fins. More beautiful is the golden rudd (*S.e.* var. *aurata*). These lovely bronze, streamlined fish can be seen circling in open patches of water, rising occasionally to take a midge or insect that alights on the surface film.

SALMO TRUTTA Trout

Trout (Salmonidae family) require much colder water and more oxygen than carp. Generally speaking brook trout will tolerate up to 17°C/62°F; rainbow trout 22°C/72°F and brown trout 24°C/75°F – as long as high oxygen levels are maintained. Brown trout (*Salmo trutta fario*) can be placed in deep ponds and lakes where they will grow slowly and, provided the numbers are small, survive on the creatures the lake can yield. Rainbow trout (*Salmo gairdneri*), however, are quick-growing voracious feeders with comparatively short lives and are usually introduced for fishing as a food source. If the two are introduced together, unless the rainbows are artificially fed to capacity, they will starve out the brownies. A lovely mood is created by the plopping sound and widening rings of water as trout of either type rise to take a fly.

TINCA TINCA Green Tench

Beautifully streamlined and velvety, these are sometimes called the doctor fish. Their reputed ability to cure other fish of various ailments is probably overrated, though they have been known to nibble the fungus growth off an infected fish. They are bottom dwellers and rarely seen. The golden tench has pretty orange coloration.

Tropical fish

Where climate permits, tropical fish that are normally confined to aquariums can be put outside in ponds over the summer. This often results in superior breeding, growth and colour.

GAMBUSIA AFFINIS Mosquito Fish

Also known as the Texas gambusia (Poecillidae family), these silvery-grey fish have a slight metallic-blue sheen and grow quickly to about 6cm/2½in. They breed quickly in tropical climates and devour midge and mosquito larvae.

ORYZIAS LATIPES AURATUS Golden Japanese Medeka

Also known as rice fish (Oryziatidae family), these tiny fish, 4cm/1½in long, multiply quickly and actively dart and nose through the water plants in their quest for food. Temperature tolerant, but favouring approximately 25°C/77°F, they can be kept in ponds in temperate climates during the summer months.

Other pond dwellers

Snails can be bought for the pond, though they may also arrive in the form of eggs attached to plants from garden centres and aquatic suppliers. Leeches, too, may arrive on plants, and anyone worried about them can disinfect the plants on purchase. They may also be carried on the feet of water birds. The pond acts as an attraction and you can do a lot to encourage visitors to stay. If space allows, a house can be installed for ducks though, endearing as they may be, ducks do not mix well with choice aquatic plants. You can also provide cover for amphibians – rocks around the pool for them to crawl beneath, and plenty of marginal plant cover, together with places where they can gain easy access to and from the water. Do not use pesticides – including slug pellets – near the pond as these will destroy natural food supplies.

ARGYRONETA AQUATICA Water Spider

This fascinating aquatic spider spins a silken dome among the weeds and proceeds to inflate it with air carried down from the surface trapped in its abdominal hairs. From its underwater balloon it can move freely around the pond, occasionally returning to the surface to restore its air supply.

ASELLUS AQUATICUS Water Louse

Very common among the weeds of slow-running streams, and similar in appearance to the woodlouse, this louse feeds on decaying plants and animal remains and is a valuable food for fish.

CORIXA and *NOTONECTA* species Water Boatman

Flat and lozenge shaped, water boatmen are pale greyish brown in colour with dark bellies and triangles on their backs. They arrive overnight to colonize a new pond and appear to row themselves around just under the water; they are dependent on air for their oxygen supply. They feed on small aquatic creatures and can kill young fish (fry).

DAPHNIA Water Fleas

Water fleas cluster in clouds, often giving a pinkish or whiteish tinge to the water. These small crustaceans feed largely on free-floating algae, clear the water and convert minute plant life into a valuable food for the higher forms of aquatic life.

DYTISCUS MARGINALIS Great Diving Beetle

This elegant beetle is a strong flyer with a ribbed, shiny brown back edged with a beautiful golden line. Both adults and larvae are fiercely carnivorous, even picking on prey larger than themselves.

EPHEMERA DANICA and other species Mayflies

Like dragonflies, these flies spend most of their lives as underwater nymphs, surfacing to shed their skins in spring or early summer. Well-known to fishermen and much-loved by trout, they moult in two stages, first becoming the familiar 'dun' and then the short-lived 'spinner' – often seen in clouds drifting across the water.

Wandering snail (Lymnaea peregra)

GAMMARUS PULEX Freshwater Shrimp

In alkaline waters these crustaceans build up in huge quantities among the weeds where they form the staple diet for many fish. The male is often seen holding on to the female as they swim about. Excellent for all ponds.

GERRIS species Pond Skaters

Like miniature hydrofoils on their broadly based legs, pond skaters dart across the surface. They will quickly adopt a new pond.

GYRINUS species Whirligig Beetle

Almost as soon as the pond is filled, these small beetles appear, spinning and darting on the surface film like silvery beads of mercury on a sheet of glass. They arrive by air and are harmless, their gyrations becoming hypnotic on a warm day.

HYDROPHILUS PICEUS Great Silver Diving Beetle

Also known as the silver water beetle, this fine silvery black beetle is about 5cm/2in long. It has grasping 'claws' on its front legs with which it seizes its prey. The huge larvae crawl around in the weeds feeding mainly on snails.

NEPA CINEREA Water Scorpion

These ruffians of the shallows attack at will, lying motionless among the weeds for hours to pounce out suddenly on prey twice their size. They can inflict wounds on quite sizeable fish.

ODONATA species Dragonflies

Anyone who has had the privilege of watching a large dragonfly undergo its metamorphosis cannot have failed to marvel. The eggs, like those of the smaller damselfly, are laid in summer on vegetation just beneath the water surface and soon hatch into nymphs, which spend up to five years growing within the pond. Sinister and scorpion-like, they behave like water scorpions, inflicting wounds on small fish. Eventually the nymph climbs a plant stem, sheds its case and, after spending half an hour or so drying off, spreads its translucent wings and takes to the sky as a beautiful dragonfly.

MOLLUSCA Mussels and Snails

Mussels feed by passing water through their bodies, absorbing harmful bacteria and filtering out nourishing organic matter, thus helping to keep the water clear. However, there is a risk of pollution if dead mussels are left to rot in a small garden pond. They are good to place in a waterfall system, separated from fish (particularly koi) who may attack them when their shells are open.

The zebra mussel (*Dreissena polymorpha*) is dark brown and beige striped. It multiplies to problematical numbers where there are no natural predators but it can be introduced to slow-running or deep water where there is plenty of room. The painter's mussel (*Unio pictorum*) is larger and has radiating rings of dark brown and greeny grey. Female bitterling deposit their eggs in a cavity beneath the mantle where they can develop in safety. The dark brown swan mussel (*Anodonta cygnea*) is the most readily available from suppliers, but it needs a large pond (it filters about 45 litres/10 gallons of water a day). It likes a small area of coarse sand in which to bury itself.

The *Elliptio crassidens*, also known as the freshwater clam, is the most common freshwater mussel in the United States. It is about the same size and colour as the swan mussel.

Snails are among the most useful pond's creatures for sifting through rotting detritus and clearing up any decaying animal matter.

The great ramshorn snail (*Planorbis corneus*), named for the shape of its spiral shell, is widely sold by aquatic suppliers. Mainly black, though other species are red and white, it lays eggs in jelly-like blisters on the underside of aquatic plants.

The wandering snail (*Lymnaea peregra*) is very common, sometimes increasing to huge numbers in ponds. These dumpy little snails vary in colour from pale brown to almost black and lay their eggs in jelly-like strips on almost any surface within the pond. Their main food is vegetation that is beginning to decay, though sometimes they will eat young shoots. When their numbers are too high, you can remove them by floating a lettuce leaf on the surface overnight. They will attach themselves to it and can be lifted out in quantity.

The great pond snail (*Lymnaea stagnalis*) resembles a spiralling icecream cone. Over 2.5cm/1in long, they lay their eggs in jelly-like strips up the stems of submerged aquatics and on the undersides of water lily leaves. Feeding mainly on decaying vegetation they will occasionally take animal food, dead or alive.

The trapdoor or Japanese mystery snail, the *Viviparous malleatus*, the most commonly sold snail in the United States, is often 2.5cm/1in in diameter. It does not reproduce as rapidly as the *Lymnaea*, and, unlike the great pond snail, does not eat growing aquatic plants.

Similar in appearance to the great pond snail, though smaller, the freshwater winkle (*Viviparus viviparus*) has a spiral shell banded brown and cream. The fleshy part bears a horny plate or operculum, with which it can close up its shell and continue to breathe through 'gills'. As the name implies, this snail gives birth to live young. It is found mainly in well-oxygenated running water.

TRITURUS Newts

Both the male and female great crested newt (*T. cristatus* or *palustris*) have black-spotted orange tummies and the male has a spiky crest along the back that is particularly prevalent in spring during the mating season. They spend more time in the

Common blue damselflies (Emallagna cythigemum) *mating. The male is an electric blue.*

pond than other newts, occasionally staying throughout the year.

The common or smooth newt (*T. vulgaris*) hunts at night. During the winter months it lives under stones and logs and in cracks in walls.

The palmated newt (*T. helveticus*), though still fairly common, tends to live at higher altitudes. It is less colourful than the preceding species but the male can be distinguished by its webbed hind feet. These newts spend a considerable amount of time on land, coming to the pond in spring to mate.

Frogs and toads

The common frog (*Rana temporaria*), once in decline in certain regions, is on the increase. Their diet of flies and slugs makes them useful garden dwellers. On wet nights in spring they move across country to their spawning ponds, where the females lay quantities of eggs surrounded by jelly. Frogs generally overwinter in pond mud or in frost-free hiding places on land.

The most common frogs in the United States are green frogs (*R. clamitans*) and bullfrogs (*R. catesbina*), both of which can readily be bought as tadpoles. Bullfrogs require two seasons to complete metamorphosis and live for several years. They can grow to more than 15cm/6in in body length and width, excluding the legs, and have been known to stalk and catch sparrows, so as adults they pose a threat to all but the largest fish in a pond. For reasons not yet determined, the pretty leopard frog (southern: *R. sphenocephala*; northern: *R. pipiens*) and the pickerel frog (*R. palustris*) are on the decline.

The marsh frog (*R. ridibunda ridibunda*), sometimes available from aquatic suppliers, is common in Europe and Asia, though rare in Great Britain. Occasionally it will take small mammals in addition to slugs and flies. The edible frog (*R. esculenta*) also spends more time in water and marshland than the common frog. Although common in mainland Europe and Asia this pretty little green frog that produces a chorus of croaking all night long in the mating season, is rare in Great Britain.

The shy and harmless common toad (*Bufo bufo*) is dumpier and flatter than a frog, and crawls more slowly on its stumpy legs. Like frogs, toads come to the ponds in spring to lay their eggs, which appear as long streamers or strings of jelly, the black eggs clearly visible inside. Their diet of slugs and insects makes them desirable in the garden.

Smaller than the common toad, the natterjack toad (*Bufo calamita*) is easily identified by the yellow stripe running down its back. It is found in drier, sandy places where it burrows to hide up by day.

Birds and wildfowl

If the pond provides sufficient cover, a pair of moorhens or waterhens may arrive and build a nest in iris leaves or rushes – usually the choicest ones that you have been nurturing. Coots may visit larger stretches of open water that provide good reed cover, and spend the winter there. A pair of mallards may move in and will soon attract others – again sometimes to the detriment of the plants. If you are stocking ducks, choose the small varieties as they do far less damage to plants and make less mess of the pond edges. Teal, mandarin, Carolina, tufted and shell ducks are all beautiful subjects for a pond.

Where small fish abound, kingfishers may frequently be seen as a flash of brilliant blue and green. Other birds, such as spoonbills, herons, storks, seagulls, terns and possibly egrets may also be attracted by this plentiful supply of food – perhaps to the pond owner's annoyance.

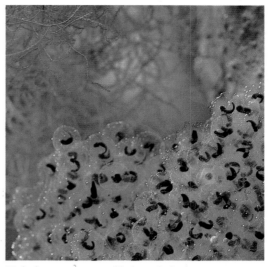

Tadpole eggs appear as black specks in frog spawn.

Frogs may travel considerable distances to reach the pond where they mate and produce spawn.

OPPOSITE *While maintaining a strong natural theme, the planting round this pond is obviously carefully planned and tended. The brilliant hues of massed candelabra primulas are offset by bold clumps of foliage presenting dramatic contrasts in shape, from the graceful curves of* Carex elata *'Aurea' to the huge, floppy, glossy leaves of* Lysichiton.

Most water plants are highly adaptable and, like the lotus BELOW *look equally well whether naturalized among native plants or grown as specimens in more formal situations.*

Planting water features

Plants have adapted to fit almost every available niche on the planet. You can therefore be sure that there are subjects to suit every possible water feature, whether in cold, temperate or tropical climates, with still or moving water, in a range of depths. While some plants will live only under the water, others flourish on its surface or beside it; yet others have adapted to survive in a combination of these situations. In addition to their beauty, certain water plants serve a useful purpose, promoting clear water or, alongside running water, helping to stabilize banks and prevent erosion.

Depending on your tastes and the style of the water feature, whether formal or informal, with still or running water, the plants you choose and the way you use them can achieve a wide variety of effects. Your choice may be far ranging or limited to a few carefully selected specimens; you may favour a particular colour theme, have a preference for native species or their close relatives, wish to encourage wildlife or simply want to link the waterside planting to the design of the surrounding garden. The key to success is to choose plants not only for their visual contribution to the garden picture, but according to their suitability for their role. Make sure, then, that they will enjoy the conditions your site has to offer.

As in any part of the garden, practical considerations must be taken into account in your choice of plants. The specific contribution of various plants in keeping the water clear and clean is discussed on p.112. At the edge of a wildlife pond, you may wish to provide cover for amphibians and small mammals who make their home in or near the water. Consider, particularly with a naturalistic pond, if you wish to deter people from approaching the water's edge or if there are places where you wish to make their passage easier. Planting around leisure pools should provide shelter, shade and seclusion.

Another practicality to bear in mind (as with any garden planting) is the amount of time and effort you are prepared to expend on upkeep. Part of the pleasure of a small formal pool is its manicured perfection: tasks such as deadheading should be part of the routine. Regular grooming is less of a priority in more informal water gardens.

PLANTING PRINCIPLES AND TECHNIQUES

Aim to keep the planting simple. Whether running or still, water is the principal focus of attention and neighbouring planting should enhance rather than confuse its impact. A restrained approach is particularly appropriate with a formal pool, where a clear geometric shape – often mirroring the sky – is an important element in the overall garden design.

Colourful annuals, biennials and the more brilliant herbaceous perennials are often too brash in tone, upstaging the more subtle colour of water plants. A satisfactory colour transition can be achieved, however, by planting in carefully considered stages: thus water margin plants can merge gradually into water associated plantings (say of trollius, hostas and iris) and thence into the drier parts of the garden.

Space and scale

The size of the plants and the way they are arranged can affect the impression of space and scale. For example, to make a medium-sized pond appear as large as possible, place, say a *Gunnera manicata* with its huge leaves in the foreground and the smaller umbrella plant (*Darmera peltata*) with its similarly shaped smaller leaves to the far side. This will create a false perspective, giving an illusion of greater distance; planting them the other way around would have a foreshortening effect. Where an informal pond is to be viewed from all round, with no particular vantage point, tall plants can be placed in groups on the promontories and lower plants used in the bays. This accentuates the bays and inlets, creating rhythms and a richly textured shoreline.

Striking juxtapositions can be achieved: slender, cylindrical shapes contrasted with globular; tall and spiky with flat and feathery.

You can plant singly or in bold groups to dramatically different effect, but always bear in mind the scale of the site and the distance from which the water feature will most often be viewed. When seen from close to, single specimens give interest but, in general, with the exception of plants such as *Rheum* or *Aruncus*, an individual plant tends to look lost on its own. Even in a small, intimate garden, I would plant in clumps of at least three. Large groups of one species can be the most dramatic, even on a small scale. Certainly when viewed from a distance, expansive masses of a single species will make more of an impression than a mixture. Remember that water and water-associated plants are often vigorous and sometimes invasive (see p.128), so ascertain before planting that a subject, when mature, is likely to be of an appropriate height and spread.

This pond is carefully sited on a steep slope to align with the house and its view of distant hills. Planting close to the house is vibrant with strong, hot colours. For the waterside, I decided to pick up on the cool, blue tones of the existing Cedrus atlantica glauca *and the receding hills.*

On the bank formed from the spoil created by a deep excavation, blue and white Iris laevigata *flower alongside the speckled* Scirpus 'Zebrinus'. *Low clumps of water forget-me-not* (Myosotis) *and bog arum* (Calla palustris) *together with the blue* Pontederia cordata *continue the theme in blue and white.*

Seen here in its second season, the pond is particularly beautiful at dawn and dusk – and magical on moonlit nights.

Making the most of reflection

Planting may be chosen to maximize reflections in still water, exploiting foliage and flower shapes and colour for beautiful and interesting effects. Remember that tall subjects planted some distance away may be mirrored every bit as clearly as those planted close to the water's edge. If you are planting a background of trees and shrubs from scratch, do so with a view to winter stem colour contrasts and summer foliage variations. In front of trees and shrubs, bog or moisture-loving subjects can be grown, with foliage and flower colour contrasts in mind. Still closer to the water, in the shallows, further interesting relationships can be explored in miniature.

When concentrating on the reflective quality of water, do not neglect those plants whose ineffable beauty enhances its surface and its depths. Around the margins, linking the water surface with the surround, small emergent plants may creep out across the water, creating patches of colour and pattern. As well as the water lily, that most distinctive and perhaps best-loved of all water plants, the surface of the pond may be graced by other fascinating subjects such as the water soldier (*Stratiotes aloides*), with its 'pineapple' tops growing on their umbilical stalks. To delight the eye beneath the surface, you might introduce *Potamogeton crispus*, with its translucent bronze fronds or, in tropical water, *Cabomba* and *Vallisneria*.

Planting to suit the site

The prevailing climate of the area affects a plant's performance (see plant hardiness zones p.191), but more localized factors include the lie of the land, how exposed it is to the sun and wind, and the nature of the soil.

Sun, shade and wind

Positioning ponds in a sunny part of the garden (see p.18) benefits water lilies and many other water plants that require several hours of sunlight each day. A few are more tolerant of shady sites. When it comes to waterside plants, particularly those suitable for the naturalistic bog garden, preferences for sun or shade vary considerably. Plants native to damp woodlands, for instance, are often adapted to the dappled light beneath the tree canopy and should be given a position where they do not receive too much direct sunlight, perhaps under a specimen tree. Plants derived from open meadows, on the other hand, enjoy full sun and may not flower freely in too shady a position. Most gardens, even small ones, offer contrasting microclimates where both shade- and sun-loving plants can be accommodated, perhaps on either side of some tall feature.

Wind can present a problem in some sites, making shelter – or the support of neighbouring plants – necessary for tall slender plants, since staking by usual herbaceous border methods is not only out of keeping with most water garden styles but is impractical in a lined bog garden. Some plants need protection from cold or drying winds, which would scorch their leaves and damage their flowers, while others, such as bamboos and some grasses, are resilient enough to make living windbreaks and shelter belts in their own right.

Soil type and structure

Certain plants are tolerant of a wide range of soil types and will grow almost anywhere; others are more fussy and must be supplied with conditions closely resembling their native habitat. Some plants have evolved in the moist, humus-rich acidity of a peat bog; others are specially adapted to the damp, gravelly alkaline soil of a limestone gorge. It is worth doing a soil test to find out the pH of your site. If your soil is one or other extreme of the pH scale, or if you want to grow plants with pronounced preference for acidity or alkalinity, then the possible choices are more limited. In containers or small beds it is sometimes feasible to adjust soil type to some extent to accommodate a special plant. This is generally easier in formal designs where plants are employed for their visual impact and do not need to appear to be growing naturally. When planning natural or naturalistic bog or water gardens on a larger scale, it is preferable to go with the prevailing conditions, choosing those plants that grow happily in them.

The structure of the soil is equally crucial to the well-being of many plants, particularly in the bog or waterside garden, since it affects moisture retention and draining properties. Well-structured soil has spaces between the particles that contain air and water, both essential to root health, and such soil can be described as being both moist and well-aerated. A few plants are happy in saturated soil, with their roots in water; others like access to plenty of moisture but will not survive being water-logged. Plants that are not naturally bog-garden subjects will often settle happily in better drained spots on the edge of the bog garden.

While absorbent materials like leaf mould, manure and peat retain water like a sponge, sand and grit improve drainage. It is often possible to modify soil structure by incorporating quantities of the texture that is lacking – in some cases, just preparing a planting hole with the right kind of soil is enough to get the plant off to a good start.

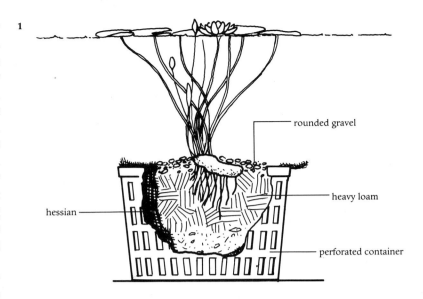

Planting in running water

Although there are fewer submerged plants that thrive in running water, those that do will greatly enhance a stream as well as provide valuable cover for insect life and small crustaceans. In a constructed stream, a good quality soil thickly covered in sharp sand or gravel will provide a growing medium for both submerged and emergent plants. New plants can be anchored with a stone over the roots until they are established.

Alongside the stream, hosts of moisture-loving subjects will flourish, many of the bog plants actually doing better with the movement of water through their roots. The advantage of a constructed stream, of course, is that water flow can be controlled so that emergent and marsh plants can be used at will to bring out the best in colour, foliage contrast and texture.

In natural running, water severe rainstorms may result in dramatic increases in flow rate and level. Where this is known to happen, use plants that root strongly and weed out those that have a loosening effect on soil, such as stinging nettles and Himalayan balsam (*Impatiens glandulifera*). If the stream is too long to plant up totally, selected areas of the banks can

be put down to grass. When strongly established, a grass bank will withstand several hours of fast-flowing flood water – and grass is, indeed, one of the best forms of planting to avoid erosion. Some bamboos, rushes and sedges are resistant to flooding and will root strongly in banks and hold the soil, but they are suitable only for situations where their invasive nature may be regarded as an advantage rather than a drawback. In warmer climates, erosion caused by flash floods is less of a problem, owing to the propensity of plants to colonize moist ground rapidly and to continue growing all year round. However, there are certain plants that are particularly good for ground stabilization when needed, such as the umbrella plant (*Cyperus alternifolius*) and the even more dramatic *C. papyrus*.

Planting in still water

As a rule all aquatics and moisture-loving plants are best newly planted or divided and transplanted in spring. Choose young plants, with their shoots just emerging, so that they have time to anchor firmly before the winter.

The old textbooks always advocated using heavy clay loam for water plants and this advice is still good today. The top spit of any good soil taken from some unused part of the garden, or from just beneath meadow turf, uncultivated and unfed by artificial fertilizers, is ideal. Special fertilizers for water plants are available in slow release form, to be applied at the beginning of the growing season each year. They come in small sachets that should be pushed down among the roots.

Ledges and containers

Although planting in perforated containers offers certain advantages, in that the plants can easily be resited or removed from the water, my own preference is to plant on soil ledges – except in the case of water lilies and the submerged aquatics – since this gives a far more natural effect.

1 Planting a container

Line perforated containers with hessian to prevent the soil running out through the holes. Plant firmly in heavy loam, taking great care not to bury the crown of the rhizome or tuber. Cover the soil with rounded gravel. Lower the basket into the pond, but do not submerge it until all the bubbles have stopped rising or the soil and plant may become dislodged.

RIGHT *Iris share the same ledge as the rock in this small, semi-formal water feature. A pump recirculates water over the rock, making an inviting corner for meditation. The tall blue* Iris sibirica *is planted just out of the water while* Iris laevigata 'Variegata' *with its striped leaves is planted slightly deeper. A rich growth of the submerged aquatic* Elodea canadensis *has also colonized the planting shelf, helping to maintain pure water and harbouring an abundance of beneficial water shrimps.*

The ledge in this simple butyl-lined pond has a covering of concrete to protect the liner and spread the load, enabling the heavy rock to sit alongside the plants.

Container planting tends to look unnatural, particularly when the containers show under the water. Plants grown in open soil in large retainers built into the pond will grow well when left undisturbed for longer periods. Container-grown plants quickly exhaust the comparatively small supply of nutrients available to them and many will rapidly outgrow their container. If you must use containers, they should be as large as possible. Plastic tubs (with a few holes pierced to allow an interchange of water through the roots) can be used, though wooden boxes, made from mature second hand timber, are ideal. Line them first with hessian, which will eventually rot away, to prevent the soil from coming straight out through the holes before the roots are established (diagram 1). Use a heavy loam with a little well-rotted cow manure (about 5 parts to 1) or a sprinkling of bonemeal for planting.

Planting water lilies

In formal ponds, water lilies are best planted in containers, rather than on planting ledges, since they never look their best when cramped up against the side of the pond. In large lined ponds it is better to restrict them by using containers or special enclosures. Brick or concrete enclosures should be about 60cm-1m/2-3ft across, either square or circular, and 15-23cm/6-9in deep. On a concrete base they can be built straight up from the concrete; where a liner has been used for the base, they can rest on an offcut of underlay or cushioning material to prevent damage to the liner. Each enclosure will take a good wheelbarrowful of planting compost. Sections of concrete pipe or concrete rings, 1m/3ft or more in diameter, also make effective water lily containers. They can be placed on top of each other until the required depth has been reached.

Choose plants with a good growing point at the crown and young leaves beginning to sprout. It is essential not to let the leaves and stalks dry out when planting, so lay them on the pool surface and cover them with newspaper until you are ready to plant. Cut back the long white anchorage roots to 15-20cm/6-8in from the tuber and make a depression in the earth in the centre of the hessian-lined container or enclosure. With the roots grasped close together and pointing downwards, place the plant in the depression and firm the earth around it. Soil must not cover the crown. Soak well, perhaps with a hosepipe, before placing in position.

In a shallow pond with a natural bottom and a complete covering of soil, plants can be pressed into the soil by hand. In deeper ponds or lakes, where this method is not possible, plants can be bundled up in soil in a weighted hessian bag with the crowns peeping out of the top, or planted up in woodchip baskets (which will have rotted away by the time the roots are established) and dropped in by boat. They are

sometimes simply tied, bare-rooted, to bricks and thrown in – a method I do not like, because the plant undergoes considerable stress while its roots are working their way into the soil. Water lilies do not like being plunged into deep water and unless there are already fairly long leaf stalks, they may die before they reach the surface. It is better to plant with two or three leaves at the surface, or not far beneath it, so that within a few days they will be on the surface and will flatten out. If the plant already has many leaves with long stalks, try to sort them out so that they are all floating the right way up (this may take a few days). Cut back any long straggly stalks to just above the crown, which will soon grow new leaves. It is sometimes necessary to contrive a method of keeping the plant raised until the leaves expand, gradually lowering it at intervals as the stems grow taller. Alternatively, start the container off in a shallow part of the pond, moving it to greater depths little by little.

Hardy water lilies should not be planted until the water reaches about 10°C/50°F, and tropicals not until the water temperature is about 21°C/70°F. (Tropicals are usually stored in a frost-free shed over winter and planted out again in spring.)

All water lilies, unless they are growing on a natural earth bottom, will need a change of soil every two years or so. They are gross feeders and established plants can be given added bonemeal. This can be applied in the form of small balls which can easily be made by rolling the bonemeal in moist soil between the palms. Always protect the hands with gloves while doing this. Bury the balls among the roots, but do not sprinkle them on the water surface. Alternatively, the plants may be given a regular feed of commercially produced water lily pellets.

When dividing water lilies that have been planted in an enclosure made from loose bricks or stones, dismantle the enclosure before attempting to cut through the roots; cutting through roots in mud is not easy if you keep running into solid material. The removal of the surround may also allow the whole fibrous mat of roots to come away from the bottom so that it can easily be divided. The bricks or stones should then be replaced and fresh soil and plants installed.

Dividing and propagating water plants

Apart from a few plants that are best propagated from seed, such as *Lobelia splendens* and candelabra primulas, most water plants are best propagated by division. The beginning of the growing season is the safest time for this as newly divided stock is vulnerable to rotting off in cold wet weather and

Where summers are hot but winters severe, planting in raised tubs within the pond is a sensible approach. Tender or tropical plants can be placed in the water in spring where they will flourish throughout the long hot summer. In the autumn some plants, such as iris and hardy water lilies, can be cut back and lowered below the ice level. Others will

have to be removed from the pond and taken to a frost-free refuge for the winter.

This pond at Wave Hill, New York, is essentially formal though it has been softened by tub planting. Sharp reflections in clear limpid water can be achieved through the use of a harmless black dye which absorbs the sunlight and thus discourages the growth of clouds of algae.

to damage from winter pests. As the plants start into growth, new shoots can be readily identified; the plant can then be split or carefully teased apart, retaining some growing roots on each piece. Some plants, such as *Butomus umbellatus* have delicate, brittle rhizomes, which must be carefully handled. Some of the tougher plants, such as *Scirpus* 'Zebrinus' particularly benefit from being cleanly cut downwards between the selected shoots with a sharp knife. Each piece, with its own section of roots, can then be planted out into the pond, where it will quickly increase into clumps of lovely fresh growth.

Plant pests and diseases

Marginal plants and floating-leaved aquatics are usually healthy plants in the first half of the growing season, but towards the end of summer their beauty can be marred by small creatures or fungal infections that attack the leaves and flowers.

Brown china mark moths (*Nymphula nymphaeta*), which can be seen hovering in clouds over ponds on late summer evenings, produce larvae that chew pieces off the edges of water lily leaves. Pick the larvae off the underside of the leaves or, in particularly severe cases, remove and destroy all floating vegetation so that fresh uncontaminated growth can eventually emerge.

Leaves and flowers riddled by holes may be caused by the small dark brown water lily beetle (*Galeruella nymphaea*), which is sometimes seen on paler petals. Hose the leaves down with a fine jet of water, washing off the beetles and their larvae. If there are fish in the pond, they will devour them; otherwise use a specially formulated proprietary product.

The water lily aphid (*Rhopalosiphum nymphaea*) is a form of blackfly that can smother the leaves of water lilies and emergent fleshy-leaved plants in late summer, causing decay. Repeated hosing down should dislodge them. If you do not have fish, which will eat them, obtain a specially formulated proprietary product to suppress them. Spray any neighbouring plum or cherry trees, where the aphids overwinter, with a proprietary fruit tree aphid wash.

Fish, particularly goldfish, are the only protection against the aquatic caddis fly larva that attacks the buds, shoots and roots of water lilies and other aquatics.

Fungal infections can affect marginal plants as well as water lilies. Most common is a harmless white mould which forms on the leaves of marsh marigolds or kingcups towards the end of summer. This does not seem to harm the plants and the new leaves will not be affected. On water lily leaves, fungal infections can be identified by disfiguring brown patches or dry shrivelled edges. It is essential that the affected foliage is removed at once and destroyed. Again, the fresh new leaves will come through unscathed.

Yellowing foliage may signal the rampant and devastating water lily crown rot, in which crown and stems turn black and jelly-like in texture and exude an evil smell. Burn infected plants and dispose of the soil they were growing in. A less drastic treatment is to lift the affected tubers and

Wildlife around this woodland pool is encouraged by the protective cover of bushes and trees, and boxes have been supplied to encourage nesting birds.

The royal fern (Osmunda regalis) and the sensitive fern (Onoclea sensibilis) thrive in the damp, shady conditions.

Sheltered waters like this can quickly become colonized in summer by floating plants such as duckweed – already visible as a green fringe round the water's edge in spring. A high-pressure water jet (from a portable water pump) or a rope pulled across will concentrate it in one spot from which it can be removed.

dose with Benlate or similar proprietary fungicide. Water lily crown rot is rarely a problem for the amateur water gardener, usually affecting commercial growers in hot weather.

Invasive plants: a warning

Most aquatic and moisture-loving plants reproduce freely and a word of warning should be given about those that may even verge on the rampageous, a quality which has led to some being banned in the United States as well as in other parts of the world. The water hyacinth (*Eichhornia crassipes*), for example, spreads rapidly and can cause so much disruption that Federal Law forbids shipping it interstate in the US and there are Movement Orders against it in many parts of the tropics and sub-tropics.

I have seen a small clump of the floating fern *Azolla caroliniana* grow in one month to cover a pond 40 sq m/48 sq yd in a green carpet that was mistaken for lawn by one visitor, with unfortunate consequences. This plant can also be reddish in colour and in autumn can give a disconcertingly convincing appearance of pink asphalt.

In temperate climates, duckweed (*Lemna minor*) can arrive spontaneously, transported on birds' feet, and rapidly cover sheltered water in a green sheet of tiny, rounded discs.

Certain plants that creep on the bottom and carpet the surface with floating leaves can also spread with undesirable rapidity. *Potamogeton natans* can cover a pond with its elliptical brown-green ribbed leaves and the humble water lily or water fringe, *Nymphoides peltata*, can also colonize small areas of a lake down to about 1m/3ft. Both of these floating-leaved plants are difficult to eradicate by hand and should not be introduced into shallow ponds with earth bottoms.

Crassula helmsii (formerly *Tillaea recurva*) is highly invasive. It needs to be kept firmly in check in gardens, and escapes into the wild have made it Britain's most menacing water plant. I would also warn against the true aquatic *Lagarosiphon major* (formerly *Elodea crispa*) that rapidly colonizes the bottoms of ponds up to 2m/6½ft deep. Its long branching stalks are bushy, with dark green leaves that run along the surface, often thickly entwined with algae.

Another plant to be treated with caution, and one of the biggest contributors to the silting up of lakes, is the reedmace or cattail (*Typha latifolia*), sometimes incorrectly called the bulrush. It grows on white sharply pointed, creeping rhizomes, working its way out into deeper water. Incomplete decomposition takes place each season, causing the water to become ever shallower and enabling the plant to creep further out during each growing period so that the pond becomes steadily smaller, while the brown pods emit thousands of airborne seeds that can start new colonies around any nearby water. Other reeds, grasses and rushes can also spread and crowd out some of the more delicate or desirable plants.

Purple loosestrife (*Lythrum salicaria*) was introduced into the United States from Europe as a decorative land plant about a century ago. It now overruns even *Typha latifolia* and it is illegal to move it in four states.

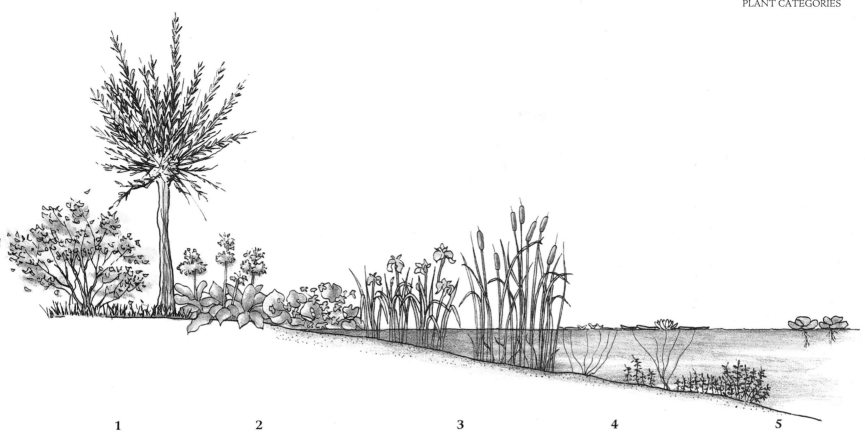

1   2   3   4   5

PLANT CATEGORIES

The plant descriptions that follow are arranged partly according to the role that each type of plant plays in the water garden and partly according to the conditions that each type prefers. They deal with planting in the wider framework of the dry garden before approaching the water itself.

1 Waterside trees and shrubs
Structural plants are a major design element in every garden, as well as providing shelter and privacy.

2 Plants for bog and marsh
Plants that relish moisture play a variety of roles in the damp ground between the water's edge and the higher drier parts of the garden.

1–3 Green foliage plants
Grown for their textural qualities, some of these thrive at the water's edge while others require good drainage and contribute to the surroundings of artificially constructed pools.

3 Emergent plants
Flourishing in a range of water depths, these plants are best established in shallower water at the edge of pools and slow-running streams.

4 Floating-leaved plants
These plants, which include the beautiful water lilies, make an ornamental display of foliage and flowers on the water's surface.

5 Aquatic plants
Surface-floating plants and the rooted submerged plants are valuable as purifiers as well as for their ornamental qualities.

The waterside habitat forms a continuum from the water itself through waterlogged and saturated soil to ground that is merely damp. Many plants will tolerate or even thrive in a wide range of these conditions. To avoid repetition I have placed plants in the category that represents them most characteristically, so if a plant seems to be missing please consult the index to see if I have allocated it to a different category. (The index will also provide enlightenment when botanical names have changed.) The figures for H (height at maturity), S (the approximate spread of a fully grown plant) and WD (the optimum water depth in which the plant will grow) are rough indications. These factors obviously vary enormously according to circumstances, as plants themselves do.

When reading about an unfamiliar plant and pondering its suitability for one's garden, sometimes it is helpful to know its place of origin, to learn that its natural habitat is a Florida swamp or a cool mountain forest, a lush watermeadow or a rocky gully. Such images convey more to the gardener than information about minimum temperatures tolerated. Climate is the deciding factor for assessing whether a plant will suit the site, and a 'Z' figure (designating hardiness zones: see p.191) is suggested for each plant.

Waterside trees and shrubs

Many trees and shrubs make admirable waterside subjects because of their ability to thrive in wet places. The willows and the swamp cypress (Taxodium distichum) are obvious candidates for a site that is naturally moist. Others are valuable for their sheer beauty in the water garden: the red-leaved dwarf Japanese maple, Acer palmatum var. dissectum, seems to have a visual affinity for small pools, and the fact that it is not moisture-loving makes it possible to plant it in ordinary garden soil beside an artificial pond.

Trees and shrubs planted to provide shelter and privacy can often be chosen for their attractive foliage or to serve as a backdrop to more colourful shrubs and marginal plants. Apart from vivid autumn leaf colour, many offer the bonus of winter display as their colourful bark glows among the season's prevailing muted tones. The obvious contrast of the red-barked dogwood Cornus alba 'Sibirica' – planted against a background of Portugal laurel (Prunus lusitanica) with its glossy dark evergreen leaves – springs to mind for winter coloration. In summer a different dogwood, Cornus alba 'Elegantissima' with its silver-variegated leaves and red stems, would lend a beautiful backdrop to the pink flowers of the flowering rush Butomus umbellatus. In more tropical climates flame-red cannas may be envisaged, lit up like fire against a green background of the cabbage palm, Sabal palmetto. Such effects acquire double the impact when the composition is seen reflected in the water surface.

Trees and shrubs are major structural elements in a garden's design and should be chosen and positioned not only for colour effects but also for the way in which their mass will balance and complement the horizontal expanse of water. Selecting plants with a suitable size at maturity is crucial. Weeping willows (Salix babylonica or S. x sepulchralis var. chrysocoma) should only be planted by rivers or the largest of lakes, but there are several smaller willows with a characteristic weeping form.

Size may also have some bearing on the choice between native and exotic trees. Trees often vary considerably in stature in a new environment. Some species of eucalyptus, native to Australia, grow moderately in temperate zones, but become impossibly vigorous in, for instance, the Californian climate. Some of the towering North American maples and tulip trees grow sufficiently soberly in the different climatic conditions of Britain to be included as modest-sized specimens, but would need a garden of vast dimensions in their native region.

Apart from the visual impact, practicalities to consider when siting trees include the shade they will eventually cast, the possibility of leaf-fall into the water and potential nuisance from roots, especially for clay ponds.

ACER Aceraceae

Mostly grown for their ornamental foliage and bark, the maples make excellent waterside subjects for their form, delicacy of leaf and general habit of growth. Most are happy on dry land, in semi-shade and well-drained soil, though a few such as *A. rubrum* will stand swamp conditions. The richest display of autumn foliage colours is achieved in slightly acidic soils.

A. davidii, Père David's maple (H to 15m/50ft or less S 10m/33ft Z6), is a snake-bark maple from central China, particularly noted for its display of striped bark in the winter garden. The dark green oval leaves of this lovely tree provide good autumn colour when they turn orange yellow.

A. palmatum Dissectum Atropurpureum Group comprises various Japanese cultivars with finely dissected deeply lobed leaves of bronze-purple, which produce a brilliant autumn display of red, orange or yellow. Their graceful weeping habit (H & S 1.5m/5ft Z5) conforms beautifully to cascading over rocks. Plant near pools, but away from damp areas, in neutral to acid soil.

A. pseudoplatanus 'Brilliantissimum' has attractive, shrimp-pink young foliage that turns to dark green by summer. This makes a dramatic reflection behind the still pond in spring time. Very slow-growing, it takes many years to reach its full stature (H 4m/13ft S 3m/10ft Z5). It grows best in full sun.

A. rubrum, swamp maple, red maple or Canadian maple, makes a magnificent tree, its size varying considerably (H to 40m/130ft S variable Z3). It has a smooth grey bark and red branches when young. Clusters of tiny red flowers cover the branches before the green ivy-shaped leaves appear in the spring. The foliage turns to a vivid scarlet in autumn, particularly in acid soils. Flourishing from the swamps of Florida to the mountains of Canada, this adaptable tree will grow in marshy ground or as a background in drier conditions.

A. saccharinum, silver maple, attracts attention when the wind rustles the leaves, which are large and deeply lobed with silver undersides. Its good autumn colour of yellow and creamy-brown with a touch of scarlet, retains this silvery contrast until leaf drop. Plant well away from the pond because of the heavy leaf-fall and their dislike of moisture. Trees are unlikely to attain full stature (H to 30m/100ft S to 40m/130ft Z3) outside the USA.

A. saccharum, sugar maple from North America, is reckoned to have the brightest autumn colouring of all the maples – a breathtaking orange and scarlet, unforgettable seen reflected in a still pond beneath a clear blue sky. Plant well back, behind cornus or nyssa, as it becomes a very large tree indeed (H 40m/130ft S 30m/100ft Z4).

ALNUS Betulaceae

Alders are moisture-loving and make popular subjects for growing in difficult wet situations, in sun or semi-shade. These hardy deciduous trees and shrubs have conical outlines and some produce attractive catkins in spring.

A. cordata, Italian alder, is native to Corsica and southern Italy (H to 15m/50ft S 10m/33ft Z6). Bright yellow catkins adorn the tree in spring, followed by dark shiny green leaves with grey undersides. Small brown cones produced in autumn remain on the branches until spring. Plant right by the lakeside, where the falling grubs of the alder fly will provide fish with a welcome food supply. It likes full sun and wet conditions.

A. glutinosa 'Aurea' (H to 25m/80ft S 10m/33ft Z2) is a cultivar of black or common alder with attractive bright yellow spring foliage. It appreciates moist soil and dappled shade. Relatively slow-growing, it looks beautiful by the lakeside or on a small island.

A. incana, grey alder, is a useful subject for poorer moist soils (H to 20m/65ft S 10m/33ft Z2). *A.i.* 'Aurea' has brightly coloured shoots and young foliage, and also provides good autumn colour. Its catkins are tinted red. *A.i.* 'Laciniata', cut-leaved grey alder, is similar, but with deeply cut leaves.

A. rubra, red or Oregon alder, makes a fine background planting (H to 30m/100ft S 20m/65ft Z6). Its shoots and buds are dark red, and it produces a profusion of long catkins.

ANDROMEDA Ericaceae

A. polifolia, marsh rosemary, is a hardy evergreen shrub (H & S 30cm/12in Z2), native to northern temperate zones, with dark glossy green pointed leaves. It bears clusters of pitcher-shaped flowers of sugar-icing pink and white in early summer. It thrives best in a moist acid soil with plenty of humus. One of the few low evergreen plants for the bog and waterside, this is particularly useful planted to provide winter disguise for necessities such as lamps and electrical sockets.

BETULA Betulaceae

These birches are popular and choice deciduous trees that provide interest throughout the year. Some are particularly suited to small gardens.

B. nigra, river or black birch, native to eastern North America, is a beautiful, neat-growing tree, ideal for wet ground (H 20m/65ft S 10m/33ft Z4). It has shaggy orange-pink and black peeling bark. The glossy green leaves turn yellow in autumn.

B. papyrifera, paper or canoe birch, is quick-growing (H 30m/100ft S 20m/65ft Z2) and will adapt to various types of soil and withstand wind,

ABOVE *BETULA PAPYRIFERA*
OPPOSITE *ACER PALMATUM*

but appreciates ample light. It forms a graceful round-headed tree with a peeling white papery bark and silvery-yellow catkins in spring. The serrated oval leaves turn a lovely clear yellow in autumn.

B. pendula, silver birch or European white birch (H to 30m/100ft S 20m/65ft Z2), forms a slender tree with a graceful pendulous habit. It has silver bark with black patches, yellow catkins up to 5cm/2in long and serrated oval leaves that turn golden-yellow in autumn. Grow singly or in a group by the pondside for reflections. The light dappled shade of their canopy is very suitable for an underplanting of blue flowers such as omphalodes or bluebells. *B.p.* 'Golden Cloud' is smaller (H to 15m/50ft S 10m/33ft Z2), with arching branches and finely dissected golden leaves. It is ideal for the smaller garden or as an ornamental island tree.

CEPHALANTHUS Rubiaceae

C. occidentalis, button bush (H & S 2m/6½ft Z6), is favoured for its beautiful fragrant cream flowers produced in late summer. Native to boggy areas of the southeastern USA and Mexico, this deciduous shrub appreciates rich, slightly acidic moist soil in full sun. It makes an ideal single specimen in the bog or surrounded by gravel.

CORNUS KOUSA VAR. SINENSIS

CORNUS ALBA 'SIBIRICA'

CORNUS STOLONIFERA 'FLAVIRAMEA'

CORNUS Cornaceae
Dogwoods make excellent waterside subjects, variously offering coloured bark or variegated leaves, or making handsome small trees with the bonus of flower interest.

Dogwoods for stem or leaf interest
These coloured-stemmed and variegated shrubs will grow near the water. The younger growth displays the brightest colours, so prune hard to encourage new shoots. Pruning at about 15cm/6in above ground level will cause a plant to send up a spray of long thin shoots to about 1m/3ft. Main

stems can be pruned or pollarded higher up, causing the plant to display at a greater height, while a combination of high and low pruning will produce a bank of colour. If not pruned each spring, the bushes grow larger and more branching, eventually becoming straggling mounds with only a haze of colour at the tips. For a good show of colour on substantial bushes with a more natural appearance, prune a proportion of stems on a two- or three-year cycle to give the bushes bursts of colour among the duller stems. Most are easily propagated from cuttings; stems cut off and pushed into the shallows will quickly form roots.

C. alba is a suckering shrub from the Far East with upright red-stemmed young growth that provides a desirable splash of colour in autumn and winter (H & S 3m/10ft Z3). The oval leaves also colour well in autumn. Small white flowers in late spring to early summer are followed by bluish-white fruits in autumn. There are several good cultivars. *C.a.* 'Aurea' has dazzling golden foliage. *C.a.* 'Elegantissima' has oval green leaves 3-8cm/1-3in long with lovely wide silvery-white margins. *C.a.* 'Spaethii' is similar, but with yellow-margined leaves that are an attractive bronze colour when young. *C.a.* 'Sibirica', the Westonbirt dogwood, has

dark coral-pink branches and green foliage and is much less vigorous (H 1.2m/4ft S 1m/3ft Z3).
C. stolonifera, red osier, is a vigorous North American shrub (H & S 2-3m/6½-10ft Z2) that spreads rapidly by putting out stolons. The smooth young shoots are dark red and will form a great mound by the lakeside. More useful is *C.s.* 'Flaviramea', a form of similar habit but with bright yellow or lime-green shoots. When hard pruned or pollarded, this looks wonderful with the red-stemmed varieties.

Flowering dogwoods

These ornamental trees and shrubs are best left to form their own lovely natural shapes; prune back only when necessary to reduce the size. They tend to prefer rather drier conditions, and are useful for planting to accentuate headlands and provide reflections.
C. florida is a fully hardy deciduous tree from the eastern USA (H to 10m/33ft S 6m/20ft Z5). In spring the insignificant green flowers are attractively surrounded by lovely white bracts. The white- and pink-edged leaves provide vivid purple autumn colour, coinciding with bright red berries. This does best in neutral to acid soils. There is also a pink form, and several beautiful cultivars, including the lovely rose-pink *C.f.* 'Apple Blossom', and *C.f.* 'White Cloud', with vivid white bracts.
C. kousa var. *chinensis* is also grown mainly for the striking white bracts surrounding the small flowers in late spring to early summer, followed later by strawberry-like fruits. The leaves turn a brilliant fiery red in autumn. It makes an upright, vase-shaped shrubby tree (H to 7m/23ft S 5m/16ft Z5).
C. macrophylla makes an attractive spreading tree or tall shrub with large oval pointed leaves (H & S 15m/50ft Z6). Tiny cream flowers, held in large clusters 10-15cm/4-6in across, look like snow dusting the branches in summer. They are followed by blue-black fruits. Grow in full sun and well-drained soil.

EUCALYPTUS Myrtaceae

Eucalyptus grown for ornament are valued for their aromatic fragrance, attractive peeling bark and distinctive juvenile foliage. Although this Australian genus of evergreen trees and shrubs is often associated with sun and well-drained soils, many species thrive in permanently boggy ground. Large trees and those long confined to pots often have difficulty 'getting away' when transplanted, and their lack of proper root anchorage makes them vulnerable to wind. Choose small young specimens for planting so that they will establish good root systems *in situ*.

KALMIA LATIFOLIA 'CLEMENTINE CHURCHILL'

E. camphora (*E. ovata* var. *glauca*), the mountain swamp gum, is a tree with lovely grey to dark brown-grey smooth bark (H 21m/70ft S 15m/50ft Z9). The juvenile leaves are oval to elliptical and green; the adult leaves are broadly lance-shaped, 13x5cm/5x2in. In its native habitat this will grow even in shallow water.
E. globulus, Tasmanian blue gum, is a tall tree that grows rapidly to its full height (H to 30m/100ft S to 21m/70ft Z8-9), but it can be kept stooled and grown as a shrub. It produces flowers throughout summer and autumn, and even later. The bark peels attractively into ribbon-like strips. The oval juvenile leaves are a beautiful silvery-blue; the adult ones long, narrow and a glossy mid-green. This provides very effective foliage contrast in moist or dry conditions. A slower-growing tree with a beautiful trunk of cream, green and grey is *E. niphophila*, the snow gum.

EUCRYPHIA Eucryphiaceae

E. lucida is an erect, bushy evergreen tree from Tasmania (H to 10m/33ft S 3m/10ft Z9). The lance-shaped glossy dark green leaves provide a good background to the nodding, open cup-shaped fragrant white flowers that appear in summer. It prefers moist but well-drained lime-free soil. It will withstand exposure when placed in mild, wet situations and makes a lovely evergreen flowering shrub for walkways around the pond. A beautiful variety with larger scented flowers is *E.x nymansensis* 'Nymansay', which tolerates alkaline soil and is slightly hardier (Z8).

EUCRYPHIA LUCIDA

ILLICIUM Illiciaceae

I. anisatum, star anise, is native to Japan and Taiwan. It makes a conical shrub or small tree (H 7m/23ft S 5m/16ft Z8), an ideal scented evergreen to plant to provide seclusion by the pondside, perhaps behind a sitting area. Both the wood and the lance-shaped leaves, up to 13cm/5in long, are very aromatic. The white or pale greenish-yellow flowers cluster densely in the leaf axils when they appear in spring, but are not fragrant. Hardy to -5°C/23°F or slightly below, plants fare better when given some protection or shelter. They prefer neutral to acid moist soils.

KALMIA Ericaceae

These hardy evergreen shrubs from North America have clusters of attractive summer flowers. Grow in sun or partial shade, in moist acid peaty soil, mulching with leaf mould or pine needles. Propagate by softwood cuttings in spring.
K. angustifolia rubra, sheep laurel, forms spreading bushy mounds (H & S 1.5m/5ft Z2) and is easily propagated by layering. Clusters of saucer-shaped red flowers are borne for many weeks in summer amid lance-shaped dark green leaves.
K. latifolia, calico bush or mountain laurel, is a gorgeous shrub (H & S 3m/10ft Z4), flowering in early summer. It has shiny dark green foliage and masses of clusters of crimped saucer-shaped flowers, opening from distinctive buds shaped like little piped icing rosettes. Cultivars have flower colours ranging from white to red and purple, often with red markings.

NYSSA SYLVATICA

NYSSA Nyssaceae

The tupelos are deciduous broadly conical trees renowned for their brilliant autumn foliage (H to 15m/50ft S 8m/25ft Z3). They do well on moist soils that are acid to neutral. *N. aquatica*, water tupelo from the southeastern USA, has long, pointed leaves with downy undersides. *N. sylvatica*, black gum or swamp tupelo from eastern North America, is one of the most beautiful small waterside trees. It has a dense crown of leathery leaves that turn a glorious orange, red or yellow in autumn. It often produces a swollen trunk when grown in water. Small blue fruits are excellent for wildlife. *N.s.* var. *biflora* bears the insignificant summer flowers in pairs.

POPULUS Salicaceae

The deciduous poplars provide quick-growing hardy specimens for the larger garden, and an interesting variety of forms. All need moist well-drained soils.

P. balsamifera, balsam poplar (H 30m/100ft S 8m/ 25ft Z2), is a North American native that rapidly reaches its full stature given moist, deeply cultivated soil with good drainage. The large oval glossy leaves are dark green with white undersides and exude a sweet aroma when unfolding. Male catkins 8cm/3in long and female ones almost twice that length drape bare branches in spring.

P. x *candicans*, balm of Gilead (H to 15m/50ft S 6m/20ft Z2), wafts a particularly delicious odour in spring when the sticky leaf buds open. *P.* x *c.* 'Aurora' (*P.* x *jackii* 'Aurora') is a variegated form, its dark green leaves splashed with creamy-white, and attractively flushed pale pink when young. Hard pruning each spring improves the coloration; the tree can be kept pollarded to any height.

P. nigra, black poplar (H 25m/80ft S 20m/65ft Z2), is a spreading tree from Europe and western Asia that likes plenty of moisture. It has dark rough bark and bright shining leaves that open bronze in spring and turn yellow in autumn. The male tree bears red catkins. The well-known slender form, *P.n.* 'Italica', the Lombardy poplar, is also moisture-loving. An even better form is *P.n.* 'Plantierensis', which is stronger, bushier, and much more resistant to disease.

P. tremula, the aspen, makes a medium spreading tree (H 15m/50ft S 10m/33ft Z2). The rounded leaves are often bronze-tinged when young, maturing to grey-green and turning a pale yellow in autumn; their flattened stems allow the slightest wind to stir them into attractive quivering motion. Long grey catkins adorn the branches in early spring. *P.t.* 'Pendula' combines the same characteristics with a weeping habit.

SALIX Salicaceae

Grown for their habit, foliage, catkins or colourful winter stems, the willows tend to prefer moist soils and do well near water, some actually growing in the shallows.

The young stems of several willows have attractive bark in winter, most colourful on new growth. The practice of pruning hard back – or pollarding – in spring ensures a supply of bright vigorous new shoots each year. These may attain 2m/6½ft or more, according to type and conditions. While they grow during the summer they are clothed with fresh new leaves, and as the stems ripen in autumn the colour intensifies ready for the show when the leaves fall.

Cut or stool willows near the ground for a low-level display, at shoulder height for convenience, or even higher, according to the setting. A maximum number of shoots is obtained by pruning a willow each spring. If left for two or more years, branches will grow longer and thicker but when cut will sprout new shoots only on the periphery of the wound. The trees can, of course, be left to attain their full natural height, but colour interest will be confined to the young tips of the branches. A multistemmed willow with trunks at slightly different heights and pollarded each year will produce a most dramatic effect.

Most willows grow easily from cuttings; branches broken off and thrust into wet mud often generate into new trees.

Shapely waterside trees and shrubs
These willows are planted primarily for the overall effect of their habit rather than for any detail of leaves, flowers or bark. They are plants chosen for the impact that their form and outline contribute to a waterside composition.

S. alba, the white willow, is a hardy deciduous tree native to Europe and northern Asia. Fast-growing and vigorous, it is conical when young, spreading in maturity (H 25m/80ft S 10m/33ft Z2). The narrow lance-shaped leaves, to 10cm/4in long, are a bright silver-grey, growing on pinkish-grey to olive-brown branches. *S.a.* var. *sericea*, the silver willow, is smaller and slower-growing, giving an even more silvery impression from a distance.

S. babylonica, weeping willow, is a graceful tree with weeping branches and long pendulous twigs that can hang down to the ground (H & S 12m/40ft Z5); most plants in cultivation are now actually forms of *S.* x *sepulcralis*. The narrow lance-shaped leaves are 8-15cm/3-6in long, green above and grey-green underneath. It bears elegant yellow-green catkins in early spring. Beware of planting this too near a pond, as branches, twigs or leaves dropped in still water have a toxic effect; it is gorgeous beside a river, where this propensity to shed does no harm.

S.b. var. *pekinensis* 'Tortuosa' (*S. matsudana* 'Tortuosa') is known as the contorted or corkscrew willow or the dragon's claw willow (H & S 15m/50ft Z5). It has upright, spiralling branches with young shoots displaying many twists and convolutions, and twisted green leaves with blue-green undersides. Plant it alone as a curiosity. The tree may lose lustre and vigour, with some dieback after a number of years; pruning branches hard back to perhaps half their length will encourage fresh new growth and renewed vitality.

S. caprea 'Kilmarnock' (*S.c. pendula*), Kilmarnock willow, is a male cultivar of the goat or pussy willow with a weeping habit (H 1.5-2m/5-6½ft S 2m/6½ft Z5). Its dark green toothed oval leaves have downy grey undersides, and it has silky grey spring catkins 2.5cm/1in long. Good by small ponds and on islands, it may be grown as a shrub or a small tree.

S. purpurea 'Pendula' is the weeping form of the purple osier, a graceful shrub or tree (H & S 5m/ 16ft Z5). It has slender drooping stems that are purple when young. In early spring catkins with red stamens that turn dark purple are borne all along last season's growth, appearing before the

SALIX BABYLONICA

SALIX ALBA 'BRITZENSIS'

leaves. This compact and pretty tree can be clipped to form a perfect umbrella shape, lovely in the smaller water garden or on a small island.

Willows for stem colour or flower interest
These willows include plants chosen primarily for qualities such as attractive catkins that merit close observation, or for the brilliant colour of young growth. They perform best during the leafless period from winter into spring.

S. alba forms and cultivars with particularly good stem colour include *S.a.* 'Britzensis', the scarlet willow with greener-tinged leaves and bright orange-red new shoots, and *S.a.* var. *vitellina*, the golden willow, with bright orange-yellow shoots. Pollard each spring for best effect.

S. elaeagnos ssp. *angustifolia* (*S. rosmarinifolia* of gardens), the hoary willow, has narrow grey leaves with white undersides on purple-brown wand-like stems. It is beautiful at the water's edge beside a pond or stream or on an island. It naturally makes a tall shrub or small tree (H 3m/10ft S 5m/16ft Z4). Forming a dense clump of arching stems, it provides good cover for ducks. It can also be pollarded at various heights annually or biennially to produce quite Chinese effects. Annual spring pruning about shoulder height on a multistemmed clump makes a wonderful contrast with cornus and bamboo species.

S. gracilistyla is a bushy shrub of Far Eastern origin (H 3m/10ft S 4m/13ft Z6). It is grown for its showy silky grey catkins, with anthers that turn from red to bright yellow, and for its silky grey lance-shaped leaves that later mature to a bright shiny green. The slightly smaller *S.g.* 'Melanostachys' (*S. melanostachys*), black willow, is an attractive and unusual shrub. It bears striking black catkins that open to reveal red anthers. These are followed by serrated glaucous leaves.

S. irrorata is a hardy upright shrub from the southwestern USA (H 3m/10ft S 5m/16ft Z5). Its dark purplish young shoots with beautiful white bloom afford very effective winter colour. The short catkins appear in spring, with red anthers gradually changing to yellow, and are followed by glossy lance-shaped green leaves. Cut this plant hard back each spring for the best winter display, either just above ground level or at 2m/6½ft high to make a short tree.

Smaller and dwarf willows
These include compact, slower-growing shrubby willows, often native to alpine habitats. They are particularly suitable for smaller gardens.

S. hastata 'Wehrhahnii' is a slow-growing, spreading shrub (H 1m/3ft S 1.5m/5ft Z6). It has smooth purple-brown upright stems prettily clothed in spring with masses of silvery-grey catkins.

S. reticulata, net-veined willow (H 10cm/4in S 30cm/12in or more Z3), is remarkable for its creeping habit on moist fibrous soil. It makes a low carpet of round, deeply textured leaves, with pink-tipped yellow catkins rising up from the male plants in spring.

S. 'Stuartii' is a slow-growing, spreading shrub (H 1m/3ft S 2m/6½ft Z3) with, oval, grey, downy leaves. Its yellow shoots in winter bear orange buds that open into fat yellowish-grey woolly catkins.

S. udensis 'Sekka' (to H & S 2.5m/8ft Z5) is sought after by flower arrangers for its curious flattened purplish coiling stems.

SORBUS Rosaceae
These deciduous trees are excellent planted in groups beside or behind ponds for their contribution of attractive form and colourful berries. They grow easily in moist soils.

S. aria, whitebeam, forms a compact, round-headed tree (H 12m/40ft S 10m/33ft Z5). Its oval leaves are greyish-white when young, maturing to dark green with felted white undersides. The silvery overall effect contrasts wonderfully with neighbouring trees in summer, and the foliage colours well to gold and russet in autumn, when deep red berries add to the display. This resilient European native withstands winds and coastal conditions. *S.a.* 'Lutescens' has creamy-white

TAXODIUM DISTICHUM

Plants for bog and marsh

The habitats known as bog, marsh, swamp, fen and a host of other evocative names conjure mysterious worlds, where plants emerge from the blackest ooze, lush, glossy and seductive. In nature these spots occupy a transitional zone between a stream or pool and higher, better-drained land. Such environments often have constantly fluctuating water levels, and plants that colonize them are consequently highly adaptable as to the degree of moisture they require. An individual plant will often both extend right out into the water and climb upward to colonize drier ground. As garden subjects, many of these versatile species (and their 'improved' descendants, the cultivars and garden hybrids) thrive in ordinary border soil, provided it never becomes too dry.

In the garden the area where these plants will grow best may be the damp zone between the edge of a natural pond or stream and the higher dry soil of the main garden or an isolated pocket of moist soil, perhaps fed by some underground spring. When creating water features artificially, it is easy to install irrigation and to inhibit drainage so that the soil can be kept permanently moist. An area adjacent to the pond makes a logical place for a bog garden, offering the benefit of reflections in the water surface and enlarging the apparent size of the pond area. Along the banks of a stream, lower-lying sections of bank or pockets of planting offer a succession of foliage contrasts and occasional bursts of colour, drawing the visitor along to enjoy clump after clump of varying form and texture, and creating a series of new frames for views of the water itself. However, an artificially made bog garden can equally well be far from water. It can be tiny, occupying the fork in a garden path in full sun, or filling a hollow in dappled shade in a woodland setting. Wherever placed, it will enable the gardener to grow a tantalizing range of different plants.

Garden plants that relish moisture in the soil are not restricted to those whose parents evolved in boggy environments. Some originated in meadows – damp, open grassland – and thus enjoy sunnier sites. Others derive from areas of damp woodland, relishing shady and moist ground, rich in leaf mould. A few plants come from high mountain pastures or gullies, the ground kept moist by melting snows from higher up. The descriptions that follow indicate whether a plant has any strong preferences for sun or shade, or for a particular type of soil.

The majority of the plants described in this section are perennials grown for the beauty of their foliage and their seasonal flowers. Many of the grassy plants and ferns in 'Green Foliage Plants' on pp.150-157 are also candidates as companion plants for the bog and marsh.

young foliage and a fine upright, branching habit, making this a most suitable tree for lakeside planting.

S. aucuparia, rowan or mountain ash (H 15m/50ft S 8m/25ft Z2), is a splendid small tree native to Europe, well loved for its attractive pinnate leaves and bright red clustered fruits in autumn. It has several beautiful cultivars, including S.a. 'Pendula', with a widely spreading weeping habit. They thrive even in very acid soils.

TAXODIUM Taxodiaceae
These large deciduous conifers from North and Central America are adapted to growing in very wet conditions, producing special spongy-textured growths or 'knees' that help the roots to breathe when they are underwater; they will tolerate a water depth of 60cm/24in once established. They make magnificent single specimens or groups by the larger pond or lake. Propagate from seed or by cuttings in late summer.

TELOPEA TRUNCATA

T. ascendens, pond cypress, makes a narrow, compact tree (H 25m/80ft S 15m/50ft Z7). It rarely produces 'knees', but broadens at the trunk base. It has spreading slender branches with pointed pale green yew-like leaves that turn a rusty brown in autumn. Although it will grow in the Florida swamps, this tree can stand drier conditions.

T. distichum, swamp cypress, is well known from the Everglades region of Florida. It grows to a fine conical shape (H 30m/100ft S 23m/75ft Z6). It has thick, smooth russet bark that peels off in strips. Alternate small pointed leaves of pale bronze-green, arranged in two rows on either side of the twigs, turn golden-brown in autumn. Small rounded greenish-brown cones are 1-2.5cm/½-1in across.

TELOPEA Proteaceae
T. truncata, Tasmanian waratah, is an upright evergreen shrub, which becomes bushy when mature (H 5m/16ft S 2.5m/8ft Z9). Large rounded heads of small crimson flowers appear in late spring and summer against a backdrop of glossy deep green leaves. It enjoys a moist, acid soil, and is ideal planted near ponds or bogs as a shelter or shade for more delicate lower-growing plants.

VACCINIUM Ericaceae
V. macrocarpon, American cranberry, is a mat-forming evergreen shrub (to H 45cm/18in S 2m/6½ft Z6). The small elliptical leaves are dark green above and white-tinged below. Pale pink flowers are followed in summer by edible but acidic red fruits; one form produces the commercial cranberry. It likes a moist, acid soil, and is attractive to clothe stream banks or provide year-round interest in the bog garden.

ARUNCUS Rosaceae

A. dioicus (A. sylvester) is a moisture-loving perennial with delicate light green foliage made up of ovate leaflets (H 1.5-1.8m/5-6ft S1m/3ft Z4). At midsummer it produces branching plumes of creamy-white flowers resembling bunches of fluffy pipe-cleaners. Female flowers are succeeded by reddish-brown seed heads. This plant will tolerate full light. Cut back the stems in autumn, propagating at the same time by dividing the clumps, or sow seed in autumn. An excellent, more compact form is *A.d.* 'Kneiffii' (H 1m/3ft S 60cm/2ft). Besides its creamy summer flower plumes, this cultivar is worth growing for its foliage alone. Its leaves are so finely cut as to give an almost skeletal but very beautiful filigree appearance, making a contrast to almost anything else in the bog garden. Propagate by division.

ASCLEPIAS Asclepiadaceae

A. incarnata, swamp milkweed (named for the white latex exuded by cut stems), is a tall tuberous-rooted perennial from North America (H 1.65m/5ft S1.2-1.5m/4-5ft Z3). It makes a strong clump of erect stems clad in lance-shaped mid-green leaves and topped in summer by slightly drooping umbels of pinky-white horned flowers. Grow in sunny but moist conditions, in humus-rich soil, propagating by division in autumn or spring.

ASTER Compositae

A. novae-angliae, the Michaelmas daisies, originate from damp, sunny habitats in eastern North America and suit large, naturalistic planting schemes. These perennials prefer fertile, well-drained but moisture-retentive soil and thrive in sun or semi-shade. The taller varieties benefit from the support of neighbouring plants when they flower from late summer. Some are prone to mildew and insect attacks in early summer. Propagate by division in autumn or spring.
A.n.-a. 'Harrington's Pink' brightens the drier parts of the bog garden with clusters of clear pink daisy-like flowers in autumn (H 1.5m/5ft S 90cm-1.2m/3-4ft Z2). Among slightly more compact cultivars, *A.n.-a.* 'Andenken an Alma Pötschke' has flowers of fiery carmine (H 75cm/30in S 60cm/24in), while *A.n.-a.* 'Herbstschnee' has yellow-centred white flowers (H 75-105cm/30-42in S 60cm/24in).

ASTILBE Saxifragaceae

A wide range of astilbes make good candidates for planting in the water garden. Attractive for both foliage and flower, these rhizomatous perennials have deeply divided leaves, often coppery red, and bear frothy spires of tiny colourful flowers in summer, followed by reddish-brown seed heads which can be used in winter flower arrangements. Astilbes enjoy a humus-rich, moist soil, but must not be waterlogged. Propagate by sowing seed in autumn or division in spring. Their delicacy of form makes excellent foliage contrast for primulas, iris and hostas, but the stronger flower colours need careful placing to avoid eclipsing the more subtle bog plants.
A. x *arendsii* 'Fanal' forms mounds of rich green ferny leaves and has fine plumes of tiny brilliant crimson flowers, succeeded by long-lasting rust-coloured seed heads (H 75cm/30in S 45cm/18in Z6). *A.* x *a.* 'Irrlicht' has dark green dissected foliage, and its flowers are delightful frothy plumes of white (H 45-60cm/18-24in S 30cm/12in Z6).
A. 'Bressingham Beauty' is a lovely tall astilbe (H 90cm/3ft S 60cm/24in Z5) with plumy panicles of deep pink flowers, borne in midsummer above broadly divided green leaves.

ARUNCUS DIOICUS

ASTILBE x *ARENDSII* 'FANAL'

A. chinensis 'Pumila' makes good ground cover for damp, shady areas. Clumps of finely dissected serrated hairy foliage bear plumes of small magenta flowers in late summer (H 20-30cm/8-12in S 30cm/12in Z5).

A.c. var. *taquetii* 'Superba' is a very useful astilbe, continuing to flower long after the others are over. A handsome plant (H 90cm/3ft S 45cm/18in Z5) with bronze-tinted foliage, it has plumes of purplish-pink flowers which are similar to those of *A.c.* 'Pumila'.

A. rivularis, from Nepal to western China, is an astilbe on a larger scale (H 1.8m/6ft S 1.2m/4ft Z7). It is an imposing foliage plant for moist well-drained soil in the wild garden or by the pool bank. Clumps of deeply divided textured leaves are topped in summer by arching plumes of tiny greenish-white flowers that mature into attractive brown seed heads.

A. 'Sprite' is an attractive low-growing astilbe (H 45cm/18in S 75cm/30in Z5) with finely dissected foliage of a bronze tint and beautifully comple-mentary panicles of shell-pink flowers.

A. thunbergii hybrids have a particularly graceful effect, better suited to mixing naturally with other waterside plants than many of the stiffer and more brashly coloured cultivars. *A.* 'Professor van der Wielen' (H & S 45cm/18in Z5) has arching, open plumes of creamy-white. Those of *A.* 'Straussenfeder' (*A.* 'Ostrich Plume') are coral-pink (H 90cm/3ft S 60cm/24in).

ASTILBOIDES Saxifragaceae

A. tabularis (formerly *Rodgersia tabularis*) from China produces great round slightly scalloped leaves of up to 90cm/3ft diameter, supported on a central stem. Drooping clusters of small creamy-white flowers are borne on stout stems above the foliage in summer. Grow this superb waterside plant (H & S 90cm-1.2m/3-4ft Z7) in moist soil, in sun or shade. Propagate by dividing the rhizomes.

ASTRANTIA Umbelliferae

A. major, masterwort, is a clump-forming perennial with mid-green divided leaves (H 60cm/24in S 45cm/18in Z6). It is grown for the sprays of beautiful and long-lasting green-tinged white flower heads produced throughout summer. Close inspection reveals each to consist of a dome of tiny florets, surrounded by a ruff of petal-like bracts. They prefer well-drained, moisture-retentive soil and do well in sun or semi-shade. Propagate by division in spring or freshly sown seed in summer. *A.m.* 'Ruby Wedding' has deep crimson flowers and purplish foliage. *A.m.* 'Shaggy' is an attractive form with particularly long bracts. The handsome leaves of *A.m.* 'Sunningdale Variegated' are splashed with cream in spring, becoming green in summer.

CAMASSIA Liliaceae (Hyacinthaceae)

C. leichtlinii is a summer-flowering bulb from western North America (H to 1-1.5m/3-5ft S 20-30cm/8-12in Z3). Its tall slender spikes of star-

shaped white or violet flowers on naked stems above tufts of bright green narrow leaves add a touch of elegance in mixed borders or by the waterside, where plants may seed and naturalize. Plant the bulbs in autumn in moist rich fertile soil in sun or part shade. *C.l.* 'Plena' has long-lasting creamy-yellow double flowers like tufts of narrow petals and increases slowly. *C.l.* 'Electra' has larger flowers of rich blue.

CAMPANULA Campanulaceae

Many of the perennial bellflowers will thrive in moist but well-drained conditions, though slugs may be troublesome. The delicate flower colours show particularly well in shade, but plants can equally well be grown in full sun. Grow the species from seed, or propagate any of the following by cuttings in summer or division in autumn.

C. x *burghaltii* produces pendent tubular flowers of palest lavender-grey that open from darker buds; they are borne in summer on erect wiry stems. The soft oval leaves have slight toothing at the edges. It forms a beautiful mound (H 60cm/24in S 30cm/12in Z6) in the drier, sunnier parts of the bog garden, where the soil is rich but well drained.

C. lactiflora (H 1.2-1.5m/4-5ft S 60cm/24in Z5) comes from moist valleys in the Caucasus. Tall stout stems clad in pointed leaves carry branching stems of many open bell-shaped flowers. There are forms in different shades of blue, plus occasional pinks and whites. Plants may need staking if grown

DIERAMA PULCHERRIMUM

in windy spots, but look glorious massed in good soil at the edge of the bog garden in sun or part shade.
C. latifolia, giant bellflower, also from moist upland areas of Eurasia, makes good basal clumps of foliage from which rise stems clad in nettle-like leaves, with long tubular purple-blue flowers borne in the leaf axils (H 1.2m/4ft S 60cm/24in Z3). Cultivars are available in white or shades of blue. They look superb beside water, in sun or shade. The species can be allowed to seed and naturalize in wilder garden areas.
C. poscharskyana (H 20cm/8in S 60-90cm/24-36in Z3) is a low, spreading perennial from Dalmatia. It has small rounded leaves with serrated edges and in summer becomes a mass of starry pale violet flowers. Essentially a rock plant, it will colonize stone walls and well-drained banks to make attractive sprawling mounds of colour.

CARDAMINE Cruciferae
C. pratensis, lady's smock or cuckoo flower, is a charming wildflower of damp meadows in northern temperate regions. In late spring and early summer it has delicate lilac flowers on tall rather straggly stems above mid-green cress-like lobed leaves. Even for informal or naturalized areas in the garden, double-flowered forms are preferable to the species. They make neater, more compact plants with showier flowers of pale lilac pink (H 25cm/10in S 30cm/12in Z4). *C.p.* 'Edith' is a superior double, sturdier than *C.p.* 'Flore Pleno' and with rather paler flowers, fading to near white. They spread slowly; propagate by leaf cuttings.

CELMISIA Compositae
C. walkeri is a summer-flowering evergreen subshrub from New Zealand (H 23cm/9in S 1.8m/6ft Z7). This loose spreading species has heads of lovely white daisy-like flowers and long tapering leaves with hairy white undersides. It thrives in cold, moist acid conditions and a sheltered site such as a well-drained streamside. Propagate by division.

CHELONE Scrophulariaceae
C. obliqua, turtlehead, makes a pretty and unusual bog plant that flowers in late summer and autumn (H 60cm/24in S 50cm/20in Z6). Stems of dark green-bronze serrated leaves bear stiff spikes of hooded rich lilac-pink flowers. From marshy habitats in the eastern USA, these perennials thrive best in moist soil and dappled shade. Propagate by dividing in spring or autumn, or taking softwood cuttings in summer. Plants may also be grown from seed sown as soon as it is ripe or in spring.

CIMICIFUGA Ranunculaceae
C. simplex (H 1.2m/4ft S 60cm/24in Z5) is grown for its rod-like panicles of tiny white faintly scented flowers held delicately on fine dark stems above glossy mid-green leaflets. It flowers in autumn. From mountain regions of northeastern Russia to Japan, this graceful perennial is well suited to woodland gardens and other damp sites. Plant in large patches in light shade and moist soil for best effect. Propagate by division or freshly sown seed. *C.s.* Atropurpurea Group has purple stems and foliage, making striking contrast with the white flowers; 'Brunette' and 'Braunlaub' are particularly good selections.

CLINTONIA Liliaceae (Convallariaceae)
C. andrewsiana (H 60cm/24in S 30cm/12in Z8) is a rhizomatous perennial with bright glossy green leaves resembling those of lily-of-the-valley. In early summer it produces deep pink to purple bell-shaped flowers clustered at the top of a stem; warm summers allow blue fruits to ripen. Native to the damp shade of woodlands in northern California, clintonias lend themselves ideally to naturalized plantings in peaty, well-drained soil with plenty of leaf mould. Propagate by division in spring.

COPTIS Ranunculaceae
C. trifolia, goldthread, is a little low-growing evergreen perennial (H 15cm/6in S 15cm/6in or more Z2) from damp woodlands in Alaska and northeast Asia. Low mats of shiny green divided leaves bear saucer-shaped white flowers of 15mm/¾in diameter in spring. Grow in cool rich moist

soil, such as at woodland edges, with ferns as companion plants.

CORNUS Cornaceae
C. canadensis, creeping dogwood (H 10-15cm/4-6in S 30cm/12in or more Z2), forms a ground cover of light green oval leaves, attractively arranged in pairs held horizontally. In early summer this leafy carpet is studded with charming four-pointed 'flowers' – conspicuous white bracts enclosing tiny greenish-purple flower clusters which later set red berries. The leaves colour rich red in autumn. Native to woodlands in northern North America and Japan, this perennial with its creeping rootstock enjoys cool humus-rich acidic soil in semi-shade. It makes a lovely underplanting for random clumps of ferns.

DARMERA Saxifragaceae
D. peltata (formerly *Peltiphyllum peltatum*), umbrella plant, is a striking large-leaved perennial (H 90cm/3ft S 60cm/24in Z6). Native to northern California, it will grow in moisture-retentive soil in sun or shade. Flat heads of pale pink flowers emerge on red-tinted stems in spring, then scalloped parasol-like leaves 30cm/12in across follow and make a dramatic mound of foliage all summer, often colouring well in autumn. Planted in a muddy stream or pond bank, the creeping rhizomes interweave to prevent erosion. Propagate by division in spring. *D.p.* 'Nana' (H & S 30cm/12in) is more suitable for smaller sites.

DIERAMA Iridaceae
D. pulcherrimum (H 1.5m/5ft S 30cm/12in Z7) earns its common names of wandflower or angel's fishing rod from the graceful arching stems supporting dangling bell-like deep pink flowers in summer. These rise above tall clumps of narrow strap-like evergreen leaves. This bulbous plant from South Africa likes full sun and grows well near water, in rich moisture-retentive soil. Propagate from seed in spring or autumn, or by dividing corms in spring. Plants resent disturbance but once established will self-seed freely.

DODECATHEON Primulaceae
D. pulchellum 'Red Wings' (H 20cm/8in S 10cm/4in Z6) bears clusters of vivid magenta flowers in late spring and early summer, on tall sturdy stems above pale green basal rosettes of oblong leaves. The downturned flowers have reflexed petals and prominent stamens, hence the name shooting star, and the plant's habit prompts the alternative name of American cowslip. Plants like moist but well-drained, humus-rich soil and shade. Propagate by dividing the roots or by seed in spring.

Drosera and other carnivorous plants

Carnivorous plants trap and digest small creatures, exhibiting varied and surprising mechanisms – usually modified leaves – for this purpose. Because they absorb nutrients from this source rather than from the soil, they do not develop large root systems. Many flourish in water or very swampy ground containing little or no nitrogen, a few grow in sand and some in sphagnum moss. Such infertile terrain is vital, and nutrients or fertilizers in either compost or water are potentially harmful to these plants. When propagating from seed or cuttings, use a growing medium of equal parts of moss peat and sharp sand that has been well washed in rainwater or soft water to remove traces of any chemicals. Plant out in a site that is similarly as nutrient-poor as possible.

DROSERA Droseraceae
The leaves of the sundews or dewplants are adapted to perform as flypapers. They are green and the sticky glandular hairs that trap the insects, red. The sun–catching drops of viscous fluid on the hair tips can create a rainbow effect that adds to the attractions of an intriguing plant. The flowers last only a day but are produced in quick succession and are often very showy. Propagate most species by seed or division in spring.

D. capensis, Cape sundew, is a large sundew with gracefully arching leaves arranged in a rosette (H & S 15cm/6in Z9). The bright green leaf blades are covered in red tentacles. A profusion of small magenta flowers is produced on 20cm/8in stems in summer. Propagate by root cuttings.

D. rotundifolia, common sundew (Z6), is one of three European species that are smaller than their exotic counterparts, but pretty none the less. It has almost circular green leaves with bright red hairs in basal rosettes and bears white flowers on stems 15-20cm/6-8in tall in summer.

D. intermedia (Z6) has more elongated leaves and white flowers.

D. anglica (Z5) is the largest, with 10cm/4in leaves.

PINGUICULA Letibulariaceae
P. grandiflora, butterwort, sheep root or bog violet (H 12-15cm/5-6in S 8cm/3in Z7), bears vivid blue violet-like flowers. They appear among clumps of pale green leaves covered in tentacles that produce a clear dewy liquid. It makes an excellent subject for the pond margin, looking effective planted among rocks or bounded by moss where the encroachment of other plants can be checked. It thrives best in equal parts of washed sand and peat and a humid atmosphere and is lime-tolerant. This hardy species withstands temperatures down to -15°C/5°F, overwintering as resting buds with few or no roots. Propagate by seed in autumn, or leaf cuttings or division in spring.

SARRACENIA Sarraceniaceae
Natives of boggy areas in eastern USA, pitcher plants are often grown as houseplants, but make good subjects for the bog garden in warmer climates; *S. flava* and *S. purpurea* ssp. *purpurea* will grow out of doors in temperate regions. The pitchers are leaves adapted to form horizontal or upright cones with hooded tops into which insects are lured by nectar. This intoxicates them so that they fall to the bottom of the pitcher and are digested by the plant. Pitcher plants thrive in a mixture of washed sand and moss peat and may be grown in sun or dappled shade. They require less water during winter. Propagate by rhizome cuttings or by seed, which is slow to germinate.

S. flava, yellow pitcher plant (H & S 75cm/30in Z7), is an unusual and extremely decorative bog plant with canary-yellow flowers and tall, stately upright pitchers.

S. purpurea ssp. *purpurea*, huntsman's cup, bears big nodding flowers of dark red. It has basal rosettes of horizontal green pitchers with reddish-purple veins (H & S 30cm/12in Z6).

DROSERA CAPENSIS

SARRACENIA PURPUREA SSP. *PURPUREA*

EUPATORIUM Compositae

E. purpureum, Joe Pye weed (H 2.1m/7ft S 1m/3ft Z4), comes from damp watersides of eastern North America. Whorls of lance-shaped mid-green leaves on tall purple stems bear wide flat terminal heads of fluffy pinkish-purple flowers from late summer into early autumn. Thriving in moist but well-drained soil in sun or partial shade, a group makes an imposing end-of-season display in a large-scale bog garden. For an even richer colour effect, plant the similar *E. maculatum* 'Atropurpureum' (Z5). Cut stems down almost to ground level after flowering, and divide between autumn and spring.

EUPHORBIA Euphorbiaceae

Moist soils suit many of the spurges or milkweeds (a name alluding to the white sap, an irritant to sensitive skins). The following make bushy perennials, mounds of arching stems crowded with narrow leaves; the terminal flowers are inconspicuous, but are framed by long-lasting brightly coloured leaf-like bracts. Grow in sun or partial shade. Propagate by division.

E. griffithii (H 60-75cm/24-30in S 60cm/24in Z5) from the Himalayas has given rise to a number of cultivars, often – like *E.g.* 'Fireglow' – too invasive for most gardens. Lance-shaped green leaves have red midribs and the flower heads are a brilliant glowing red, eye-catching in 'hot' colour schemes. Showier and far less rampageous is *E.g.* 'Wickstead', with dark leaves. *E.g.* 'Dixter' is an intense reddish-orange form with dark foliage, luxuriant but non-invasive.

E. palustris (H & S 1m/3ft Z5) is a handsome plant from marshy regions from Europe to western Asia. Stems clad in dark green leaves terminate in distinctive heads of greeny-yellow flowers and bowl-shaped bracts.

FILIPENDULA Rosaceae

Meadowsweets have attractive fern-like foliage and bear large frothy flat-topped heads of tiny flowers. They need moist soil but will grow in sun or shade. Propagate by division or by seed in autumn.

F. kamtschatica (H 1.5m/5ft S 2.5m/8ft Z3) makes a striking robust clump above most of the bog subjects, its heads of white or pale pink flowers held above large divided leaves.

F. rubra 'Venusta' is a magnificent plant (H 2.1m/ 7ft S 1.2m/4ft Z2) for large-scale bog gardens. This cultivar of the queen of the prairies forms splendid large clumps of divided leaves, topped in summer with huge pink flower heads.

F. ulmaria is native to Europe and Asia. Two cultivars (H & S 30cm/12in Z2) provide good foliage contrasts in the smaller bog garden.

F.u. 'Aurea' has golden-green leaves, brightest in spring. Removing the creamy-white flowers in summer prompts fresh yellow leaf growth and pre-empts green-leaved seedlings. *F.u.* 'Variegata' has dark green leaves striped with yellow; divide and replant regularly to retain its character.

FRANCOA Saxifragaceae

F. appendiculata, bridal wreath (H 60cm/24in S 45cm/18in Z7), is a clump-forming perennial from Chile. The oval basal leaves are dark green, crinkled and hairy. In summer and early autumn tall graceful branching stems bear spikes of small bell-shaped pale pink flowers with deep pink spotted bases. It requires full sun and well-drained fertile soil. In frost-free climates plants can grow in damp areas beside pools; in cold regions, grow them in pots and protect in winter. Propagate by division.

GENTIANA Gentianaceae

G. asclepiadea, the willow gentian, is a perennial from central to eastern Europe with arching stems thickly clothed in narrow bright green leaves (H 90cm/3ft S 60cm/24in Z6). From late summer sprays of trumpet-shaped flowers of richest blue appear in the upper leaf axils. Plant in shade or part shade, in moist, well-drained soil enriched with humus; chalky soil is tolerated, though neutral to acid is preferred. Plants look effective among the shorter grasses or in groups with ferns. Propagate by seed or division.

GERANIUM Geraniaceae

G. 'Johnson's Blue' is a vigorous clump-forming perennial (H 30cm/12in S 60cm/24in Z5). It has the characteristic divided cranesbill foliage and deep blue flowers all summer. Like all the herbaceous geraniums, this will grow in all soils except those that are waterlogged, providing ground cover and bright summer colour. A group makes good transition planting between the dry earth of the main garden and the moist edges of the bog area. Propagate by division.

GEUM Rosaceae

G. rivale, water avens, is a small upright hairy perennial from marshes and watermeadows of northern temperate zones to the Arctic. The species is grown for its delicately nodding cup-shaped red flowers borne in summer (H & S 30-45cm/12-18in Z3). *G.r.* 'Leonard's Variety' has copper-pink flowers tinted with orange, and *G.r.* 'Lionel Cox' has apricot-tinted primrose flowers. Grow in cool moist soil in sun or part shade. Divide clumps every two years in spring.

EUPATORIUM PURPUREUM

GENTIANA ASCLEPIADEA

GUNNERA MANICATA

GUNNERA Haloragidaceae

Gunneras are South American perennials grown for their striking foliage, which ranges in scale from dwarf to giant.

G. magellanica (H 8cm/3in S to 30cm/12in Z7) spreads on creeping stems to make a carpet of toothed kidney-shaped green leaves, bronze when young, and bears little reddish-green flower spikes in summer. It prefers peaty soil. Propagate by dividing plants in spring.

G. manicata (H & S 2.1-3m/7-10ft Z7) is a huge plant with lobed toothed leaves, borne on sturdy prickly stems. At 1.5m/5ft across, its leaf is the largest that can be grown in a temperate climate. Brownish-green flowers appear in spring on club-like stems and resemble great cones. Plant in deep rich moist soil; this will grow right at the water's edge to make a marvellous feature on a grand scale. Foliage may suffer wind damage in exposed areas. Provide winter protection by inverting the leaves over the crowns and pegging them down securely, and in cold areas cover with a further insulating mulch. Propagate from seed sown as soon as it ripens, or by dividing the crowns in spring. *G. tinctoria* (syn. *G. chilensis*) is smaller than *G. manicata* and a useful alternative where space is limited. Its rather smoother leaves 60cm/24in across are borne on stalks about 1.5m/5ft high.

HELLEBORUS Ranunculaceae

Hellebores are moisture-loving perennials that grow best in semi-shade and reasonably well-drained fertile soil. They thrive in chalk or clay, though they dislike sand and gravel.

H. orientalis hybrids, the Lenten roses (H & S 45cm/18in Z6), flower in winter or early spring and their attractive divided foliage makes handsome evergreen ground cover all year – excellent under taller plants and in damp wooded areas. Gracefully nodding saucer-shaped flowers come in greenish- or creamy-white and gradations of pink from palest blush to murky purple. They may be purple-spotted within or green-flushed outside. Plants are best chosen in flower from selected strains such as Ballard hybrids or Washfield hybrids. Remove straggling or damaged foliage to foster new growth and flowers. Propagate by dividing the plants after flowering but before new leaves appear, or in late summer in moister soils. Alternatively sow ripe seed to produce seedlings in varying colours.

HELONIAS Liliaceae (Melanthiaceae)

H. bullata, swamp pink or stud flower, is a spring-flowering bog plant from northeastern North America (H 38-45cm/15-18in S 30cm/12in Z6).

Rosettes of strap-shaped shiny dark green leaves produce dense heads of little starry pink scented flowers on 30cm/12in stems. Grow in full sun. Propagate by sowing seed in autumn or by dividing established plants in spring.

HELONIOPSIS Liliaceae (Melanthiaceae)

H. orientalis makes clumps of narrow lance-shaped leaves above which sturdy stems bear clusters of nodding mauve-pink flowers in spring (H & S 30cm/12in Z7). This perennial bog plant looks best against a neutral surround of peat or moss. Increase by sowing seed in autumn or spring, or by division in autumn. Plants will not tolerate temperatures below -15°C/5°F.

HEMEROCALLIS Liliaceae (Hemerocallidaceae)

Day-lilies are hardy herbaceous perennials with arching strap-shaped leaves of fresh pale green; the lily-like trumpet flowers are borne in long succession, though each lasts only a day. For such exotic-looking plants, day-lilies are remarkably tough and adaptable. They will grow in sun or part shade in a variety of soils, but must have moisture. Propagate by division in autumn or spring. There is an immense breadth of choice in stature, colour and flowering time among the vast range of hybrids offered by specialist nurseries: the following presents a purely personal selection.

H. dumortieri (H & S 60cm/24in Z4) has fragrant flowers in late spring, deep yellow opening from brown buds.

H. fulva 'Kwanzo Variegata' (H 75-90cm/30-36in S 75cm/30in Z4) has rich orange double flowers enhanced by variegated strap-shaped leaves.

HIBISCUS GRANDIFLORUS

HELLEBORUS ORIENTALIS

Replant only the best portions when dividing to prevent reversion to plain green foliage.

H. 'Golden Chimes' (H 75cm/30in S 60cm/24in Z4) has small golden-yellow flowers, with brown contrast outside, borne on branching stems to create a dainty and elegant effect in midsummer.

H. 'Corky' is similar, with soft yellow flowers.

H. lilioasphodelus (H. flava) is one of the best scented species, with beautiful clear yellow trumpet-shaped flowers in spring (H & S 75cm/30in Z4).

H. 'Marion Vaughn' (H 90cm/3ft S 60cm/24in Z4) is a vigorous and long-flowering hybrid. Fragrant clear yellow trumpet-shaped flowers with green throats are borne at midsummer.

H. minor is a more compact species (H 25cm/10in S 45cm/18in Z4), forming clumps of grass-like foliage and bearing brown-backed fragrant yellow flowers in late spring.

HEUCHERA Saxifragaceae

These perennials are often grown for their evergreen foliage, which can be colourful and decorated with a metallic marbling. They provide good ground cover in woodland or damp, sunny areas. Propagate by dividing plants between autumn and spring.

H. cylindrica 'Greenfinch' is a vigorous clump-forming plant (H 60cm/24in S 45cm/18in Z4) with basal rosettes of kidney-shaped lobed leaves, dark-veined and with a greyish sheen. Stiff narrow stems carry terminal spires of tiny greenish-white or lemon-green flowers in summer.

H. micrantha 'Palace Purple' makes beautiful colour contrast in drier parts of the bog. It has rich purple leaves and bears delicate sprays of tiny white flowers in early summer. H.m. 'Bressingham Bronze' has striking, shining, purple-black leaves.

HIBISCUS Malvaceae

H. grandiflorus, swamp hibiscus (H 2.5m/8ft S 1.8m/6ft Z9), is a robust woody-based perennial that is particularly suited to waterside plantings. Large lobed leaves, broader than they are long, have white hairs on the underside. The flowers up to 15cm/6in long are white, pink or pinkish-purple. Plants are usually frost-hardy to -5°C/23°F.

HOSTA Liliaceae (Funkiaceae)

Grown for their luxuriant foliage, hostas – also known as plantain lilies or funkias – love plenty of moisture and so are eminently suitable for waterside planting, though they do not like to be waterlogged. Many also enjoy some shade, making them ideal candidates for damp woodland areas, where their large leaves contrast boldly with overhanging ferns.

From left to right: *HOSTA SIEBOLDIANA* VAR. *ELEGANS, H. FORTUNEI* F. *AUREA, H. CRISPULA* and *H. FORTUNEI* VAR. *ALBOPICTA*

There are 40 species and over 1,000 cultivars, with an enormous variety of colour, form, size and texture. Some have the added attraction of elegant trumpet-like flowers, often scented, borne in racemes on slender stalks above the foliage. It is important to choose a hosta of the right appearance and scale for a site; for example the large and beautiful H. sieboldiana would completely dominate a petite planting scheme.

Plant the rhizomes in spring or autumn in a pH of 6-7 and in partial shade. Give plenty of compost or manure. Propagate by dividing three- to four-year-old plants in early spring, taking care not to damage the fresh growing points. Although hostas thrive in moisture, take care when watering, as droplets on the leaves may cause scorch marks. Evening watering also makes hostas doubly attractive to slugs and snails, which relish the gorgeous foliage and riddle it with holes. Sprinkle slug bait liberally around plants as soon as the leaves begin to emerge, and again when tell-tale holes appear. Surrounding plants with coarse materials such as sharp sand, grit, eggshells etc. also helps to deter these pests. Following is a small personal selection of the many possibilities.

H. fluctuans 'Variegated' (H 50cm/20in S 60cm/24in Z4) is an outstanding large variegated cultivar. Its soft green leaves are edged with cream.

H. fortunei var. albopicta (H 75-90cm/30-36in S 90cm/36in Z4) has fresh pale green leaves that look, when they open in spring, as though their centres have been painted with irregular areas of creamy-white, leaving the margins and veins in dark green. This variegation gradually darkens to green in summer. Attractive lilac-coloured trumpet-shaped flowers are held in nodding racemes on slender stalks from early summer.

H.f. f. aurea has leaves slightly smaller than in the preceding example (H & S 45cm/18in Z4). They open a lovely bright yellow, turning a pale green by midsummer. Protect this delicate foliage from bright sun, which will turn it brown.

H. 'Honeybells' (H & S 90cm/3ft Z4) has large green wavy-edged leaves that keep their fresh appearance right into autumn. Beautifully fragrant pale lilac bell-like flowers hang gracefully from the arching stems.

H. montana 'Aureomarginata' (H 45cm/18in S 75cm/30in Z4) is the brightest and brassiest of the variegated hostas. Its rich deep emerald-green leaves, edged with brilliant gold, are among the earliest to emerge.

H. plantaginea var. grandiflora (H & S 45-60cm/18-24in Z4) is a hosta for sunny situations and retentive soil. The long narrow leaves remain a fresh glossy green through the season. Trumpet-shaped white flowers borne in late summer are sweetly scented.

IRIS ENSATA 'METEOR'

KIRENGESHOMA PALMATA

H. sieboldiana var. *elegans (H. glauca)* is an ideal waterside plant (H 90cm/3ft S 1.5m/5ft Z4). The heart-shaped leaves are green-blue, deeply textured and with conspicuous veins. Large pale lilac flowers are borne in mid- to late summer.

H. 'Snowden' (H & S 90cm/3ft Z3) is a handsome greyish-leaved cultivar with white flowers in late summer. It has a strikingly different upright growth.

H. 'Sum and Substance' (H 50cm/20in S 75cm/30in Z4), with outstanding golden-yellow foliage, is one of the best large-leaved yellow hostas.

H. undulata var. *albomarginata (H.* 'Thomas Hogg') makes vigorous clumps of smooth pointed green leaves with creamy-white margins that extend some way into the leaf stalk. The centre of the leaf is two-toned dark and pale green. Lilac trumpet-shaped flowers are borne in early summer (H 45cm/18in S 60cm/24in Z4).

H. venusta (H 8cm/3in S 10cm/4in Z3) is a tiny hosta that spreads by stolons. It is quick to increase and good for ground cover, though not invasive. It gives an outstanding display of trumpet-shaped purple flowers in summer.

HOUTTUYNIA Saururaceae
H. cordata (H 15-30cm/6-12in S indefinite Z5) has aromatic bluish-green heart-shaped leaves, red stems and spikes of small white flowers in spring. Its creeping rhizomes spread in wet soil or shallow water to form attractive ground cover in damp areas, preferably in semi-shade. Propagate by division or by removing runners in spring. The double-flowered variety *H.c.* 'Plena' makes beautiful carpeting. Colourful *H.c.* 'Chameleon' has eye-catching leaf variegation of red, green, yellow and cream that is most vivid in sites in full sun. It makes an attractive and unusual underplanting.

IRIS Iridaceae
While some irises qualify as 'emergent' plants and are described on pages 159-160, the following like moist soil but dislike standing permanently in water – particularly in winter.

I. chrysographes 'Black Knight' (H & S 60cm/24in Z5) is a well-shaped dark velvety-purple iris, similar to *I. sibirica*. It forms lovely strong clumps in deep moist soil. Propagate by division in spring.

I. ensata (I. kaempferi), Japanese flag (H 60cm/24in S 30cm/12in Z4), prefers acid soils and plenty of water in summer, but drier conditions in winter. The leaves are narrow with a prominent midrib that aids identification. The species has purple flowers with a golden blaze, but many different colour forms and some new Japanese cultivars are available. Varieties include Higo strain and hybrids in white, mauve, purple and pink, often with a blaze or blotch of a contrasting or complementary colour. *I.e.* 'Variegata' has purple flowers and thin white-striped leaves.

I. sibirica makes elegant clumps of thin deep green leaves (H 60cm-1.2m/2-4ft S 90cm/3ft Z4). The type has blue flowers, but many forms are available including white, purple and different blues, and many are decorated with a blaze or attractive veining. They do well in the drier parts of the bog or marsh in sun or shade, as well as succeeding in ordinary garden conditions, which makes them a very useful transition plant. Propagate by splitting clumps in early spring.

JEFFERSONIA Berberidaceae
J. diphylla, twinleaf, from eastern North American woodlands is a slow-growing perennial (H & S 23cm/9in Z5) that slightly resembles epimedium. The leaves are a distinctive butterfly shape. Cup-shaped white flowers, each on a slender stem, stand erect from the basal clump in late spring. Grow in shade in rich moist soil.

KIRENGESHOMA Hydrangeaceae
K. palmata (H 90cm/3ft S 60cm/24in Z5) is a beautiful herbaceous perennial with light green palmate leaves arranged in pairs on tall slender dark purple stems. Arching panicles of delicately nodding pale yellow shuttlecock flowers appear in late summer to autumn. It will not tolerate very alkaline soils, but makes an ideal and graceful plant for shady acid bog gardens or for planting under large rhododendrons.

LEUCOJUM Liliaceae (Amaryllidaceae)
L. aestivum, summer snowflake (H 50cm/20in S 30cm/12in Z4), is a slender bulbous perennial native to wet and swampy habitats in central Europe. Its spring flowers, borne on leafless stems above strap-shaped basal leaves, brighten bog and waterside gardens. The pendent bell-shaped flower, white with green tips, resembles a tall snowdrop, but is firmer and waxier in texture. *L.a.* 'Gravetye Giant' is a superior form. Propagate by division in autumn or by seed.

LIGULARIA Compositae
These handsome herbaceous perennials thrive in deep moist soil in dappled shade or in sun, though plants tend to flop in strong afternoon sunlight. Their foliage needs protection from slugs and snails, and shelter from damaging winds. Propagate by division.

L. dentata 'Desdemona' (H 1.2m/4ft S 60cm/24in Z4) bears clustered shaggy orange daisy-like flowers on purple-black stalks in midsummer. With heart-shaped green leaves that are maroon underneath, this makes an extremely eye-catching plant. *L.* 'Gregynog Gold', a hybrid sharing the

LOBELIA CARDINALIS

same *dentata* parentage, has handsome green leaves, and its flowers are arranged in pyramidal spikes. *L. przewalskii* (H 1.2-1.8m/4-6ft S 1m/3ft Z4) has dissected leaves and tall black stems supporting spires of small yellow flowers in summer. *L.* 'The Rocket' has less deeply cut leaves, of a good dark green.

LILIUM Liliaceae
L. superbum, the swamp or Turk's-cap lily (H 3m/ 10ft S 30cm/12in Z3), comes from eastern North America. It blooms in late summer and early autumn above whorls of lance-shaped or elliptical leaves. The loose clusters of pretty nodding flowers with recurved petals are orange, usually flushed with red and spotted with maroon. They look wonderful with the larger ferns, *Iris pseudacorus* and petasites. Grow in well-drained but moist, deep, neutral to acid soil, rich in humus.

LOBELIA Campanulaceae
Lobelias offer a fine display of long-lasting flowers from mid to late summer. They need deep rich soil, in sun or part shade. While all are moisture-loving, *L. cardinalis* will thrive in soil that is actually waterlogged, and makes a dramatic emergent plant. The water also provides protection from slugs, to which all these lobelias are vulnerable. Propagate by division, cuttings or seed in spring.

L. cardinalis, cardinal flower (H 60-90cm/24-36in S 30cm/12in Z3), is an extremely handsome perennial for moist soil or water to a depth of 10cm/4in. Spires of brilliant red flowers are borne above a rosette of glossy red-bronze foliage. *L.c.* 'Alba' is a white-flowered variety, and *L.c.* 'Rosea' has pink flowers. *L. splendens (L. fulgens)* has red flowers like those of *L. cardinalis*, but its foliage is green. It is similar in stature, less hardy (Z8), and also grows in shallow water.
L. 'Bees Flame' and *L.* 'Queen Victoria' are good hardy hybrids (Z5) with bronze-red leaves and scarlet flowers, to grow in moist ground. *L.* 'Compliment Scarlet' which is raised from seed, is a superb hybrid with flowers of an astonishing deep red that glow among dark green leaves.
L. x *gerardii* 'Vedrariensis' (H 75-90cm/30-36in S 30cm/12in Z5) has lance-shaped dark green leaves and bears tall spires of rich crimson-violet flowers.
L. syphilitica (H 90cm/3ft S 30cm/12in Z5) is a perennial from damp meadows in the eastern USA. Its habit is similar to that of *L. cardinalis*, though with green leaves and two-lipped clear blue flowers the effect of this plant is altogether more subtle. It is best divided and replanted every few years.

LYCHNIS Caryophyllaceae
L. flos-cuculi, ragged robin (H 45cm/18in S 30cm/ 12in Z6), grows in temperate water marshes and meadows and brightens the wild garden with its

LILIUM SUPERBUM

delicate shaggy-petalled flowers. Appearing in early summer, these emerge above narrow oval leaves from a tube-shaped calyx, each of the five petals deeply cut into four. The type is rose-pink; *L. flos-cuculi* var. *albiflora* has white flowers. Grow in full sun in moist, well-drained soil. Propagate by division in autumn or seed in spring.

LYTHRUM Lythraceae
L. salicaria, common purple loosestrife (H 1.2-1.5m/4-5ft S 1m/3ft Z3), looks attractive among grasses and reeds beside water. However, it is often regarded as a pernicious weed for its invasiveness, and growing it is banned in parts of the USA. Cultivars and crosses with the smaller *L. virgatum* offer superior garden plants with subtler variations on the type's magenta-purple tones and in scale with the smaller bog garden. *L.s.* 'The Beacon' has closely packed racemes of small dark rose-coloured flowers and *L.s.* 'Feuerkerze' has rose-pink flowers (H 90cm/3ft S 45cm/18in Z3). *L. virgatum* 'The Rocket' has slender flower spires of vivid rose-pink (H 75cm/30in S 45cm/18in Z3).

MECONOPSIS Papaveraceae
Blue poppies are beautiful clump-forming perennials that decorate the cool, shady garden with exquisite papery flowers in early summer. Native to moist mountain regions from the Himalayas to China, they can be difficult to

MECONOPSIS GRANDIS

accommodate in harsher climates than their own, disliking intense summer heat and drying winds. Where conditions suit them, such as in the Pacific northwest of the USA or in some relatively moist western areas of the British Isles, they thrive in rich retentive soils that are lime-free. Propagate from seed sown as soon as it ripens, or by division when the flowering period is over.

M. betonicifolia, the Tibetan poppy (H 90cm-1.2m/3-4ft S 45cm/18in Z7), bears nodding sky-blue poppy flowers clustered on tall stems above downy leaves. Give plants at least a year to establish themselves before allowing them to flower, and protect from harsh winds The white form, *M.b. alba*, has flowers of exceptional purity and delicacy, and handsome glaucous foliage.

M. grandis is a slightly larger plant (H 90cm-1.5m/3-5ft S 60cm/24in Z5), and bears large four-petalled flowers singly on stout stems. Plants are best divided and replanted every three years.

M. x *sheldonii*, a hybrid between the previous two species, is a magnificent plant of greater poise, with shapely clear blue flowers (H 1.2-1.5m/4-5ft S 45-60cm/18-24in Z5).

MIMULUS Scrophulariaceae
The perennial monkey musks as a rule prefer sun and moisture. Potentially invasive, they carpet damp soil with rosettes of fresh green leaves decorated with colourful snapdragon-like flowers in summer. Propagate the following three species in spring by dividing the tiny rosettes.

M. cardinalis (H 75-90cm/30-36in S 60cm/24in Z7) from western USA is upright-growing, with hairy leaves and flowers of bright scarlet. This species will grow in soils that are just damp.

OMPHALODES CAPPADOCICA

M. guttatus (H & S 60cm/24in Z6) from western North America has bright yellow flowers with red-brown spots above lush green foliage. It relishes very damp sites.

M. ringens, Allegheny monkey flower from eastern North America, spreads more slowly on moist ground. Spires of lilac flowers are borne on square stems above narrow oval dark green leaves (H 75-90cm/30-36in S 30cm/12in Z3).

M. 'Whitecroft Scarlet' is very free-flowering, with vivid scarlet blossoms borne above small oval green leaves (H 10-15cm/4-6in S indefinite Z6). This short-lived perennial may not overwinter in colder areas; propagate from seed brought on under glass in spring or by division. Allow it to spread in a sheltered corner near an ornamental pool where its qualities can be appreciated.

MONARDA Labiatae
Bergamots are hardy clump-forming perennials from North America that thrive best in sun and moist soil to flower in summer. They are lovely growing at the bog edges to provide a transition into the drier planting. Propagate by division in spring. Among hybrids of *M. didyma*, bee balm or Oswego tea (H 75-90cm/30-36in S 45cm/18in Z4), *M.* 'Cambridge Scarlet' has bright red shaggy-headed flowers on tall stems above mid-green aromatic foliage; *M.* 'Beauty of Cobham' has soft pink flowers with darker calyces. Shorter and neater in habit, *M.* 'Mrs Perry' has coral-red flowers above dark green foliage. *M.* 'Prärienacht' has rich violet flowers and *M.* 'Schneewittchen', white.

NARTHECIUM Liliaceae (Asphodelaceae)
N. ossifragum, bog asphodel (H 20-30cm/8-12in WD 0-5cm/0-2in Z6), has spear-shaped leaves and clusters of bright yellow flowers in summer. Native to northern temperate regions and often found in peat bogs, it is an attractive subject to grow in the boggy parts of a natural or wildlife pond. It is happy in sphagnum moss. Propagate by dividing rhizomes, or by sowing seed in spring.

OMPHALODES Boraginaceae
O. cappadocica (H 15-20cm/6-8in S 25cm/10in or more Z6) is a carpeting perennial from Turkey with attractive mid-green ribbed oval leaves growing from spreading stems underground. Large five-petalled flowers like forget-me-nots of a lovely intense blue are borne in spring. Excellent planted beneath trees in retentive soil (for example as vivid blue carpeting to silver birches), it will grow in sun if the soil is sufficiently moist and will tolerate drier soils in cool shade. Propagate by seed or division in spring.

Orchidaceae

The beautiful and unusual flowers of the orchid family are wonderful in the variety of their forms and colours, ranging from subtle to spectacular. The many thousands of species are widely distributed, from the Arctic to Australasia, and from high cloud forests to mountains with prolonged snow cover. Many can only be obtained from specialist nurseries. It is now illegal in many countries to take orchids from the wild, and anyway those collected in the field usually grow less well than nursery-propagated ones.

The warm moist atmospheres of gardens in the tropics (or of conservatory water gardens in temperate regions) make it possible to grow epiphytes such as phalaenopsis cultivars, attached to tree branches or rocks and perhaps dangling down beside a waterfall, as well as some of the more spectacular terrestrial orchids. However, the species included here are all terrestrial, best allowed to naturalize in a pocket of suitable soil in the natural or wild bog garden where their subtle charms can be appreciated.

The hardy orchids suitable for growing in temperate gardens are deciduous, dying down over winter to re-emerge in spring and flower in summer. They thrive best in a situation that closely resembles their natural habitat. Some enjoy dappled shade, some prefer chalk or lime, and all require less water during the dormant period.

Plant the rhizomes or tubers 5cm/2in deep in fibrous loam with an equal amount of sharp sand and leaf mould. The leaf mould is important to their well-being, because it encourages the mycorrhizal fungi which help to provide sustenance for the orchids and without which the seeds cannot germinate. Propagate in spring, by division or by planting pseudobulbs.

ANACAMPTIS Orchidaceae
A. pyramidalis, pyramid orchid, is native to Europe and North Africa (H to 75cm/30in Z6). Growing from round tubers, plants take three to five years to produce pyramids of pink, violet or purple summer flowers, which attract pollinating butterflies. Spear-shaped leaves are held in a loose rosette. It thrives in open grassland, if mowing is delayed until the flowering period is over. The grassy fringes of a natural or wildlife pond make an ideal site.

ARETHUSA Orchidaceae
A. bulbosa, swamp pink, bog rose or dragon's mouth, is an attractive fragrant orchid (H 20cm/8in Z3). Showy rose-pink to purple flowers are borne above grass-like leaves. Native to Canada and Japan, these orchids withstand low temperatures but not drought. Plant the corms in peaty soil in the bog garden or alongside streams.

Alternatively, bring on in pots under glass, transferring the pots to the garden for the flowering season and returning to shelter to overwinter when the growth dies back. Repot in peaty soil with some leaf mould every three years.

BLETILLA Orchidaceae

B. striata, hyacinth orchid from China and Japan (H 50cm/20in Z5-9), bears slender two-toned bright pink flowers with white throats 2.5cm/1in or more across in late spring or early summer. *B.s.* f. *gebina* has delicate stems of white flowers normally slightly blushed with pink. The lance-shaped leaves are mid-green. Grow among ferns at the bog edges, planting the flattened pseudobulbs in soil enriched with leaf mould. It requires a sheltered position, and new foliage is susceptible to damage by late frosts; protect crowns in winter in cold areas.

CALOPOGON Orchidaceae

C. tuberosum (C. pulchellum) is a choice orchid bearing loose clusters of gorgeous big pink or white flowers with bearded lips (H 45cm/18in Z3). The mid-green leaves are lance-shaped. Preferring damp acid soil, this native of eastern North America, Cuba and the Bahamas can vary in hardiness and may need some protection.

CALYPSO Orchidaceae

C. bulbosa (H 20cm/8in Z3) is a delightful orchid from damp mossy woodlands of Finland and Sweden. In early spring to summer each tuber bears one showy 2cm/1in pink or white flower with purple markings and a saffron fringe above a single broad dark green leaf. Grow in damp slightly acid soil and mulch with leaf mould.

CLEISTES Orchidaceae

C. divaricata, spreading pogonia or funnel-crest, is a lush terrestrial orchid native to northeastern USA (H 75cm/30in Z5). The 10cm/4in leaves are strap-shaped, and striking clusters of large dark pink flowers are sweetly perfumed. Grow the rhizomes in damp slightly acid soil and mulch occasionally with leaf mould.

CYPRIPEDIUM Orchidaceae

C. reginae, showy lady's slipper (H 1m/3ft Z4), is native to damp peaty woodlands of eastern North America. It has downy mid-green oval ribbed leaves and bears delicate white flowers with a pink pouched lip or third petal in late spring to early summer; *C.r.* var. *album* has creamy-white flowers. Grow the rhizomes in semi-shade in the bog garden. Plants resent disturbance and can be slow to establish.

ANACAMPTIS PYRAMIDALIS

DACTYLORHIZA Orchidaceae

D. fuchsii, common spotted orchid from northwestern Europe (H 20-60cm/8-24in Z6), has smooth green lance-shaped leaves spotted with purple. In late spring to early summer densely packed flower spikes bear a profusion of dark to light pink flowers with dark red or purple markings. These orchids love marsh-like conditions; grow in humus-rich damp soil in sun or semi-shade. Propagate by dividing the tubers in autumn.

EPIPACTIS Orchidaceae

E. palustris, marsh helleborine (H 50cm/20in Z6), occurs mainly in wetland areas of Europe, temperate Asia and North Africa. From summer to early autumn attractive subtly coloured flowers grow in loose clusters from stems bearing ribbed lance-shaped leaves. Each flower consists of three maroon sepals surrounding three creamy-white petals, often with dark red lines leading into the centre. Plant in semi-shade; the spreading underground rhizomes can quickly establish themselves over large areas.

LIPARIS Orchidaceae

L. liliifolia, mauve slickwort, has smooth oval leaves 13cm/5in long and racemes of relatively showy mauve flowers in summer. This hardy species (H

CYPRIPEDIUM REGINAE

25cm/10in S 15cm/6in Z4) is native to areas of sphagnum moss in moist peaty soil, with a range from Sweden to North America. Plant the pseudobulbs in a special corner of the bog garden with other sphagnum-loving plants.

PLATANTHERA Orchidaceae

These hardy orchids grown from tubers prefer a moist chalky soil. Both have mid-green oval leaves surmounted by a stem bearing a loose spike of hooded flowers in late spring or early summer (H 25cm/10in S 15cm/6in). *P. bifolia*, lesser butterfly orchid from the Mediterranean and the former USSR (Z6), has delicate starry fragrant flowers that make a charming addition to a green and white planting scheme. *P. chlorantha*, greater butterfly orchid (Z7) from Europe and the Mediterranean, has bigger but fewer greenish blooms.

SPIRANTHES Orchidaceae

S. cernua, lady's tresses, is a lovely autumn-flowering orchid from eastern North America (H 50cm/20in S 30cm/12in Z3). It produces a display of fragrant dainty white flowers with yellow throats, arranged in a spiral at the top of the tall stem. The lance-shaped mid-green leaves form a basal rosette. Plant the tubers in well-drained humus-rich soil in dappled shade and mulch with leaf mould.

PERSICARIA Polygonaceae

These knotweeds are moisture-loving plants, thriving in sun or shade. Formerly included in the genus *Polygonum*, they are related to the ineradicably invasive Japanese and giant knotweeds, but proportioned to smaller gardens and spread slowly.

P. amplexicaulis 'Firetail' (*Polygonum amplexicaule* 'Firetail') makes a big clump of heart-shaped leaves (H & S 1.2m/4ft Z4) above which rise numerous flower spikes of bright red. These make a colourful display from midsummer until the first frosts.

P. bistorta 'Superba', (*Polygonum bistorta* 'Superbum') is a vigorous clump-forming leafy perennial (H & S 60cm/24in Z4) whose 15cm/6in long fat pink flower spikes look particularly fine when grown in the bog garden near one of the white and green variegated grasses. It produces mats of light green leaves and flowers in late spring or early summer, sometimes with a second flowering.

PETASITES Compositae

P. japonicus var. *giganteus* (H & S 1.5m/5ft Z5), giant butterbur, is a large-leaved perennial native to streamsides in northern Japan. The spreading roots are useful for binding the clay banks of ponds or streams but are potentially invasive. They make a spectacular display where space permits. Tightly packed knobs of creamy-white daisy-like flowers emerge in early spring, followed by large elegant pale green leaves that form imposing mounds, and provide shading for low underplanting.

PHLOX Polemoniaceae

P. maculata from eastern North America produces a lovely burst of summer colour for the drier parts of the bog garden, when cylindrical panicles of fragrant mauve-pink flowers appear on erect stems clad in oval leaves. *P.m.* 'Alpha' is lilac-pink and *P.m.* 'Omega' white with a lilac eye. These elegant perennials (H 90cm/3ft S 45cm/18in Z5) like moist but well-drained soils. Propagate by division.

PHYSOSTEGIA Labiatae

P. virginiana, the obedient plant (H 90cm/3ft S 60cm/24in Z5), is a rhizomatous perennial native to damp areas of eastern North America. It forms a dense clump of erect stalks clad in lance-shaped toothed leaves. Through summer into autumn tight stiff spikes of pinky-mauve tubular flowers (white in *P.v.* 'Alba', reddish-pink in *P.v.* 'Vivid') are held on stems that obediently stay in place when bent. Propagate by division.

PODOPHYLLUM Berberidaceae

P. hexandrum (*P. emodi*) is an intriguing perennial with a creeping rootstock (H & S 30cm/12in Z6). A native of the Himalayas to Sichuan, it thrives in shady places where the soil is moist and humus-rich. The foliage resembles small furled umbrellas as it emerges through the soil in spring, opening into pairs of three-lobed brown-mottled leaves. White saucer-shaped flowers appear on top of the leaves in summer, followed by shining red egg-shaped fruits. Propagate by division.

POLYGONATUM Liliaceae (Convallariaceae)

P. odoratum, Solomon's seal (H 60cm/24in S 30cm/12in Z4), is a rhizomatous perennial native to Europe and northern Asia. It thrives in shady woodland areas with well-drained humus-rich soils. Oval to lance-shaped leaves are borne on elegant arching stems, and pairs of bell-shaped greenish-white flowers hang from the leaf axils in late spring. The leaves are prone to sudden attack by sawfly larvae in summer. Propagate by division.

PRIMULA Primulaceae

This genus embraces some of the most desirable waterside flowering plants, with a wide range of gay colours, shapes and sizes. Those described here generally need partial shade and moist, heavy soil with plenty of humus. Primulas dislike the intense summer heat of continental climates, though irrigation teamed with skill can produce good results in sites that are relatively cool. They are best suited by moist temperate regions such as western Scotland and the Pacific northwest of the USA. Propagate by sowing fresh seed in a fine compost, or by division in autumn or spring. The candelabra types look best planted in gentle drifts. Cross pollination between different cultivars can often result in seedlings of many diverse shades and hues.

P. alpicola forms a compact specimen (H 40cm/16in S 20cm/8in Z6), the leaves varying from oval to lance-shaped. Loose terminal clusters of pendent flowers appear in early summer. They are cream-coloured in *P.a.* var. *luna* and violet-toned in *P.a.* var. *violacea*. Both are sweetly scented.

P. denticulata, the drumstick primula from the Himalayas (H 20-45cm/8-18in S 30cm/12in Z5), forms neat rosettes of pale green leaves above which globular flower heads are held on stout stalks, like drumsticks, in spring. The colour varies from white through shades of pink and lavender to violet or claret-red.

P. florindae from Tibet resembles a giant cowslip (H 60-90cm/24-36in S 30-60cm/12-24in Z6). Large clumps of lush leaves are topped in summer by several stems bearing long-lasting heads of pendent pale yellow flowers. It is beautiful planted in the wetter parts of the bog or at damp streamsides, where it can naturalize and extend into the water.

P. 'Inverewe' (*P.* 'Ravenglass Vermilion') is a clump-forming candelabra type (H 90cm/3ft S 45cm/18in Z6). Numerous whorls of flowers in a

CANDELABRA PRIMULA HYBRIDS

PRIMULA VIALII

deep glowing orange-red are set off to perfection by the dark green basal rosette of oval leaves, to make this a particularly radiant primula. Propagate by division as the plant is sterile.

P. japonica is an early-flowering candelabra type, with abundant whorls of flowers on a tall stem (H 60-75cm/24-30in S 30-45cm/12-18in Z5) in late spring. Colours include white and many different shades of pink and red, some with a contrasting eye. Plants are fairly short-lived, but seed freely. *P.j.* 'Miller's Crimson' has vivid red blooms; *P.j.* 'Postford White' is pure white with yellow centres.

P. prolifera (P. helodoxa) is a candelabra primula from Burma and western China (H 60-90cm/24-36in S 45cm/18in Z6). It retains its light green glossy leaves throughout the winter and produces whorls of clear strong yellow flowers on tall stems in midsummer.

P. pulverulenta is a candelabra primula from Sichuan (H 60-90cm/24-36in S 30-45cm/12-18in Z6). Whorls of crimson flowers are borne on mealy stems in summer above rosettes of small coarse leaves. The slightly more delicate *P.p.* Bartley Hybrids have whorls of flowers in shades of soft peachy pink with darker centres.

P. sikkimensis, the Himalayan cowslip (H 45-75cm/18-30in S 30-45cm/12-18in Z5), is similar to *P. florindae* but smaller.

P. vialii from southwest China is an unusually shaped primula with very dramatic colouring (H 30cm/12in S 20cm/8in Z7). The blooms in densely flowered spikes resemble a miniature pink kniphofia, with 8-13cm/3-5in 'pokers' of mauve flowers opening from scarlet calyces in late spring or early summer. The tufts of lance-shaped leaves are slightly mealy.

RANUNCULUS Ranunculaceae

Two moisture-loving perennials from the buttercup genus make small-scale contributions in sunny or partially shady sites in the bog or waterside garden.

R. aconitifolius 'Flore Pleno', fair maids of France (or of Kent), is slow-growing, forming a clump of divided dark green buttercup leaves (H 60cm/24in S 45cm/18in Z6). Above these, branching stalks bear many pure white pompon-like double flowers in late spring to summer. This makes a handsome companion for a wide range of plants.

R. ficaria albus (H 5cm/2in S 15cm/6in plus Z5) is a white-flowered form of the lesser celandine, with a blue-green tinge on the underside of the petals. Spreading to form a carpet of glossy green leaves, it is suitable for naturalizing in a moist place, or planting beneath later-leafing subjects such as hostas. *R.f. flore-pleno* has attractive double flowers with shiny yellow petals. *R.f.* 'Brazen Hussy' has

sulphur-yellow saucer-shaped flowers above purple-black leaves.

RHEUM Polygonaceae

R. palmatum 'Atrosanguineum' is an ornamental rhubarb (H & S 2m/6½ft Z6) with handsome deeply cut leaves which are dark red when they first appear, turning green from the top later. Large fluffy plumes of bright red flowers are borne in early summer, but for the best foliage effects, the flowers should be removed before they sap the energy resources of the plant. This large plant calls for plenty of space. A vigorous grower, it needs deep moist soil with plenty of humus, in sun or partial shade. Propagate by dividing the thick woody roots in spring or by seed in autumn.

RODGERSIA Saxifragaceae

Rhizomatous perennials native to China and Japan, rodgersias like moist soils. They are grown primarily for their handsome foliage, but plume-like flowering heads add interest and textural contrast in the summer months. Propagate by seed or division.

R. aesculifolia (H & S 90cm-1.2m/3-4ft Z6) forms clumps of leaves resembling those of horse chestnuts, each with five to nine leaflets some 25cm/10in long. Rusty-brown hairs over the veins and leaf stalks give a bronzish tinge, adding to the attraction of the foliage. Tall plumes of creamy-white flowers appear at midsummer.

R. pinnata 'Superba' (H 90cm/3ft S 75cm/30in Z6) has abundant deep pink flowers. The bronze leaves are less distinctively chestnut-shaped, but nevertheless handsome.

SIDALCEA Malvaceae

S. malviflora 'Jimmy Whittet' makes a tall graceful plant (H 1.2m/4ft S 1m/3ft Z6) for the sunny, drier areas at the edges of the bog garden. The spires of delicate purple-pink mallow-like flowers are carried on erect stems above a basal clump of bright green leaves. Other cultivars provide a range of colours from pale pinks to rich reds.

SMILACINA Liliaceae (Convallariaceae)

S. racemosa, false Solomon's seal or false spikenard (H 75-90cm/30-36in S 45cm/18in Z4), is a perennial of graceful habit which comes from North American woodlands. Fresh green ribbed leaves grow alternately up the arching stems, and fluffy sprays of creamy-white flowers that smell like lily-of-the-valley are borne from spring to midsummer, followed by spherical reddish fruits. This lovely plant thrives in damp shady garden areas, favouring slightly acid conditions. It makes beautiful companion planting to meconopsis or

RANUNCULUS FICARIA ALBUS

Matteuccia struthiopteris. Propagate by division in spring or by sowing seed in autumn.

SOLIDAGO Compositae

S. 'Golden Wings' (H 1.5m/5ft S 1m/3ft Z4) is a tall golden rod with large feathery panicles of yellow flowers atop stems clothed in lance-shaped and toothed mid-green leaves. These vigorous plants have colonized vast tracts of swamp in the southern USA, but will thrive in well-drained soil or on poor ground, in sun or shade. Where space permits, a group makes a welcome splash of colour in late summer and early autumn. Golden rod is a good choice for furnishing the bare expanses beside a newly excavated lake.

SYMPHYTUM Boraginaceae

S. grandiflorum (H 25cm/10in S 60cm/24in Z5) is a small spreading perennial native to the Caucasus. It has oval to lance-shaped hairy green leaves and in spring bears bell-shaped flowers of a lovely creamy colour held in one-sided racemes. Preferring moist soils and shady habitats, this plant makes a good evergreen ground cover, beautiful in winter as underplanting to *Cornus alba* 'Sibirica' on stream banks or in the wild garden. The variegated variety *S.g.* 'Goldsmith' has cream outlining on the leaves. Propagate by division in spring or autumn.

TIARELLA Saxifragaceae

T. wherryi, foamflower (H 30cm/12in S 25cm/10in Z6), is a carpeting perennial native to woodlands of the southeast USA. This attractive plant has lobed and serrated ivy-shaped leaves that turn from pale green to bronze in the autumn. Racemes of small white to pink flowers appear in late spring to early summer, sometimes with a repeat flowering. Spreading by runners, plants make a carpet in deep shade provided the soil is moist. Propagate by dividing and replanting in spring or autumn.

TRADESCANTIA Commelinaceae
T. ohiensis, blue spiderwort (H & S 60cm/24in Z7), forms large green clumps of grass-like leaves amid which three-petalled triangular flowers of an intense violet-blue are borne throughout the summer. Adaptable to sun or partial shade, and compact-growing, this perennial will thrive in all parts of the bog garden and even extend into the shallows.

TROLLIUS Ranunculaceae
The globe flowers form clumps of divided buttercup-like leaves and bear double or cup-shaped flowers in spring and summer. *T.* x *cultorum* cultivars have spherical flower heads with incurved petals rising above attractive foliage (H 90cm/3ft S 60cm/24in Z5). *T.* x *c.* 'Golden Queen' has warm orange flowers, while the pale citron of *T.* x *c.* 'Lemon Queen' looks good among bog plants or by the streamside. Grow in rich moist but well-drained soil. Propagate by seed or division in spring.

UVULARIA Liliaceae (Uvulariaceae)
U. grandiflora, bellwort or merry-bells (H 60cm/24in S 30cm/12in Z3), is a clump-forming rhizomatous perennial from rich woodlands in eastern North America. It has fresh green oval leaves, and clusters of beautiful pendent bell-shaped yellow flowers are produced in the spring from graceful stems. Grow in cool peaty or leaf-mould soils in a shady position. Propagate by division.

VIOLA Violaceae
V. riviniana purpurea (wrongly known as *V. labradorica purpurea*) is a little perennial (H 10-15cm/4-6in S indefinite Z5), a variant of the European wood violet. It suckers and seeds to make pretty ground cover in sun or shade, in moist but well-drained soil. The ovate or kidney-shaped leaves are dark purplish green, sprinkled with toning lavender-purple flowers in spring and summer. Propagate by seed or division.

WAHLENBERGIA Campanulaceae
W. gloriosa (H & S 10cm/4in Z9) is a beautiful little perennial, the emblem of the Australian Capital Territory. Bell-shaped flowers up to 3cm/1½ in diameter are a deep blue and arise on slender stems above the ovate dark green leaves. It prefers well-drained, peaty, sandy soils: grow in the drier parts of the bog or stream bank. Propagate by division.

Green foliage plants

Ferns, grasses and grassy-leaved plants such as sedges, and bamboos (which are related to grasses) contribute foliage shape and texture. They look handsome among gravel, pebbles and boulders, and complement all kind of architectural features. They also make a fine neutral foil or surround for more decorative and colourful plants and flowers.

While some of the grassy plants are distinctively moisture-loving (juncus and cyperus will thrive in shallow water and could qualify as emergents), others will grow in quite dry soil. The bamboos are not only decorative but also useful for screening purposes, and their hollow stems and gentle rustlings make excellent noise barriers when planted as a thick boundary belt. The graceful habit of many grasses similarly enhances the surrounds of formal ponds and swimming pools where the soil is not moist. Several of the grasses and reeds and most of the bamboos have sharply pointed rhizomes and young shoots that can penetrate a flexible pond liner and damage a clay-lined pond. Do not, therefore, plant them within the confines of a planting shelf. When planted close to the pool, a concrete or metal barrier sunk into the ground around them will protect vulnerable liners.

Choose species carefully, matching scale and vigour to the size of the site. Some grassy plants are invasive, and some of the bamboos attain tree-like proportions in their native tropics, although they remain smaller when grown in rather colder climates. Bamboos flower very occasionally and many die right back. Cut them off close to the ground, give them a nitrogenous feed and new shoots will usually soon emerge. Grasses keep their dead leaves throughout the winter, and this brown or straw-coloured herbage can be a late-season bonus. Cut it to the ground before the new shoots emerge in spring.

Ferns are beautiful and venerable plants that are found all over the world except in dry or cold deserts – so wherever you live, there will be a fern to suit your water garden. Although a few ferns will thrive in full sun and dry ground, most are woodland plants that prefer semi-shade. With their refreshing variety of greens and lovely uncurling fronds, they are capable of flourishing among moss and rocks in spots that are too damp and shady for many other plants. Some, like Onoclea and Osmunda, enjoy saturated soil or even shallow water.

Harsh winds can scorch the fronds, and although ferns enjoy humidity they dislike being planted beneath the outer overhanging branches of trees that steadily drip on them in wet weather. You can propagate ferns from spores, but it is simpler to divide plants in winter or early spring, when they are resting.

ACROSTICHUM Adiantaceae
A. danaeifolium, giant leather fern (H & S 3m/10ft Z10), is native to coastal mangrove swamps in tropical and subtropical regions of the Americas. This imposing fern forms clumps of tall mid-green pinnate leaves. It needs humidity and many hours of sunlight – albeit partially shaded – in summer. Useful for maritime plantings in hotter areas, grow in a large greenhouse in temperate climates.

ADIANTUM Adiantaceae
Maidenhair ferns are widespread in a variety of habitats in both temperate and tropical areas. Wiry stems bearing delicate fan-like leaflets arranged on either side emerge from slowly spreading rhizomes. The new growth is often of a startling pink. The hardier species thrive in semi-shade, planted in moist soil containing some composted tree bark. They need humidity and movement of air, though too much wind will scorch the fronds.
A. capillus-veneris, common maidenhair (H & S 15-25cm/6-10in Z9), has graceful, delicate fronds and pale green triangular leaflets with deeply indented edges. It is evergreen in sheltered sites.
A. pedatum, northern maidenhair fern, has glossy black stems topped with delicate bright green leaflets to give an overall appearance of fans of green feathers (H & S 30cm/12in Z3). *A.p.* var. *aleuticum* is an attractive form with arching strap-shaped fronds and close-packed mid-green leaflets. Semi-evergreen in temperate regions, these ferns from North America and Japan can withstand temperatures down to -5°C/23°F and thrive best in dappled shade.
A. venustum is a deciduous inhabitant of mountainous wooded areas of Nepal, Kashmir and Afghanistan (H 20cm/8in S 30cm/12in Z9). An abundance of tiny triangular leaflets held on dark stalks look like sprays of delicate pale green gems. The foliage turns brown after frost but retains its decorative silhouette.

ARUNDO Gramineae
A. donax is a giant reed native to southern Europe and thriving best in rich damp soil in warm situations (H to 6m/20ft S 1m/3ft plus Z8). Although seen as an untidy mound of tangled stems in Mediterranean watercourses, when tamed and cultivated this grass is fresh and quite desirable. Grey-green bamboo-like leaves are arranged alternately up stout hollow culms (stems) and have a lush tropical appearance. Given shelter from strong winds, this makes an effective screen in temperatures down to -10°C/14°F. Cut back hard in autumn to encourage attractive new growth. Propagate by seed or division. *A.d.* var.

versicolor 'Variegata' has attractively striped leaves edged in creamy white. This is a very handsome plant but smaller-growing and less hardy than the type (H 3m/10ft S 60cm/24in Z9).

ASPLENIUM Aspleniaceae

The spleenworts are a large and varied genus of evergreen ferns adapted to a wide range of habitats. They spread by means of rhizomes, sometimes creeping and sometimes upright.
A. nidus, the bird's-nest fern from tropical Asia and the Pacific, sends out shuttlecocks of lovely bright green shiny leaves (H 90cm/3ft S 45cm/18in Z10).
A. scolopendrium, hart's-tongue fern (H & S 60cm/24in Z5), is native to northern temperate zones. The type has long wavy pale leaves with distinctive rows of brown spore cases on the undersides. Their clean lines make an invaluable foil for finely dissected foliage and contrast well with rocks. Chalk-tolerant, this fern can be grown near water in well-drained soil. *A.s.* Crispum Group is more decorative, the leaves with frilled edges resembling seaweeds such as sea lettuce.
A. trichomanes, maidenhair spleenwort (H 20cm/8in S 30cm/12in Z2), is native to temperate zones. Its attractive pinnate silhouette with dark brown midrib looks effective among rocks or in walls.

ATHYRIUM Dryopteridaceae

A. filix-femina, lady fern (H & S 90cm/3ft Z2), is a slender pale green deciduous fern, bipinnate or doubly divided fronds giving it a particularly delicate, lacy appearance. There are crested forms with flamboyant tips to their fronds, curly and feathery forms; *A.f.-f.* 'Clarissimum' has typical fern-like fronds and long slender leaflets. *A.f.-f.* 'Plumosum Druery' is a beautiful feathery form and grows to only 50cm/20in. Native to temperate zones, these ferns thrive in moist humid conditions, preferring acid soils and light shade.

BLECHNUM Blechnaceae

These moisture-loving evergreen or semi-evergreen ferns thrive best in damp lime-free soils with some shade.
B. fluviatile, the ray water fern (H 15cm/6in S 75cm/30in Z8), is native to Australia and New Zealand. It forms rosettes made up from many low-growing dark green sterile fronds. The upright fertile fronds are much shorter.
B. penna-marina is a small Antarctic fern (H 30cm/12in S 45cm/18in Z3). Its creeping rhizomes quickly send up clusters of glossy evergreen fronds to form an excellent dark green ground cover, very useful for damp shady places and a charming contrast to rock work. The leaflets are arranged symmetrically in opposite pairs up the stems, those of the fertile fronds being wider and more rounded than the infertile ones.
B. spicant, hard fern or deer fern (H 75cm/30in S 45cm/18in Z5), is native to forests and damp moorland of northern temperate zones. It is an extremely useful evergreen garden plant, hardy to -25°C/-13°F, and flourishing in fibrous soil with peat or composted tree bark. It has narrow divided fronds with dark green leathery leaflets, the outer infertile leaves spreading, the inner leaves upright, with narrower leaflets that bear spore cases on the undersides. There are crested and serrated forms; *B.s.* 'Cristatum' has little tufts at the tip of each frond, and *B.s.* Serratum Group is smaller (H 20cm/8in), with lobed leaflets on either side of the central axis.

CAREX Cyperaceae

Grass-like rhizomatous perennials, many sedges are too invasive for gardens, but these more decorative forms are particularly attractive for the bog garden, either standing in shallow water or in moist soil.

ASPLENIUM SCOLOPENDRIUM

CAREX ELATA 'AUREA' and *IRIS SIBIRICA*

CYPERUS PAPYRUS

C. buchananii, leather-leaf sedge (H & S 30-60cm/ 12-24in Z7), is an imposing sedge from New Zealand with narrow leathery blades of a subtle coppery-brown, sometimes red-tinted. It will flourish in rich well-cultivated moisture-retentive soil as well as in shallows, and prefers some shade. It increases slowly. Propagate by division.
C. elata 'Aurea' (C. stricta 'Aurea'), golden tufted sedge or Bowles' golden sedge, forms handsome tufts of evergreen yellow leaves (H 40cm/16in S 60cm/24in Z7). These look beautiful among green waterside foliage and magnificent reflected in dark water. They also contrast strikingly with red-leaved Lobelia cardinalis. This sedge prefers semi-shade. Propagate by division, but do not split too finely. It is not invasive and is often slow to establish.
C. riparia 'Variegata' (H 60-90cm/24-36in S indefinite Z7) is a cultivar of the greater pond sedge, with elegant arching leaves striped with

white. It is suitable for the larger garden, where it can spread beween other coarse-leaved waterside plants. In confined spaces, restrict its root run by planting it in a buried or submerged container.

CHIMONOBAMBUSA Gramineae
C. marmorea (H 2m/6½ft S 1m/3ft Z6) is an elegant bamboo for the streamside, sufficiently compact to be planted in groups or used as hedging. It has smooth purplish culms (stems), usually with three branches, with well-defined nodes. The young shoots are lime-green, dappled with red-brown and white, and have pink tips. The species has long slender bright green leaves; C.m. 'Variegata' has leaves with white stripes. This bamboo thrives best in moist soil and withstands temperatures down to -20°C/-4°F; new stems appear so late that they may have difficulty overwintering in colder climates.

CORTADERIA Gramineae
Pampas grass is a tussock-forming evergreen perennial with showy silky flowering plumes often used in dried flower arrangements. Plant in a sunny site in rich well-drained soil in spring, and remove straggly growth annually in spring. Propagate by division in spring, as seed does not always come true.
C. richardii (H & S 3m/10ft Z8) forms tussocks of gracefully arching narrow blades surmounted by lofty creamy-white plumes from midsummer. This species may be grown close beside the water in frost-free locations. (Most plants under this name in the British Isles turn out to be C. fulvida.)
C. selloana (H 1.5-3m/5-10ft S 1m/3ft Z7) has rough-edged narrow green leaves above which silky plumes are borne in late summer. There are many named forms which vary in stature or flower colouring, and some have leaf variegation. C.s. 'Monstrosa' bears large creamy-white plumes. C.s. 'Pumila' (H 1.2m/4ft) is a useful compact plant for limited space. C.s. 'Rendatleri' has plumes coloured silvery-purple. C.s. 'Sunningdale Silver' has dense erect stems of feathery creamy-white open plumes. Among variegated sorts (hardy to Z8-9), C.s. 'Silver Comet' (H 1.2m/4ft) has leaves with white edges and silvery-white plumes; C.s. 'Albolineata' ('Silver Stripe') is similar but slightly taller, and C.s. 'Aureolineata' ('Gold Band') (H 1.2m/4ft), has yellow stripes.

CYPERUS Cyperaceae
Members of this huge and diverse family of perennials have graceful grass-like leaves and an inflorescence resembling the ribs of an opened umbrella. Grow in very moist soil or a water depth of up to 15cm/6in. Propagate by division in spring.
C. alternifolius, the umbrella plant, is a popular houseplant in temperate areas. (Plants seen in cultivation under this name in the British Isles are often C. involucratus.) Numerous bright green stems terminate in whorls of graceful weeping bracts beneath rather insignificant pale flower spikes which appear in summer (H 90cm/3ft S 30cm/12in Z10).
C. eragrostis (C. vegetus), American galingale, is a very attractive species from southwest USA and warm temperate South America (H 60cm/24in S 30cm/12in Z8) that will grow happily in water or almost dry land. The interesting green spikelets are useful for drying for winter flower arrangements.
C. haspan, dwarf papyrus from central Asia, bears spikelets of reddish-brown flowers (H 45-75cm/ 18-30in S 30cm/12in or more Z9).
C. involucratus has tapering bracts on pale green stems with reddish-brown umbels (H 1-1.5m/3-5ft S 45cm/18in Z9).

C. longus, sweet galingale or medium umbrella palm from Europe, is the original 'strewing rush' used to cover floors in the Middle Ages. Attractive grown at pond margins where space allows, it produces graceful grassy tufts terminating in brown umbels (H 1.5m/5ft S indefinite Z7).
C. papyrus, Egyptian paper reed, is a tall, graceful plant (H 2-5m/6½-16ft S 1m/3ft Z9-10) that rockets up to bear clusters of bracts with brown spikelets resembling a huge brown-tipped green dishmop. *C.p.* 'Variegatus' is a boldly variegated form with white markings (Z10). *C.p.* 'Nanus' (syn. *C. isocladus*) is a smaller form (H 75cm/30in S 45cm/18in or more Z9), suitable for a tiny water garden in a tub or small enclosure. Confine the roots in a 20-30cm/8-12in pot.

CYRTOMIUM Dryopteridaceae
C. falcatum (Polystichum falcatum), fishtail fern or Japanese holly fern from southern Asia, East and South Africa (H 60cm/24in S 45cm/18in Z9), has pointed dark green glossy leaflets resembling holly leaves, borne alternately up the stem. Its bulky appearance makes a foil to the more feathery ferns. Occurring naturally in damp woodland areas, these evergreen ferns thrive best in humus-rich soils in shady sites. *C. fortunei (Polystichum fortunei)* from Southeast Asia is a very hardy species (Z4), tolerating temperatures down to -30°C/-22°F.

DICKSONIA Dicksoniaceae
D. antarctica, soft tree fern from Australia and Tasmania (H to 20m/65ft S 4m/13ft Z9), makes a truly spectacular evergreen fern for a shady woodland streamside or a large rocky waterfall site. With its great hairy upright rhizome and spreading fronds, it resembles a palm tree at first glance. It needs plenty of moisture during summer; sprinkle the roots and trunks with water in hot dry conditions. Mulch with good organic compost. Stature varies according to conditions; in temperate regions this fern is best grown under glass. Propagate by spores in summer.

DREPANOSTACHYUM Gramineae
These tender bamboos from the Himalayas do best in light sandy soils, as they resent waterlogged conditions during winter.
D. hookerianum (H 10-12m/33-40ft S 3m/10ft Z9) is an exotic-looking bamboo, well worth growing as an impressive specimen clump. The young canes begin green and yellow before turning pink, and are attractively decorated with a blueish circle beneath each node.
D. falconeri (H 5-10m/16-33ft S 2.5m/8ft Z9) is a desirable slightly smaller species. The slender stems have a mealy texture when young but turn pale green, with purple rings beneath each node.

ERIOPHORUM Cyperaceae
E. angustifolium, common cotton grass, is a tufted sedge-like perennial (H 30-45cm/12-18in S 20cm/8in or more Z4) which thrives in acid conditions such as peat bogs and in water to a depth of 15cm/6in. The silky white tufts of fine hairs 3cm/1¼in long attached to the seeds in summer look like cotton wool, and the plants make a beautiful sight when massed by the waterside. Propagate by division in spring.

GLYCERIA Gramineae
G. maxima var. *variegata*, variegated manna grass, (H 75cm-2m/30in-6½ft S indefinite Z5), is a handsome tall grass for marshland or a water depth to 30cm/12in. It can be invasive among weaker plants. The creamy-yellow stripes are pink-tinged in spring, leaves colouring best in semi-shade. Propagate by dividing the rhizomes.

ERIOPHORUM ANGUSTIFOLIUM

GLYCERIA MAXIMA VAR. *VARIEGATA*

MATTEUCCIA STRUTHIOPTERIS and *PRIMULA JAPONICA*

OSMUNDA REGALIS

HAKONECHLOA Gramineae

H. macra 'Aureola' (H 35cm/14in S 45cm/18in Z7) is a beautiful small-growing grass that is ideal beside tiny water features, where the golden-striped leaves can embrace smooth boulders and pebbles or sit in a squat clump as a specimen among leaf mould. Later in summer the myriad striped leaves take on red tints to complement the reddish-brown flower spikes, colouring best in sun. Grow in deep moist humus-rich soil. The smaller *H.m.* 'Alboaurea' (H 23cm/9in) has golden leaves finely striped with green, and prefers a shadier site.

HYPOLEPIS Dennstaedtiaceae

H. millefolium (H 45cm/18in S 30cm/12in Z8) is a deciduous fern from damp forests and swampy grasslands of New Zealand. Finely dissected dark green fronds are 25cm/10in wide. It likes rich moist soil. Creeping rhizomes make this a good carpeting fern where conditions are sufficiently warm; it will increase by spores to naturalize at shady streamsides, but can become invasive.

JUNCUS Juncaceae

Grassy bog plants mainly from acid soils in temperate regions, the rushes spread vigorously by rhizomes. They make cover for wildfowl at the margins of larger lakes, growing in water to a depth of 15cm/6in.
J. effusus, soft rush, forms dark green perennial clumps on smooth slender stems with brown inflorescences. More useful than the species in smaller gardens is *J.e.* 'Spiralis', a lower-growing contorted form that twists over the ground (H 30-45cm/12-18in S 45-60cm/18-24in Z4). *J.e.* 'Aureostriatus' is an eye-catching variety with cream and green banded stems (H 75cm/30in Z5). *J. inflexus*, hard rush (H 30-60cm/12-24in Z4), forms evergreen clumps of slender grey-green stems with brown inflorescences. It is useful as one of the few plants that retains its character while overwintering in water in colder regions.

LUZULA Juncaceae

The woodrushes have grass-like flat leaves edged with white hairs and bear clusters of brown or creamy-white flowers in summer. Many species are attractive but extremely invasive; the following spread slowly enough to be accommodated in garden displays.
L. x borreri 'Botany Bay' (H & S 20cm/8in) is a cultivar with broad leaves that are parchment-coloured when young.
L. nivea, snow rush (H 60cm/24in S 45-60cm/18-24in Z6), has loose panicles of shining white flowers in summer followed by reddish-brown seeds. This graceful evergreen is most effective making neat clumps among the cool greens of contrasting foliage. Grow in sun or shade in moisture-retentive soil.
L. sylvatica 'Marginata' (H 30-45cm/12-18in S indefinite Z6) is a form of great woodrush with leaves narrowly edged with white. Spikes of little brown flowers are borne in summer. It spreads slowly in dense tufts, carpeting damp shade.

MATTEUCCIA Dryopteridaceae

M. struthiopteris, ostrich fern or shuttlecock fern (H 90cm/3ft S 45cm/18in Z2), is a spectacular deciduous fern with fresh green fanning fronds resembling shuttlecocks. The fertile fronds in the centre are shorter than the peripheral infertile ones. Widely distributed in moist shady habitats in the temperate northern hemisphere, it is an excellent fern for the bog garden or stream bank, especially with meconopsis, smilacina, *Iris sibirica* or kirengeshoma. It colonizes rapidly via underground rhizomes. Mulch occasionally with leaf mould.

MISCANTHUS Gramineae

These large graceful perennials are valuable both as windbreaks and as attractive specimen plants. Although tall, they need no staking. The thick rhizomes increase more rapidly (and plants flower most profusely) in warmer climates. They enjoy retentive soil and are particularly useful in waterside plantings. Grow in a sunny position. Propagate by division in spring. Cut back dead stems in spring to ensure tidy new growth.
M. sacchariflorus, Amur silver grass, sugar flower grass, (H 3m/10ft S 1m/3ft Z5), is native to eastern Asia. With a creeping rootstock that is potentially invasive, it forms tall imposing columns of attractive fluttering mid-green leaves that often turn bronze as they die down in autumn. The effect is reminiscent of bamboo. Given sufficient warmth, flowers are produced in loose panicles of mauve-brown. *M.s.* 'Variegatus' has leaves with a cream stripe down the centre.
M. sinensis from China and Japan (H 2m/6½ft S 60cm/24in Z5) makes a graceful clump of wiry, erect stems. It will flourish in better drained soil and is not invasive. It has a number of coloured and variegated forms. *M.s.* var. *purpurascens* has small leaves with a pink-tinted central vein and turns brown and orange-red in autumn. *M.s.* 'Variegatus' (H 1-1.5m/3-5ft S 45-60cm/18-24in Z5) forms clumps of elegantly arching leaves with longitudinal stripes of ivory and green; *M.s.* 'Cabaret' has perhaps the boldest variegation, with

broad stripes of cream and green, and *M.s.* 'Morning Light' has very narrow graceful leaves. *M.s.* 'Zebrinus', tiger grass (H 2m/6½ft S 1.5m/5ft Z5) develops transverse bands of creamy-white on the leaves during summer, giving the clump a distinctively speckled appearance from a distance. Feathery flower heads are produced in late autumn. The very similar *M.s.* 'Strictus', of more upright habit (S 1m/3ft), makes a useful alternative for smaller gardens.

ONOCLEA Dryopteridaceae
O. sensibilis, sensitive fern or bead fern, is a moisture-loving deciduous fern from northeast North America and eastern Asia (H 45cm/18in S 90cm/3ft Z4). Carpets of single fronds growing up from long spreading rhizomes make fine foliage contrast among emergent plants and, if allowed, will form a mat out over the water surface. Its common names derive from its susceptibility to frost, which colours it an attractive ochre, and to the bead-like dark globules formed in winter when leaflets of the fertile fronds curl up to enclose the spore cases.

OSMUNDA Osmundaceae
O. regalis, royal fern or flowering fern, is a majestic deciduous fern (H 2m/6½ft S 1m/3ft Z2) from boggy habitats in many parts of the world. Growing from massive erect rhizomes, it unfurls tan-coloured crosiers in spring to form tall pale green fronds, which take on glorious orange-russet tones in autumn. The fertile leaflets held at the tops of the fronds are so heavily covered with spores that they resemble panicles of tiny light brown flowers. *O.r. purpurascens* has purple new growth and *O.r.* 'Crispa' has curly foliage. Unfussy as to sunlight and soil type, these ferns need plenty of moisture. They contrast well with iris and darmera (peltiphyllum) at the waterside.

PENNISETUM Gramineae
P. alopecuroides (P. compressum, P. japonicum), Chinese fountain grass, is a perennial from eastern Asia and eastern Australia (H 90cm/3ft S 45cm/18in Z9). It forms clumps of slender mid-green leaves and in autumn bears bristly purple plumes that stand well into the winter. They fountain upwards from the centre of the plant, as the name implies. It prefers a light well-drained soil and a sunny position, and will withstand temperatures down to -5°C/23°F. Propagate by division. *P.a.* 'Burgundy Giant' (Z10) is of similar stature, with bronze leaves and red flowers. These grasses make beautiful specimens in gravel or as large clumps near ponds and swimming pools. *P.a.* 'Hameln' (H 45cm/18in S 25cm/10in Z9) is a small variety with

greeny-white flowers and leaves which become golden yellow in autumn.

PHALARIS Gramineae
P. arundinacea var. *picta*, reed canary grass or gardener's garters, is an imposing perennial grass with waving flower spikelets during summer and handsome white-striped leaves (H 1m/3ft S indefinite Z4). It tolerates dry and wet conditions, and will grow happily to the water's edge but can become invasive if left unchecked. Divide and replant between autumn and spring. The bright variegation makes this particularly attractive beside *Persicaria bistorta* 'Superba' and *Iris sibirica*. *P.a.* var. *picta* 'Aureovariegata' is similar, but with golden-yellow variegation. *P. a.* var. *picta* 'Mervyn Feesey' has better white foliage than *P.a.* var. *picta* and spreads more slowly.

PHEGOPTERIS Thelypteridaceae
P. connectilis, beech fern, is a shade-loving deciduous fern (H 23cm/9in S 30cm/12in Z5). The dissected foliage is pale yellowish green, with lower leaflets curving towards the ground. Spreading slowly on long creeping rhizomes, this makes a good carpeting plant in humus-rich soil, preferably acid, which is moist but not waterlogged.

PHRAGMITES Gramineae
P. australis (P. communis), common reed or Norfolk reed, is a swamp-loving perennial that grows from creeping rhizomes (H 4m/13ft S indefinite Z6). It will grow as an emergent in up to 1.5m/5ft of water. Long downward-bending leaves are attached by loose sheaths to lofty stout stems, and glossy purplish flower plumes throughout summer look wild and graceful bending to the wind. Plant these very invasive grasses only where they can be contained; they afford shelter to fish and wildfowl and are valuable for consolidating shifting dunes, as well as for thatching and fodder. The variegated *P.a.* 'Variegatus', with golden-yellow stripes on its leaves, is less rampant but spreads and naturalizes if given the chance. Propagate by division.

PHYLLOSTACHYS Gramineae
Some of the loveliest bamboos, with branching grooved stems, phyllostachys are generally less invasive in cooler climates and do not grow as tall, making manageable but spectacular garden plants. They prefer a sheltered position in damp fertile soil, and enjoy an occasional mulch of well-rotted compost or manure. Propagate by division. *P. aurea*, fishpole bamboo, is a compact clump-forming evergreen bamboo from southeast China (H to 6-8m/20-25ft S indefinite Z6). It has

PHALARIS ARUNDINACEA VAR. PICTA

yellowish-green leaves and upright grooved culms (stems), with a swollen ridge below each node. This hardy and adaptable plant will thrive in relatively dry conditions. *P.a.* 'Albovariegata' has white-striped leaves, while *P.a.* 'Violascens' has fine purple stripes and will grow to no more than 6m/20ft.
P. aureosulcata, yellow groove bamboo, forms clumps of evergreen olive-green canes with yellow grooves and dainty 17cm/7in long leaves; *P.a.* 'Spectabilis' has yellow canes with green grooves (H to 6-8m/20-25ft S indefinite Z6).
P. bambusoides, giant timber bamboo, forms clumps of stout canes with large broad evergreen leaves (H to 6-30m/20-100ft S indefinite Z7). *P.b.* 'Holochrysa' is a smaller form (H to 6m/20ft) with yellow stems, often striped with green.
P. nigra, black bamboo (H to 6-8m/20-25ft S indefinite Z7), is a superbly elegant evergreen plant that spreads slowly. It has graceful arching culms and a profusion of small leaves. The canes, green at first, become black in time, *P.n.* f. *punctata* having maroon spots. *P.n.* var. *henonis* is one of the most beautiful bamboos for garden use, with green culms and luxuriant shining feathery foliage (H to 10m/33ft S 2-3m/6½-10ft Z7).

PLEIOBLASTUS AURICOMA and EUPHORBIA GRIFFITHII

SPARTINA PECTINATA 'AUREOMARGINATA'

PLEIOBLASTUS Gramineae
Some of these small- to medium-sized bamboos from Japan and China are too invasive for smaller gardens, but in more extensive sites low-growing varieties can make good ground cover and afford nesting sites for wildfowl. Plant in moist soil and shelter from harsh winds. Mulch occasionally with well-rotted manure or compost.
P. auricoma (P. viridistriatus) is most effective against a dark background. The broad yellow leaves striped with green are most conspicuous on young growth, which is encouraged by cutting hard back each spring (H 1m/3ft S indefinite Z7). It spreads slowly.
P. variegatus (Arundinaria variegata, Sasa variegata), dwarf white-striped bamboo, is a compact branching species (H 75cm/30in S 60cm/24in or more Z7). It has dark green leaves striped with creamy-white and downy purple-lined sheaths.

POLYPODIUM Polypodiaceae
P. vulgare, common polypody, is an attractive evergreen fern with long leathery leaflets arranged alternately up the stems (H & S 30cm/12in Z3). It grows equally happily in soil, on the branches of trees in damper areas and even in dry stone walls. It does best in acid conditions and semi-shade.

Given a moist but well-drained soil, it will form an attractive evergreen ground cover. The similar *P. cambricum*, Welsh polypody (Z6), has wider fronds, and there are variants with crested, curly or feathery forms. *P. scouleri* (Z9) from the northwest United States has large glossy leaflets on fronds growing up to 45cm/18in from creeping rhizomes.

POLYSTICHUM Dryopteridaceae
P. setiferum, soft shield fern from south, west and central Europe (H 60cm/24in S 45cm/18in Z4), is a lovely pale green evergreen fern. *P.s.* Divisilobum Group has leaflets so divided as to resemble small ferns in themselves, creating a rich fluffy appearance. A covering of silky scales gives the newly emerging crosiers an attractive furry sheen. These ferns thrive best in moist but well-drained neutral to alkaline soils; enjoying a stony terrain in semi-shade, they are choice plants to grow in the rocks near a waterfall. Remove dead fronds, which are susceptible to fungal disease.

PSEUDOSASA Gramineae
P. japonica, arrow bamboo or metake, is a sturdy species from Japan and Korea (H 5m/16ft S indefinite Z6). Tough thickets of smooth green canes sheathed in light brown have large broad

evergreen leaves. Capable of growing in shade and very boggy conditions, this highly wind-resistant bamboo is useful for providing shelter for less robust subjects. Propagate by dividing the rhizomes. Cut back and feed copiously when flowering occurs: there is a tendency for plants to die after flowering, so this bamboo is best avoided for permanent hedging or screening.

PTERIS Pteridaceae
P. cretica, Cretan brake (H 45cm/18in S 30cm/12in Z9), is an evergreen fern native to a zone stretching east from southwestern Europe to Japan. Its undivided pale green leaflets are sometimes forked near the base of the stem, giving them a chunky, saw-toothed outline. Decorative forms include *P.c.* 'Albolineata' with white variegation, *P.c.* 'Childsii' with ruffled or wavy fronds and *P.c.* 'Wilsonii' with distinctive crests at the tip of each frond. *Pteris* prefer alkaline soils, humidity and movement of air.

SASA Gramineae
S. veitchii is an evergreen bamboo from southern Japan (H to 1.5m/5ft S indefinite Z7). Potentially invasive, its thickets of yellow stalks with contrasting purple sheaths bear a canopy of rich green leaves. The leaf margins become parchment-coloured in autumn and retain this handsome variegated effect all winter, standing out well against a dark background. Plant in rich moisture-retentive soil in semi-shade. Plants tolerate temperatures down to -20°C/-4°F. Propagate by division in spring, keeping new plants well misted.

SCIRPUS Cyperaceae
S. lacustris, the true bulrush, is native to bogs or shallow water all over the world. Growing from short creeping roots, it quickly forms colonies of slender spiky cylindrical leaves with reddish-brown flower spikelets. It is suitable for wild schemes on a large scale. *S. l.* ssp. *tabernaemontani (Schoenoplectus lacustris* ssp. *tabernaemontani)* is a more elegant form, taller and blue-green in colour (H 3m/10ft Z4). It also has a number of fine cultivars. *S.l.* ssp. *t.* 'Albescens' (H 1.8m/6ft) has stripes running vertically along the length of the leaves. With its cylindrical white stems, this form makes beautiful, graceful clumps by watersides. *S.l.* ssp. *t.* 'Zebrinus' (H 1.5m/5ft) has transverse white and green stripes on the leaves. Its decorative quality and more compact stature make it one of the most useful and dramatic rushes for the garden pond.

SPARTINA Gramineae
S. pectinata 'Aureomarginata' (*S.p.* 'Variegata') is a robust cord grass (H 2m/6½ft S indefinite Z5). Its

graceful long arching leaves are mid-green with gold edges. The numerous narrow flower spikes have pendulous purple stamens. The whole turns an attractive russet-yellow in autumn, and the flowers dry well. Preferring moist, sunny situations, this tough herbaceous grass spreads via running rhizomes and can be invasive, but is valuable for consolidating mud banks.

STIPA Gramineae
These clump-forming evergreen grasses are hardy, easy to grow and generally trouble-free. Known as needle grass or spear grass, they have sturdy narrow leaves and tall slender stems, with attractive loose panicles of pendent spikelets remaining until late into the winter. Propagate by seed or division.
S. arundinacea, pheasant grass (H 1.5m/5ft S 1.2m/4ft Z8), forms clumps of narrow olive-green leaves and bears purplish inflorescences in autumn, when it assumes an attractive orange coloration. *S.a.* 'Autumn Tints' becomes suffused with red towards the end of summer.
S. gigantea, golden oats (H 2.5m/8ft S 1m/3ft Z8), is a truly wonderful grass with great panicles of silvery-gold flower spikes held aloft on long straight stems from a slowly spreading clump.

THELYPTERIS Thelypteridaceae
T. palustris, marsh fern or marsh buckler fern, is a North American deciduous fern for really wet situations. Pale green much-divided lance-shaped fronds grow from creeping rhizomes (H 75cm/30in S 30cm/12in Z4). Though inclined to be invasive, it is an excellent lakeside subject, ideal naturalized among sedges and rushes in sun or shade.

TYPHA Typhaceae
Reedmaces or common cattails are deciduous perennial marginal plants, suitable for the edges of larger pools, lakes and wild gardens. Handsome, stately plants, making large clumps of strap-like green foliage, their late-summer flowers are followed by highly decorative chocolate-brown seed heads shaped like fat pokers on tall slender stems. Accommodating plants, which grow in sun or shade, they are unfortunately very invasive.
T. angustifolia, the lesser reedmace or narrow-leaved cattail, with more elegant, slender foliage (H 2.1m/7ft S 60cm/24in Z3), is the species to choose for medium to large ponds.
T. latifolia, greater reedmace (H 1.2-2.5m/4-8ft S 60cm/24in Z3), is a larger, broader-leaved species. Light brown flowers are followed by dark brown seed heads. Seeds germinate freely and will quickly colonize any shallow water where there is soil for them to grow. They are among the principal

contributing factors to the silting of lakes, so use with care. *T.l.* var. *elatior* has narrower leaves and shorter spikes.
T. minima, dwarf reedmace (H 30-45cm/12-18in S 30cm/12in Z6), is the 'baby' of the genus, and less invasive. The rusty-brown seed heads are more spherical. With its grass-like leaves, it makes a pretty plant for the small pond.

WOODSIA Aspleniaceae
W. alpina, northern woodsia, is a heavily dissected tufty little deciduous fern (H & S 20cm/8in Z5), native to rocky mountainous areas of southeast Canada and eastern and central USA. This is a good candidate for shady, moist stony situations where any surface moisture will drain away rapidly. The crowns rot in waterlogged ground. Stone troughs or the rocks beside a small waterfall show these endearing ferns to advantage.

WOODWARDIA Blechnaceae
W. radicans is a magnificent fern with elegant arching fronds and finely serrated leaflets (H 2m/6½ft S 1.5m/5ft Z9). The spores form a chain-like pattern, hence the common name of chain fern. Native to North America, southwestern Europe and the Atlantic islands, it grows extremely well by running streams, preferring moist, slightly acid soil of fibrous texture and light shade. Plants can need some winter protection in cold districts. Propagate easily by pinning down the plantlets that grow at the tips of the fronds.

YUSHANIA Gramineae
Y. anceps (formerly *Arundinaria anceps*), anceps bamboo (H 3m/10ft S indefinite Z8), is a most attractive evergreen with arching branches that bear pointed leaves of mid-green. The arrangement of canes gives a pleasant fresh, open appearance to the foliage, allowing wind to pass through and keep the plants quivering. This bamboo is happy to grow beneath trees, and likes humus and leaf mould. Plants sometimes die out after flowering, so are not recommended for important structural planting, permanent screening or shelter.

ZIZANIA Gramineae
Z. aquatica, Canada wild rice or water oats, is an attractive lofty annual grass (H 3m/10ft S 45cm/18in WD 0-23cm/0-9in Z6). It has lush flat soft green leaves and pale green terminal flower heads in summer, followed by rice-like seeds that attract waterfowl. Grow in full sun at the water margins. Propagate from seed sown in spring in pots of mud sunk in water.

Emergent plants

This group of plants may be found wherever the water is shallow enough to permit their growth, usually around pond margins and along lakes and slow-running streams. They root in the mud and emerge out of the water, holding their leaves and flowers above the surface.

In their natural habitat, fluctuations in water level are likely to occur. During drier periods they may have to survive on land where the soil is only just moist; however, after sudden storms or annual rains they may be inundated and remain submerged for days or even months. It follows that many of these plants, by the very circumstances in which they grow naturally, can flourish in a range of water depths. In the list that follows I suggest an average water depth for each plant, but this should be taken only as a rough guide – useful in the rather more stable environment of an ornamental pond. Most species establish better in shallow conditions and gradually work their way into deeper water, so do not plant too deeply at first. Allow for natural spreading in all directions.

In temperate countries the plants are often submerged during the winter months, during which they are dormant. The foliage will have died away in the autumn to prevent them from being dragged out by strong currents or ice. As the water recedes in spring, they put out fresh leaves and begin to flower, and the diversity of species and cultivars provides colour and foliage right through until late autumn. Tropical types receive their water in the summer, often in the form of regular thunderstorms in the afternoons. Flowering begins with the arrival of the water, and usually the drier months are their resting periods.

Clear up and remove old leaves as the plants die down or go into their dormant phase. This prevents a build up of leaf matter which may only partially rot down, gradually making the water shallower around the plants. If this is allowed to happen they will gradually encroach out into the pond on a raft of their own making. In time this can cause a pond to become completely covered and finally silt it up. Eventually land plants will take over, spreading outwards from the progressively drier shores.

There is such a wealth of emergent plants available that something can be found to suit every planting position.

ACORUS Araceae
Pleasantly aromatic in all parts, these semi-evergreen perennials look handsome at the water's edge in shallow water or moist soil. Propagate by dividing the rhizomes.
A. calamus, sweet flag or beewort (H 60cm-1.2m/2-4ft WD 0-30cm/0-12in Z3), has been used in medicine since the time of Hippocrates; its candied

roots are a popular sweetmeat in Turkey. The 5-8cm/2-3in long spike of green flowers appears below the tips of the foliage. The apple-green leaves, sweetly scented when rubbed, are slightly crimped along the upper edge, differentiating them from an iris. In large sunny ponds or lakes, it forms a strong spreading clump. *A.c.* 'Variegatus' is more compact (H to 90cm/3ft) and suited to smaller ponds; its cream-striped leaves, flushed red at the base, are attractive next to the pink flowers of butomus.

A. gramineus, a diminutive species from Japan (H 30cm/12in WD 0-10cm/0-4in Z6), is available with several sorts of variegation. *A.g.* 'Variegatus' is striped cream and yellow and *A.g.* 'Ogon', chartreuse and cream; *A.g.* 'Oborozuki' is gold. Their fans of compact leaves look attractive near small water features or among stones and pebbles.

ALISMA Alismataceae

Water plantains are attractive marginal perennials with bright green leaves and wide panicles of small whitish flowers borne in summer on stems high above the water. They grow best in an open sunny position and in humus-rich soil. Propagate by root division or by sowing seed as soon as it is ripe.

A. plantago-aquatica, mad dog weed or great water plantain (H 45-75cm/18-30in WD 0-30cm/0-12in Z6), was formerly used in North America as an antidote to rattlesnake bites; in Europe it was used to treat rabies – hence one of its common names. In deeper water, linear leaves remain below the surface; in shallower water, light green spoon-shaped leaves and loose panicles of small rose-lilac to white flowers stand above the surface. Seedlings may become invasive in natural earth ponds.

A. lanceolatum, narrow-leaved water plantain (H 30-60cm/12-24in WD 0-20cm/0-8in Z6), is a species with dark green tapering leaves and pinkish-white flowers, suitable for smaller ponds.

BUTOMUS Butomaceae

B. umbellatus, the flowering rush (H 60cm-1.2m/2-4ft WD 5-40cm/2-16in Z5), has pretty bronze shoots that grow up into slender rush-like olive-green leaves. Umbels of rose-pink flowers are borne above the leaves on tall cylindrical stems in summer. This perennial looks splendid beside silver or white foliage. It does best in open ground; if containerized, it needs frequent repotting. Propagate by division. Handle the rhizomes carefully: they are extremely brittle.

CALLA Araceae

C. palustris, the water or bog arum (H 15-30cm/6-12in WD 5-30cm/2-12in Z4), has heart-shaped glossy dark green leaves and white arum-like flowers in spring, followed by red or orange berries. Expanding on creeping rhizomes, it thrives in lime-free moist soil or in shallow water, where it spreads to form rafts. It prefers full sun. Propagate by cutting rhizomes into sections or by sowing seed as soon as it is ripe.

CALTHA Ranunculaceae

With their profusion of yellow or white buttercup-like flowers above mounds of shiny rounded leaves, marsh marigolds are a welcome spring sight at a sunny water's edge. Propagate these perennials by sowing seed soon after ripening or by division in the growing season.

C. palustris (H 45cm/18in WD 0-15cm/0-6in Z3) has a wealth of common names including marsh marigold, kingcup, meadow rout; may-blob, water-blob or horse-blob; water dragon, water cowslip or meadow gowan. Its clusters of single golden yellow flowers look equally well among rushes by the wild pond and beside the more formal ornamental pool. *C.p.* var. *alba* is a smaller form (H 30cm/12in WD 5cm/2in). It makes a neat clump of saw-toothed rounded leaves and bears endearing white flowers with gold centres. It looks very pretty planted with *Primula rosea* 'Micia Visser-de Geer' at the water's edge. *C.p.* 'Plena' is another compact variety (H 15-30cm/6-12in WD 5cm/2in). The bright orange-yellow of its double flowers requires more careful placing than the softer tones of the other forms. *C. polypetala* is a larger species (H 45-75cm/18-30in WD 0-30cm/0-12in Z3) with 8cm/3in diameter yellow blooms from late spring through summer. Suitable for large ponds or lakesides, it forms great mounds and increases by rooting at each node.

CANNA Cannaceae

Tender perennials from the warmer regions of North America, cannas have showy leaves and bright exotic flowers in summer. Clumps make attractive bold specimens in a formal pond and provide splashes of colour among green foliage. They require a minimum temperature of 10-15°C/50-59°F and some will grow up to 5m/16ft given sufficient warmth and a retentive humus-rich soil. Cannas will grow equally well in the bog, in soil that is not waterlogged, provided it is sufficiently moist and rich. To propagate, keep the rhizomes just moist in slightly damp peat or soil during winter, cut into shoot-bearing sections in spring and plant each in moist soil at 16°C/60°F, repotting as necessary. Many excellent hybrids are now available, such as *C.* 'Endeavour' (H 1.2m/4ft WD 0-15cm/0-6in Z10), with vivid light red flowers.

COLOCASIA Araceae

The tubers of taro or poi are grown for eating in humid tropical regions; the plant is grown as an ornamental in temperate zones.

CALTHA PALUSTRIS

CRINUM AMERICANUM

C. esculenta 'Fontanesii', the violet-stemmed taro, makes a fine foliage plant for water margins (H 90cm/3ft WD 0-30cm/0-12in Z10). Its elephantine deep green leaves up to 60x35cm/24x14in are strikingly enhanced by conspicuous violet veins, and the stalks are the colour of aubergines; the summer flowers are insignificant. It spreads easily by runners in rich soil to form a bold area of pattern. Propagate by division in spring.

COTULA Compositae
C. coronopifolia, brass buttons, has masses of small yellow disc-shaped flowers in summer above small lance-shaped mid-green leaves (H 15cm/6in WD 0-10cm/0-4in Z7). Seedlings of this annual or short-lived perennial usually appear spontaneously each spring; as an insurance save some seed and resow in spring in trays of damp soil.

CRINUM Liliaceae (Amaryllidaceae)
C. americanum, the bog lily, Florida swamp lily or string lily (H 60cm/24in WD 0-15cm/0-6in Z9), bears fragrant white flowers with six elongated petals on stout stalks above strap-shaped leaves. The flowers stand out strikingly against the black water and ferns of its native Florida, and look equally good planted in gardens among the royal fern (*Osmunda regalis*). These tropical bulbous plants thrive in full sun or partial shade.

GALAX Diapensiaceae
G. urceolata (*G. aphylla*), the wandflower from southeast USA, is a most impressive low-growing evergreen foliage plant (H 15-20cm/6-8in WD 0-10cm/0-4in Z5). It has large glossy heart-shaped leaves of rich green, which turn an attractive reddish-bronze in winter, and dense spires of white flowers in early summer. It needs a lime-free soil. Thriving in shade, it makes an attractive carpet below shrubs.

HYMENOCALLIS LIRIOSOME

HYMENOCALLIS Liliaceae (Amaryllidaceae)
Tender bulbous plants with large fragrant flowers, the native American hymenocallis flourish as bog plants or in shallow water. In temperate gardens lift and dry the deciduous varieties for winter storage; keep the more tropical evergreen varieties moist, overwintering them in a cool greenhouse.
H. liriosome, spider lily (H 60cm/24in WD 0-15cm/0-6in Z8-10), has fragrant exotic white flowers and strap-like foliage. It looks wonderful grown among aquatic ferns.
H. caribaea 'Variegata' H 60cm/24in WD 0-15cm/0-6in Z8-10) has similar flowers and variegated evergreen foliage.

HYPERICUM Guttiferae
H. elodes, marsh or bog St John's wort, has downy heart-shaped leaves and clusters of pale yellow summer flowers 15mm/¾in across, they make useful carpeting plants (H 30cm/12in WD 0-10cm/0-4in Z7). Propagate in spring by seed or division, or in summer by stem cuttings.

IRIS Iridaceae
Several species in this stately and colourful genus are suitable for growing in moist soil or shallow water. Distinctive leaf variegation makes many of them among the most arresting waterside plants even when not in flower.
I. laevigata is a majestic plant (H 60-90cm/24-36in WD 0-10cm/0-4in Z5), native to marshy areas of Japan. Flowers appear in early to midsummer; the purple-blue outer petals have yellow markings at the base. Planted in baskets of rich loam or on planting ledges, this iris is very effective in merging a pond with its surroundings. It is lime-tolerant. Propagate by dividing the rhizomes after flowering or in early spring. When replanting, cut the leaves back to 10cm/4in to prevent the plants from being blown over. As with all iris, never plant too deeply, as soil rots the leaf bases. *I.l.* 'Dorothy Robinson' (H 45cm/18in WD 0-10cm/0-4in Z5) is one of the most beautiful forms, worthy of any poolside. Plant it beside *Scirpus lacustris* ssp. *tabernaemontani* 'Zebrinus' or the white *S.l.* ssp. *t.* 'Albescens'. *I.l.* 'Variegata' (H 75cm/30in WD 0-10cm/0-4in Z5) is a 'bonus' plant; it has spectacular green and white striped leaves and a lovely blue flower, and sometimes blooms twice. Compact-growing, it is ideal for small ornamental ponds.
I. 'Snowdrift' (H 75cm/30in WD 0-10cm/0-4in Z5) has gorgeous large snow-white flowers elegantly

LYSICHITON AMERICANUS

IRIS PSEUDACORUS

borne on tall stems; they look particularly attractive when planted with blue forms and appear luminous by the poolside at dusk. Louisiana Iris belong to the beardless Hexagonae series of the genus, from swamp lands in southern USA, and are widely grown in the USA and Australia. The spectacular colour range includes red, yellow, blue, purple and white as well as deep tan; some forms are single, others fully double. Popular varieties of these superb plants include 'Black Gamecock', a deep velvety-purple, and 'Bayou Comus', an elegant rich yellow (H 60cm/24in WD 10cm/4in Z5-9). Most are tender; as climatic conditions vary so enormously, seek advice from nurserymen when purchasing one of these iris as to its best siting. The Louisiana Iris Society of America and the Species Iris Group of North America also provide information.

I. pseudacorus, yellow flag (H 90cm-1.2m/3-4ft WD 0-30cm/0-12in Z5), is a luxuriant and vigorous yellow-flowered beardless iris from Europe and Asia. The colonizer of many river banks and natural pools, it is suitable only for large ponds. It adapts to most soil types. It seeds freely, or can be propagated by dividing rhizomes. *I.p.* 'Flore Pleno' is a double form. *I.p.* var. *bastardii* is less vigorous than the species, and has pale creamy-yellow flowers that provide an interesting contrast to *I.*

pseudacorus when planted in bold clumps around a lakeside.

I. x *robusta* 'Gerald Darby' (H 60-90cm/24-36in WD 0-10cm/0-4in Z5-6) is a most distinctive iris with purple coloration in the stems and leaves. This plant forms a neat clump of fine foliage and the branching stems carry small mauve flowers.

I. setosa, bristle-pointed iris (H 25-30cm/10-12in WD 0-10cm/0-4in Z3), thrives in the wetter parts of the bog or shallow water. It forms a low carpet of grey-green leaves. The flowers, borne in profusion in early summer, are blue-mauve with light centres.

I. versicolor, blue flag (H 60cm/24in WD 0-15cm/0-6in Z4), is a free-flowering smaller beardless iris from eastern North America, more suitable for the average garden pool. Small rich blue-purple flowers with white and yellow centres are borne on branching stems above neat green sword-shaped leaves. Propagate as for *I. laevigata*. *I.v.* 'Kermesina' has lovely claret-coloured flowers. The slightly less vigorous *I.v.* 'Rosea' has pinky-purple flowers, and looks very pretty planted near blue and white irises.

LUDWIGIA Onagraceae

These floating and creeping swamp-loving plants are mostly from warm climates.

L. adscendens (H 10cm/4in WD 0-45cm/0-18in Z9-10) is an attractive plant whose mid-green leaves 6cm/2½in long and large yellow flowers float on the water surface. Spongy respiratory roots grow vertically upwards. Propagate from cuttings and pot up some shoots in autumn to overwinter in a cool but frost-free situation.

L. palustris, water purslane (H 5cm/2in WD 0-45cm/0-18in Z3), has pale green oval leaves 2.5cm/1in long, which turn an attractive reddish colour as they reach the air. Stems 5-30cm/2-12in long are creeping on wet soil but grow vertically when submerged, becoming excessively leggy in a heated tank or warm pond. The green flowers are insignificant. Propagate from cuttings.

LYSICHITON Araceae

The spathes of the skunk cabbage, skunk lily or bog arum emerge dramatically from bare mud in early spring, unfurling (like the 'loose cloak' of their Greek name) to display large arum-like flowers. These are succeeded in summer by huge paddle-shaped green leaves. Plants will grow in deep mud or in still or running shallow water; they flower better in a sunny situation. Plant with ferns and *Iris sibirica* for foliage contrast. Propagate by sowing seed in very wet mud in mid to late summer, as soon as it is ripe.

ORONTIUM AQUATICUM and IRIS PSEUDACORUS 'VARIEGATA'

MENTHA AQUATICA

Z3) from pond margins in far northern and arctic regions. Spires of deep pink buds open into fringed white flowers above tripartite mid-green leaves. Foliage and flowers are held erect and extend out over the water surface on long branching rhizomes. Propagate by cutting stems into sections, each with a root, and planting into wet earth.

MYOSOTIS Boraginaceae
M. scorpioides (M. palustris), water forget-me-not (H 20cm/8in WD 0-10cm/0-4in Z5), is a marsh-loving relative of the well-known garden plant with its endearing small blue flowers with a yellow eye. Planted by the pondside, it will creep some way out over the water surface and flower on branching stems throughout the summer. Propagate by sowing seed in well-watered pots or by striking young shoots in spring. Plants vary in quality and some forms have larger and darker flowers than the type. *M.s.* 'Mermaid' has sturdy stems and deep green leaves. *M.s.* 'Sapphire' is a good strong blue.

ORONTIUM Araceae
O. aquaticum, golden club (H 30cm/12in WD 10-45cm/4-18in Z7), is a perennial grown for its attractive large waxy blue-green leaves and extraordinary flower spike. Appearing in spring, this consists of a long, slender spadix covered with small yellow flowers and resembles a white club with a golden-yellow top. Grow it as a marginal or in submerged baskets; the oval leaves float on the surface in deeper water. Propagate by division or by sowing fresh seed in underwater containers or trays of mud.

PARNASSIA Saxifragaceae
P. palustris, grass of Parnassus or bog star (H 15-30cm/6-12in WD 0-10cm/0-4in Z4), is a perennial from marshes and wet meadows in northern temperate zones. It bears charming snow-white buttercup-like flowers 2.5cm/1in diameter in late spring and early summer on long slender stems above a shiny rosette of leaves. Usually evergreen, it will not tolerate lime and prefers to grow near running water. Propagate from seed sown in small pots in late autumn or by division in spring.

PELTANDRA Araceae
P. sagittifolia (P. alba), arrow arum (H 45cm/18in WD 0-20cm/0-8in Z7), is a rhizomatous arum-like perennial from marshes and springs in southeastern USA. With clumps of glossy dark green arrow-shaped leaves, plants give a fine effect when grown in shallow water; the white flower spathes 8-10cm/3-4in long are followed by clusters of red berries. Propagate by division in early spring.

L. americanus (H 90cm-1.2m/3-4ft WD 0-10cm/0-4in Z7) from peaty swamps of northwest North America has large flowers of rich yellow, followed by tall oval leaves.
L. camtschatcensis (H 75-90cm/30-36in WD 0-10cm/0-4in Z7) from Japan and Siberia has smaller pure white flowers. Crosses between the two species produce attractive cream forms.

MENTHA Labiatae
Several species of mint thrive in shallow water or damp soil. They look attractive softening pool edges and smell delicious when touched in passing. Propagate by division or by short stem cuttings in spring, and plant in wet soil.
M. aquatica, water mint (H 30-45cm/12-18in WD 0-10cm/0-4in Z6), has oval serrated leaves and lilac flowers in summer. The aromatic leaves are edible, and look attractive at a natural pondside, but the creeping rhizomes can become invasive.
M. cervina (H 30cm/12in WD 0-20cm/0-8in Z7) is a daintier, low-growing plant that forms clumps of leafy stems with spikes of blue or lilac flowers in whorls during late summer.

MENYANTHES Menyanthaceae
M. trifoliata is a pretty little creeping deciduous perennial (H 20-30cm/8-12in WD 5-30cm/2-12in

SAGITTARIA SAGITTIFOLIA

PONTEDERIA CORDATA

SCHIZOSTYLIS COCCINEA

PERSICARIA Polygonaceae
P. amphibia, amphibious persicaria or amphibious bistort (H 10cm/4in WD 0-45cm/0-18in Z5), will grow in or out of water. It is from northern temperate regions, with floating lance-shaped green and reddish leaves and characteristic pink flower spikes held above the water surface. Propagate by division in spring.

PONTEDERIA Pontederiaceae
P. cordata, pickerel weed or wampee (H 60-90cm/ 24-36in WD 5-30cm/2-12in Z4), is an imposing perennial marginal aquatic from North America. Large clumps with their attractive lance-shaped glossy leaves offer striking foliage effects and flower spikes of a lovely intense blue are borne over a long period in late summer and autumn. *P.c.* 'Alba' is a white-flowered variety (WD 10-20cm/4-8in).

162

RANUNCULUS Ranunculaceae

R. lingua, greater spearwort (H 45cm-2m/1½-6½ft WD 0-30cm/0-12in Z4) is a tall, narrow perennial native to Europe with thin lance-shaped green leaves. In late spring pinkish stems bear clusters of large flat buttercup flowers. Potentially invasive, large clumps of plants are effective beside lakes and larger ponds, but in small groups stalks tend to flop over and then grow upright from the tip, giving a sprawling, untidy appearance.

SAGITTARIA Alismataceae

The arrowheads thrive in shallow water or marshy areas and prefer full sun. The underwater foliage of this genus is useful for oxygenating and purifying, and plants are believed to sweeten the soil in which they grow. Increase by separating the scaly young shoots (known as turions) in early spring, or divide vigorously growing plants in summer.

S. lancifolia (H 60cm-1.5m/2-5ft WD 0-30cm/0-12in Z9) has lance-shaped leaves and several whorls of white flowers. They provide a lovely fresh foliage contrast around the margins of either small or large ponds. *S.l. ruminoides* is a striking red-stemmed form with bright green leaves.

S. latifolia, duck potato (S 45cm/18in or more WD 10-90cm/4-36in Z7), has bright green arrow-shaped floating and aerial leaves; the narrow strap-like underwater foliage is valuable for oxygenating.

S. sagittifolia (S. japonica), arrowhead (H 45cm/18in WD 0-30cm/0-12in Z7), bears three-petalled white flowers with dark centres that emerge above attractive arrow-shaped leaves. This plant will colonize large areas of the water margins but never becomes a problem like the more strangulating rushes and reeds. *S.s.* 'Flore Pleno' has gorgeous fluffy white double flowers. It is an excellent plant for small ornamental ponds and looks good planted beside blue *Pontederia cordata*.

S. subulata (Z4) is a good oxygenator, spreading rapidly by runners beneath the surface to form a dense covering of fine grass-like leaves. It may also produce small elliptical dark green aerial leaves.

SAURURUS Saururaceae

S. cernuus, lizard's tail or swamp lily (H 20cm/8in WD 0-30cm/0-12in Z5), is a pretty summer-flowering perennial for the smaller pond. Clumps of heart-shaped bright green leaves make a foil for fragrant nodding flower spikes resembling large fluffy white caterpillars. Propagate by division in early spring.

SCHIZOSTYLIS Iridaceae

S. coccinea, Kaffir lily (H 60cm/24in WD 0-10cm/0-4in Z8) is a beautiful moisture-loving rhizomatous plant from South Africa, which resembles a small gladiolus. Sheaves of light green grassy foliage make good ground cover before spikes of warm crimson flowers appear in autumn, continuing into winter in mild weather. There are named forms in scarlet, shades of pink and white; *S.c.* 'Major' is a good coral-red free-flowering form. Plants need full sun and plenty of moisture to flower really well. They increase readily; divide frequently to prevent the rhizomes from becoming congested.

SCROPHULARIA Scrophulariaceae

S. auriculata, water betony or water figwort, is a rather insignificant plant with nettle-like leaves. Its variegated form *S.a.* 'Variegata' (H 30-60cm/12-24in WD 0-15cm/0-6in Z5) is, however, very decorative. A broad band of creamy-white running around the edges of the rich green leaves makes this an outstanding evergreen marginal plant. Spikes of greenish-purple flowers are borne in summer. Cut these down immediately after flowering to encourage new foliage growth. Grow in a sheltered, partly shaded site. Propagate by dividing in spring or by softwood cuttings in summer.

SENECIO Compositae

S. smithii is an imposing perennial (H 90cm-1.2m/3-4ft WD 0-15cm/0-6in Z7) from southeast South America. Leathery dark green spinach-like leaves form a bushy clump, topped in early summer by white daisy-like flowers in terminal clusters 15cm/6in across. It thrives in muddy situations and in full sun. Propagate by division in spring.

THALIA Marantaceae

Marginal perennials with attractive oval leaves carried on tall slender stems, and violet flowers in summer, thalias need a sunny situation. Most require at least 7°C/45°F, though some withstand cooler water. Propagate by seed in spring.

T. dealbata (H 1.5m/5ft WD 0-30cm/0-12in Z9) is a tall, graceful foliage plant with broad oval leaves 8-10cm/3-4in long, dusted with a mealy white

THALIA GENICULATA

ZANTEDESCHIA AETHIOPICA

Floating-leaved plants

An important component of the water garden is provided by plants whose shapely floating leaves break up the reflective water surface with areas of pattern; many offer the additional bonus of flowers in season. These plants are useful as well as beautiful. In wildlife ponds their leaves and numerous stalks act as a haven for many of the smaller aquatic creatures. Moreover, by shading the surface, the leaves inhibit the growth of algae.

Water lilies (the genus Nymphaea*) are the undisputed stars of the floating-leaved plants, with an unrivalled spectrum of flower colours and shapes. Cultivars can be chosen to suit a range of pools, formal and informal, and their proportions and vigour can be scaled to the size of the pond. If the site is not sunny enough for water lilies, other more shade-tolerant plants with floating leaves can be chosen instead.*

Always be sure to select plants of a suitable scale and vigour for the space available, and monitor their progress to keep them within bounds. These plants grow mostly in the shallows, between and just beyond the emergent plants, flourishing in the mud between the shore line and the deep water of perhaps 1.5m/5ft or so. Given a naturally sloping edge with rich soil, they will strain to the very limits of their zone in order to occupy fresh space. A large pond can quickly develop a fringe of floating vegetation from its muddy edges out into quite deep water, and a smaller pond might soon become completely covered by one or more kinds. However attractive the marbled light green leaves and bright yellow flowers of Nymphoides peltata, *they can form a carpet entirely smothering the water surface of a clay-lined pond which can only be detrimental to other plants.*

coating. Violet flower spikes are followed by decorative seed heads. It tolerates a cooler pond. *T. geniculata* needs warm water. It is a showy plant with blue-green leaves and spires of violet flowers (H 2m/6½ft WD 0-30cm/0-12in Z10).

VERONICA Scrophulariaceae
V. beccabunga, brooklime (H 10cm/4in WD 0-15cm/0-6in Z5), a perennial, is the best of the swamp-loving veronicas. It has a profusion of white-centred flowers of an intense blue, borne in the leaf axils, and luxuriant foliage on procumbent stems. Plants are extremely useful for disguising the edges of artificial pools and merging them into their surroundings. *V.b.* 'Blue Spire' is a very fine form, with more conspicuous flowers of intense blue. Propagate by stem cuttings, complete with roots, planted in trays of mud.

ZANTEDESCHIA Araceae
Z. aethiopica, arum lily from South Africa (H 75-90cm/30-36in WD 0-30cm/0-12in Z8-9), has rich green heart-shaped leaves and bears pure white spathes, each surrounding a yellow spadix, in summer. Plants look handsome beside formal or informal pools. Evergreen and more vigorous in warmer countries, it needs a winter minimum of 10°C/50°F; it will survive in Z8 if submerged, planted deeply or if well mulched when grown in moist soil. Propagate by dividing the tubers during the dormant season or by dividing plants in spring. *Z.a.* 'Crowborough' seems to differ little from the type species.
Z.a. 'Green Goddess' (H 60-75cm/24-30in WD 0-25cm/0-10in Z8-9) is a highly elegant form. Its green spathes each have a large splash of white at the centre.

APONOGETON Aponogetonaceae
A. distachyos, Cape pondweed or water hawthorn (S 60cm/24in WD 10-60cm/4-24in Z5-9), is native to South Africa. Its attractive strap-shaped leaves are often marbled with purple and have purple undersides. It blooms in spring and autumn, but in some situations will continue to produce some flowers throughout the year. These are pure white and forked, with black anthers; occasionally they come up pink. They have a delicious smell of hawthorn or vanilla, and on a still, warm evening scent the whole pond area. Plants grow from onion-shaped tubers and will succeed in partial shade. They seed freely, sometimes in sheltered ponds producing too many seedlings. They can also be propagated by division as the tubers multiply.

APONOGETON DISTACHYOS

EURYALE FEROX

HYDROCLEYS NYMPHOIDES

BRASENIA Cabombaceae
B. schreberi (B. peltata), water shield (S 60cm/24in or more WD 10-30cm/4-12in Z10), is a pretty little plant with almost circular floating leaves like a tiny tropical water lily, borne alternately on stalks from the running stems. The upper surface is dark green, attractively edged with brown, while the undersides are reddish. Small mauve to purple flowers are produced during the summer. Propagate from cuttings or rooted runners. This plant can be grown in the shallows and looks pretty among clumps of emergent plants such as butomus.

EURYALE Nymphaeaceae
E. ferox, prickly water lily or Gorgon (S 2.5m/8ft WD 30-90cm/12-36in Z5B-10), is grown mainly as a curiosity for its extraordinary great flat circular floating leaves, which resemble giant sanding discs. The entire dark green upper surface is veined in red and raised into horny ribs, while the undersides are deep purple. Deep magenta-violet flowers, small in relation to the leaf size, have vicious pointed thorns on the outside of sepals and stalks.

HYDROCLEYS Limnocharitaceae
H. nymphoides, water poppy (S 60cm/24in or more WD 10-60cm/4-24in Z9-10), is a creeping plant from the tropics worthy of a place in any informal pool. Three-petalled primrose-yellow flowers, each 5cm/2in across, are poppy-shaped, hence its common name. They are borne above the water in succession from clusters of buds like those of *Nymphoides peltata*. The shiny bright green leaves are evergreen in hotter climates and plants will occasionally overwinter in Z9. It enjoys a rich soil. Propagate by removing and planting the runners.

MARSILEA Marsileaceae
Non-flowering aquatic or marsh plants related to the ferns, marsileas spread on creeping rhizomes. *M. mutica*, nardoo plant or water clover (S 60cm/24in or more WD 10-45cm/4-18in Z9) has pretty four-lobed leaves, each divided into inner, lighter and outer, darker zones of bright greens. Some of the leaves stand just above the water on fine stalks. The plant creeps about in the shallow pool margins. Propagate by sowing the bean-shaped spore pods in shallow water, or by division. *M. quadrifolia* (H 60-75cm/24-30in WD 0-30cm/0-12in Z5) is a small amphibious fern from eastern North America. It can be overwintered as a floating plant, or grown as a decorative border plant. Propagate by breaking off and planting the side shoots.

MARSILEA MUTICA

NELUMBO Nymphaeaceae

An ancient and revered plant, the lotus has been cultivated for thousands of years. Apart from the garden attraction of leaf and flower, the chocolate-brown seed pods, with edible seeds like small hazelnuts each rattling in its own little compartment, are good in flower arrangements. Lotus run a considerable distance on their creeping rhizomes, and when grown in open soil in the pool bottom can reappear the next season in a completely different place. Propagate and grow plants as for tropical water lilies, or sow seeds in pots in warm tanks. Plants can be quite hardy, especially if the rhizomes are down below the ice level, but need hot summers to flower well.

N. nucifera, sacred lotus (S 1.5m/5ft or more WD 15-90cm/6-36in Z6-10), has large plate-like leaves on sturdy stems and soft pink flowers in summer. N.n. 'Alba Grandiflora' has immense fragrant single flowers, with broad oval petals of pure white and tufts of golden stamens. The young seed capsule rests in the centre, a pale duck-egg green. N.n. 'Rosea Plena' has enormous deep rosy-pink double flowers like full-blown peonies, 30cm/12in or more across, with a profusion of curving petals. N.n. 'Shiroman' is similar in size, with creamy-white green-centred double blossoms. The small numerous petals are reminiscent of swan feathers. N. 'Mrs Perry D. Slocum' freely produces large-petalled flowers. They open deep pink, and turn through apricot to yellow by the third day, so that all three colours are often on display at once. N. 'Momo-botan' is a smaller cultivar (S 1m/3ft WD 10-30cm/4-12in Z10-11). It bears a profusion of rose-red fully double flowers with yellow centres, large in comparison with the circular apple-green leaves. This will grow successfully in tiny outdoor ponds in warm climates, or in conservatory tubs in temperate zones.

NUPHAR Nymphaeaceae

Compared to water lilies, nuphars have insignificant flowers, but offer the advantages of growing in shade, in running water and in deep water. Their beauty is in their habit and foliage. Some species produce lovely wavy, translucent rounded leaves underwater; others emerge right up above the surface. Plants grow strongly from creeping rhizomes. Propagate by breaking off pieces of rhizome with a growing point, or sowing ripe seed in shallow pans.

N. advena, common or American spatterdock (S 1.5m/5ft WD 30cm-1.5m/1-5ft Z3), will grow in still or running water. Its thick spade-shaped leaves some 30cm/12in across stand right out of the water. The small globular yellow flowers are tinted copper by reddish stamens.

N. japonica, Japanese pond lily (S 1m/3ft WD 30-90cm/1-3ft Z7), is for still water. It has large round crimped submerged leaves and more elongated emergent ones. The globular flowers are up to 8cm/3in across. N.j. var. variegata is an attractive variegated form.

N. lutea, brandy bottle or yellow pond lily (S 2m/6½ft or more WD 45cm-2.5m/1½-8ft Z6), has beautiful wavy submerged foliage of translucent pale green throughout the year. In summer distinctive dark green egg-shaped leaves float on the surface, and tight yellow cup-shaped flowers stand erect, smelling faintly of brandy. Native to ponds and slow-moving waters in Europe and western Asia, this can become a pernicious weed; a variegated form is less vigorous. N. pumila is also similar but smaller, so more suited to moderate-sized ponds. These prefer acid conditions.

NYMPHAEA Nymphaeaceae

Preferring still water and an open position, water lilies are classic candidates for the pond or lake. The vast range of hybrids, some fragrant, makes it possible to choose form and flower colour quite precisely and in scale with the size and depth of the pool. Water temperature must also be taken into account. The following lists distinguish between hardy water lilies and tropical or tender water lilies, this second group being divided according to whether they bloom by day or by night. Tropical water lilies require summer and winter minima of 21°C/70°F and 10°C/50°F. In temperate climates they will grow happily in conservatory pools. In regions with hot summers but cold winters, remove the tubers for overwintering in moist sand at the minimum winter temperature.

Once established, water lilies are usually long-lived and generally need little attention. They are best grown in perforated containers, which can conveniently be lifted out when necessary for tasks such as replacing the soil and dividing the rhizomes, or for overwintering. Remove old flower heads and leaves regularly to promote new growth. Feed at two- to four-weekly intervals during the growing season.

LEFT *NELUMBO NUCIFERA*   ABOVE *NUPHAR LUTEA*

Propagate by dividing rhizomes of three- to four-year-old plants or by separating offsets. Viviparous kinds produce plantlets in the centres of leaves; propagate by detaching these and growing them on in pots in shallow warm water. Seedlings sometimes germinate spontaneously, but producing good new hybrids from seed entails painstaking work.

The measurements given below are approximate; size depends on water depth, age and the number of crowns that have developed per clump.

Hardy water lilies

The most colourful water lilies flourished only in warmer climates until the late nineteenth century when the French plant breeder Latour-Marliac began to experiment in the cross-pollination of *N. alba* – until then the only hardy water lily available to European gardeners – with the more brightly coloured tropical species, producing over seventy hardy varieties. Some excellent hybrids have been produced subsequently, and there are now hardy water lilies to suit every depth from 10cm/4in to 2m/6½ft or more. Some, such as *N. x helvola*, are tiny and suitable for a small tub on a terrace. Others, such as the vigorous *N.* 'Gladstoneana', form rafts of leaves upon the largest ponds. Many of these water lilies will withstand a considerable degree of cold provided that their roots are not frozen.

N. 'Amabilis' (S 1.2m/4ft WD 45-75cm/18-30in Z5) is a dramatic hybrid, whose elongated smooth, pointed petals of coconut-ice pink appear to have been delicately sprayed with red on their undersides. The colour appears as a dusting of tiny speckles on the white background. Stamens of a rich cadmium yellow radiate from its orange centre, making a striking contrast with the starry pink flowers and the large green lily pads. The blooms, which are some 23cm/9in across, gradually deepen in colour with age.

N. 'American Star' (S 1.2m/4ft WD 45-60cm/18-24in Z5) is a superb semi-double American hybrid. As its name implies, the sugar-candy–pink petals are extremely sharply pointed. About 10cm/4in across at their widest point, they are held well above the leaves, which turn with age from bronze to a bright green.

N. 'Andreana' (S 1m/3ft WD 45-75cm/18-30in Z5) has very free-flowering terracotta-coloured blooms, streaked with yellow, giving this French lily an unusual appearance. The glossy dark green leaves, heavily blotched with red, have distinctive overlapping lobes.

N. 'Atropurpurea' (S 1.5m/5ft WD 30-60cm/12-24in Z5) is one of the darkest red water lilies to

NYMPHAEA 'AMABILIS'

NYMPHAEA 'ATROPURPUREA'

NYMPHAEA 'CHARLES DE MEURVILLE'

NYMPHAEA 'FIRECREST'

NYMPHAEA TUBEROSA VAR. *MAXIMA*

NYMPHAEA 'WILLIAM FALCONER'

date, raised by Marliac in France. An excellent water lily for the small pond, its brilliant deep crimson flowers appear freely among the dark red leaves that change to green with maturity.

N. 'Attraction' (S 2m/6½ft WD 60cm-2.5m/2-8ft Z5) freely produces large star-shaped flowers 20cm/8in across that vary so considerably in shade that their identification often causes difficulty. Colours range from almost white with crimson streaks to a richly suffused carmine. Flowers darken in colour with each successive day.

N. 'Caroliniana Nivea' (S 1.5m/5ft WD 45cm/18in Z5) is excellent for the smaller pond. It bears a profusion of large, fragrant pure white blooms with yellow stamens. The leaves are pale green.

N. 'Charles de Meurville' (S 2.5m/8ft WD 60cm-1.2m/2-4ft Z5) is a very early-flowering vigorous water lily. It has wine-red blooms, slightly suffused with white, and huge olive-green leaves. The flowers may reach 25cm/10in across.

N. 'Escarboucle' (S 2-2.5m/6½-8ft WD 60cm-2m/2-6½ft Z5) is an adaptable and glorious hybrid, suitable for large ponds. Its crimson flowers can grow as large as 30cm/12in across. Faintly apple-scented blooms enclose a rich crown of golden stamens and the leaves range in colour from purple to deep green. The initial flowering is slightly paler in colour than subsequent years' flowers, which are a deep red.

N. 'Fabiola' (S 2m/6½ft WD 45-60cm/18-24in Z5) has rich chocolate brown stamens crowning suffused deep pink petals. The leaves are dark green.

N. 'Firecrest' (S 1.5m/5ft WD 45-75cm/18-30in Z5) is a very pretty North American variety, conspicuous for its beautiful deep orange centre that glows amidst the clear, even, pink petals of semi-double flowers. The lobes of the green leaves are wide open.

N. 'Froebelii' (S 1.5m/5ft WD 30-45cm/12-18in Z5) is a compact plant producing a profusion of small single wine-red flowers with dark orange stamens. The leaves are a matt purple-green.

N. 'Gladstoneana' (S 2.5m/8ft WD 60cm-1.5m/2-5ft Z7) is one of the finest water lilies for deep ponds, its broad incurving creamy-white petals offset by a large central cluster of golden stamens.

N. 'Gloire de Temple-sur-Lot' (S 1.5m/5ft WD 45-90cm/18-36in Z5) opens from a delicate pink to resemble an immense white chrysanthemum with papery petals curved at the tips and bright yellow stamens. It is scented.

N. 'Gonnère' (S 1.2m/4ft WD 45-75cm/18-30in Z5) is a free-flowering plant; the lovely snow-white double flowers have rich golden centres surrounded by green sepals. Rounded mid-green leaves form a compact group on the water surface.

N. x helvola (S 30cm/12in WD 10-20cm/4-8in Z4) is a perfect miniature. It is very free-flowering, sometimes bearing as many of its clear yellow star-shaped flowers with buttercup-yellow centres as it has tiny green leaves mottled with maroon.

N. 'Hollandia' (S 1.5m/5ft WD 45-90cm/18-36in Z5) has double flowers of a gorgeous peach-pink, strong-growing with orange-reddish stamens setting off the broad, well-formed petals, and slightly fragrant.

N. 'James Brydon' (S 1m/3ft WD 45-75cm/18-30in Z7) is compact in growth, with distinctive round copper to dark green leaves flecked with purple. The cup-shaped flowers open from maroon buds and are deep velvety carmine, with orange stamens. Attractive in the small pond or massed in large patches, it will flower in partial shade.

N. 'Laydekeri Fulgens' (S 1m/3ft WD 30-60cm/12-24in Z5) is a choice compact water lily for the small pond. Its fragrant crimson flowers have red stamens, and the leaves are a distinctive dark green with purple undersides.

N. 'Marliacea Chromatella' (S 1.5m/5ft WD 45-90cm/18-36in Z5) is one of the most accommodating and easily grown water lilies. The flowers are primrose-yellow with golden stamens, and the petals wide and pointed. The young leaves are copper-coloured with purple streaks, remaining faintly flecked even when the leaves turn greener. The leaf undersides are speckled with purple.

N. odorata (S 1.2m/4ft WD 45-75cm/18-30in Z5) has distinctive round apple-green leaves. The pure white cup-shaped scented flowers are set within four sepals, green on the outside. The plant creeps along on a horizontal rhizome, from which growing eyes develop at right angles.

N. 'Peter Slocum' (S 1.2m/4ft WD 45-75cm/18-30in Z5) is an exquisite pink water lily for the medium-sized pool. The flowers are fully double with lovely wide petals and orange centres. The leaves are copper, turning to deep green.

N. 'Perry's Pink' (S 1.2m/4ft WD 45-75cm/18-30in Z5) produces blooms of intense mauve-pink, once the plant is established. They are fully double and have golden-red stamens and centres. The leaves, opening copper, become a rich green.

N. 'Pygmaea Rubra' (S 45cm/18in WD 20-30cm/8-12in Z6) is a miniature water lily for the tub or pool edge. Light rose flowers darkening to blood-red appear in summer among the copper-green leaves with distinctive reddish undersides.

N. 'Ray Davies' (S 1m/3ft WD 30-45cm/12-18in Z5) is named after the founder of Stapeley Water Gardens. This superb introduction has double flowers of an even pink with conspicuous golden

yellow centres. The leaves are a rich deep green.

N. 'Rose Arey' (S 1.2m/4ft WD 45-75cm/18-30 in Z7) is a lovely acid-tolerant cultivar. Its flowers of an even sugar-icing pink have pointed petals. The leaves open bronze-purple, and change to mid-green with age.

N. 'Sioux' (S 1m/3ft WD 20-45cm/8-18in Z4) makes an attractive display when several blooms are open at once. They begin warm yellow with an orange glow and gradually darken until the pointed petals become a rich peach-red. The green leaves are purple-spotted.

N. 'Sulphurea' (*N. odorata sulphurea*) (S 90cm/36in WD 30cm/12in Z6) is a rich deep yellow water lily with wide pointed petals. The flowers stand up from the surface amid deep green leaves which are flecked with brown markings.

N. tetragona (S 30cm/12in WD 10-20cm/4-8in Z3) is a miniature water lily for the tub or small pool with perfectly formed blooms of snow-white with a yellow centre, little more than an inch across. The leaves are dark green with purple undersides, and the plant is free-flowering.

N. 'Texas Dawn' (S 1.2m/4ft WD 45-75cm/18-30in Z6) has a profusion of large pale primrose-yellow flowers with elegant slender petals and rich butter-yellow centres. The leaves are deep green.

N. tuberosa (S 1m/3ft WD 20-45cm/8-18in Z5) is a strong-growing North American water lily with white blooms and pure green leaves. Some varieties, such as *N.t.* var. *maxima* are so vigorous they are best suited to large pools.

N. 'William Falconer' (S 1.2m/4ft WD 45-75cm/18-30in Z5) is one of the darkest red water lilies and very compact-growing. The flowers are a lovely port-wine colour, with prominent bright yellow centres. The leaves open deep maroon and turn dark green, with purple veining.

Tropical day-blooming water lilies

It is surely the sky-blue colours and the shades of purple and violet that make the tropical water lilies so glorious. Flowers are produced profusely throughout summer; the spectacular veining and mottling of maroon or brown on leaves with saw-toothed edges add to their glory. Many beautiful hybrids are now readily available, thanks to the dedicated work of people like George H. Pring of the Missouri Botanic Garden.

This group of water lilies enjoys full sun and warm water: summer minimum of 21°C/70°F and winter minimum of 10°C/50°F. They are best planted in the warm shallows, but will also succeed in deeper conditions, preferably in containers. Lift these out and fill with new soil each season. Feed regularly during the flowering period.

N. 'Albert Greenberg' (S 1.8m/6ft WD 30-60cm/ 12-24in) is a beautiful plant with unusual peach-coloured flowers of 15-20cm/6-8in diameter, which deepen to copper at the tips of the petals and have bright orange centres. Buds are held above the water. The elegant light green leaves blotched with purple have bright red undersides.

N. 'Aviator Pring' (S 2.5m/8ft WD 45-75cm/18-30in) is a fine water lily with lovely rich yellow flowers, reaching a full 25cm/10in diameter, held high above the water. The slightly crimped elongated petals have incurving tips. The wavy edges of the mid-green leaves are toothed.

N. 'Bagdad' (S 2m/6½ft WD 60-90cm/24-36in) is a strikingly beautiful plant, sometimes viviparous. Its sky-blue flowers, borne in profusion on stout stalks 15cm/6in above the water, have orange stamens tipped with mauve. The green leaves are strongly marbled with purple and have slightly upturned serrated edges.

N. 'Blue Beauty' (*N.* 'Pennsylvania', *N.* 'Pulcherrima') is a water lily with a most distinctive appearance. Profuse clusters of single star-shaped sky-blue flowers 15cm/6in across open up from black-streaked buds resembling writhing snakes' heads. The small green leaves are black-spotted on the undersides (S 2m/6½ft WD 45-75cm/18-30in).

N. 'Bob Trickett' (S 2m/6½ft WD 45-75cm/18-30in) has well-formed plumbago-blue flowers beautifully complemented by the rich green-yellow centres and blue-tipped stamens. The large green leaves have green-veined red undersides.

N. capensis (N. emirensis, N. scutifolia) is the Cape water lily from southeast Africa and Madagascar (S 3-4m/10-13ft WD 45-75cm/18-30in). The startling star-shaped fragrant blooms up to 30cm/12in across are lilac-blue, fading with age. It has great lettuce-green leaves with saw-toothed edges, purple underneath with green veins.

N. 'Daubeny' (*N.* 'Daubenyana'), the Madagascar dwarf lily, is a tiny viviparous plant (S 30-60cm/12-24in WD 10-30cm/4-12in), ideal for the small pool or tub when confined to a small container. The blue star-shaped flowers with yellow stamens have a sweet, pungent aroma. The leaves, more pointed than most, are olive-green splashed with brown.

N. 'Director George T. Moore' (S 2-2.5m/6½-8ft WD 45-75cm/18-30in) holds its most handsome deep damson-blue flowers 20-23cm/8-9in across well above the water. They have golden centres and blue stamens. The round green leaves have horned wavy edges and occasional purple flecks.

N. 'Evelyn Randig' (S 2-2.5m/6½-8ft WD 45-75cm/18-30in) is a striking plant. Its great fragrant blossoms of a rich magenta-pink measure 25cm/10in across and are held well above the water. The

NYMPHAEA 'ALBERT GREENBERG'

NYMPHAEA 'LEOPARDESS'

NYMPHAEA 'GENERAL PERSHING'

NYMPHAEA 'SHELL PINK'

NYMPHAEA 'ISABELLE PRING'

NYMPHAEA 'ST LOUIS GOLD'

NYMPHAEA 'EMILY GRANT HUTCHINGS'

NYMPHAEA 'MISSOURI'

green leaves are circular, with spectacular purple stripes radiating like the spokes of a wheel.

N. 'General Pershing' (S 2.5-3m/8-10ft WD 60-90cm/24-36in) has magnificent pink flowers, fully 25-30cm/10-12in across, containing a great cluster of pink-tipped yellow stamens. The leaves have occasional blotches of purple and red splashes underneath.

N. 'Isabelle Pring' (S 2-3m/6½-10ft WD 45-75cm/18-30in) has finely pointed creamy-white flowers 20-25cm/8-10in across with butter-yellow centres. They are held 30cm/12in above the pale green oval leaves, which have occasional maroon blotches and overlapping lobes. It is viviparous.

N. 'Leopardess' (S 2m/6½ft WD 45-75cm/18-30in), produced by Martin Randig of California, has speckled buds held well above the water. These open to reveal lilac blossoms with yellow centres. Spectacular rounded apple-green leaves have radiating maroon stripes and their undersides are blotched with bright purple.

N. 'Midnight' (S 2m/6½ft WD 30-60cm/12-24in) has tulip-shaped buds that open into sweetly scented star-shaped flowers 25cm/10in across of rich blueberry-blue. The dark green leaves, flecked with chocolate-brown, are small and rounded, with horned edges and overlapping lobes.

N. 'Panama Pacific' (S 2-2.5m/6½-8ft WD 45-75cm/18-30in) is a resilient hybrid produced by Tricker. It has light bluish-purple flowers 10-15cm/4-6in across that become redder with age. They tend to rest a little below the buds, which are held well aloft. The lobed leaves are an even apple-green, with horny edges.

N. 'Pink Platter' (S 2.5-3m/8-10ft WD 45-75cm/18-30in) holds above the water its vast, wide-open pink blossoms 25-30cm/10-12in across, with gorgeous yellow centres and multitudes of pink stamens. This viviparous water lily has large green wavy-edged leaves with light brown splashes and overlapping lobes.

N. 'St Louis' (S 2-3m/6½-10ft WD 45-75cm/18-30in), produced by Pring, has huge star-shaped lemon-yellow flowers 30cm/12in across with rich gold centres. They are held elegantly well above the water. The great leaves are an even green, with slight brown spotting when young, and have overlapping lobes.

N. 'St Louis Gold' (S 2-2.5m/6½-8ft WD 45-90cm/18-36in), produced by Pring, has rich mustard-yellow flowers that fade to lemon. They have strong yellow centres, measure 20cm/8in across and are held 15cm/6in above the water. The oval dark green leaves 25-30cm/10-12in across appear with maroon marbling that fades with age.

N. 'Shell Pink' (S 2m/6½ft WD 45-75cm/18-30in) is a lovely plant raised by Pring. It has flat blooms 25cm/10in across of a subtle shell-pink, with a most distinctive mass of pinky-gold stamens resembling a sea anemone. The leaves are slightly oval with overlapping lobes; they are grass-green with maroon flecks.

N. 'Yellow Dazzler' (S 2-2.5m/6½-8ft WD 45-90cm/18-36in) has large rich yellow star-shaped flowers with multitudes of matching stamens, giving a fully double appearance to the abundantly produced blooms. The huge leaves are an even apple-green.

Tropical night-blooming water lilies

On a hot summer's night, the flowers of these plants seem to glow from within, so radiant and pure are their spectacular colours. The blooms open in the evening and remain open until early to mid-morning. They can be enjoyed in tropical countries, in regions with hot summers and, in temperate climates, in conservatories and green-houses. Planting is the same as for day-blooming varieties.

At night individual flowers can be lit by means of small low-voltage lamps. These are held on long spikes that can be pressed into the earth beside the plant and angled to best effect. Hooded black holders prevent the light from shining upwards.

N. 'Antares' is a beautiful hybrid raised at Longwood Gardens, Pennsylvania (S 2m/6½ft WD 45-75cm/18-30in). The flowers are a bright velvet carmine, 15-20cm/6-8in across and held a similar distance above the water. Almost round, copper to moss-green leaves have spiked edges and heavily veined undersides.

N. 'Emily Grant Hutchings' (S 2m/6½ft WD 30-60cm/12-24in) is an excellent nocturnal water lily raised by Pring. It will tolerate a little shade. The rounded flower petals are a light mauvish-red, contrasting with rich reddish-brown stamens. The small leaves are a beautiful bronze-green and have undulating margins.

N. 'Missouri' (S 2.5-3m/8-10ft WD 60-90cm/24-36in) keeps its huge creamy-white flowers, 30cm/12in or more across, open through the following day for those who missed its nocturnal glory. The rounded petals flop on to the water to lie back among the spiky-edged green leaves. Young leaves are tinged with purple and brown.

N. 'Red Flare' (S 1.2-1.8m/4-6ft WD 45-75cm/18-30in) is a most distinctive plant. It has fragrant star-shaped flowers of brilliant magenta 15-20cm/6-8in across that are held above the water. Its beautiful circular leaves are deep maroon and have spiked edges.

N. 'Trudy Slocum' (S 2-2.5m/6½-8ft WD 45-75cm/18-30in) is a vigorous and easily grown water lily. It bears a profusion of white blooms that open so wide that they turn back on themselves, making the flower's centre and yellow stamens very conspicuous. The puckered leaves are a smooth rich green, with toothed edges.

NYMPHOIDES (Limnanthemum) Menyanthaceae
These creeping aquatics have rounded water lily-like floating leaves. *N. peltata (Villarsia nymphoides)* is known variously as yellow floating heart, water fringe or humble water lily. This hardy summer-flowering deciduous perennial (S 60cm/24in or more WD 10-75cm/4-30in Z6) has small bright green heart-shaped leaves, attractively mottled and marbled with brown or lemon and lighter green, particularly in full sun when plants have run out of good soil. (The cultivar *N. peltata* 'Bennettii' has leaves without this mottling.) The lovely clear yellow fringed flowers are held above the water and open successively into funnel shapes from clusters of buds borne at the ends of long stolons. Spreading on runners, plants can completely cover shallow muddy-bottomed pools, so beware of introducing them to clay ponds. Propagate from the runners. *N. aquatica*, fairy water lily or banana plant, from the northeast United States, has white flowers and leaves that are more kidney-shaped (Z6). *N. indica (N. cristata)*, water snowflake, is of similar habit (WD 10-45cm/4-18in Z10), but the leaves are smaller, with beautiful brown and green patterning. The pure white flowers with yellow centres are delicately frilled and crimped around the edges. *N. germanica* has yellow flowers with pretty frilled edges (WD 15-30cm/6-12in Z10).

VICTORIA Nymphaeaceae
This genus of tropical plants of astonishing size includes the spectacular *V. amazonica* with a spread of 6m/20ft. Its 2m/6½ft diameter leaves with upturned edges are buoyant enough to carry the weight of a small person. The huge pineapple-scented nocturnal flowers 30cm/12in across have prickly sepals. They open pure white at first,

turning to pale pink and by the end of the second night deepening to a rich purple. This species requires a temperature of 30°C/85°F to bloom. In temperate countries victorias are usually treated as annuals, with fresh seed sown each spring. They grow rapidly: pot on young plants regularly and provide fresh doses of well-rotted cow manure and fertilizer. *V. cruziana*, Santa Cruz water lily, is similar to *V. amazonica* but blooms earlier. It tolerates cooler temperatures, and will flower at 21-24°C/70-75°F. The outsides of the flowers are less prickly. The rough-textured leaves are deeply rimmed and have purple undersides.

V. 'Longwood Hybrid' is a magnificent plant raised by Patrick Nutt of Longwood Gardens from seed obtained from Kew Gardens, combining the best features of both *V. cruziana* and *V. amazonica*. It is even hardier and more prolific, the flowers coming in quick succession. The upturned edges of the leaves display heavily pink-veined and spined undersides.

NYMPHOIDES PELTATA

VICTORIA CRUZIANA

Aquatic plants

This group includes both plants that float freely on the surface of the water and submerged oxygenating plants, usually anchored by roots at the bottom of the pond. Apart from their decorative effect, both types are important for combating the cloudiness caused by algae – indeed they are the chief natural contributors to water clarity. Floating aquatics provide shade, which discourages algae. Most aquatic plants, whether floating or rooted, absorb large quantities of dissolved salts and nutrients directly from the water, thus starving the competing algae out of existence. Bottom-rooting plants perform a further purifying function by using detritus such as fish droppings, dead plants and animal remains as fertilizers.

Bottom-rooting aquatics are particularly valuable in fishponds. Thick clumps of these plants provide excellent cover for fish and their fry. They harbour food in the form of aquatic insects, and their leaves make useful spawning areas. Most importantly, as they liberate oxygen and absorb carbon dioxide under the action of sunlight on their tissues, they replace the oxygen used up by the fish. Their submerged leaves are often finely dissected to maximize the surface area for this exchange of gases. The feathery foliage, offering little water resistance, is sufficiently flexible to withstand the erratic movements of currents, but lacks hard tissue and relies on the water for support, rapidly collapsing and deteriorating without it. For this reason, plants should be exposed to air as little as possible when being transplanted. They should be thinned out in autumn if they become overgrown and congested.

Free-floating aquatics can be introduced as an interim measure in a new pond, to provide shade until a stock of permanent floating-leaved plants becomes established. They are the easiest of all to plant – simply drop a handful into the water. They multiply correspondingly rapidly, by budding off. Some plants can be very vigorous, so choose carefully and monitor their progress regularly. In small ponds, scoop up superfluous plants with a hand net; on larger stretches of water, skim them off with a rope or remove with a water jet or herbicide. In temperate climates most free-floaters die down in the winter, a few submerged particles remaining dormant to reappear the following year. In the tropics they continue to grow unchecked. In the descriptions of floating aquatic plants that follow, the 'spread' factor is indicated in terms of the likely speed of growth (slow, moderate or rapid) rather than as a measurement.

ANUBIAS Araceae
A. afzelii, water aspidistra – often sold as African cryptocoryne – is a submerged aquatic plant from tropical West Africa (S 30cm/12in WD 10-60cm/4-24in Z10). Leathery elliptical leaves with a strong midrib extend from stout stalks to form an attractive dark green border beneath the pool edges or a specimen in an aquarium. Occasionally, a short white spadix appears above the water. These slow-growing plants flourish in rich soil, lime-free water and good sunlight with partial shade. Propagate by sowing seed in shallow pans in mud.

APONOGETON Aponogetonaceae
A. madagascariensis (A. fenestralis), Madagascar lace plant or laceleaf, is a beautiful submerged aquatic plant for the aquarium or the shallows of a tropical pond (S 60cm/24in WD 15-60cm/6-24in Z10). The oval olive-green leaves are a delicate tracery of longitudinal and transverse veins forming tiny oblong squares like a net. Fluffy forked white flowers are held just above the water surface. Plants are quite difficult to grow, requiring moving warm water and dark, shady conditions, and tubers often seem to rot away in an aquarium. Propagate by seed, or by separating offsets, though these are infrequent. A. crispus is more easily grown, in sun or shade, and also beautiful, though with less openwork between the leaf veins. The leaves are more elongated, up to 30cm/12in long, and the flower is a small white spike.

AZOLLA Azollaceae
A. caroliniana, floating fairy fern, is a small floating perennial fern with lacy leaves 5-15mm/¼-¾in across (S rapid Z7). Its initial pale green colour changes to deep rusty red in full sun and in autumn. In small patches it provides welcome shade to both fish and water. However, never allow azolla to cover a pond completely if fish are present, as it will prevent oxygen from reaching the water. If unchecked, this rapid colonizer will quickly coat a small pool with a crust of deceptively substantial-looking foliage.

BACOPA (Herpestis) Scrophulariaceae
B. caroliniana (B. amplexicaulis), water hyssop (S 15cm/6in WD 15-60cm/6-24in Z10), is a submerged aquatic native to coastal regions of southern and central North America. Its oval green leaves with rose-pink markings are closely arranged around the stems in opposite pairs. They form fresh clumps that are attractive in the sunny pond or aquarium. Bright blue flowers are borne above short stalks bearing tough aerial leaves. Grow in rich soil and propagate by cuttings, division or seed.

CABOMBA Cabombaceae
These submerged plants from South, Central and southern North America have tufts of long finely dissected foliage. Beautiful plants for a tropical pond or coldwater aquarium, they make good oxygenators. Propagate from cuttings.
C. aquatica, fanwort (Z10), comes from the Amazon estuary. It has deeply cut underwater leaves and floating kidney-shaped foliage, with occasional dark yellow buttercup-shaped flowers held above the water.
C. caroliniana, Washington grass (Z10), is found from North Carolina through to Florida and Texas. It is pretty, though more robust than C. aquatica. Beautiful rich green stems bear deeply dissected fan-shaped underwater leaves and narrow surface leaves; yellow-eyed white flowers 15mm/¾in across are borne occasionally (S 20cm/8in or more WD 15-60cm/16-24in Z10).

CALLITRICHE Callitrichaceae
Distributed worldwide, members of this genus are found in ponds, swift streams and on mud in places that periodically dry out. Their mode of growth makes them among the loveliest submerged plants: in clear running water they form trailing 'beards' of waving green foliage; in winter, hardy species grow happily beneath the ice in mounds of fresh brilliant green. The following grow in still or running water and dislike heat. They spread by fruiting and by adventitious roots near the stem bases.

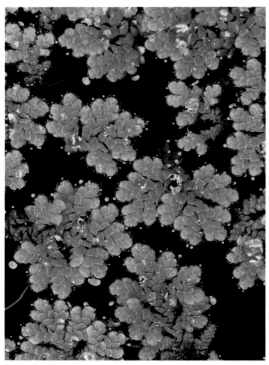

AZOLLA CAROLINIANA

C. hermaphroditica (C. autumnalis), autumnal starwort (Z6), is one of the 'dwellers beneath the ice'. It is bright green, composed of small thin lance-shaped leaves arranged in pairs up the delicate stalks. *C. platycarpa* is similar, but has secondary surface leaves in the form of a bright green rosette (S 60cm/ 24in WD 5-60cm/2-24in Z2).

CERATOPHYLLUM Ceratophyllaceae

Submerged aquatic plants with brittle leaflets and almost worldwide distribution, hornworts make useful oxygenators and purifying plants for small ponds or deep lakes. They seldom clog the water surface, preferring to remain well submerged. Drop the rootless plants straight into the water, or weight them down on to the mud.

C. demersum has forked dark green leaves arranged in whorls up the stems. At the tips are very congested leaves which in autumn draw up starch and form resting buds, which sink to the bottom in winter and reappear as new plants in spring (S 30cm/1ft plus WD 30cm-3m/1-10ft Z8).

C. submersum is a rarer form with more finely dissected foliage. It flops about at the pond bottom on pale brown or black leafless stems.

CERATOPTERIS Adiantaceae

C. thalictroides, watersprite, is a tender tropical or subtropical fern (S moderate Z10) consisting of dense rosettes of spreading feather-shaped fronds with wavy edges. It may root at the bottom of the pond or be free-floating. Used in temperate zones mostly as an aquarium plant, it also grows to good effect as a marginal plant at a minimum of 10°C/ 50°F; the delicate pale green submerged foliage contrasts with the darker, more substantial surface fronds that stand erect. Grow in a sunny situation. Propagate by division in summer, or plant buds and plantlets that develop on the leaves no deeper than 30cm/12in at 20-22°C/68-72°F.

CHARA Characeae

C. vulgaris, stonewort (S 30cm/1ft plus WD 30cm-3m/1-10ft plus Z4), is a primitive and ancient submerged aquatic belonging to the algae. Mostly found in calcareous waters, plants are often coated with lime scale, giving them a harsh feel and chalky appearance. This species makes rapid growth of fine twiggy stems and sparsely arranged whorls of thorny-looking spikes of a pale greyish green. Good for oxygenating and clearing the water, it may congest the shallows for short periods before spontaneously dying back, perhaps to reappear some months later. A very similar plant, with sparser whorls, is *Nitella*, which often coexists in the water just below the *Chara*.

BACOPA CAROLINIANA

CABOMBA AQUATICA

CRASSULA Crassulaceae

C. helmsii (Tillaea helmsii, T. recurva), Australian swamp stonecrop, is a bright green compact mound-forming plant with narrow lance-shaped leaves and tiny white star-like flowers (S indefinite WD 0-45cm/0-18in Z7). Underwater it is less dense, with long thin stems reaching the surface, but at pond edges it creeps inexorably to form a thick mass that smothers other plants. Highly invasive, any tiny piece broken off can root and found a fresh colony, and plants escaping into the wild pose a severe threat to native species. However, it is excellent for masking the rims of small domestic ponds where it will make a lovely light green carpet.

CRYPTOCORYNE Araceae

These pretty submerged aquatic plants from the tropics enjoy the subdued light and warmth of an aquarium. They spread slowly as fresh plantlets appear on runners or around the main rhizome. The lance-shaped leaves vary in width and colour according to species, and scented flowers are borne as spathes above the water (S 30cm/12in WD 15-45cm/6-18in Z10).

C. beckettii from Southeast Asia has slightly wavy broad green leaves that have an attractive sheen and a hint of purple on the undersides.

C. cordata is native to the Malay Peninsula. The pale olive-green leaves are very well marked, with conspicuous veining. Their edges are slightly crimped and the undersides a dull beetroot-red.

C. crispatula (C. balansae) from India to southern China has very elongated crimped green leaves borne on mahogany-brown stalks. It prefers brighter conditions.

C. purpurea is a large and variable Malayan species with yellow to scarlet spathes. Elliptical to heart-shaped dark green leaves held on long red stalks are patterned with blotches or dots and have contrasting undersides of light green to purple. Preferring soft water conditions, these plants produce a magnificent underwater garden when grown in the clear shallows of a tropical garden or the aquarium.

C. x willisii from Sri Lanka is of a distinct reddish hue, and bears attractive tall tubular spathes.

ECHINODORUS Alismataceae

Growing submerged or as bog plants, some species form large rhizomes and produce slow-spreading tall plants with emergent leaves; others have adventitious roots bearing plantlets, which root like spider plants into the substrate to make a dense carpet.

E. amazonicus (Z10) forms a rosette of narrow pale green leaves, sometimes 1m/3ft long, which curve gently upwards and then level off to grow just beneath the water surface. Enjoying strong light, this submerged plant provides shade and cover and purifies the water. It makes a spectacular foliage plant for the shallows of tropical ponds.

E. osiris (S 30cm/12in WD 15-90cm/6-36in Z10) is attractive for the small pool or aquarium. It has broad lance-shaped or elliptical leaves with a conspicuous midrib, bright red when young but changing gradually to olive green. Flowers about 3cm/1in across are produced just above the surface, accompanied by plantlets. *E. parviflorus*, black Amazon sword plant, is similar, but produces numerous leaves 30cm/12in long.

EGERIA Hydrocharitaceae

E. densa (Elodea densa) is a lovely soft, lush plant that remains completely submerged, an ideal oxygenator for sunny ornamental ponds (S 30cm/12in plus WD 30-90cm/12-36in Z8). Whorls of slightly recurving grey-green leaves arranged up delicate stems culminate in a thick wide trumpet of fresh new leaflets. Occasional white flowers borne on fine shoots near the tips project above the water surface. Plants root easily from cuttings, or when pieces break off the brittle stems.

EICHHORNIA Pontederiaceae

E. crassipes var. *major*, water hyacinth (S rapid Z10), is a glossy green buoyant plant that bears exquisite mauve flowers like large hyacinths with gold and violet eyes. Native to tropical South America, it is now widely naturalized elsewhere, making rafts of mauve across lakes and rivers. In some places it has become such a troublesome weed that its cultivation is banned by law. In a controlled environment, however, it is a most desirable and ornamental plant, providing shade and shelter for fish and absorbing nitrates, phosphates and other mineral salts on which unsightly algae thrive. Increase by detaching plantlets borne on runners during summer. In colder climates overwinter indoors in artificial light and a minimum temperature of 15-20°C/59-68°F.

ELODEA (Anacharis) Hydrocharitaceae

E. canadensis, Canadian pond weed, is probably the best of the submerged oxygenators, with whorls of fresh mid-green slightly curving leaves arranged up soft branching stems (S 30cm/12in or more WD 15cm-2m/6in-6½ft Z3). Tiny white flowers are produced in summer at the end of fine white threads. The plant gained a bad reputation for invasiveness when introduced to England in the mid nineteenth century. After initial vigour in a new site, it seems to use up the trace elements it requires, or somehow exhaust its strength, and settles back to grow modestly. It is preferable to *Lagarosiphon major* because it dies back each winter and does not congest the surface with woody stems. *E. callitrichoides* forms dense clumps of light grey-green stems with slightly shorter leaves.

FONTINALIS Fontinalaceae

F. antipyretica is a delightful submerged moss of cold running water and spring-fed ponds (S 30cm/12in WD 15-90cm/6-36in Z5). The stems are fine, branched and thickly covered in rows of short leaves. Its dark green/grey makes a superb colour contrast to elodea and callitriche. Transplant this moss complete with a piece of the material on which it is growing – stones, old bricks, rotting wood or willow tree roots. The common name, incombustible willow moss, derives from this last host and the Scandinavian use of this moss to plug the air gaps between stones in chimneys as fireproofing.

HIPPURIS Hippuridaceae

H. vulgaris, mare's tail, cat's tail, joint weed, paddock pipe, bottle brush or knotgrass, (S 15cm/6in plus WD 15-60cm/6-24in Z6), has whorls of bright green leaves that stick out horizontally from the stiff vertical stems that rise above the water. The submerged parts are paler and the leaves longer and softer. Rooting in the bottom mud, plants are easily propagated by division or cuttings.

HOTTONIA Primulaceae

H. palustris (S 30cm/12in WD 30-90cm/12-36in Z6) has descriptive common names of water violet, water feather, featherfoil and water yarrow. These submerged aquatic plants billow up from the depths of the pond in early spring after the ice melts, making an unforgettable sight. They swell from winter resting buds to form great bright green mounds just beneath the surface, soon followed by very pale lavender flowers borne on thin stalks 20cm/8in above the water. The dissected foliage forms a wide rosette at the growing tip, with finer leaves below. Plants can be slow to establish. Propagate by inserting rooted pieces into the soil, preferably in slightly acid water.

EICHHORNIA CRASSIPES VAR. *MAJOR*

HOTTONIA PALUSTRIS

HYDROCHARIS MORSUS-RANAE

HYDROCHARIS Hydrocharitaceae

H. morsus-ranae, frogbit, is a dainty little floating perennial resembling a miniature water lily with its nymphaea-shaped leaves and small three-petalled white flowers (S slow Z4). The parent plants reach a spread of only 10cm/4in on the surface, but plantlets on stems may stretch to 1m/3ft. Seldom invasive, plants disappear to the pool bottom in winter, and turions or young shoots lie dormant until spring, when resting buds float to the surface and gradually expand. It is a good plan to overwinter a plant or two in soil at the bottom of a container of water, reintroducing them to the pond when all danger of frost is over.

HYGROPHILA Acanthaceae

H. difformis (S 30cm/12in WD 10-45cm/4-18in Z10) is a beautiful submerged plant from tropical or subtropical parts, often grown in aquariums. Its leaves, light green on the upper surfaces and paler beneath, vary in shape; some are singly or doubly pinnate, others toothed with deep indentations. *H. polysperma* is similar, with lance-shaped leaves with rounded tips that can take on reddish tints in strong sunlight. Propagate by division.

LAGAROSIPHON Hydrocharitaceae

L. major (formerly *Elodea crispa*) is a submerged aquatic (S 30cm/12in or more WD 30-90cm/12-36in Z8). It resembles a large, rich bright green *Elodea canadensis*, with very pronounced recurving leaves thickly arranged up firm stems. It is a good oxygenator, if kept under control in small ponds. The stems continue to grow horizontally and congest the water surface, becoming woody when they do not die back completely in mild winters; cut back each autumn close to the bottom, and remove old stalks. Propagate by cuttings.

LEMNA Lemnaceae

The duckweeds are tiny perennials, each with a frond and root, which form a floating green carpet on the water surface. Although excellent food for fish and waterfowl, they can be extremely invasive, depriving submerged plants of vital sunlight.
L. minor, common duckweed (S rapid Z4), is often introduced to a pond on the feet of visiting waterfowl. Each plant consists of a pale green flat oval frond about 5mm/¼in long. It is a troublesome weed world-wide in all temperate climates except Australia and east Asia. Keep removing it with a net if it multiplies faster than the fish can eat it.
L. trisulca, ivy-leaved or star duckweed (S slow to moderate Z4), is a much more desirable form, less invasive and often forming branched chains of attractive translucent green fronds 3-15mm/⅛-¾in

HIPPURIS VULGARIS

long just below the water surface. It is excellent for clearing the water in garden ponds, and is a good type for a cold aquarium.

LIMNOBIUM Hydrocharitaceae

L. spongia, American frogbit (S slow Z5), consists of rosettes of little rounded floating leaves up to 10cm/4in long, often with spongy undersides. The trailing roots have a reddish-purple coloration. Plants jostle on the water surface but will also root themselves in mud at the pool bottom. This is an effective shade-producing plant, often used in aquatic nurseries. Propagate from offshoots.

LIMNOPHILA Scrophulariaceae

L. aquatica is a pretty tropical plant (H 30cm/12in WD 10-45cm/4-18in Z10), often used in aquariums. Its submerged whorls of finely divided pale green leaves shoot to the surface and produce simple aerial leaves in the deeper or shadier parts of the pond. Propagate from cuttings, which root quickly.

MAYACA Mayacaceae

M. fluviatilis (*M. vandellii*) is a curious delicate little submerged aquatic from tropical and subtropical waters (S 20cm/8in WD 10-45cm/4-18in Z10). Thin horizontal leaves radiate from fine strands, ending in a dense tuft at the growing tip. Attractive

for the pond shallows or aquarium, this plant enjoys plenty of light. Propagate by cuttings or thinning out.

MYRIOPHYLLUM Haloragidaceae

Milfoils are submerged plants with numerous whorls of feathery leaves cladding the stems. Valuable oxygenators, many species are used by fish to harbour their eggs, but some are equally attractive to clinging algae. In some ponds calcium deposits form on the fine foliage, and shaking the plant releases a cloud of white dust into the water. Propagate by plantlets or cuttings in spring.
M. aquaticum (*M. proserpinacoides*), parrot's feather, has finely dissected bright green leaves arranged in whorls to give a delicate feathery effect (S indefinite WD 15-60cm/6-24in Z10). Stems may reach up to 2m/6½ft long, and will climb out of the water to clothe the pool edges. Plants thrive in a sandy soil with plenty of decaying organic matter. Although intolerant of frost, some protected plants usually survive beneath a thin layer of ice in Z9.
M. pinnatum (*M. scabratum*) from central and southern North America has fine feathery bronze-red leaves and small purple flower spikes held just above the water (S 30cm/12in or more WD 15-60cm/6-24in Z6). *M. hippuroides* (Z7) is a beautiful green form, with fine long hair-like

MYRIOPHYLLUM AQUATICUM

PISTIA STRATIOTES

leaves. *M. spicatum*, spiked water milfoil (Z6), has pale green or bronze dissected leaves, usually arranged in whorls of four up the delicate stems. It bears small spikes of red flowers 2.5-5cm/1-2in above the surface. *M. verticillatum*, whorled water milfoil (Z3), is similar, but has leaves usually in whorls of five and darker green, with greeny-yellow flowers in a long spike above the water.

PISTIA Araceae
P. stratiotes, water lettuce, is a most ornamental tropical floating perennial (S moderate to rapid Z10), with rosettes of pale downy blue-green leaves each measuring some 20x8cm/8x3in and bunches of feathery white roots. Plants make attractive groups on tropical and subtropical ponds or in large aquariums, though they can increase to become a nuisance in polluted waterways. Plants remain evergreen only at 15-22°C/59-72°F. They thrive in good light in temperate zones, but need protection from strong sunlight in hotter areas. Propagate by detaching plantlets in summer and placing them in shallow water where their roots can reach soil.

POTAMOGETON Potamogetonaceae
P. crispus, curled pondweed (S 30cm/12in or more WD 15-60cm/6-24in Z7), is a submerged aquatic that is at its best in winter and spring, when translucent bronze, mahogany or green leaves branch out on either side of long waving stems. Tiny crimson flower spikes are held just above the surface before the plant becomes brittle and disintegrates at midsummer. These seaweed-like aquatics will grow in deep shade, often succeeding in ponds severely congested with oak leaves, where no other plants survive. Propagate early in the season by cuttings or by stems bearing a few roots at the nodes. *P. pectinatus*, fennel-leaved pondweed, has fine branching stems and leaves that wave like hair beneath the surface of slow running water.

PROSERPINACA Haloragidaceae
P. palustris, mermaid weed (S 30cm/12in or more WD 15-60cm/6-24in Z10), grows completely submerged. Dark green leaves, variously deeply cut or serrated, are arranged alternately up the occasionally branching stems. Any that appear on the surface tend to be narrower with a saw-tooth edge, and have insignificant white flowers in the leaf axils. The plants form beautiful clumps and are effective grown in the margins of natural ponds.

RANUNCULUS Ranunculaceae
R. aquatilis, water crowfoot, is a superb submerged aquatic from temperate climates (S 30cm/12in plus WD 10-60cm/4-24in Z5). Underwater it forms sprays of fine hair-like foliage on long branching stems. On the surface rounded three-lobed leaves are formed, some deeply segmented. A profusion of white buttercup-like flowers with yellow centres decorates the pond surface in spring. Varieties for running water include *R. fluitans*, river crowfoot. Propagate by division in early spring.

RICCIA Ricciaceae
R. fluitans, crystalwort, forms thick mats of tightly packed segmented green foliage floating just beneath the water surface (S moderate Z10). These are appreciated by carp as a good spawning ground and provide good cover for the fry. The plant likes a temperature of 18-25°C/65-77°F.

SALVINIA Salviniaceae
S. natans is an annual floating fern with pale green round hairy leaves up to 15mm/¾in long (S slow to moderate Z10). This interesting plant bears no true roots, their place being taken by one of its three leaves which is finely divided and grows down into the water. Native to the tropics, where it has no winter dormancy, it has become naturalized in some warmer temperate areas, where its spore cases can overwinter on the pool bottom.

STRATIOTES Hydrocharitaceae
S. aloides, water soldier, is a fascinating floating perennial (S slow to moderate Z5). Rosettes of stiff narrow serrated leaves up to 40cm/16in long resemble pineapple tops floating on the water. Small male and female flowers appear on separate plants. An abundance of spidery plantlets is produced on long stolons. In the autumn the plant descends to the pool bottom, where the plantlets and dormant buds will overwinter. Propagate by detaching plantlets. *S.a.* var. *rubrifolia* is an attractive variety in which the baby plants in particular are a deep bronze colour.

TRAPA Trapaceae
T. natans, water chestnut, is a decorative annual native to Europe (S slow Z9). Dense floating rosettes of toothed diamond-shaped leaves bear

rather inconspicuous whitish flowers, followed by spiny dark brown nuts – these are the chestnuts of the common name – which are edible when cooked. To propagate, collect some of the nuts in autumn and keep them damp during the winter to ensure successful germination the following spring.

UTRICULARIA Lentibulariaceae

Bladderworts are attractive free-floating aquatics bearing lovely yellow pouched flowers above the surface and are widespread throughout the northern hemisphere. Tiny disc-shaped bladders distributed on the sides of stems use a vacuum mechanism to catch small insects that the plant digests, though it can survive without this source of nutrient. Carefully lifting a plant from the water causes an audible crackle as the changing pressure triggers the insect traps. Bladderworts thrive best in strongly acidic waters. Adding well-rotted cow dung to the water assures extremely rapid growth. With their penchant for mosquito larvae and beautiful appearance, these must be among the most desirable floating plants available. Propagate by division in spring.

U. inflata, swollen bladderwort, is found in the swamps of Florida and elsewhere in southern North America (S slow Z9-10). It has long, bushy underwater foliage and bears deep yellow flowers rather like small sweet peas.

U. vulgaris, common bladderwort (S slow Z5), has beautiful foliage, appearing as feathery green or bronze branching strands. Rich yellow flowers are produced abundantly above the water.

VALLISNERIA Hydrocharitaceae

V. spiralis, wild celery (S 30cm/12in WD 30-90cm/ 12-36in Z8), is an accommodating submerged aquatic that will grow even in a substratum of washed gravel. The long tape-like leaves grow upwards in clumps, which gradually multiply as more plants develop on runners. In shallow water the leaves may grow flat along the surface. *V.s.* 'Contorta' has shorter, thinner leaves twisted like a corkscrew and makes a pretty plant for the pond or aquarium. The larger *V. americana (V. gigantea)* is excellent in lakes but unsuitable for tanks or small ponds. Plants require good light and are best propagated by division.

RANUNCULUS AQUATILIS

STRATIOTES ALOIDES

UTRICULARIA VULGARIS

Maintenance and repairs

A well-constructed water feature requires only the seasonal maintenance outlined in the chart (opposite) and protection against severe winter weather.

SEVERE WINTER-WEATHER PRECAUTIONS

As the surface of a pond warms up, the water forms an upper layer of variable thickness called the epilimnion. Next is a transition level, where the temperature falls abruptly, known as the thermocline. Below this, in the bottom hypolimnion layer, the water is very cold. In the autumn, when the temperature begins to fall, these distinctive layers merge and the water mixes up throughout the pond. Further cooling then results in a curious phenomenon. At temperatures below 4°C/39°F cold water floats above less cold water, so that the surface freezes first.

The diagram shows some of the strategies for overwintering a pond. Where prolonged and thick ice is anticipated, an immersion heater or two can be installed to keep an open area in the ice. Black floats placed on the surface will absorb sunlight and quickly melt a hole in thin ice. They also help to absorb the pressure of the expanding ice, which could save the structure of a weaker concrete pool. An excellent way of absorbing ice pressure is to float containers of 25 litre/5gallon capacity, half-filled with sand or soil so that they are partially submerged.

A large surface area can be kept free of ice by roofing over a third or half of the pond, using wooden planks – supported so that they do not touch the water. Cover these with canvas, then straw, fir branches or bracken. Spread over this a sheet of polythene to trap warmer air. Alternatively, drape polythene or bubble wrap over a framework of hoops, as for a cold frame, ensuring some edges are left open to allow air to circulate.

In severe weather, a hole up to 30cm/1ft can be cut, once 5-8cm/2-3in of ice have formed, and 2-5cm/1-2in of water siphoned off to provide an air gap. This acts rather like double glazing, and should prevent the water beneath it from freezing. The hole itself can be roofed over to prevent too much cold air from entering the cavity while allowing an exchange of oxygen to take place on the surface so that the pond can breathe. An immersion heater can be used in conjunction with all of these methods.

In any event the ice should *never* be hit with a hammer, or any other hard object, to break it. Water cannot be compressed and the hydraulic action transmits the blow through the water to compress any soft-bodied object within the pond. The shock will certainly injure or kill the fish.

PONDS

As a general rule ponds should be cleaned out as infrequently as possible, because refilling invariably results in green water due to proliferation of algae and the process of creating a well-balanced ecosystem must start again.

However, there may be reasons for completely emptying a pond: to repair a leak; to remove a build up of silt and mud; or, possibly, to deal with an invasion of an undesirable species of plant. In very rare circumstances you may need to empty the pond to eradicate a pernicious fish disease.

If possible, clean out only one half of a pond, stream or ditch at a time. That way you ensure that some of the small creatures escape to recolonize the freshly cleaned part. With a very small pond scoop out some bucketsful of mud without emptying it completely: most of the small creatures and organisms will remain and after topping up the pond will quickly return to normal.

When repairs have to be effected, provided the leak is not at the bottom, the water can be lowered to just below the damage and the repair site cleaned and dried.

If you have to empty the pond completely you may need to find temporary accommodation for its inmates. If no suitable tank or pond is available, improvise one in a shady spot close by, using either heavy-duty builders' polythene (which is inexpensive) or a piece of pond liner draped over a wall of old boards, blocks or bricks. Into this siphon or pump some of the pond water. Once the water level has been lowered, waft the fish into washing-up bowls and transfer them to the holding tank.

Before hauling out the muck, spread a groundsheet over the lawn or paths to avoid making a mess and to allow small creatures such as newts and shrimps to be caught and transferred to a safe place.

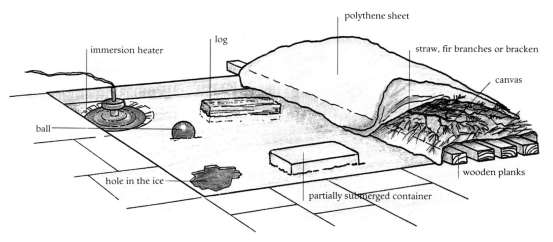

Overwintering a pond
Floats that absorb the pressure of expanding water as it freezes help keep part of the surface area of a small pond ice free. On larger ponds, cover a section of the surface with canvas or a polythene sheet hanging down almost to water level to prevent chill winds blowing beneath it. A hole cut in the ice with a saw enables you to siphon off some water to make an air gap that prevents the water beneath from freezing.

An immersion heater can be used with any of these methods.

MAINTENANCE THROUGH THE SEASONS

Spring	Summer	Autumn	Winter
PLANTS			
Consider replacements of bog and marginal plants in good time to order. Divide and transplant aquatics and moisture-loving plants. Work well-rotted leaf mould or compost into the soil before replanting bog plants. Mulch bog areas to reduce weed growth and hold in moisture. Propagate lobelias and primulas. Pollard willows and dogwoods.	Weed; dead head self-seeding plants. Remove algae and dead and dying leaves. Be on alert for and treat pest and fungal infections in second half of growing season. Add new plants. Use fertilizer tablets to boost growth. Divide and transplant water lilies.	Cut down and remove excessive growth of such plants as *Elodea* and *Myriophyllum*. Remove tender water lilies for overwintering. Carry out any heavy pruning of waterside trees. Remove excessive leaf fall from pond bottom.	Clear untidy or dead foliage. Apply compost or manure to bog or moisture-loving plants outside the pond; mulch. Spray plum or cherry trees that may harbour water lily aphids.
POND LIFE			
Increase rate of filtration. After the nesting season, clear away excessive growth on the shoreline of large ponds and lakes. Apply barley straw to suppress algae. Start feeding fish as weather warms up.	Top up water lost through evaporation. Introduce fish. Feed fish with high protein foods when water temperature rises above 15°C (60°F). Watch for signs of fish disease, parasites, etc.	On large natural ponds, clear some vegetation from the shoreline, leaving cover for small creatures and food for ducks. Feed fish when the weather is warm and bright.	Stop feeding fish when water temperature drops below 5°C/40°F. Set up nesting boxes for ducks. Lift tender plants and cover tender subjects such as *Gunnera* before frost.
EQUIPMENT, SURFACES AND STRUCTURES			
Remove any winter netting. Check electrical equipment and cables. Service pumps: check glands and bearings; dismantle, clean and replace as necessary. Inspect oil for signs of emulsification. Send out for repairs if in doubt. Check bridges and decking for rot or corrosion; repair or replace. Treat softwoods with preservative and clean off/oil hardwoods. Remove slippery leaves/algae from paths and timber walkways.	Clean biological filters and pump strainers. Total pond clean out if necessary. Install any new lighting so you have it to enjoy during the season. Clean pump filter and fountain jets as necessary.	Set nets in position (see p.115) before the onset of leaf fall. Remove excessive quantities of fallen leaves before the onset of winter. Drain, or remove, clean and store, pumps if not in use. Remove underwater lights and clean lenses. Drain pumps, heaters and pipework before onset of frosts.	Take precautions against frosts (see **Severe winter-weather precautions**, opposite).

Remove the mud and silt with a plastic dustpan. Skim across the bottom to scoop up the last of the water and mud. Cart the mud away in buckets or a wheel-barrow and use it in the garden, but save a little for replanting as this will reintroduce worms and microscopic pond creatures.

If there are problems of disease or harmful bacteria, swill the empty pond round with a solution of potassium permanganate or proprietary pond antiseptic, or simply leave it to dry in the sun for a few days before refilling it. Add some de-chlorinating or maturing fluid and leave the pond to stand for a few more days before checking the water temperature, replanting and returning the fish and other creatures to the clean pond.

Otherwise, replant the pond and siphon or pump back the original water from the holding tank and then replace the fish in their own water, or refill with fresh water and leave to settle as you would for a new pond (see p.111) before planting and returning fish.

Natural and clay-lined ponds
The degree of maintenance required for natural or clay-lined ponds is largely governed by their depth and the amount of leaf fall and silt they receive. A deep pond with little leaf fall or silt reaching it will be the easiest to maintain. Shallow ponds, or ponds receiving large influxes of leaves and silt, will require more frequent clearing out and, perhaps, dredging.

A sudden storm could add 30cm/1ft or more of silt in some situations and silt may build up in ponds that are subject to sudden influxes of dirty water or that are fed from ditches and land drains. The beauty of the natural or clay-bottomed pond is that, when it is drained, it is simple to move about the bottom with a tracked machine. The silt can be dug away with a tracked excavator and dumper and taken to some chosen area nearby, where it can be spread out to dry and form a nutritious and friable soil. Great care must be taken when using machinery, however, not to go through the clay bottom.

In shallow ponds, encroachment can be a problem, because with a natural bottom the plants spread to their very limits. Each year as the plants die down the water will be made that little bit shallower, and the next year's growth will be able to encroach a little more, so that year by year the pond becomes slightly smaller. To curb this, pull out the offending plants in late summer and remove the seed heads of free-seeding species.

Some floating-leaved aquatics and some water lilies, such as *Nymphaea tuberosa* and *N. odorata*, are unsuitable for shallow ponds, as they spread quickly, leaving no clear water surface whatsoever.

Ponds with gently sloping sides – say 1:4 – are more water retentive than steep ones – for all the minute soil particles, pieces of decayed matter, rotting detritus and dead microscopic animals that are constantly raining down within the pond will lodge or collect and gradually block or seal the pores in the pool structure. You can actively help this process by agitating the surface and stimulating the movement of particles that will settle and clog the open pores. It is possible to make improvements simply by vigorously raking the banks by hand.

A steep pond side offers no resting place for descending particles. Any agitation of the water washes particles away from the side, exposing fresh fissures and open pores in the ground. I call this phenomenon 'self-leaking'.

A very steep side may also be eroded by wave action until it becomes completely undercut. It will then continue to erode beneath the edge of the pond unless a solid edging (see pp.61-8) is applied or the bank is graded back to a much shallower profile.

Finding and repairing leaks
Repairing leaks is usually the easy part. Finding them can be much more difficult; even when you can see the water coming out, it is hard to tell where it is coming from. Vegetable dyes, or proprietory fluorescent water-tracing dyes can be applied to suspect places. But although dyes are good at showing where water is going, they are not so good at indicating where it is coming from.

If the water is clear, a careful examination of the bottom may reveal the source. One indication is the presence of water shrimps, which congregate in areas of gently moving water. I have often succeeded in locating a leak thanks to the hyperactivity of these little creatures. Sometimes they can be seen darting in and out of the hole through which the water is flowing.

Be on the alert, too, for patches of exposed gravel or leaves congregating in one spot. Where there is no water loss at all, the base of the pond will be covered in a rich sediment. This may be only 2-3cm/1in deep, but it is still clearly there – a fine, powdered coating. Where water is leaking away, this will be washed through and the gravel or loose-textured, granular earth will be exposed, while leaves will be drawn to the spot by the movement of water. These leaks can be blinded over with fine soil or clay. If the water is moving through a bank made of large stones, then finer stone or gravel might need to be applied first.

Tree stumps at the edge of the pond are always suspect, for the earth around them becomes eroded as the stump rots, leaving hollows where the roots were and providing exit points for large quantities of water. Stumps should be removed and the area carefully battered up in good clay. If this is not possible, clay should be banked up against the stump to make a shallow batter.

Tree roots can also be the source of leaks. Those of willow, for example, planted by water quickly work their way out into the pond, and whole sections of the bank become a porous, fibrous mat of root that acts like a sponge. Here a layer of clay should be smeared up the bank, preferably over a sheet of polythene, to discourage the progress of the roots.

Preformed ponds
Because this type of pond is comparatively small, maintenance is quick and easy. Planting is usually contained in crates and baskets, and these can be lifted out in the spring for repotting and dividing. Fallen leaves can be taken out once a year with little likelihood of damage to the pond.

If you are the kind of person who cannot resist getting into the water, take great care, because these premoulded forms are extremely slippery. Also, the sand or soil on which the pond is bedded may have settled to some extent, leaving the ledge without support: and your weight could cause the shell to fracture.

The smooth, shiny surface of these structures greatly facilitates cleaning. Once the pond has been emptied, any silt can easily be scooped out with a dustpan and brush and the shell rinsed with a hose.

Repairs
Most preformed shells can simply be cleaned with solvents and repaired with a two-part resin compound, which usually consists of a resin and a hardener. Car body repair kits usually work well on these structures. They include a small piece of glass or stainless steel matting that can be used to reinforce the break. Test the product first – say on the top outer lip – to make sure that the materials are compatible. If only a small hole has been made, an epoxy resin glue, which also consists of a resin and a catalyst and hardens rapidly, is ideal. Again, you must first do a test on a non-essential section of the shell.

To use any of these substances, first thoroughly score the area to be repaired and roughen it with glass paper. Clean out splits with a file and carefully brush or blow out all loose powder. Do not run your fingers over a rough break: tiny glass fibres are extremely difficult to remove from flesh.

Concrete ponds

The smooth, hard surface of a concrete pond is ideal for shovelling on, and the digging and cutting of plants can be carried out without damaging the structure. If a major clean out is needed, dredging can be carried out with assurance. A well-constructed pond should be able to withstand a small machine on rubber tracks.

Repairs

A properly made concrete pond, unless it is very large, is an integral, independent structure and should not develop cracks even if the ground beneath it moves or cracks. If cracks do occur, the traditional method of repair is still one of the best. First cut away the rendering coat from the area, then chisel out the crack, making sure it is clean and free from debris or soil. A high-pressure jet from the hosepipe can be used for this.

Fill the crack with a 3:1 mix of sharp sand and cement, mixed with cement additive. Used in accordance with the manufacturer's instructions, this causes the mortar to expand instead of shrink on curing. Work this well into the crack and then re-render the whole area back to the original.

You can also use a proprietary mastic and sealant. For most of these it is essential that the surface be dry as well as clean and dust-free, and here a blowlamp or hair-drier will be useful.

Completely coating the pond with GRP (see p.45) or with a flexible sealant is a solution that enables you to preserve the original shape without having to remove a paved surround. Several coats, applied by a professional team, will be needed to build up the laminate to a good strength.

Alternatively, line the concrete with a high-quality flexible pond liner made of butyl or EPDM. If you have a level rim with overhanging slabs, a liner can be positioned beneath them. Otherwise you will need to remove the top 20cm/8in of the rim to bring the liner up behind the stone or brickwork facing so that it is invisible, protected and well fastened. Punch a hole through the bottom of the shell first, to allow any water to drain away and prevent it from collecting between the concrete and the new liner.

Flexible liner ponds

Routine maintenance in liner ponds presents no problem, although care is needed when thinning plants with a knife or garden fork. When dividing plants on ledges, first ease your hand or a blunt spade underneath the fibrous root mat and prise it off the liner. Once it is lifted a few centimetres or inches, the mat can be cut – sideways, rather than downwards – with a knife or trowel. Planting on ledges and in bog gardens may be done on an extra protective layer of liner or a cushioned underlay to facilitate subsequent maintenance.

Planting baskets can be lifted out, dealt with, then carefully replaced (once the ledge has been cleaned off carefully) on a further protective layer of liner or underlay. This extra protection is worthwhile, as even plastic containers may have sharp edges that could tear a liner.

Repairs

If a split occurs in a polythene lining it probably means that the whole sheet has become brittle, which makes repair work futile. So this is probably a good time to reline, using a material of better quality.

PVC and vinyl-based liners are quite easily repaired with adhesive patches, or by heat welding, using a hot iron or roller – or, in the case of vinyl, a hot air gun and patch. However, if a PVC liner has become brittle through age and exposure to ultraviolet light, repair is fairly pointless, and a new liner should be considered.

Butyl, rubber and EPDM are also easily repaired. They are unlikely to become brittle and should last a lifetime, but they can be torn, and it is a good idea to set aside a small piece of liner to be used if this should occur. These take adhesive easily and can be patched. Butyl is best repaired with special cold butyl tape, which is a double-sided sticky strip of raw butyl. A butyl patch is applied to one side of the tape and the other side is placed over the tear.

Take special care in preparation; cleanliness is essential. First scrub with water and a slightly abrasive pad. Then dry this off and clean the area with a clean rag moistened with a suitable solvent, such as acetone or petrol. When this has evaporated completely, apply the patch, pressing or rolling it firmly into position. It can be finished off with the heel of your shoe for good measure.

Long or awkward tears and splits can be welded using a strip of uncured butyl and a butyl welder that applies heat and pressure so the raw butyl is welded on to the two edges of the tear. If properly prepared and executed, this will make the strongest of all repair jobs.

MOVING-WATER FEATURES

Fountains, waterfalls and cascades need to be freed from dirt and debris with regular cleaning once or twice a year and especially after leaf fall. Running water does not freeze as easily as still water so, except under extremely severe conditions, it may be kept running to prevent pipes freezing. Check the pump and pipework.

Repairs

To repair frost damage to stonework, thoroughly clean off the area to be repaired and remove any algae. Mix lime, sand and cement in equal proportions with a bonding agent to the consistency of putty and remodel the damaged area. Finish off with a wet paintbrush, dragging some of the green patina off the surrounding surfaces over the new work.

If an old fountain ornament needs extensive repair work, take the opportunity to check internal pipework. Very often the diameter of the original pipe is too small. Modern pumps tend to work on a higher volume and lower pressure than the old systems so, if possible, insert a new pipe of as large a diameter as can be accommodated. For most small fountains, a 20mm/¾in diameter pipe is adequate. This will be bushed down (reduced) at the very top of the ornament to take the required nozzle.

Pumps

Modern submersible pumps are usually made from non-corrosive materials, are self-lubricating and require little maintenance. In dirty water or ponds with much filamentous algae, pumps may need to be brought to the surface and the filter cleaned weekly. The pump should be stripped down and cleaned and serviced at least once every year. Bearings and glands should be inspected for signs of wear and tear and cleaned and reassembled or replaced as necessary. Pumps that contain oil should be carefully inspected for signs of emulsification indicating water entering the motor which could lead to expensive damage.

Water deeper than 60cm/24in is unlikely to freeze and so submersible pumps can be left running in winter to operate a fountain or waterfall. Run the pump at least once a month to prevent it from seizing.

Surface pumps need annual maintenance by a pump specialist. All moving parts should be kept greased or oiled to prevent clogging and seizing up and, like submersible pumps, they operate with fewer problems if run frequently. Where winter operation is not required, the pump can be drained or removed, cleaned, dried and stored.

You must be careful with surface pumps that you do not run them dry or forget to turn on the tap or valve that allows water from the pond to reach the pump. Nearly all models have a bleed screw or priming plug that enables the impeller housing to be filled with water before the pump is turned on, but these vary and it is best to check with your supplier. When restarting, remember to turn on the valves from the pool.

Further reading

Bring, Mitchell and Wayembergh, Josse *Japanese Gardens* McGraw-Hill, New York, 1981

Brookes, John *Gardens of Paradise* Weidenfeld & Nicolson, London, 1987

Chatto, Beth *The Damp Garden* J.M.Dent & Sons, London, Melbourne and Toronto, 1982

Fitter, R et al. *Grasses: Collins Pocket Guide* Collins, London, 1992

Hobhouse, Penelope *Colour in Your Garden* Collins, London, 1985
— *Garden Style* Frances Lincoln, London, 1988

Ito, Miwako (ed.) *Aquascape: water in Japanese landscape architecture* Process Architecture, Tokyo, 1990

Keble Martin, W. *The Concise British Flora in Colour* Ebury Press and Michael Joseph, London, 1965

Keswick, Maggie *The Chinese Garden* Academy Editions, London, 1986

Lacey, Stephen *Scent in Your Garden* Frances Lincoln, London, 1991

Macan, T. T. and Worthington, E. B. *Life in Lakes and Rivers* Fontana, London, 1972

Mühlberg, Helmut *The Complete Guide to Water Plants* translated by Ilse Lindsay, E. P. Publishing, London, 1982

Perry, Frances *Water Gardening* Country Life, London, 1938

Swindells, Philip *Water Lilies* Croom Helm, London, 1983

Verey, Rosemary *Good Planting* Frances Lincoln, London, 1990

Williams, Robin *The Garden Planner* Frances Lincoln, London, 1990

Useful addresses

Anthony Archer-Wills Ltd
Broadford Bridge Road
West Chiltington
Sussex RH20 2LF
Tel. 0798 813204
Specialists and consultants in the design and construction of ponds, lakes and water gardens. Wholesale and retail suppliers of butyl, EPDM and geotextile underlays of any size; pumps and fountain equipment; and a wide selection of water plants from their own nurseries.

National Trust
36 Queen Anne's Gate
London SW1H 9AS
Tel. 071 222 9251

Royal Botanic Gardens
Kew
Richmond TW9 3AB
Tel. 081 940 1171

Royal Horticultural Society
80 Vincent Square
London SW1P 2PE
Tel. 071 834 4333

For all services to the landscape industry see also:
Landscape Specification directory
Landscape Promotions
Stirling University Innovation Park
Scottish Metropolitan Beta Centre
Innovative Park
Stirling FK9 4BR

Bentonite

Volclay Ltd
Birkenhead Road
Wallasey
Merseyside L44 7BU
Tel. 051 638 0967

Consulting engineers to the leisure industry

P.G.B. Barber
Ramridge Dene
Ramridge
Nr. Weyhill
Hants
Tel. 0264 772465

Filtration

Aqua Med Ltd
14 Boxhill Way
Strood Green
Betchworth
Surrey RH3 7HY
Tel. 0737 842 921

Fish biologist

Bernice Brewster
91 Fleeming Road
Walthamstow
London E17 5ET
Tel. 081 531 2423

Flexible pond and lake liners and geotextile underlays

Gordon Lowe Plastics Ltd
Dragonfly House
Rookery Road
Wybaston
Beds MK44 3UG
Tel. 0480 405433

Fountains and jets

Anglo Aquarium Plant Co. Ltd
Strayfield Road
Enfield
Middlesex EN2 0EX
Tel: 081 363 8548

International Aquatic Centre
26/127 West Bar
Sheffield
South Yorkshire S38 PN
Tel. 0742 750147

Lotus Water Garden Products
260/300 Berkhamsted Road
Chesham
Bucks HP5 3EY
Tel: 0494 774451

PLS Products Ltd
PO Box 114
Croydon
Surrey

Stapeley Water Gardens
Stapeley
Nantwich
Cheshire CW5 7LH
Tel. 0270 623868

Ustigate
3 Berkeley Crescent
Gravesend
Kent DA12 2AD
Tel. 0474 363012

WDT
No.5 Focus 303
Walworth Industrial Estate
Andover
Hants SP10 5NY
Tel. 0264 333225

Garden designers

Veronica Adams
Lower Hopton Farm
Stoke Lacey
Bromyard
Hereford HR7 4HX
Tel. 0885 490294

Rosemary Alexander
Chelsea Physic Garden
66 Royal Hospital Road
London SW3 4HS
Tel. 071 352 4347

John Brookes
Clock House
Denmans Gardens
Fontwell
Nr. Chichester
West Sussex BN18 0SU
Tel. 0243 542808

Edmonde Cannon
Orchard Cottage
Willow Vale
Chiselhurst
Kent BR7 5DF
Tel. 081 467 3280

Penelope Hobhouse
The Coach House
Bettiscombe
Bridport
Dorset DT6 5NT
Tel. 0308 68560

Lucy Huntington
2 Manor Farm Cottages
Cothelstone
Taunton
Somerset
Tel. 0823 433215

A. du Gard Pasley
Dornden
Langton Road
Tunbridge Wells
Kent
Tel. 0892 27836

Nicola Parsons
The Parsons Garden Ltd
10 Nayland Road
Colchester
Essex C04 5EG
Tel. 0206 853242

Rosemary Verey
Barnsley Close
Barnsley
Cirencester
Glos GL7 5EE

Robin Williams
Rowan House
Winterton Drive
Speen, Newbury
Berks RG13 1WD
Tel. 0635 32910

Landscape architect

Andy Nichols
Hutton Nichols Brown
Pond House
North End
Henley-on-Thames RG9 6LG
Tel. 0491 638536

Landscape contractors

The British Association of Landscape
Industries
(Landscape Contractors' Trade
Association) Landscape House
9 Henry Street
Keighley
West Yorkshire BD21 3DR
Tel. 0535 606139

Lighting

Hoffmeister Lighting
Units 3 and 4, Preston Road
Reading
Berkshire RG2 0BE
Tel. 0734 866941

Outdoor Lighting Supplies
Argent Court
Hook Rise South
Tolworth KT6 7LD
Tel. 081 974 2211

Plants

aquatic, bog and moisture-loving

Stapeley Water Gardens
Stapeley
Nantwich
Cheshire CW5 7LH
Tel. 0270 623 868

carnivorous

The Carnivorous Plant Society
174 Baldwins Lane
Croxley Green
Herts WD3 3LQ
(s.a.e. postal enquiries only)

nymphaea/water lilies

International Water Lily Society
Wycliffe Hall Botanical Gardens
Barnard Castle
County Durham DL12 9TS

International Water Lily Society
P.O.Box 104
Buskeytown
Maryland 21717-0104, USA

International Water Lily Society
c/o School of Science
601 University Drive
South West Texas State University
San Marcos
Texas 78666-4616, USA

National Collection of Water Lilies
Burnby Hall Gardens
Pocklington
North Yorkshire YO4 2QE
Tel. 0759 302068

Bennett's Water Lily and Fish Farm
Putton Lane
Chicherell
Weymouth
Dorset DT3 4AA
Tel. 0305 785150

Stapeley Water Gardens
Stapeley
Nantwich
Cheshire CW5 7LH
Tel. 0270 623 868

orchids

American Orchid Society
6000 South Olive Avenue
West Palm Beach
Florida 33405, USA

The British Orchid Council
20 Newbury Drive
Davyhulme
Manchester M31 2FA

The Cymbidium Society of America
6881 Wheeler Avenue
Westminster
California 92683, USA

The Orchid Society of Great
Britain
120 Crofton Road
Orpington
Kent BR6 8HZ
Tel. 0689 741549

unusual

Coombelands Gardens
Coneyhurst
Billinghurst
Sussex
Tel. 0403 741549

Beth Chatto Gardens
Elmstead Market
Colchester
Essex CO7 7DB
Tel. 0206 822007

Steam dredging

James Lowther
Ramridge Dene
Ramridge
Nr. Weyhill SP11 0QP

Swimming pools, spas and hot tubs

Crosdil Leisure
16 The Mews
Downlands
Pulborough
Sussex RH20 2DQ
Tel. 0798 25643

Fowler Bros (Cowfold) Ltd
Henfield Road
Cowfold
Sussex RH13 8BS
Tel. 0403 864373

Guncast Ltd
Moorcraft
Abinger Common
Dorking
Surrey RH5 6HZ

Hot Tubs
Coldharbour
Wisborough Green
Sussex RH14 0EX
Tel. 0403 700769

Imperial Swimming Pools Ltd
World's End Nurseries
Aylesbury Road
Wendover
Aylesbury
Bucks HP20 6BD
Tel. 0296 623116

Penguin Swimming Pools Ltd
Bakers Lane
Galleywood
Chelmsford
Essex

Pennine Swimming Pools Ltd
Oak Hill
Dunnockshaw
Nr. Burnley
Lancs BB11 5PW

Waterfowl

The Wildfowl and Wetlands Trust
Mill Road
Arundel
Sussex BN18 9PB
Tel. 0903 883355

Regional Branches:

78 Ballydrain Road
Camber
Newtownards
Co. Down B23 6EA
Tel. 0247 874146

Slimbridge
Cambridge
Gloucester GL2 7BT
Tel. 0453 890333

Eastpark Farm
Caerlaverock
Dumfriesshire DG1 4RS
0387 77200

Water sculpture

Jonathan Froud
(sculpture in glass)
44 Denman Road
London SE15 5NR
Tel. 071 703 5177

The Hannah Pescar Sculpture Gallery
Black and White Cottage
Standon Lane
Ockley, Surrey

Water treatment

Hamish Sneddon
The Complete Water Treatment Co. Ltd
5d The Tanneries
East Street
Titchfield
Hampshire PO14 4AR
Tel. 0329 843160

Wood preservatives

BP Aquaseal
Kingsnorth Hoo
Rochester
Kent ME2 2AG
Tel. 0624 716654

Cuprinol
Adderwell
Frome
Somerset BA11 1NC
Tel. 0373 465151

Langlow Products Ltd
P.O.Box 22
Asheridge Road
Chesham
Bucks HP5 2QF
Tel. 0494 784866

Rentokil Ltd
Products Division
Felcourt
East Grinstead
West Sussex
Tel. 0342 327 171

Plant index

Page numbers in *italics* refer to illustrations.

A

B

C

General index

Figures in *italics* refer to illustrations, diagrams and their captions.

Hardiness zones

The hardiness zone ratings given for each plant – indicated in the text by the letter 'Z' and the relevant number – suggest the appropriate minimum temperature a plant will tolerate in winter. However, this can only be a rough guide. The hardiness of a plant depends on a great many factors, including the depth of its roots, its water content at the onset of frost, the duration of cold weather, the force of the wind, and the length of, and the temperatures encountered during, the preceding summer. The zone ratings are based on those devised by the United States Department of Agriculture.

Approximate range of average annual minimum temperatures

°CELSIUS	ZONE	°FAHRENHEIT
below -45	1	below -50
-45 to -40	2	-50 to -40
-40 to -34	3	-40 to -30
-34 to -29	4	-30 to -20
-29 to -23	5	-20 to -10
-23 to -18	6	-10 to 0
-18 to -12	7	0 to 10
-12 to -7	8	10 to 20
-7 to -1	9	20 to 30
-1 to 4	10	30 to 40
above 4	11	above 40

Acknowledgments

AUTHOR'S ACKNOWLEDGMENTS

First my admiration and thanks go out to Frances Lincoln Limited and all its staff for their enormous help, kindness and hard work which made the successful production of this beautiful book such a pleasurable experience.

My thanks to Frances Perry for providing the first real inspiration with her wonderful book *Water Gardening*. My gratitude, also, to John Brookes, who had for years entreated me to write this book, for kindly writing the foreword. In addition, I must thank John Brookes and all the garden designers and architects for their loyalty and support in providing me with stimulating and challenging water garden designs to create - for it is by taxing one's abilities that greater skill and knowledge are acquired. Among these, Robin Williams deserves special mention here for his beautiful plans and perennial good humour. In the same vein, I would like to thank all my loyal customers who keep providing me with interesting commissions.

For their help and support I would also like to thank the National River Authorities, Kew Gardens and its helpful staff, Wisley Gardens, Harlow Carr Gardens, Christopher Brickell, Rosemary Alexander and Sir Francis Avery-Jones. A special thank you goes to Christopher Lloyd for increasing my plant awareness and doing 'plant swaps'.

In the United States, my sincere thanks go out to John Meeks and Jim Lawrie for their thorough scrutiny of my manuscript. To Charles B. Thomas of Lilypons Water Gardens, Margaret Wright (Great Gardens), Mr and Mrs Hubert McDonnell, and The Horticultural Society of Maryland, my thanks are due for all their help and hospitality. My special thanks to Linda R. Lawrence for all her time and kindness spent introducing me to the sub tropical plants of Florida in their native swamps, and to all the people who were able to assist me in my studies of these fascinating plants.

To Patrick Nutt, I am indebted for a magical introduction to the tropical water lilies at Longwood Gardens and for all the personal help given by him and his staff.

I am most grateful to Elizabeth and Howard Aldridge, Sir Francis Avery-Jones, Alan Bayne, Jo and Ian Burns, Angela and Richard Graves, Sue and Peter Holland, Gilly Hopton, and Pam and John Kenway, who allowed us to photograph their gardens.

Also a big thank you to Tony Lord, who gave invaluable assistance with plant names; to all those who cannot be named here, and to my own staff, particularly Martin Kelley, who have been so supportive during the writing of this book.

Finally, I doubt if the book would ever have been written had it not been for the unstinting support and encouragement given by my long-suffering wife, and for the endless hours she spent in plant research and for all the things both she and my daughter had to go without during the long periods I was ensconced, hampered by an importunate cat, and unable to join in any activities with them.

PHOTOGRAPHIC ACKNOWLEDGMENTS

b=bottom, c=centre, t=top, l=left, r=right

Anthony Archer-Wills: 97, 153r, 165br, 169tl,cr,bl,br, 170r
Deni Bown: 134, 136t, 142bl, 149
Neil Campbell-Sharp: 22, 45, 85
Geoff Dann: 160l © FLL
Garden Picture Library: Brian Carter 2, Marijke Heuff 11, Clive Boursall 12, Bob Challinor 70, Gary Rogers 101, Henk Dijkman 104, Ron Sutherland 106, 107
Mick Hales: 30
Jerry Harpur: 5 (Laver Hall, Worfield), 6-7 (Denmans), 13 (Beth Chatto), 36 (Brenthurst, Johannesburg), 42, 47 (Wave Hill, NY), 72, 77 (designer: Bill Wheeler, NY), 102, 126 (Wave Hill, NY)
Marijke Heuff: 17 (designer: Jacques Wirtz), 55 (Jaap Niewenhues and Paula Thies), 128 (Mr & Mrs Voorwaijk-Luca)
Saxon Holt: 109, 176
Holt Studios International: 172
Impact Photos: Pamla Toler 35
Michèle Lamontagne: 10, 73, 76, 80, 81, 87, 94, 95, 105, 111, 119b, 120, 132tr, 135l, 137t, 138, 141r, 143, 144, 145t and br, 147r, 152, 153l, 159r, 161t, 162, 165cl, 166l
Andrew Lawson: 41, 90, 131, 133, 135r, 136b, 139, 140l, 141l, 142br, 145bl, 146, 148l, 154b, 156, 167tl, tr, cr, and bl, 171b
Georges Lévêque: 14, 18, 26, 43, 92
Christopher Lloyd: 29
Tony Lord: 65
Marianne Majerus: 62
S & O Mathews: 33, 121, 130, 132br, 151t, 154t, 155, 158, 167cl, 171t, 177tl
NHPA: Stephen Dalton 108, Silvestris 115, George Bernard 117, Stephen Dalton 118 and 119t, A.N.T. 140r, Jane Gifford 147l, John Hayward 161b, Laurie Campbell 166r, Gerard Lacz 173, Stephen Dalton 174l, David Woodfall 174c, Martin Garwood 174r, Walter Murray 177bl, Laurie Campbell 177r
Clive Nichols: 8 © FLL, 24, 27 © FLL, 59 © FLL, 60 © FLL, 83, 88 © FLL, 96 © FLL, 99, 122 © FLL, 125 © FLL, 132l, 137b © FLL, 142t, 148r © FLL, 151b © FLL, 160r © FLL, 164 © FLL
Oxford Scientific Films: Hans Reinhard 116
Gary Rogers: 175
Stapeley Water Gardens: 1, 159l, 163, 165tl and bl, 167br, 169tr and cl, 170l
Elizabeth Whiting and Associates: 19, 68

PUBLISHERS' ACKNOWLEDGMENTS

The Publishers would like to thank the following people for their help in producing this book: Sally Cracknell, Sue Gladstone, John Laing, Niki Medlikova, Claudine Meissner, Sarah Mitchell, Annabel Morgan and Caroline Wright. Particular thanks for their creative input are due to Margaret Crowther, Penny David and Eleanor van Zandt. Horticultural advice from Stapeley Water Gardens was much appreciated.

Illustrations by Sharon Bradley-Papp
Horticultural consultants Tony Lord, Patrick Nutt
Technical consultants John A. Meeks, James A. Lawrie

Editors Anne Kilborn, Penelope Miller
Art Editor Louise Tucker
Picture Editor Anne Fraser
Art Director Caroline Hillier
Editorial Director Erica Hunningher
Production Adela Cory
Production Director Nicky Bowden